THE BAGLEYS AND RELATED FAMILIES OF WASHINGTON COUNTY, MAINE, AND BEYOND

A GENEALOGICAL PROFILE OF OUR ANCESTRAL FAMILIES

VOLUME 3 – ANCESTRAL CHARTS

by

Timothy W. Bagley

The Bagleys
and Related Families
of
Washington County, Maine, and Beyond

The Bagleys and Related Families of Washington County, Maine, and Beyond

A Genealogical Profile of Our Ancestral Families

Volume 3 – Ancestral Charts

Timothy W. Bagley

DEDICATION

This book is dedicated to the loving memory of my mother, Ethel Marie Bagley, and my father, Abraham Leroy Bagley. My mother was taken from those she loved far too early in life. While she was with us she suffered more than anyone will know, but throughout it all, she was determined to give me the foundation I would need to survive without her, to grow strong and to become the man I was destined to be. I am proud to be their son and everything I have ever done that has been good; every accomplishment I have ever made; every award or recognition; has been done because of how much I loved my Mom and Dad and wanted to make them both proud. I am the legacy of my parents and all that I have accomplished in my life is thanks to them and can never compare to what they gave during their lives to me.

Growing up, the extended Bagley family in Washington County and throughout New England and beyond of aunts, uncles, cousins, and more was a large part of my life as were the memories of those who were no longer here. I became interested in researching our family history as every year my Mom, Dad, and I would make crosses and baskets decorated with flowers that we would place on all of the family graves in Down East (Washington County), Maine. Those visits, stories, and old photos were the only way I knew who my grandparents and many other members of the family were. After my Mom passed away, I found a stack of notes she had made on the dates of births, marriages, and other life events of my grandparents in the family Bible. I wanted to document our family history as best I could before any more of it was lost, and while this book took many years of work to research, compile, and write, it was a joy and honor to do it in remembrance of my Mom, Dad, and all our family.

- Timothy W. Bagley

Abe and Ethel Bagley

TABLE OF CONTENTS

PREFACE AND ACKNOWLEDGMENTS

I began the process of research for the Bagleys and related families in 1998, and the information found in this book and the related volumes has been developed and built on over the past 20+ years. ***The Bagleys and Related Families of Washington County, Maine, and Beyond: A Genealogical Profile of Our Ancestral Families Volume 1 – In America*** contains a narrative family tree with over __850 direct ancestors from the Bagleys and over 140 other families__ that are all related and part of the direct familial line, and much more including thousands of additional siblings.

Volume 2 – In Europe contains a narrative family tree with over __490 direct ancestors from the Bagleys, as well as 25 of the immigrant families and dozens of others__ that are all related and part of the direct familial lines, and much more.

Volume 3 – Ancestral Charts contains a series of graphic family tree/pedigree charts that show __the direct ancestors from the Bagleys and other families__ that are all related and extending back to 27 generations for some of the familial lines.

Special thanks and acknowledgment go to members of my family, friends, fellow researchers and institutions that over the years have helped support this effort. This includes Dr. Norton Bagley who was the foremost authority in the country on Bagley genealogy and with his blessing and support I have strived to continue some of his work and to make it available to others interested in the Bagley lines. I would also like to acknowledge the support from my cousin Gloria Hayward; The Clayton Genealogical Library in Houston, Texas; the Town Clerks of Washington, County; and assorted aunts, uncles and cousins.

I have found through the years that although I started what I thought was a family tree; it was often more of a family wreath. The lives and relationships of many ancestral families were weaved together generation after generation and have created a rich tapestry of history.

- Timothy W. Bagley

INTRODUCTION TO USING THIS BOOK AND RELATED VOLUMES

WHY DID OUR FAMILIES COME TO AMERICA?

In researching my family tree and my ancestors, I was enthralled by the history that added a level of richness and depth to the names. Many of our ancestors came to the colonies during the Great Migration (1620-1640s): a time during which English puritans migrated to New England, the Chesapeake and the West Indies. English migration to Massachusetts consisted of a few hundred pilgrims who went to Plymouth Colony in the 1620s and between 13,000 and 21,000 emigrants who went to the Massachusetts Bay Colony between 1630 and 1642.

Our ancestors immigrated to the colonies for many reasons: from those seeking religious and political freedom to those who came for economic gain or adventure. Some of our ancestors came from wealthy and titled backgrounds while others landed in New England as indentured servants. Coming to the colonies was not cheap and cost about 5 pounds per person for fare, plus a charge for any personal goods that were shipped. Once they arrived, the hard work often began as they set to building a new life. As you follow the generations that came after the immigrant ancestor in *Volume 1* you begin to discern the familial and geographic migration patterns as the colonists spread out from Massachusetts and ultimately up into Washington County, Maine, and beyond.

THE ANCESTRAL FAMILIES

In researching our genealogy, I found many of the reference books to be difficult to follow and not always easy to find the specific information I needed. I have written and organized this book in a way that is different than many family genealogies to help make it easier to navigate, find what you want, and document the historical information in a logical manner. The narratives on each family and ancestral generation are not exhaustive, but provide a snapshot and highlights of the information that may be available as my goal was not to duplicate the work already well done by others, but to create a focused and unique guide and resource. While I have made every effort to accurately document and provide what was known and recorded, I expect that as new records and resources have become available online there may be some variances in the information.

In *Volumes 1* and *2*, each family's genealogical summary begins with the name of the family and is followed by the origin or meaning of the family name. Please see the **INTRODUCTION** in each volume for additional, specific details.

Volume 3 is a combination of the information found in *Volumes 1* and *2* distilled down to family tree/pedigree charts. These charts trace the direct paternal and maternal lines of the Bagleys and related immigrant ancestors both in America and in Europe when possible. There are instances in which no name is recorded or, especially for the wives, only their first name is documented so those instances are indicted with UNKNOWN.

Please note that *Volume 3* includes some generations and ancestral lines that are noted as 'possible', or 'maybe' within the narratives found in *Volumes 1* and *2*. The family tree charts show the names of the direct ancestors only and do not include titles, dates, siblings, and other details that may be found in the family narratives in *Volumes 1* and *2*.

Dr. Norton Russell Bagley spent years researching every Bagley line descended from our immigrant ancestor Orlando Bagley I. Detailed information on Orlando and his descendants may be found in Dr. Norton Russell Bagley and Martha Bagley Anderson's *Some Descendants of Orlando Bagley of Amesbury, Massachusetts*, and also their *Families Related to the Bagley and Floyd Families*, both of which are listed in the Bibliography. Their research was printed and revised between 1973 and 1990 and may be found in many libraries and repositories on the internet where I have tried to make sure the hard copies of his work and research that Norton provided me will continue to be accessible to future Bagley generations.

ANCESTOR NAMES

The names of our ancestors often provide clues to where they came from, what type of work they or their families may have done, and connections to other families. While we benefit greatly from the detailed town, church, and other records from New England going back to the earliest colonial days, trying to identify an ancestor by their name alone can still be a frustrating and difficult process even if they did not change their name for some reason during their life time.

The colonies were comprised of immigrants from many different countries so often times the names of one person were spelled in records in various ways especially as vowels were often interchanged. For example: Jackson - Jacksen - Jacksin. Sometimes the person keeping the record spelled it phonetically, or maybe they or the ancestor had minimal writing skills and one letter was easily mistaken for another, or the information written down and attested to at a later date as sometimes happened with town records that might have been lost or destroyed as in the case of Centerville, Maine.

GIVEN OR FIRST NAMES

The given or first names of our immigrant ancestors often appear familiar or similar to ones we know and still use today. In the family genealogical notes in the chapters of this book, you will find many variations of names from John and Mary, to those with religious or virtue overtones or qualities like Hatevil/Hateevil and Patience. Some female children are referenced in the records as Daughter, and it was not uncommon to see multiple children within the same family with the same first name – often because the children had died young.

Given and middle names are often a clue as well to family linkages and might be a grandparent's name or the mother's maiden name, all of which may be important clues when trying to confirm a specific ancestral line.

SURNAMES OR LAST NAME

The Chinese were among the very first cultures to adopt the use of hereditary surnames (around 2800 B.C.). However, the custom didn't quite catch on in Europe until the Venetian aristocracy made it popular sometime between the 10th and 11th centuries A.D.

Types of surnames: Most surnames fall into one of four categories: patronymic surnames such as Johnson pass from father to son (literally, "Son of John"); occupational surnames such as Cook or Miller stem from an individual's livelihood; topographic names such as Forest or Ford identify where someone lived; and there are also a few surnames that derive from individual characteristics or nicknames such as Small and Stern.

Patterns in surnames: There are many ways a surname could have evolved over centuries. One possibility is migration. A Roman name may have traveled to France and then to England where it was later Anglicized. For example, the surname Lawrence went from Laurentius (Roman) to Laurent (French) to Lawrence (English) and then to Lowry (Scottish). There is natural change and evolution to how a name a name may be spelled over hundreds of years. For example, a Middle English spelling may have evolved to a modern English spelling, such as Stiward to Stewart. In the colonies, many immigrant surnames were also Anglicized including our ancestral family O'Tierney that became Turner.

GENERATIONS

The family tree/pedigree charts in *Volume 3* begins with myself, and follows each direct ancestor back in the paternal and maternal lines for the Bagleys and related families. Each individual in the charts is assigned a unique identifying number. Those individuals whose lines continue past the page they are first shown on have a number and arrow to the right that indicates the page number on which their line continues.

MULTIPLE ANCESTRAL LINES

Many families include multiple, direct ancestral lines and ancestors who are related to the Bagleys and those lines or branches of the families are noted and numbered with a reference **(see Ancestral Line #)** in *Volumes 1* and *2*.

The family tree/pedigree charts in *Volume 3* only trace these multiple lines to the common ancestor. The common ancestor is shown only once and their continued lines are not duplicated, but may be cross referenced using the individual's unique identifying number and the narratives in *Volumes 1* and *2*.

ANNEXES, BIBLIOGRAPHY, AND INDEX OF DIRECT ANCESTORS

To provide some compiled reference lists and some additional historical information I found interesting and helpful, I have created a set of Annexes that contain summaries including the names of the ships that the immigrant ancestors arrived to New England on, notes on military service, and more.

A Bibliography containing a sampling of the books, records, and other reference sources used in writing these books is also provided.

In addition, an Index of all of the names included in the family tree/pedigree charts is included that specifies the page(s) on which each ancestor may be found.

COAT OF ARMS, HERALDY, AND OLD PHOTOS AND HISTORICAL IMAGES

There are now many companies and websites that claim to have, or can find, a family coat of arms or family crests based on the surname alone. While some of those may be accurate, in the colonial records and histories of the families in *Volume 1 – In America* I found only a few that were documented and referenced including the Bagleys, Allens, Chutes, Dodges, Tenneys, and Wilders. While I found some old photos and many historical images, maps, drawings, and other materials, I only included a few of those related to the most recent Bagley generations in *Volume 1* in order not to duplicate work already done by others and to help minimize reproduction costs of the printed Volumes or related eBooks.

In Europe, many of the families of our immigrant ancestors and those they were related to have a coat of arms identified for them. There are also multiple photos, paintings, or other images of them, their families, their manors or castles, and more in many books and on the internet. For example, there are some great photos on the internet of Baguley Hall. The Hall is a 14th-century timber framed hall in Baguley, Greater Manchester, England (grid reference SJ81628874). It is listed as a Grade I listed building and a Scheduled Ancient Monument. The current hall may be on the site of an earlier hall, possibly from the 11th or 12th century.

VOLUME 1 – IN AMERICA AND VOLUME 2 – IN EUROPE

The Bagleys and Related Families of Washington County, Maine, and Beyond: A Genealogical Profile of Our Ancestral Families - Volume 1 contains the genealogical profiles of our ancestors who came to the America. Some of the families are traceable further back into Europe and these may be found in *Volume 2 – In Europe.*

FAMILY TREE/PEDIGREE CHARTS

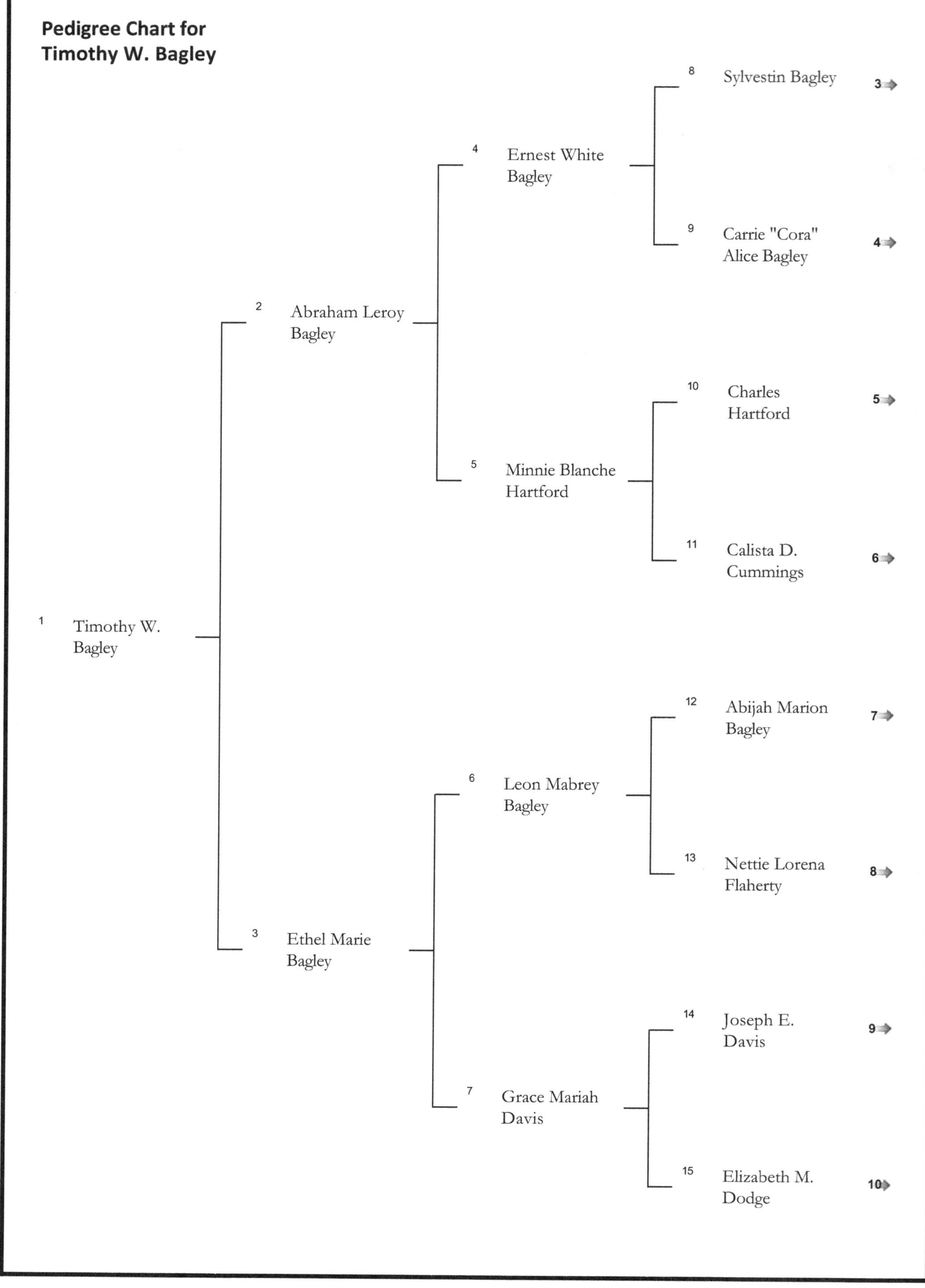

1 Timothy W. Bagley
2 Abraham Leroy Bagley
4 Ernest White Bagley
8 Sylvestin Bagley 3
9 Carrie "Cora" Alice Bagley 4
5 Minnie Blanche Hartford
10 Charles Hartford 5
11 Calista D. Cummings 6
3 Ethel Marie Bagley
6 Leon Mabrey Bagley
12 Abijah Marion Bagley 7
13 Nettie Lorena Flaherty 8
7 Grace Mariah Davis
14 Joseph E. Davis 9
15 Elizabeth M. Dodge 10

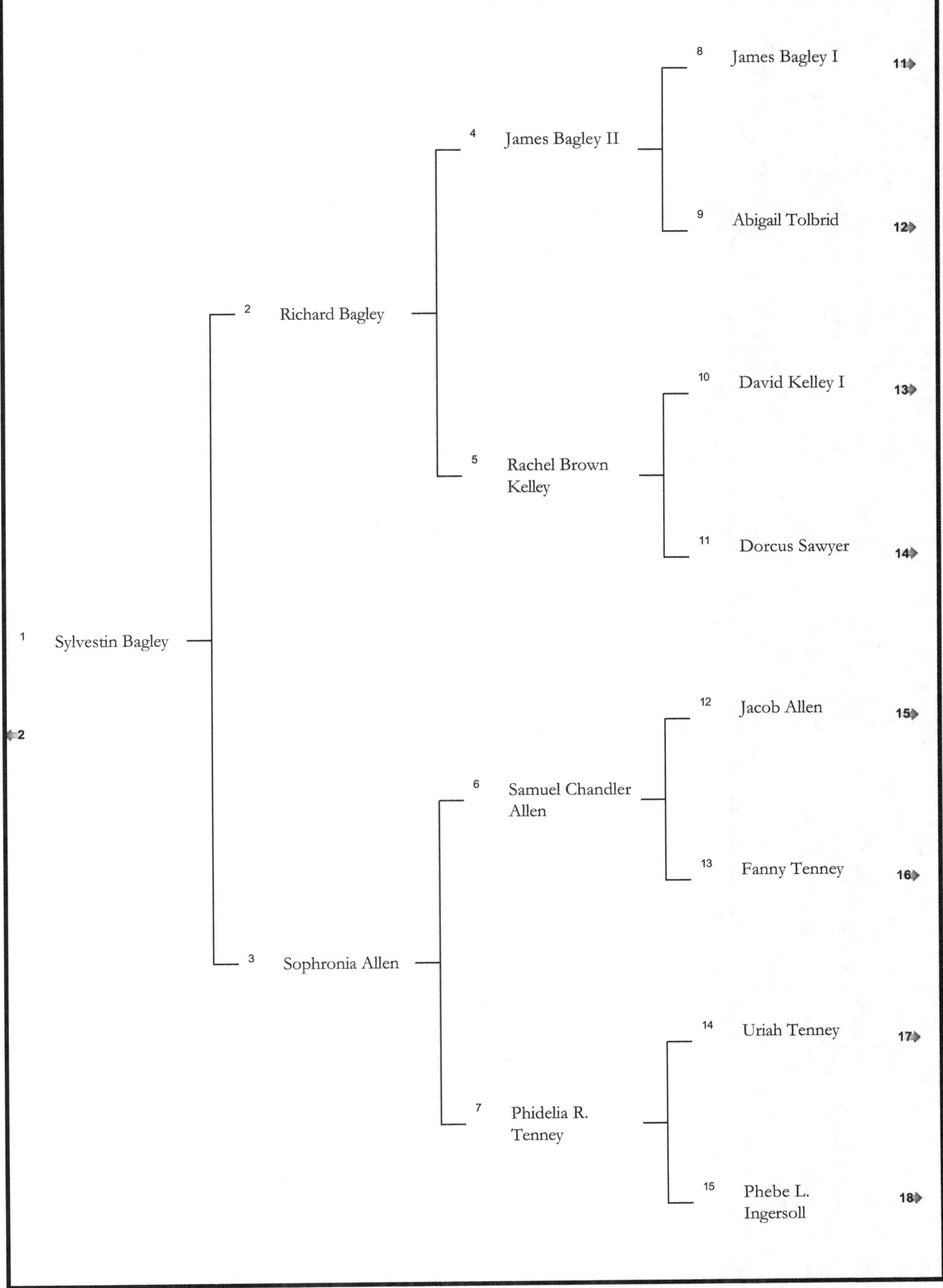

1 Sylvestin Bagley
2 Richard Bagley
3 Sophronia Allen
4 James Bagley II
5 Rachel Brown Kelley
6 Samuel Chandler Allen
7 Phidelia R. Tenney
8 James Bagley I
9 Abigail Tolbrid
10 David Kelley I
11 Dorcus Sawyer
12 Jacob Allen
13 Fanny Tenney
14 Uriah Tenney
15 Phebe L. Ingersoll
11
12
13
14
15
16
17
18
2

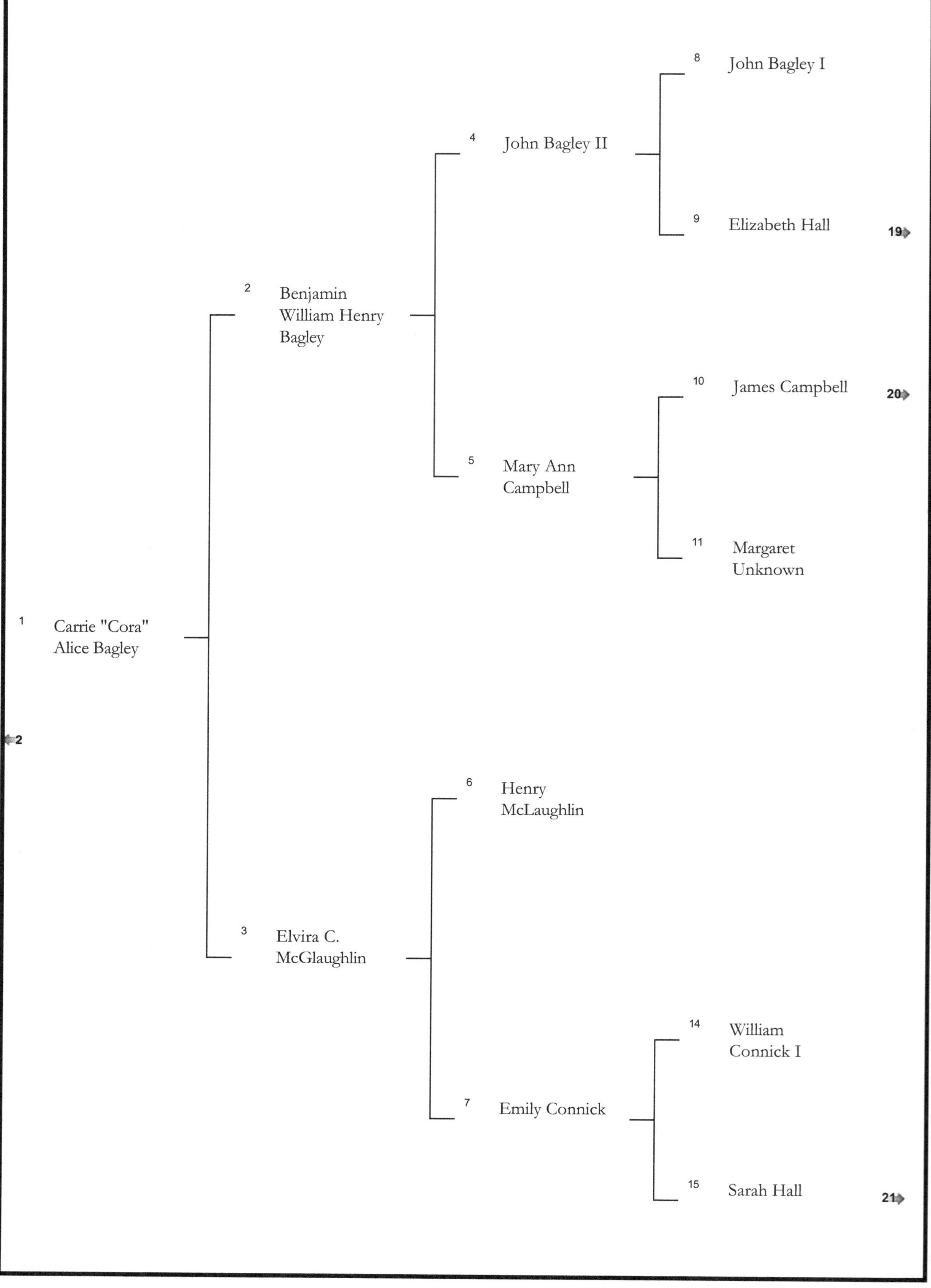

8 John Bagley I
4 John Bagley II
9 Elizabeth Hall
19
2 Benjamin William Henry Bagley
10 James Campbell
20
5 Mary Ann Campbell
11 Margaret Unknown
1 Carrie "Cora" Alice Bagley
2
6 Henry McLaughlin
3 Elvira C. McGlaughlin
14 William Connick I
7 Emily Connick
15 Sarah Hall
21

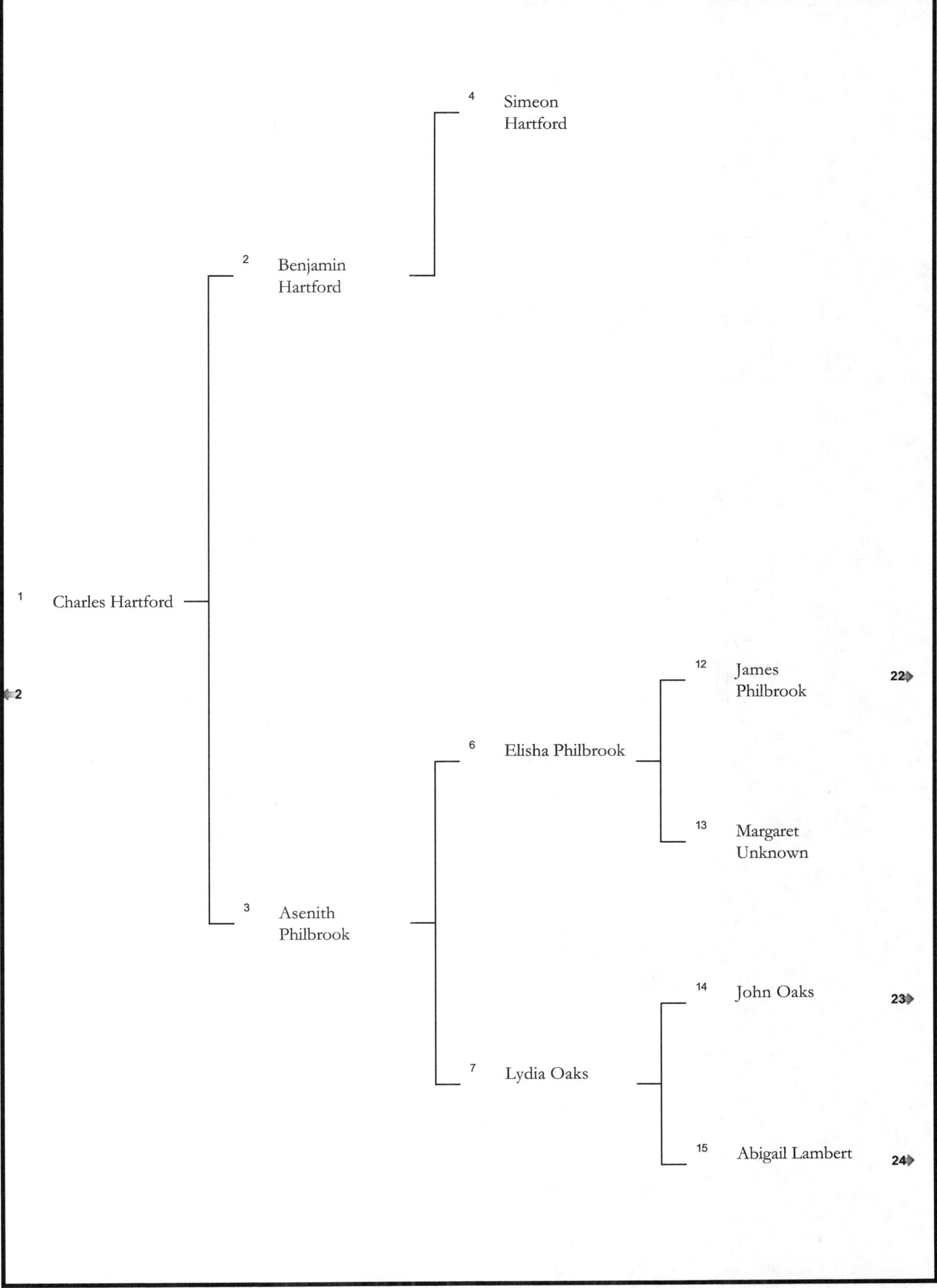

4 Simeon Hartford
2 Benjamin Hartford
1 Charles Hartford
12 James Philbrook 22
6 Elisha Philbrook
13 Margaret Unknown
3 Asenith Philbrook
14 John Oaks 23
7 Lydia Oaks
15 Abigail Lambert 24
2

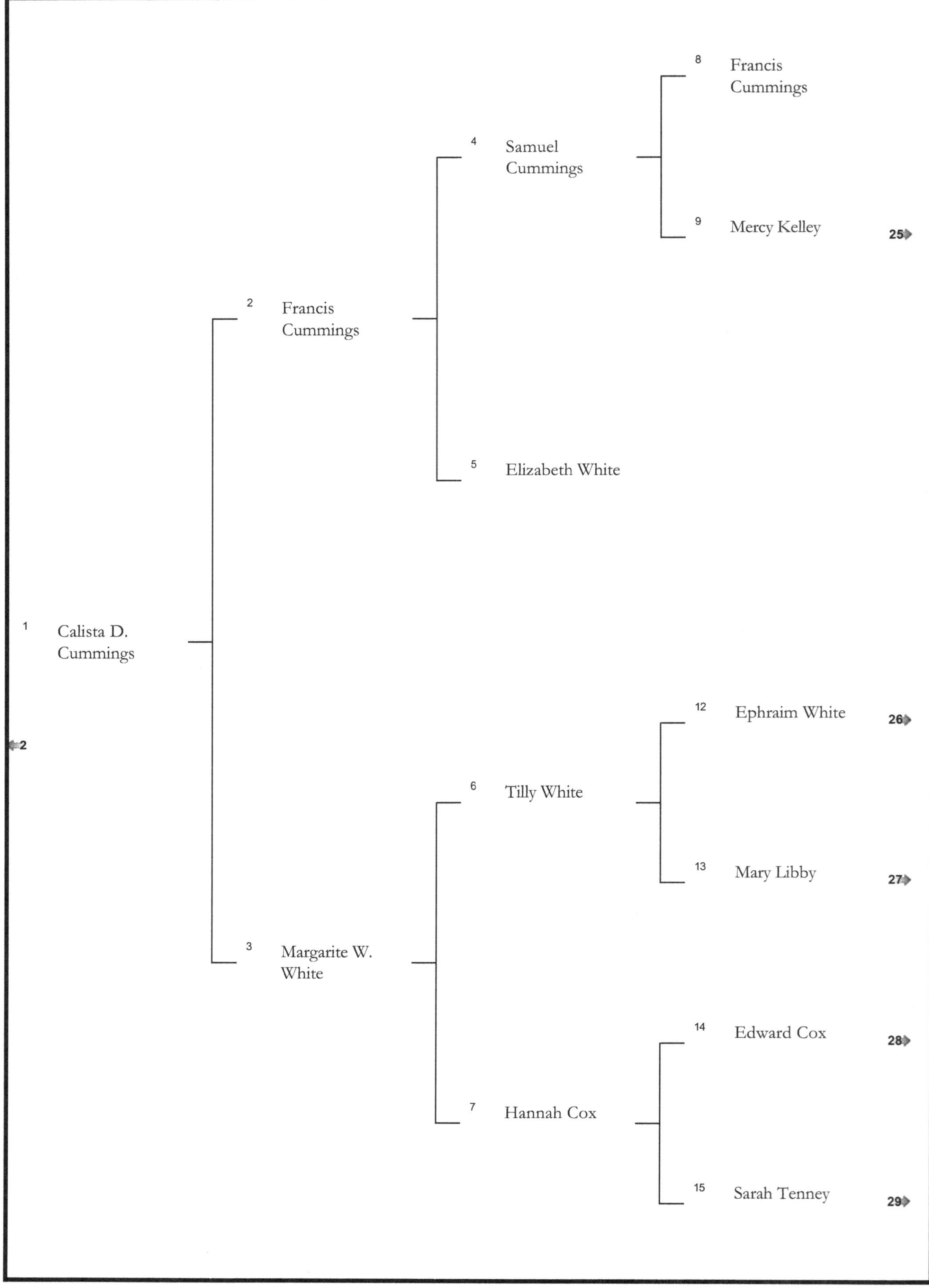

1 Calista D. Cummings
2 Francis Cummings
4 Samuel Cummings
8 Francis Cummings
9 Mercy Kelley
25
5 Elizabeth White
3 Margarite W. White
6 Tilly White
12 Ephraim White
26
13 Mary Libby
27
7 Hannah Cox
14 Edward Cox
28
15 Sarah Tenney
29
2

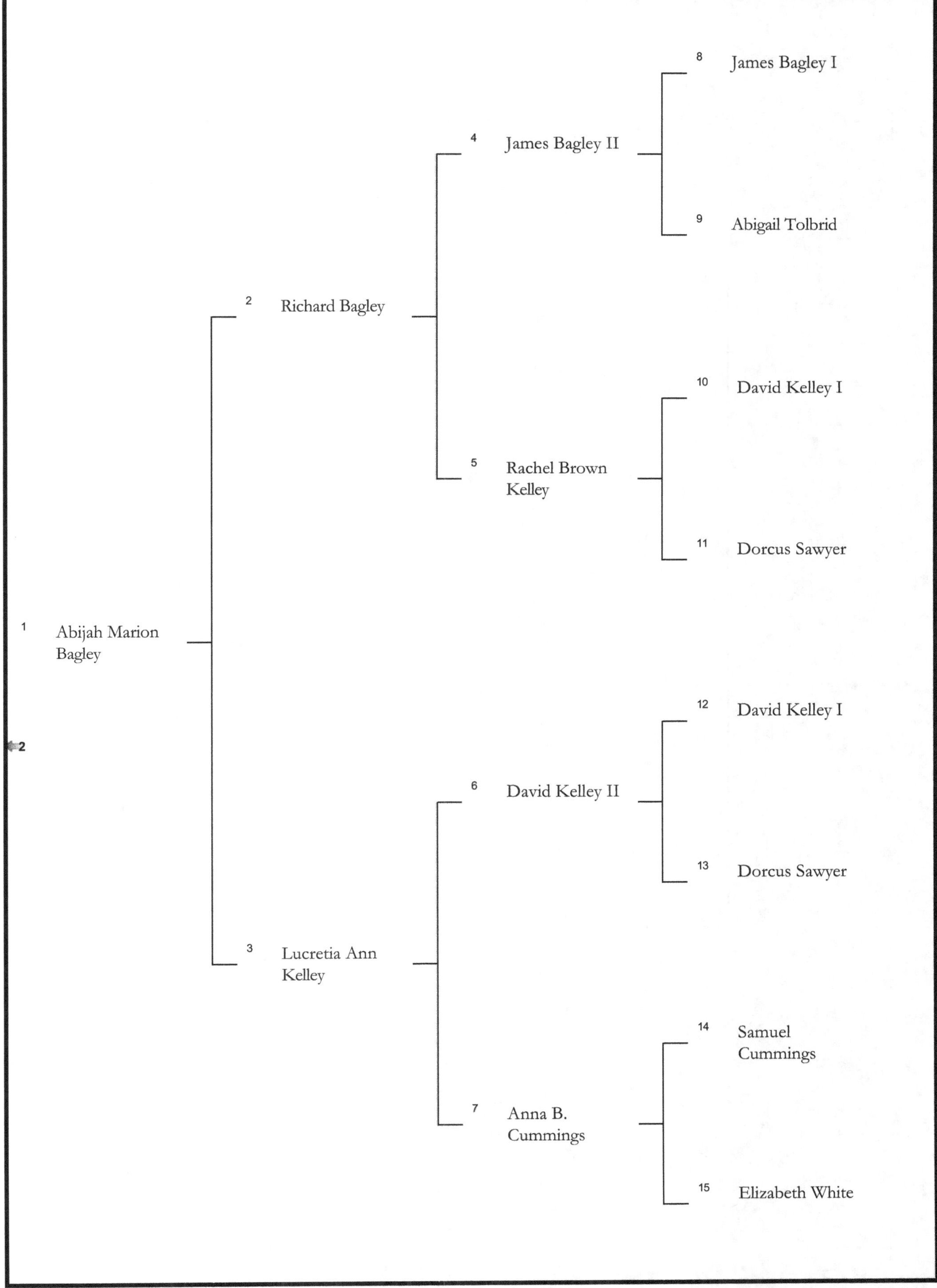

1 Abijah Marion Bagley
2 Richard Bagley
3 Lucretia Ann Kelley
4 James Bagley II
5 Rachel Brown Kelley
6 David Kelley II
7 Anna B. Cummings
8 James Bagley I
9 Abigail Tolbrid
10 David Kelley I
11 Dorcus Sawyer
12 David Kelley I
13 Dorcus Sawyer
14 Samuel Cummings
15 Elizabeth White

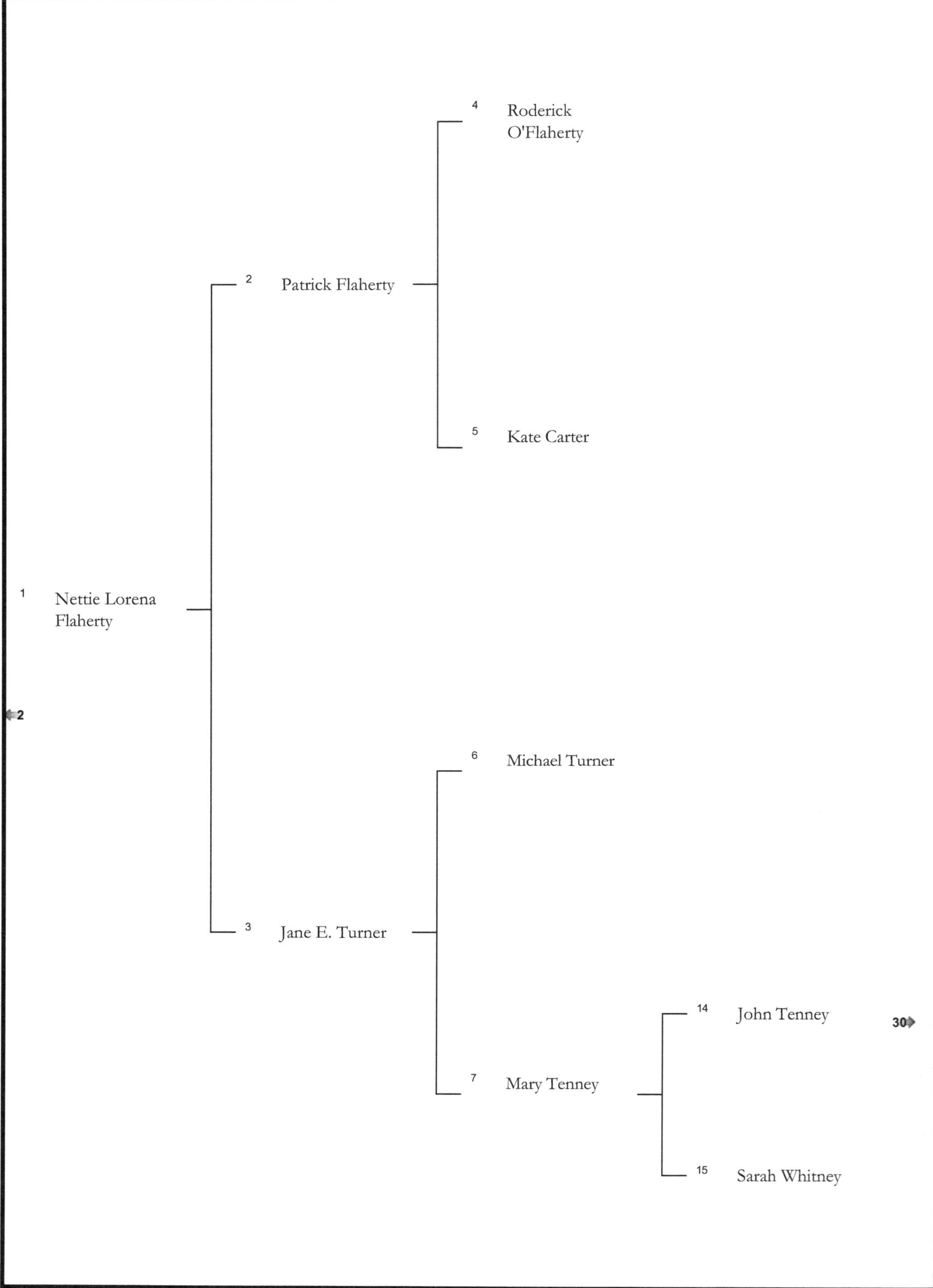

4 Roderick O'Flaherty
2 Patrick Flaherty
5 Kate Carter
1 Nettie Lorena Flaherty
2
6 Michael Turner
3 Jane E. Turner
14 John Tenney
30
7 Mary Tenney
15 Sarah Whitney

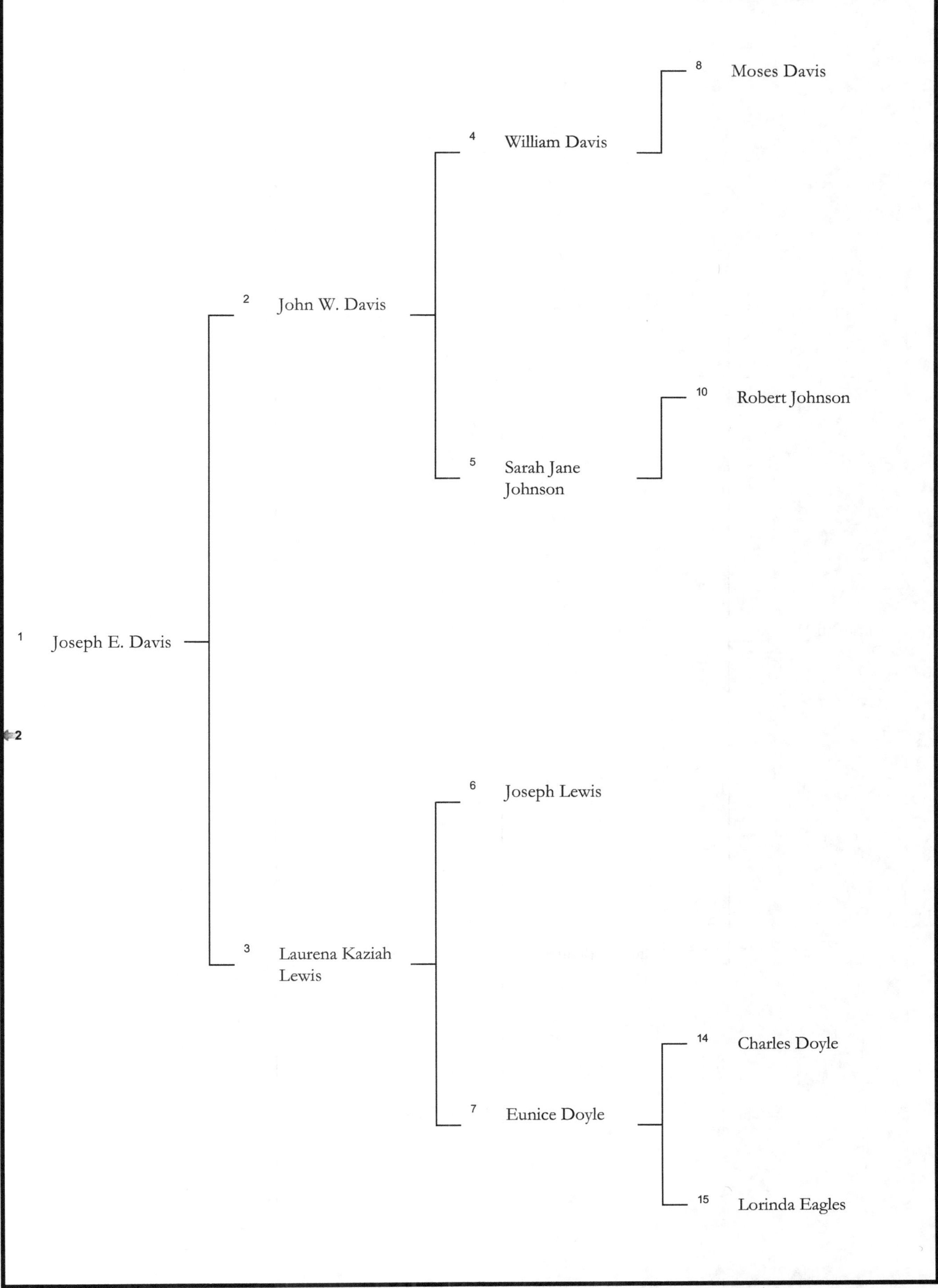

1 Joseph E. Davis
2 John W. Davis
3 Laurena Kaziah Lewis
4 William Davis
5 Sarah Jane Johnson
6 Joseph Lewis
7 Eunice Doyle
8 Moses Davis
10 Robert Johnson
14 Charles Doyle
15 Lorinda Eagles

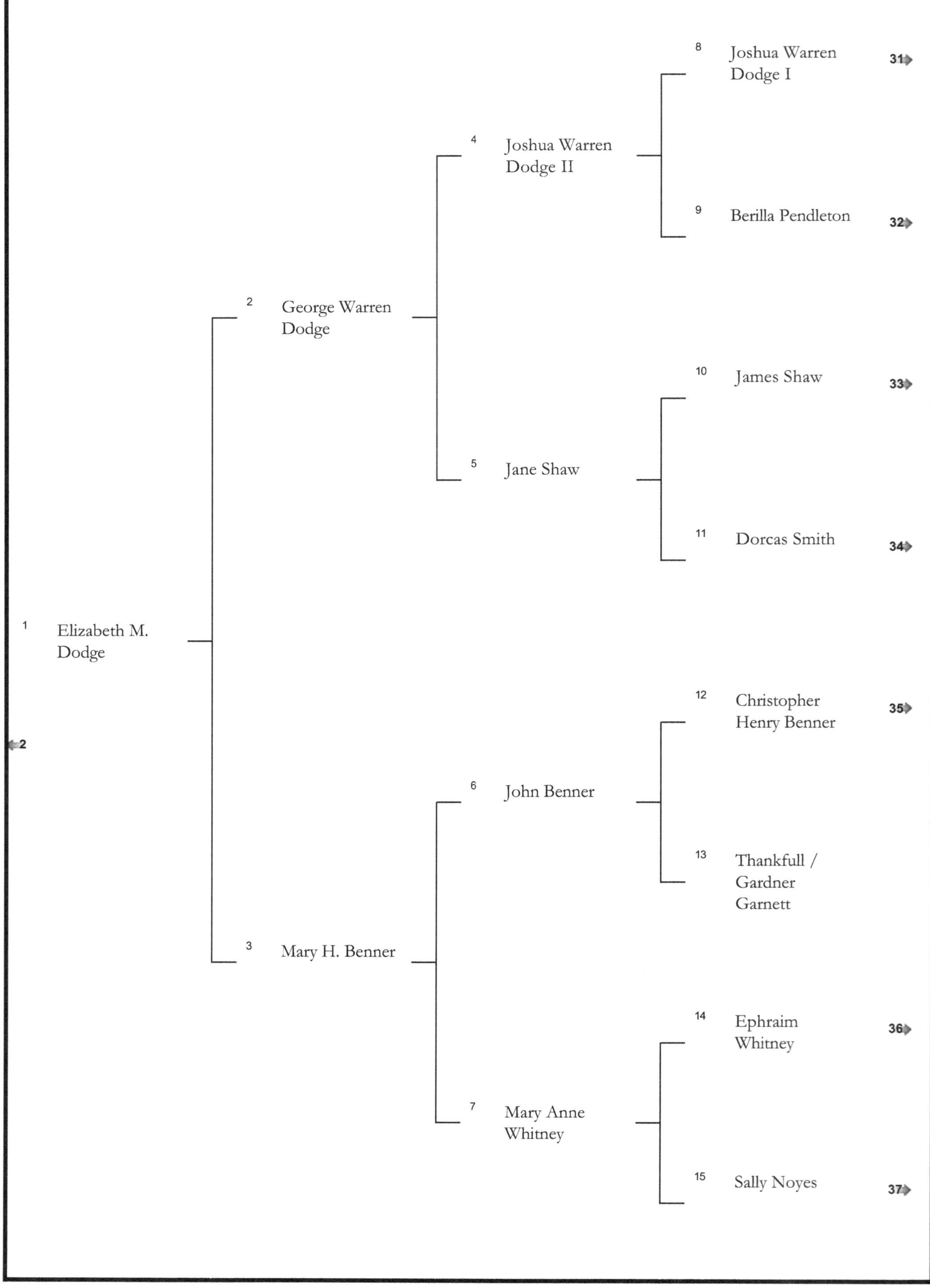

1 Elizabeth M. Dodge
2
2 George Warren Dodge
3 Mary H. Benner
4 Joshua Warren Dodge II
5 Jane Shaw
6 John Benner
7 Mary Anne Whitney
8 Joshua Warren Dodge I 31
9 Berilla Pendleton 32
10 James Shaw 33
11 Dorcas Smith 34
12 Christopher Henry Benner 35
13 Thankfull / Gardner Garnett
14 Ephraim Whitney 36
15 Sally Noyes 37

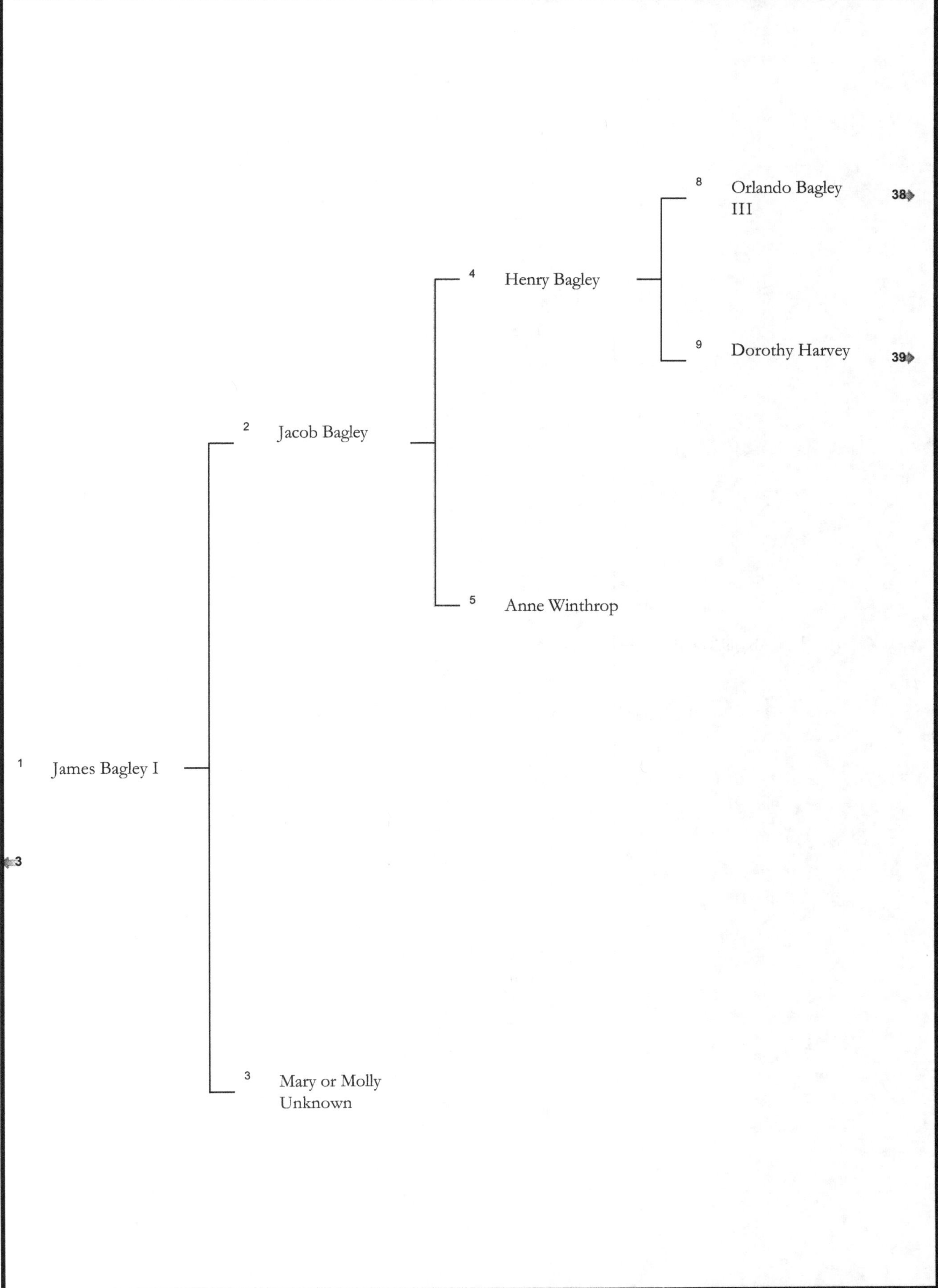

8 Orlando Bagley III 38
4 Henry Bagley
9 Dorothy Harvey 39
2 Jacob Bagley
5 Anne Winthrop
1 James Bagley I
3
3 Mary or Molly Unknown

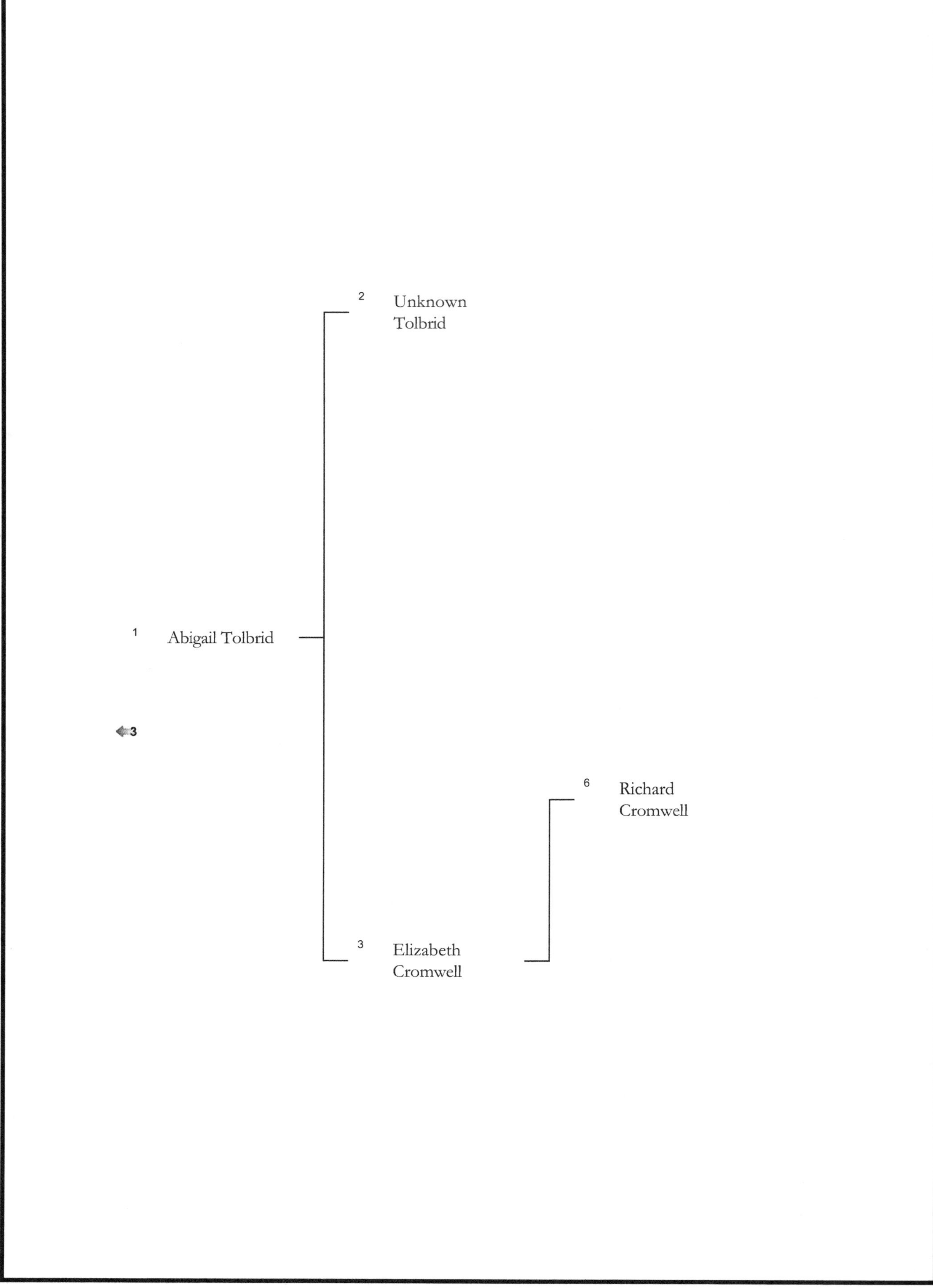

2
Unknown
Tolbrid

1
Abigail Tolbrid

3

6
Richard
Cromwell

3
Elizabeth
Cromwell

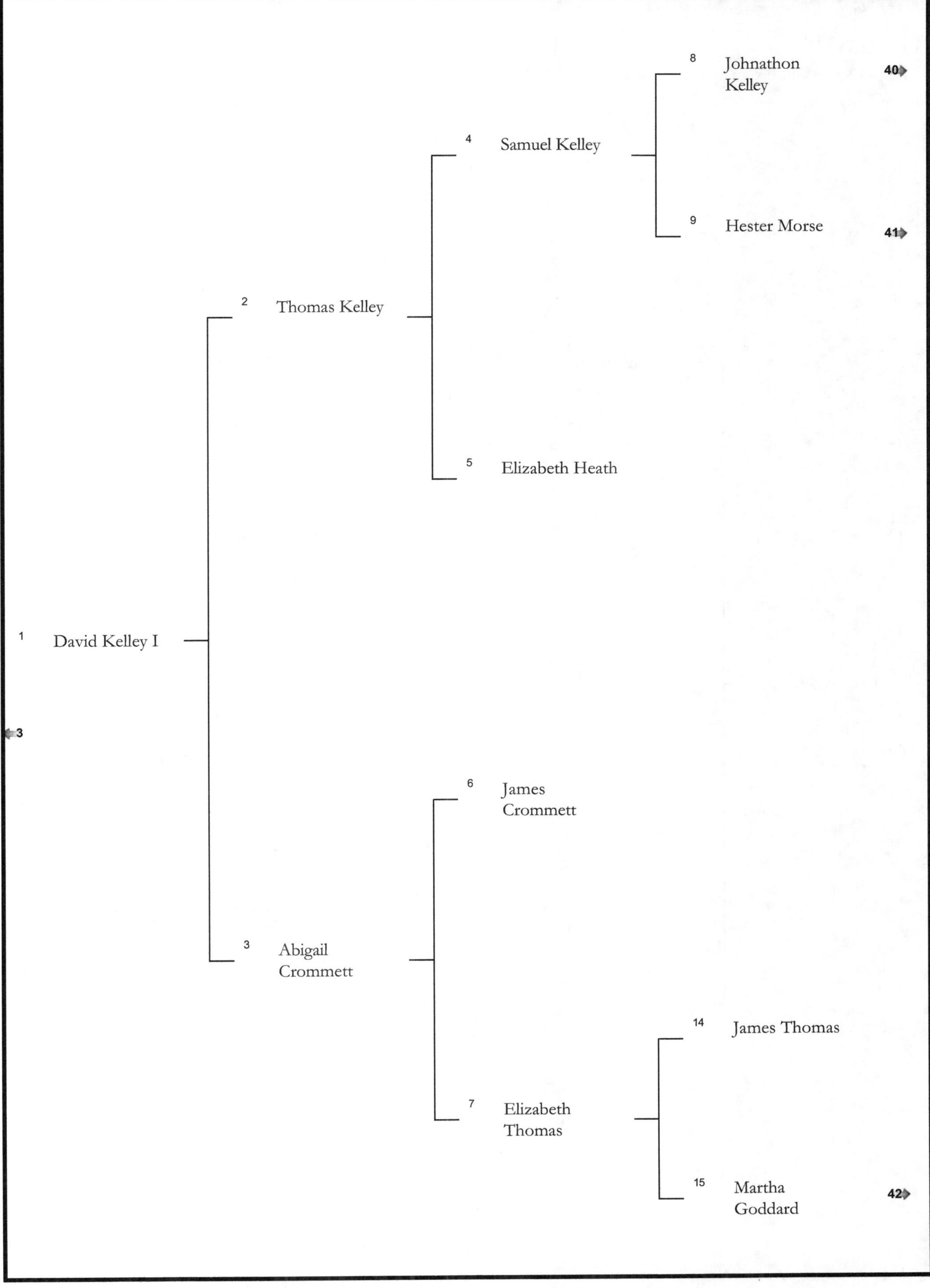

1 David Kelley I
2 Thomas Kelley
3 Abigail Crommett
4 Samuel Kelley
5 Elizabeth Heath
6 James Crommett
7 Elizabeth Thomas
8 Johnathon Kelley
9 Hester Morse
14 James Thomas
15 Martha Goddard
40
41
42
3

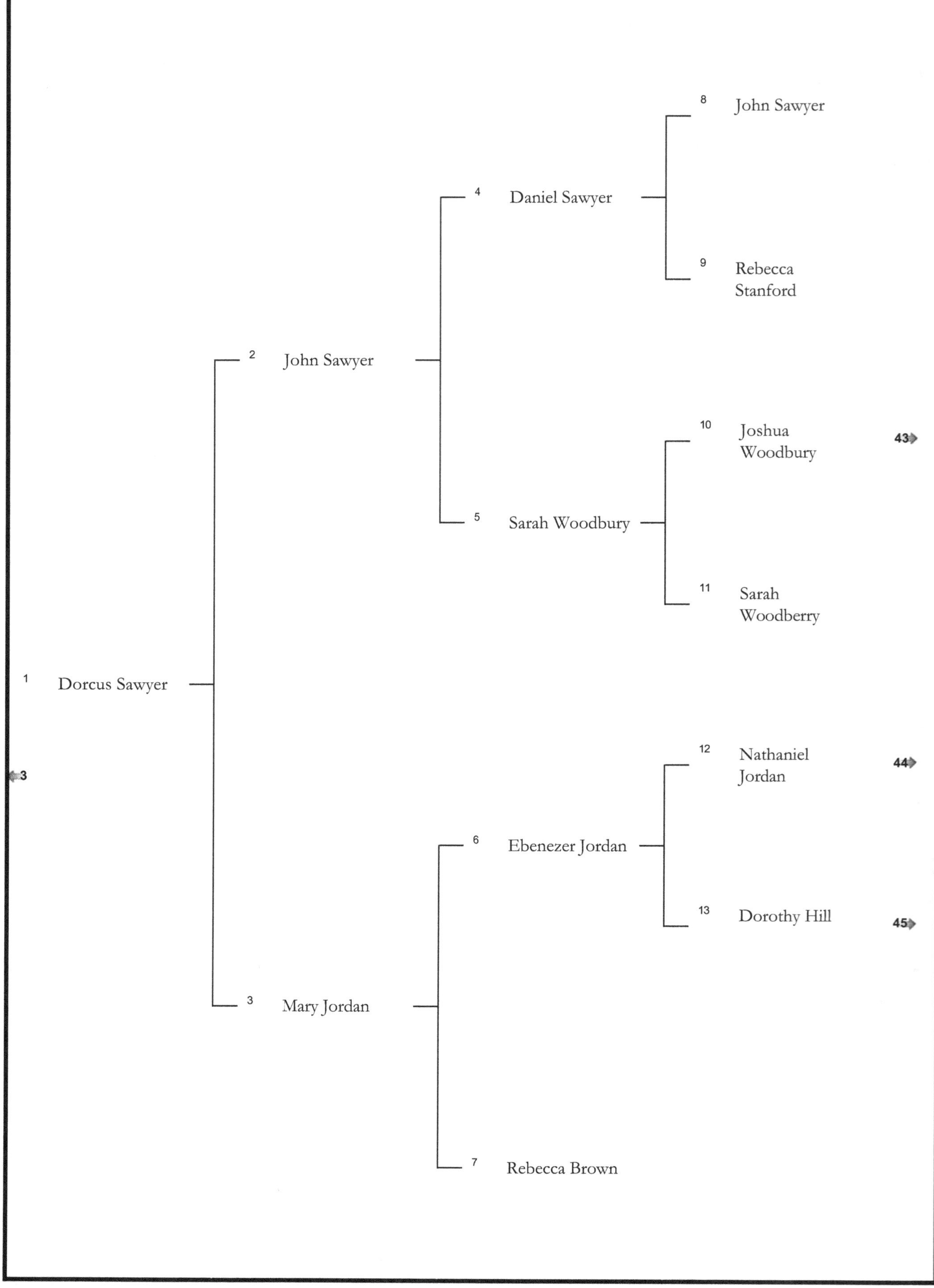

1 Dorcus Sawyer
2 John Sawyer
3 Mary Jordan
4 Daniel Sawyer
5 Sarah Woodbury
6 Ebenezer Jordan
7 Rebecca Brown
8 John Sawyer
9 Rebecca Stanford
10 Joshua Woodbury
11 Sarah Woodberry
12 Nathaniel Jordan
13 Dorothy Hill
3
43
44
45

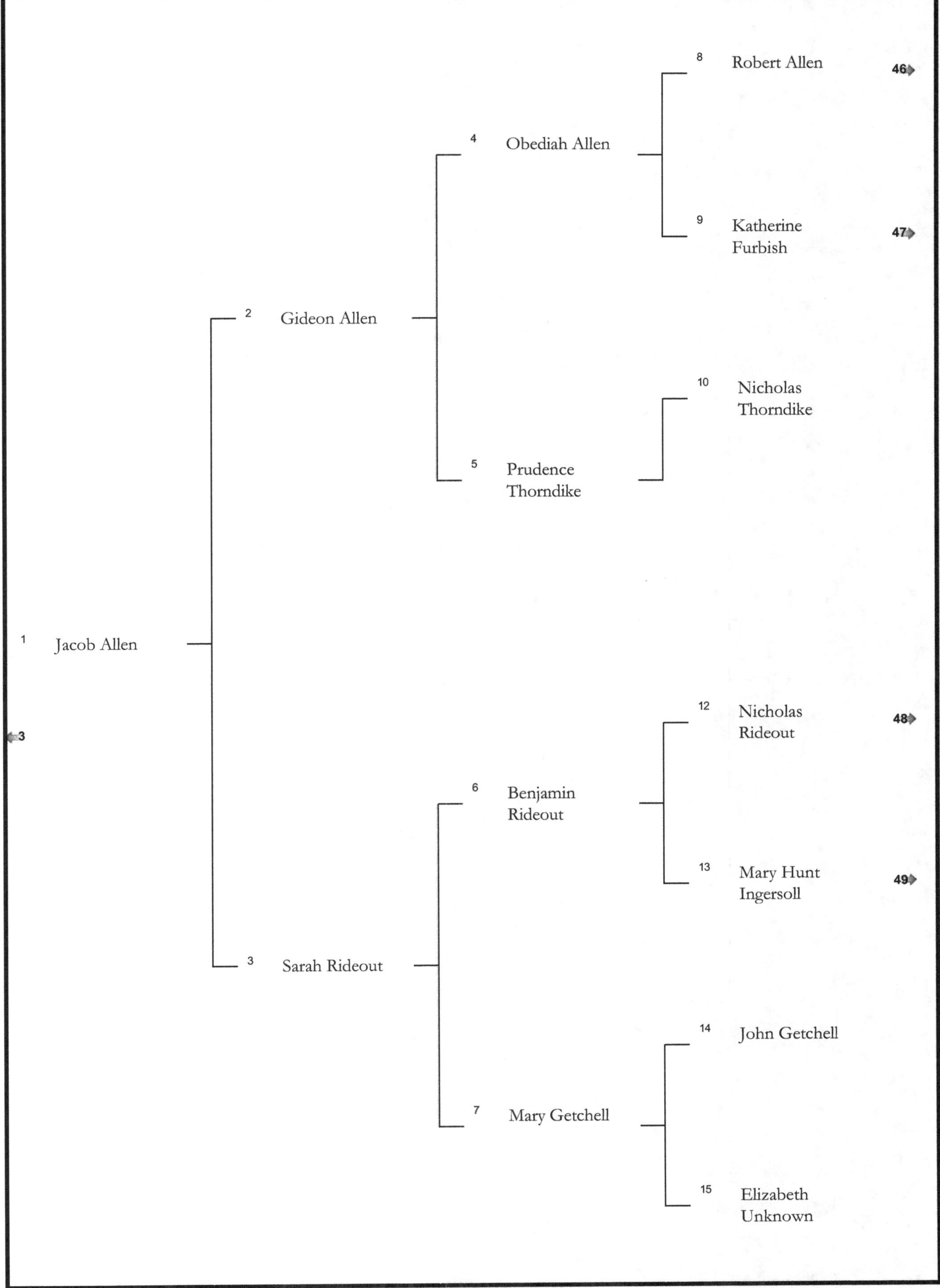

8 Robert Allen 46
4 Obediah Allen
9 Katherine Furbish 47
2 Gideon Allen
10 Nicholas Thorndike
5 Prudence Thorndike
1 Jacob Allen
3
12 Nicholas Rideout 48
6 Benjamin Rideout
13 Mary Hunt Ingersoll 49
3 Sarah Rideout
14 John Getchell
7 Mary Getchell
15 Elizabeth Unknown

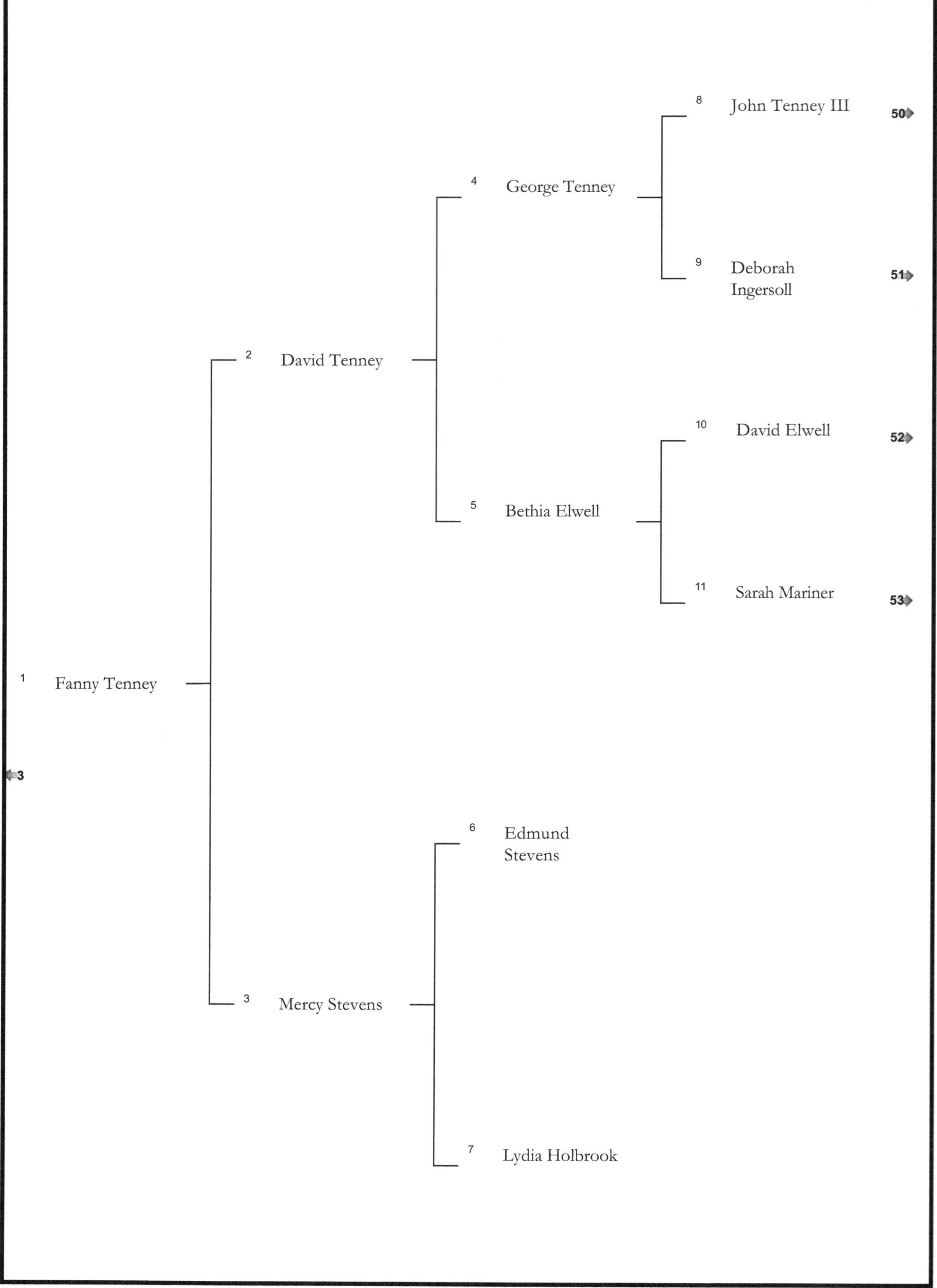

1 Fanny Tenney
3
2 David Tenney
3 Mercy Stevens
4 George Tenney
5 Bethia Elwell
6 Edmund Stevens
7 Lydia Holbrook
8 John Tenney III 50
9 Deborah Ingersoll 51
10 David Elwell 52
11 Sarah Mariner 53

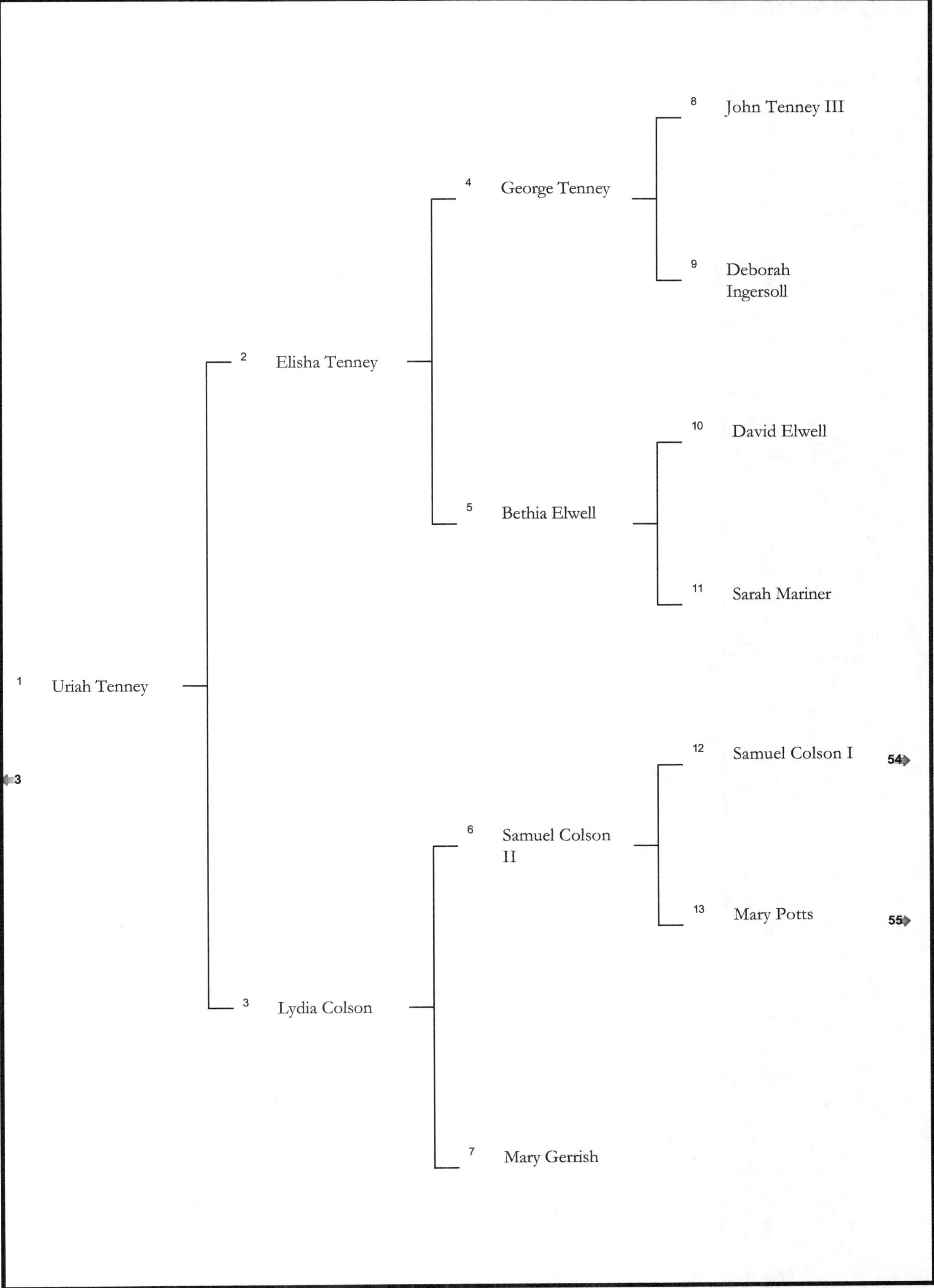

1 Uriah Tenney
2 Elisha Tenney
4 George Tenney
8 John Tenney III
9 Deborah Ingersoll
5 Bethia Elwell
10 David Elwell
11 Sarah Mariner
3 Lydia Colson
6 Samuel Colson II
12 Samuel Colson I
54
13 Mary Potts
55
7 Mary Gerrish
3

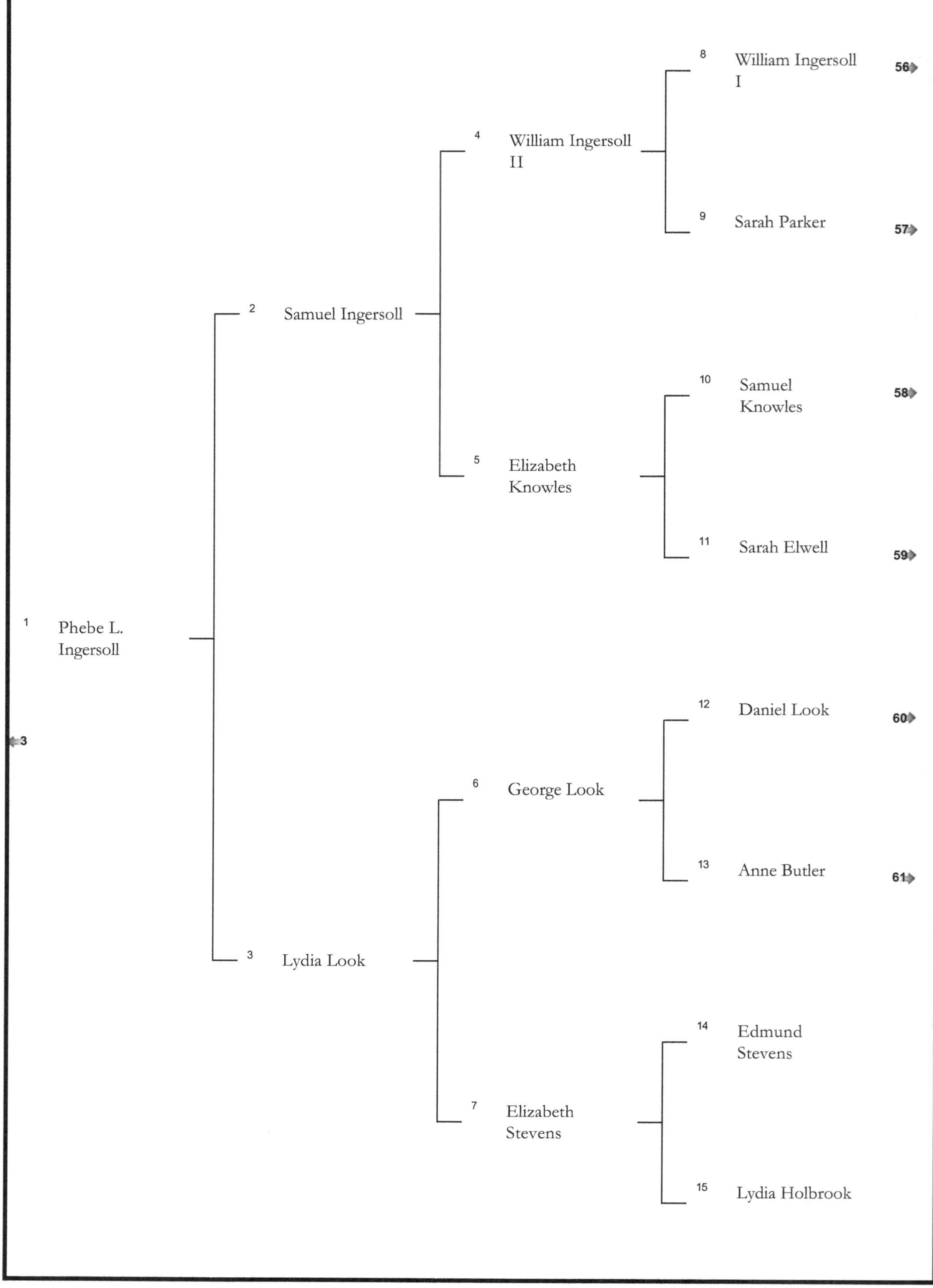

1 Phebe L. Ingersoll
3
2 Samuel Ingersoll
3 Lydia Look
4 William Ingersoll II
5 Elizabeth Knowles
6 George Look
7 Elizabeth Stevens
8 William Ingersoll I
56
9 Sarah Parker
57
10 Samuel Knowles
58
11 Sarah Elwell
59
12 Daniel Look
60
13 Anne Butler
61
14 Edmund Stevens
15 Lydia Holbrook

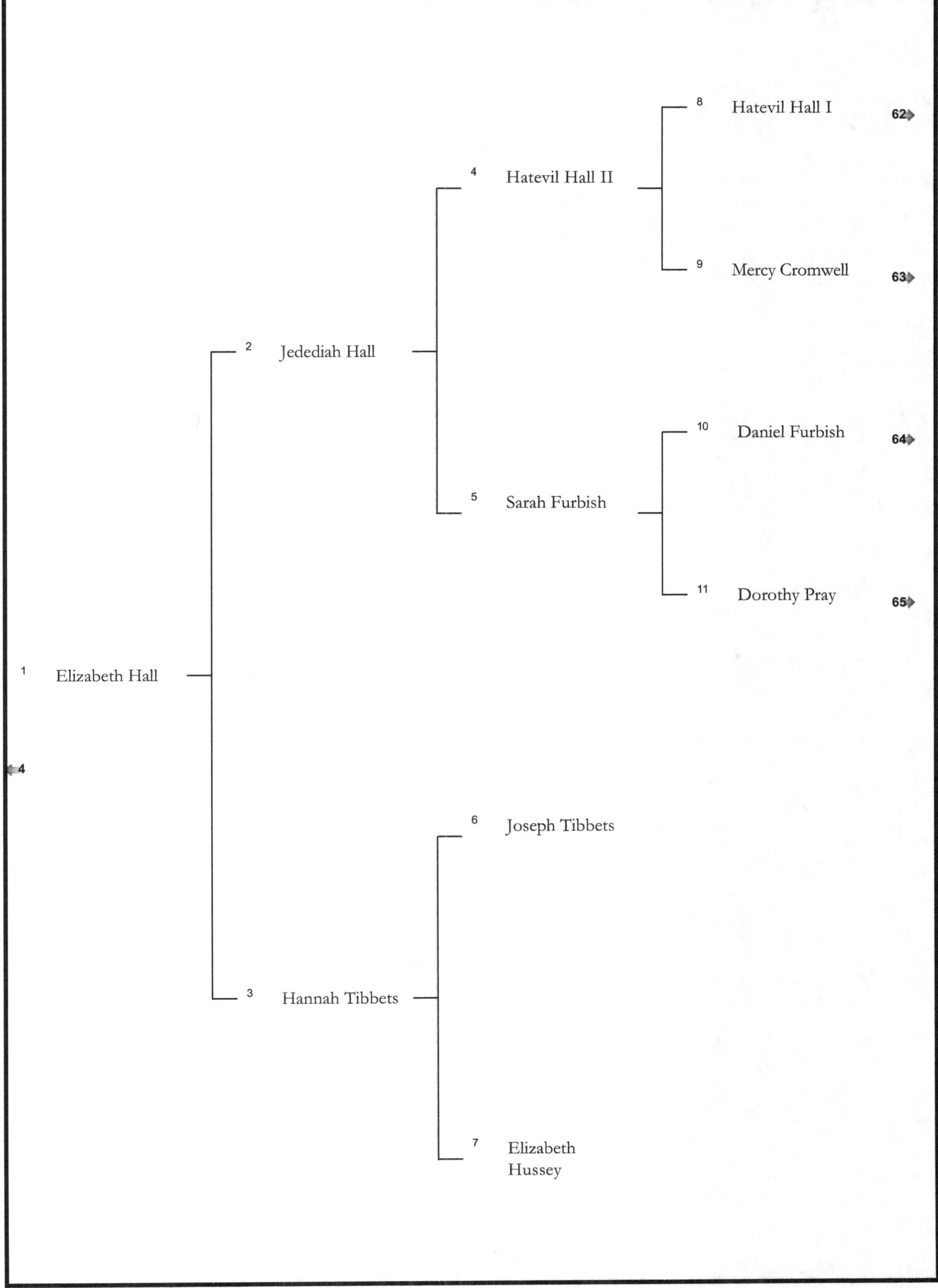

1 Elizabeth Hall
2 Jedediah Hall
3 Hannah Tibbets
4 Hatevil Hall II
5 Sarah Furbish
6 Joseph Tibbets
7 Elizabeth Hussey
8 Hatevil Hall I
62
9 Mercy Cromwell
63
10 Daniel Furbish
64
11 Dorothy Pray
65
4

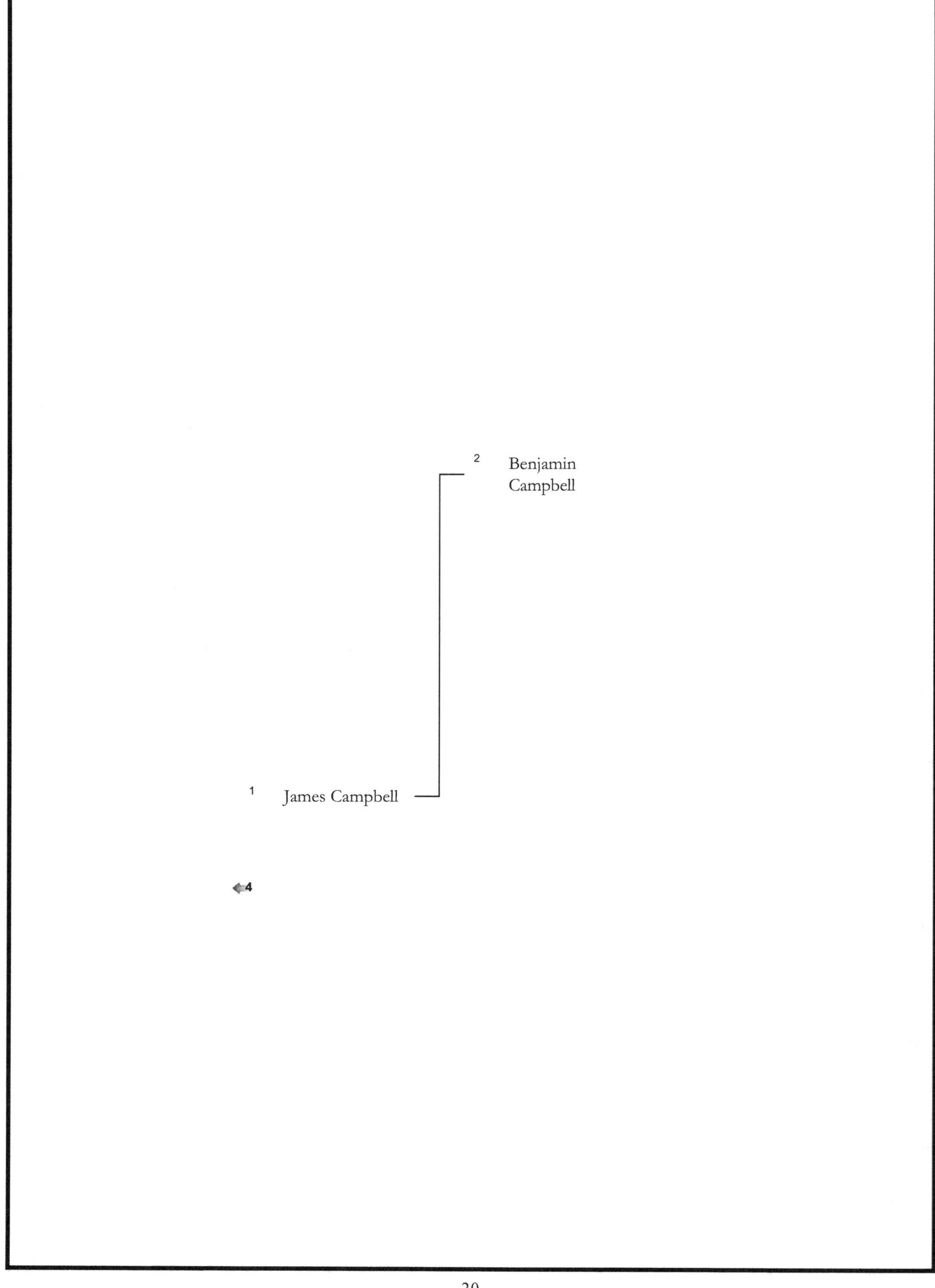
2
Benjamin
Campbell
1
James Campbell
4

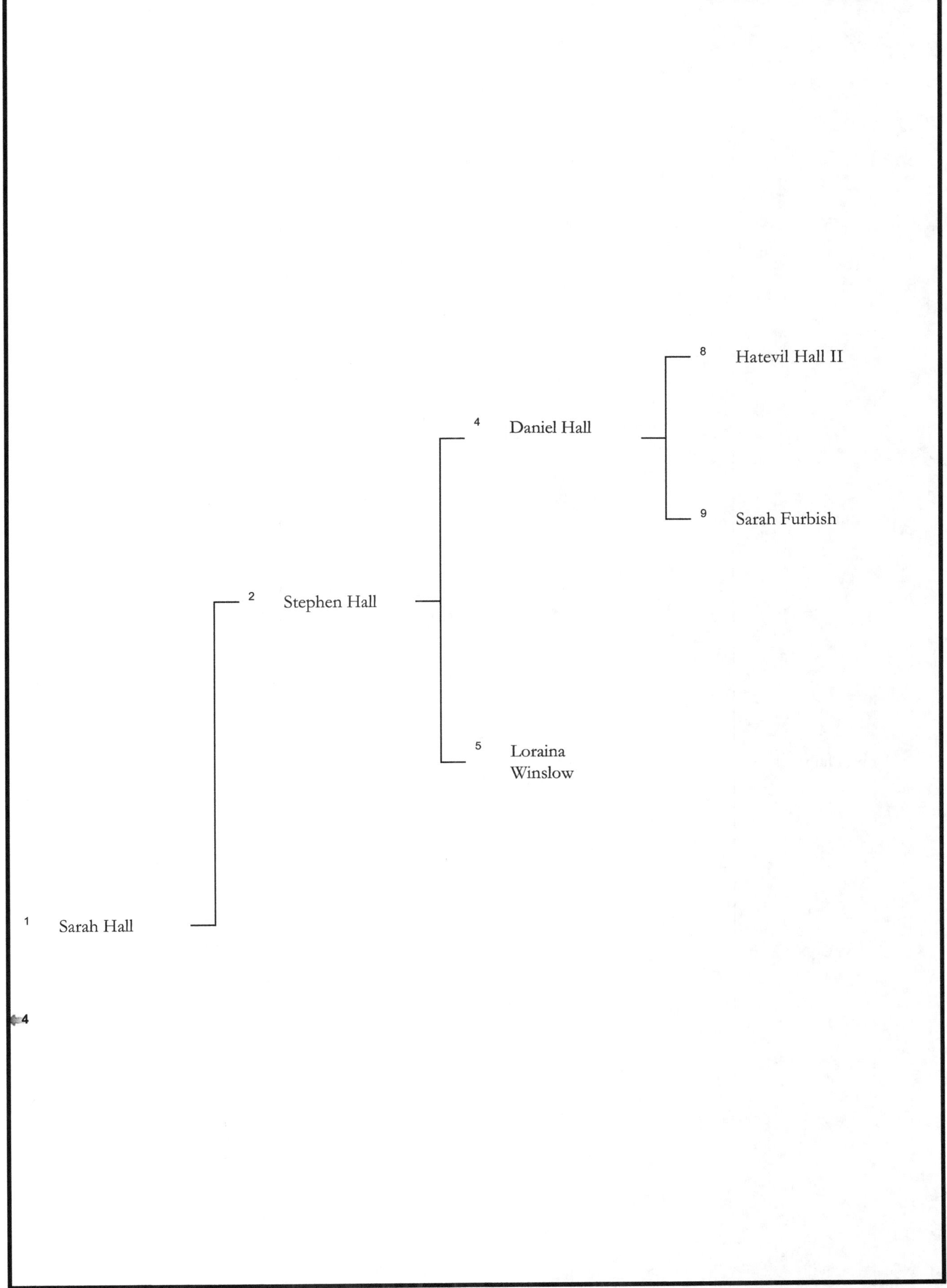

1 Sarah Hall
2 Stephen Hall
4 Daniel Hall
5 Loraina Winslow
8 Hatevil Hall II
9 Sarah Furbish

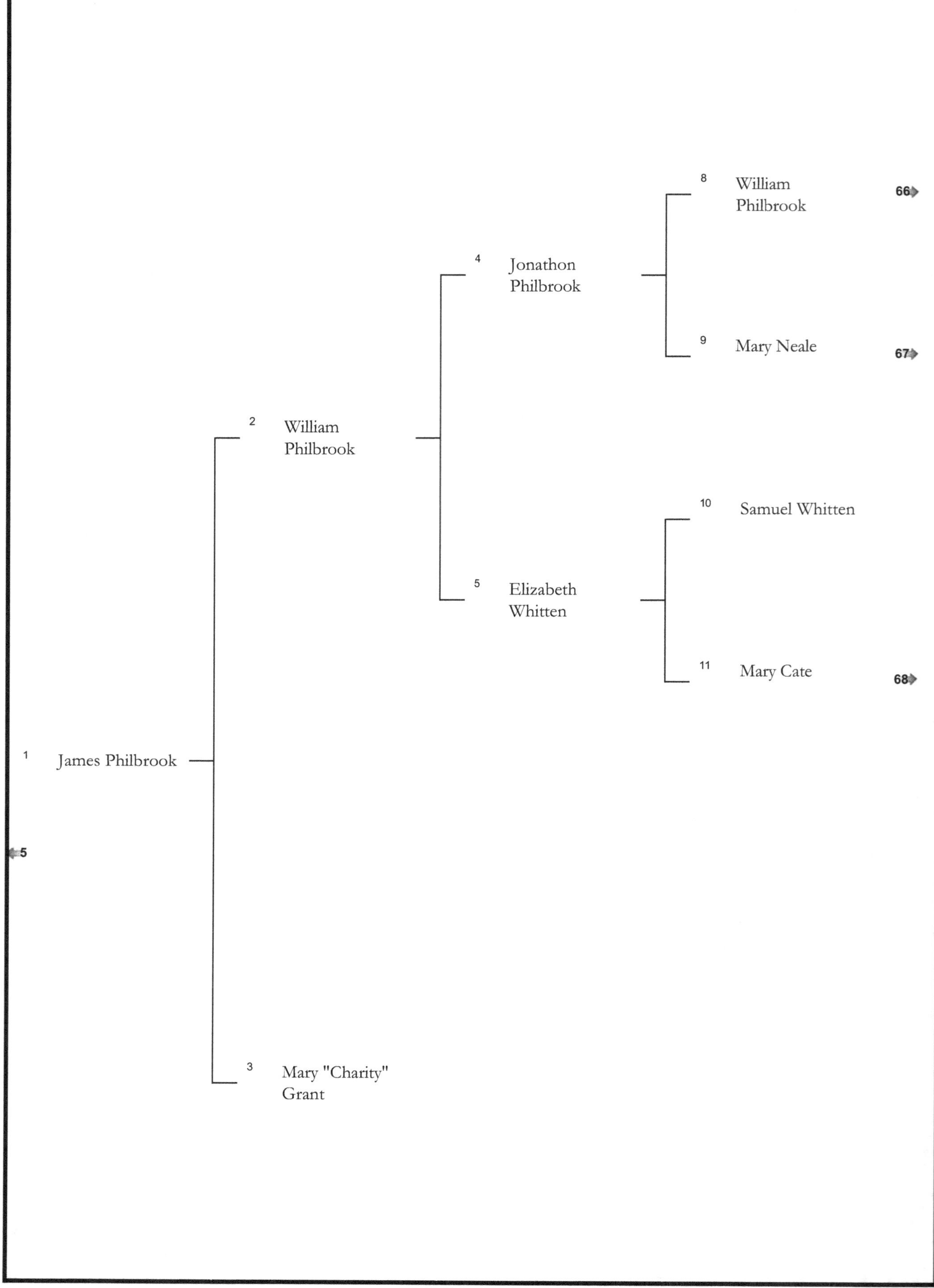

8 William Philbrook
66
4 Jonathon Philbrook
9 Mary Neale
67
2 William Philbrook
10 Samuel Whitten
5 Elizabeth Whitten
11 Mary Cate
68
1 James Philbrook
5
3 Mary "Charity" Grant

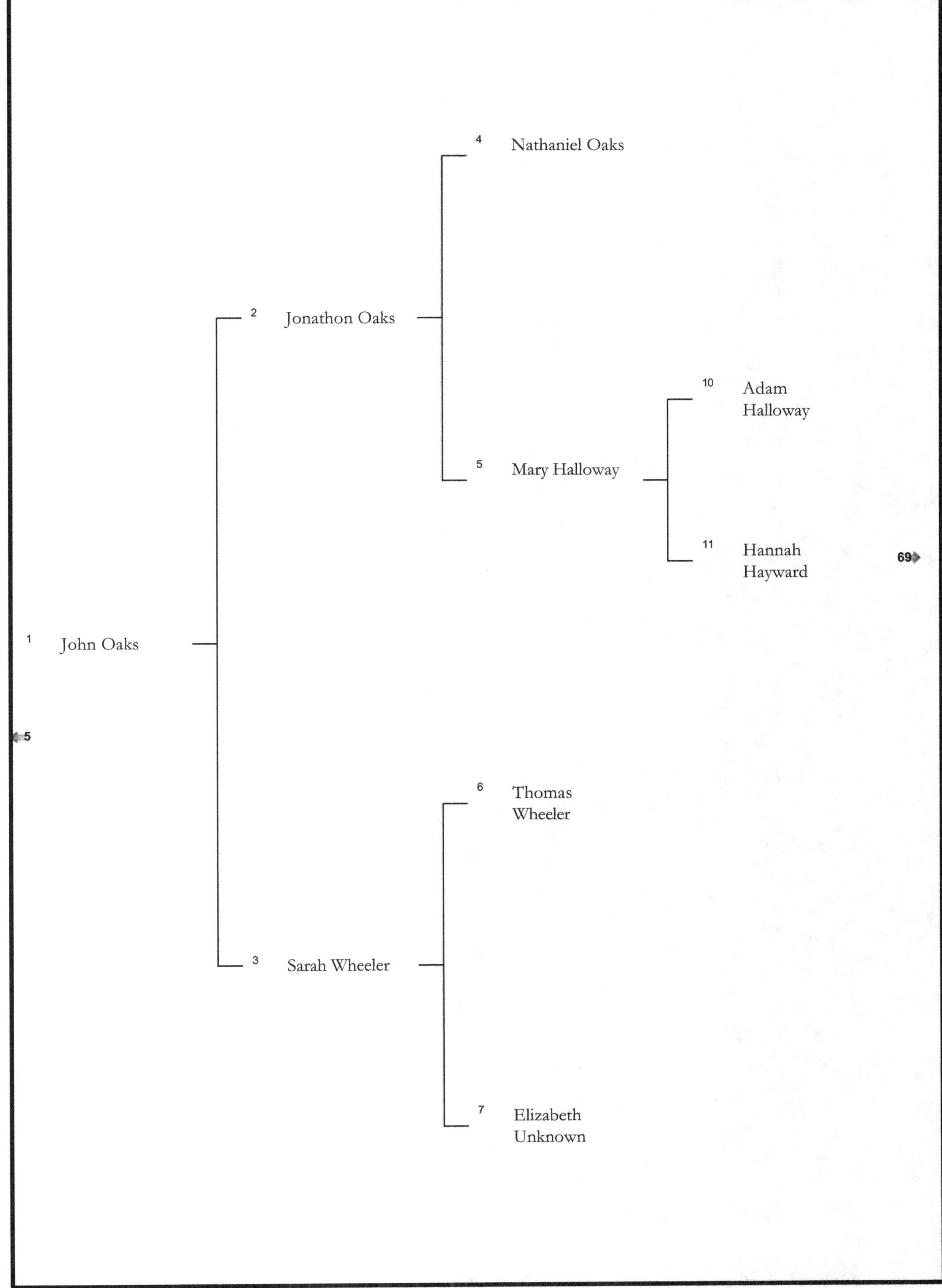
5
1 John Oaks
2 Jonathon Oaks
4 Nathaniel Oaks
5 Mary Halloway
10 Adam Halloway
11 Hannah Hayward
69
3 Sarah Wheeler
6 Thomas Wheeler
7 Elizabeth Unknown

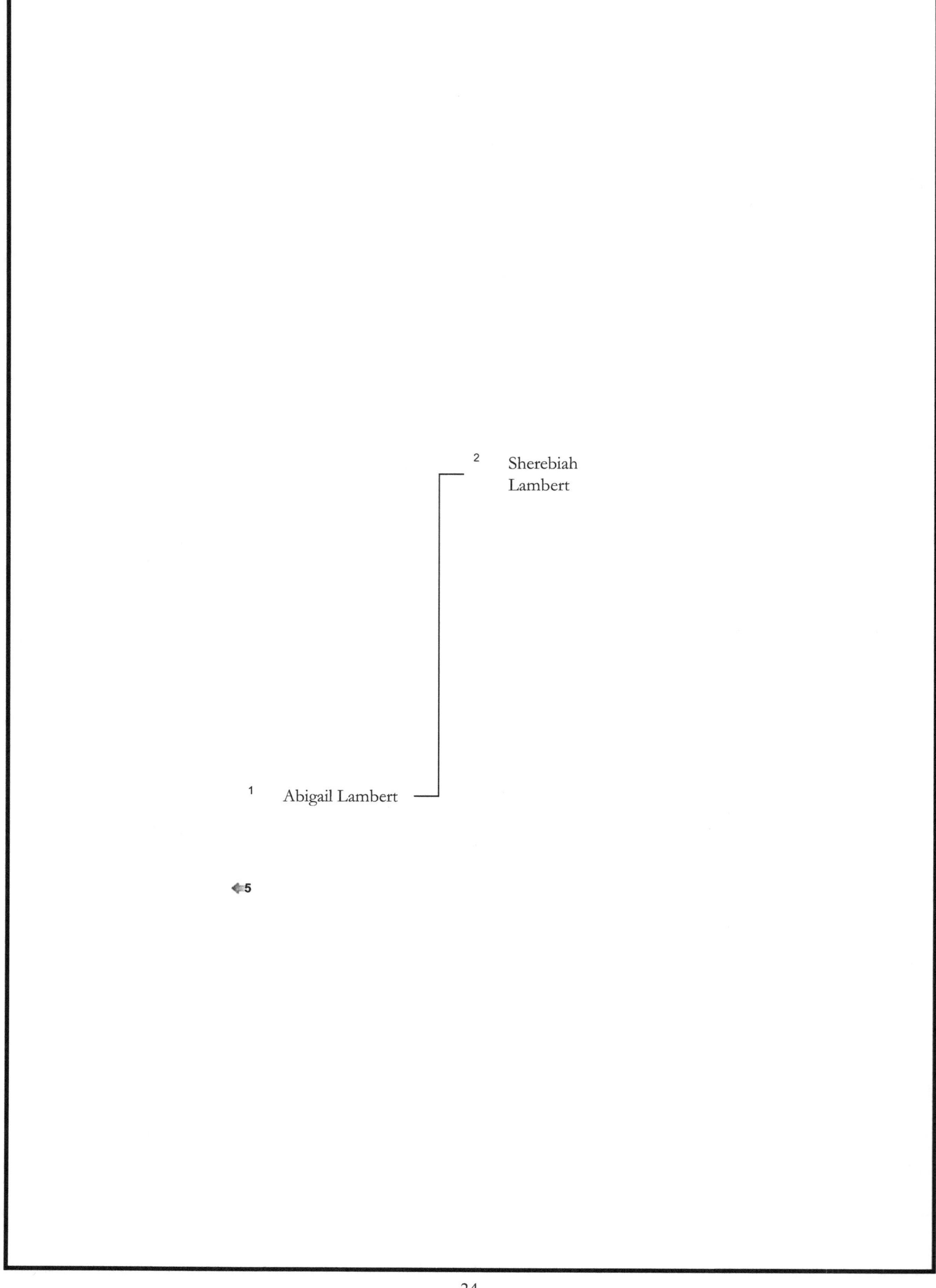

2
Sherebiah
Lambert

1
Abigail Lambert

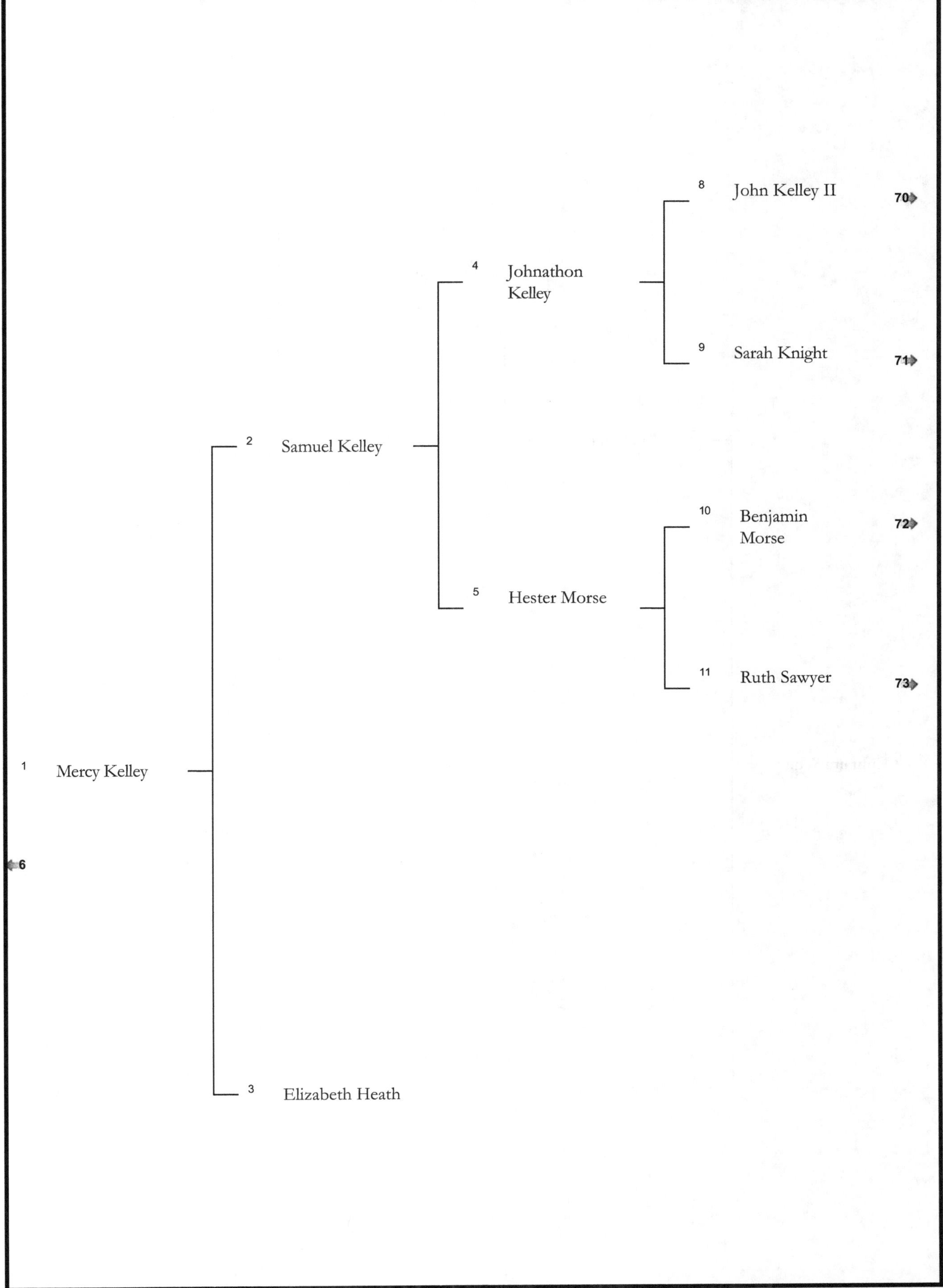

1 Mercy Kelley
6
2 Samuel Kelley
3 Elizabeth Heath
4 Johnathon Kelley
5 Hester Morse
8 John Kelley II
70
9 Sarah Knight
71
10 Benjamin Morse
72
11 Ruth Sawyer
73

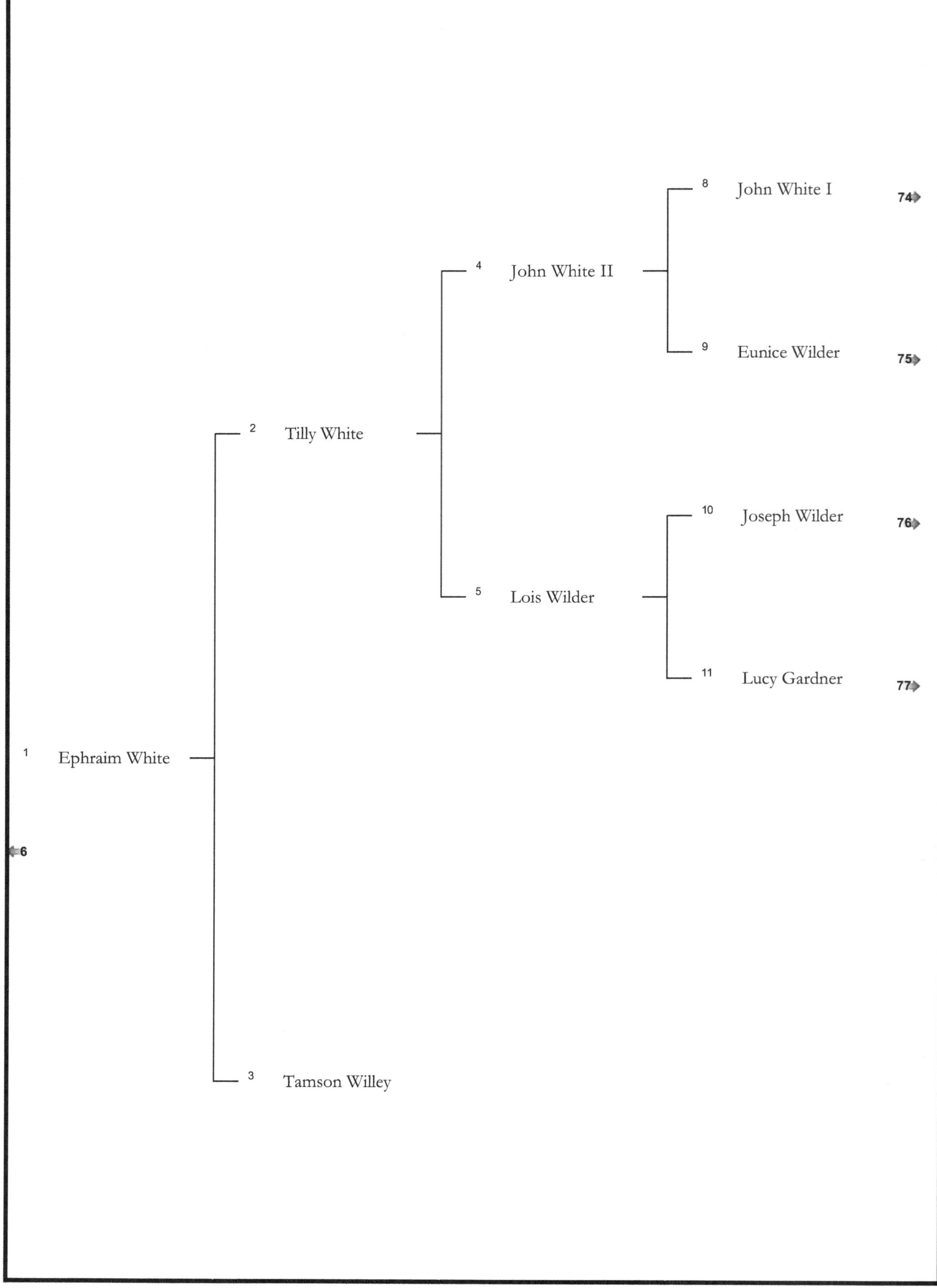

1 Ephraim White
6
2 Tilly White
3 Tamson Willey
4 John White II
5 Lois Wilder
8 John White I 74
9 Eunice Wilder 75
10 Joseph Wilder 76
11 Lucy Gardner 77

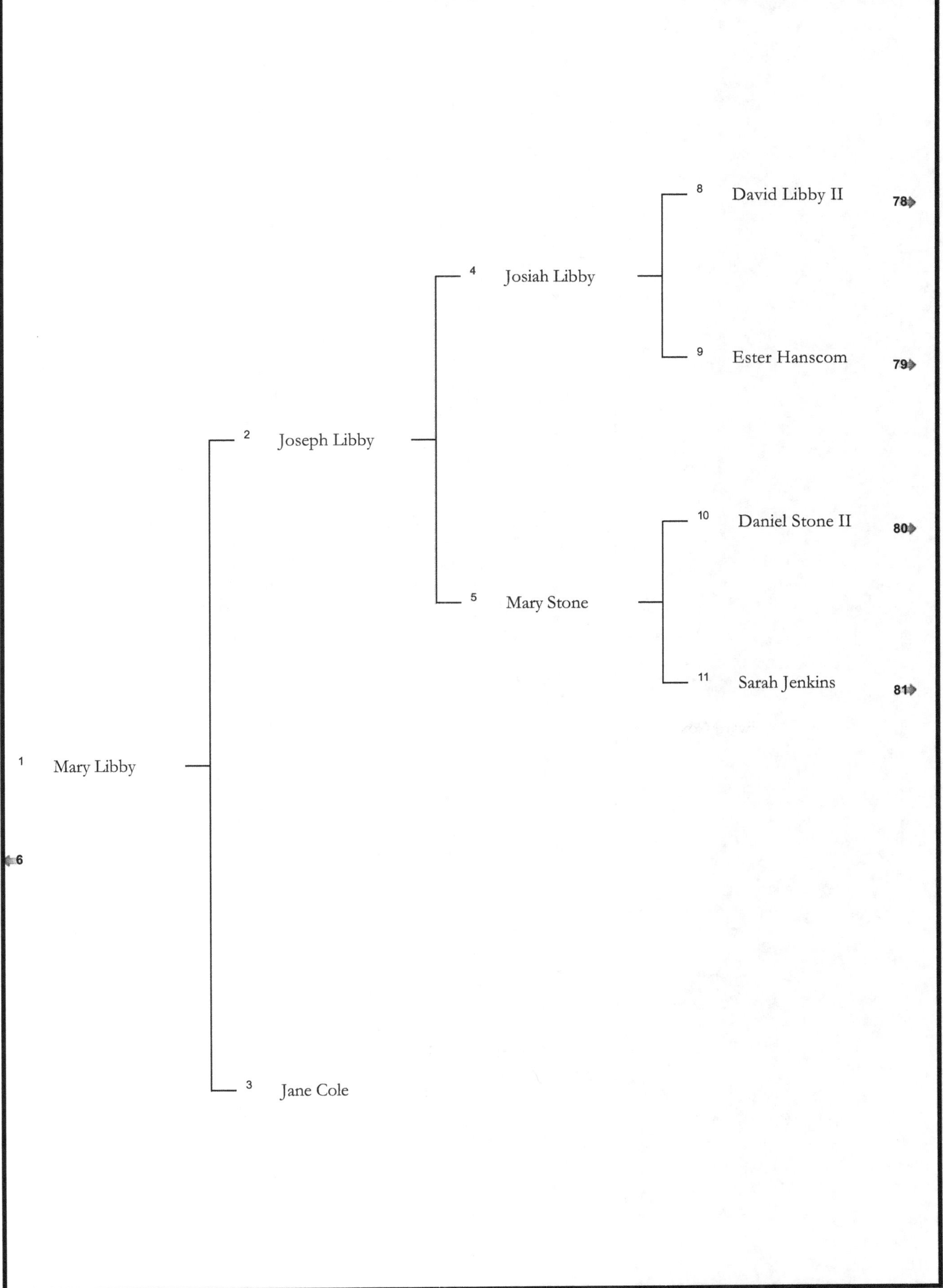

1 Mary Libby
6
2 Joseph Libby
3 Jane Cole
4 Josiah Libby
5 Mary Stone
8 David Libby II
78
9 Ester Hanscom
79
10 Daniel Stone II
80
11 Sarah Jenkins
81

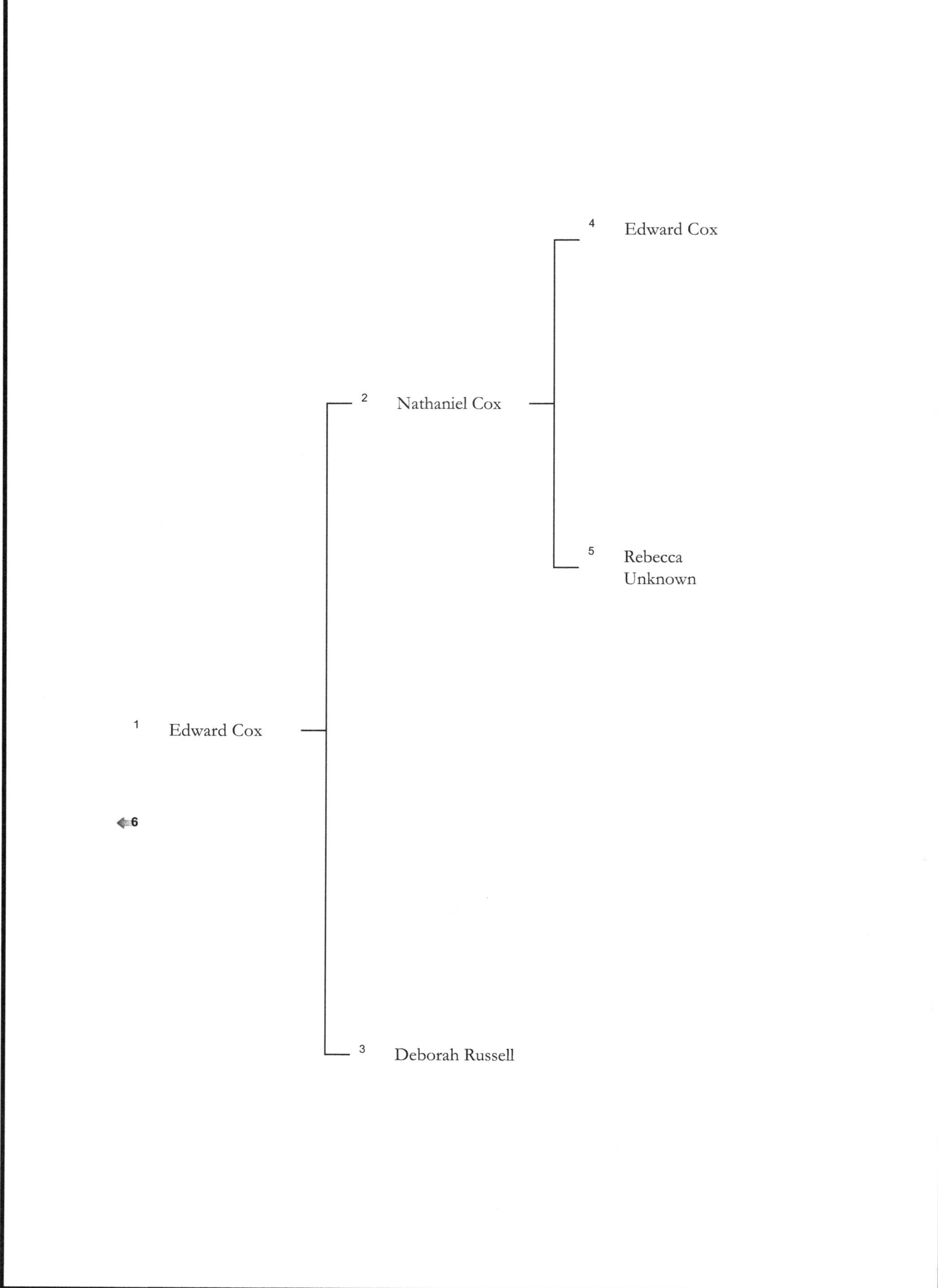

4 Edward Cox
2 Nathaniel Cox
5 Rebecca Unknown
1 Edward Cox
6
3 Deborah Russell

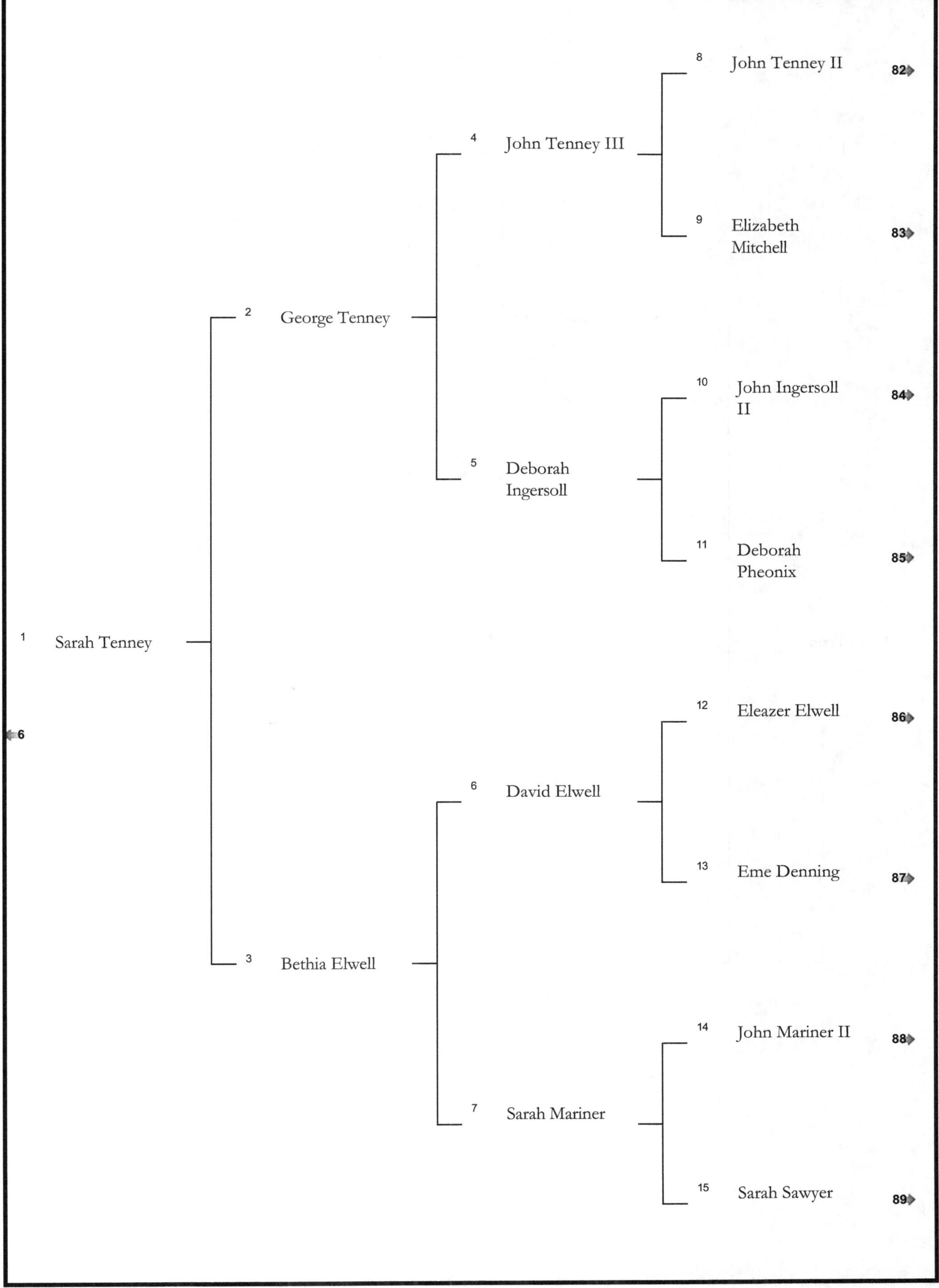

1 Sarah Tenney
6
2 George Tenney
3 Bethia Elwell
4 John Tenney III
5 Deborah Ingersoll
6 David Elwell
7 Sarah Mariner
8 John Tenney II 82
9 Elizabeth Mitchell 83
10 John Ingersoll II 84
11 Deborah Pheonix 85
12 Eleazer Elwell 86
13 Eme Denning 87
14 John Mariner II 88
15 Sarah Sawyer 89

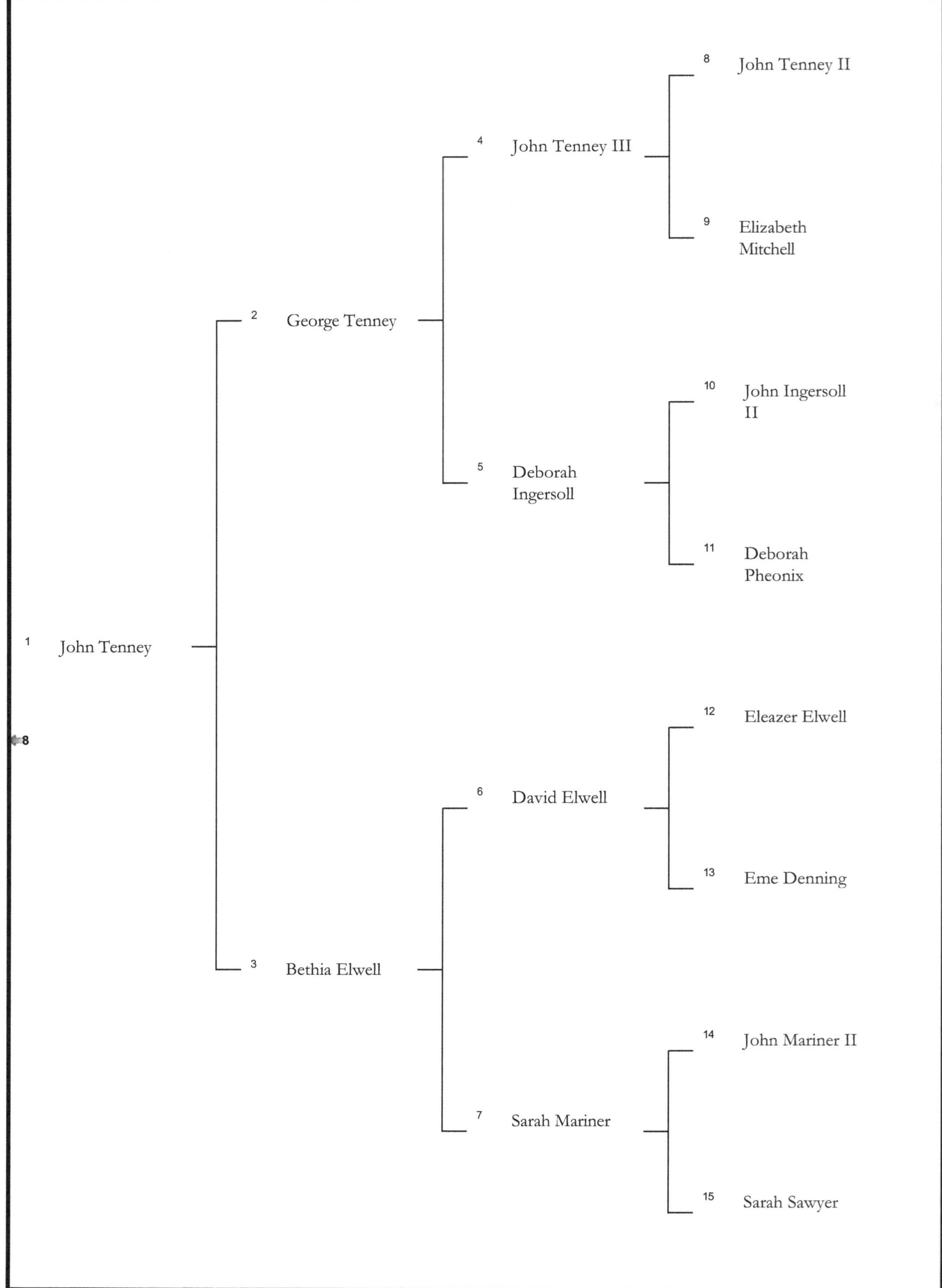

1 John Tenney
2 George Tenney
3 Bethia Elwell
4 John Tenney III
5 Deborah Ingersoll
6 David Elwell
7 Sarah Mariner
8 John Tenney II
9 Elizabeth Mitchell
10 John Ingersoll II
11 Deborah Pheonix
12 Eleazer Elwell
13 Eme Denning
14 John Mariner II
15 Sarah Sawyer
8

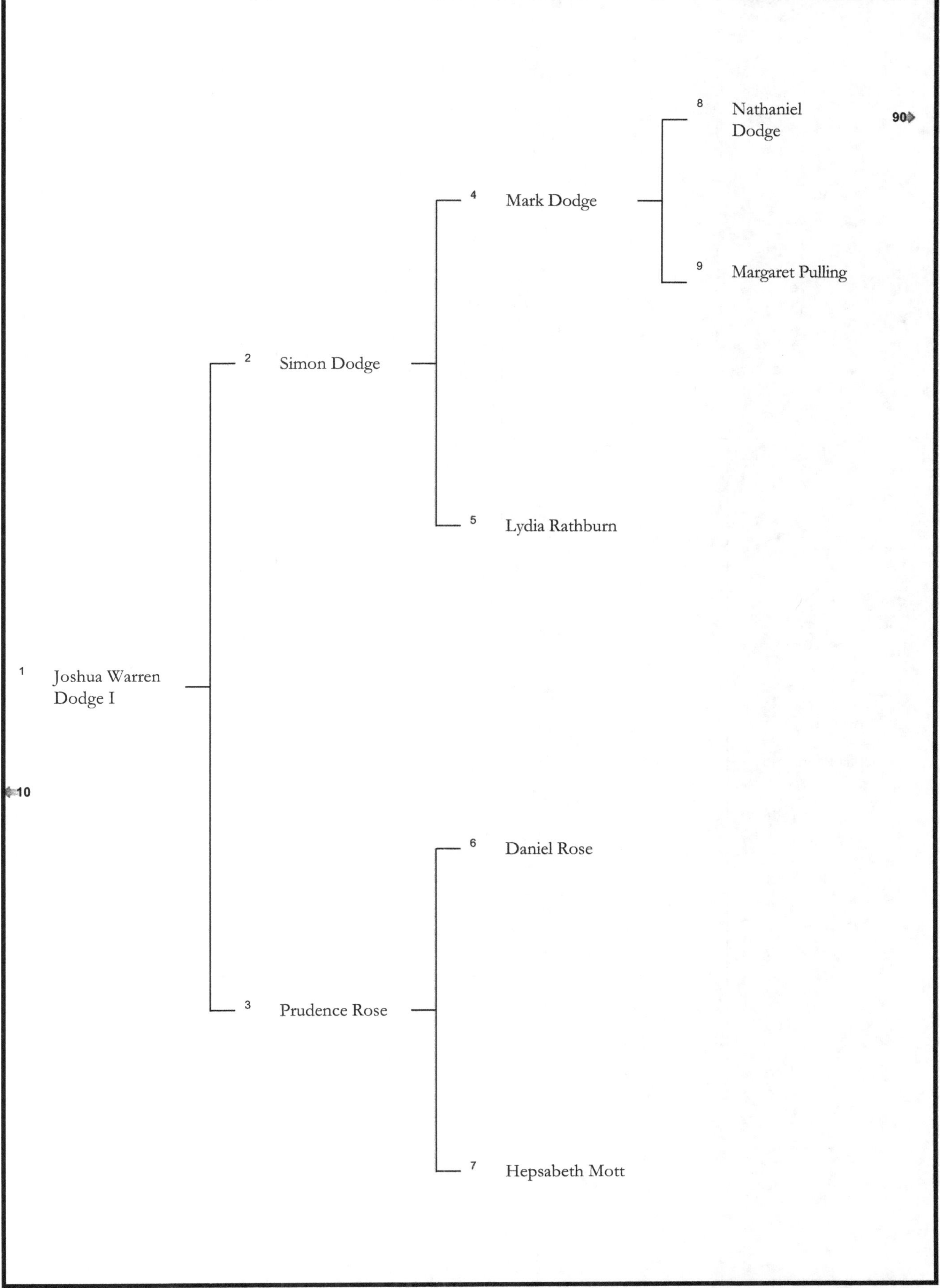

8 Nathaniel Dodge
90
4 Mark Dodge
9 Margaret Pulling
2 Simon Dodge
5 Lydia Rathburn
1 Joshua Warren Dodge I
10
6 Daniel Rose
3 Prudence Rose
7 Hepsabeth Mott

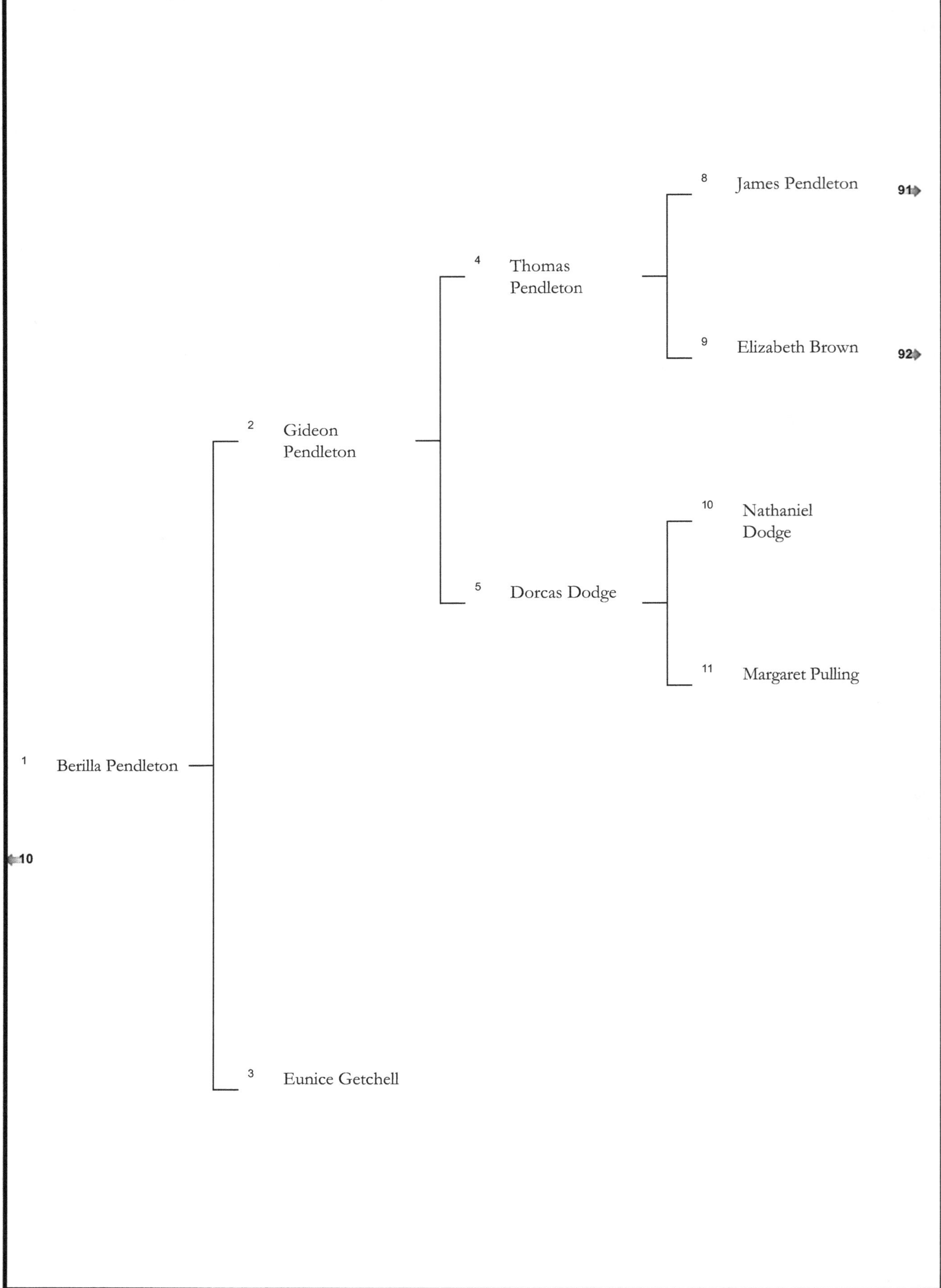

8 James Pendleton 91
4 Thomas Pendleton
9 Elizabeth Brown 92
2 Gideon Pendleton
10 Nathaniel Dodge
5 Dorcas Dodge
11 Margaret Pulling
1 Berilla Pendleton
10
3 Eunice Getchell

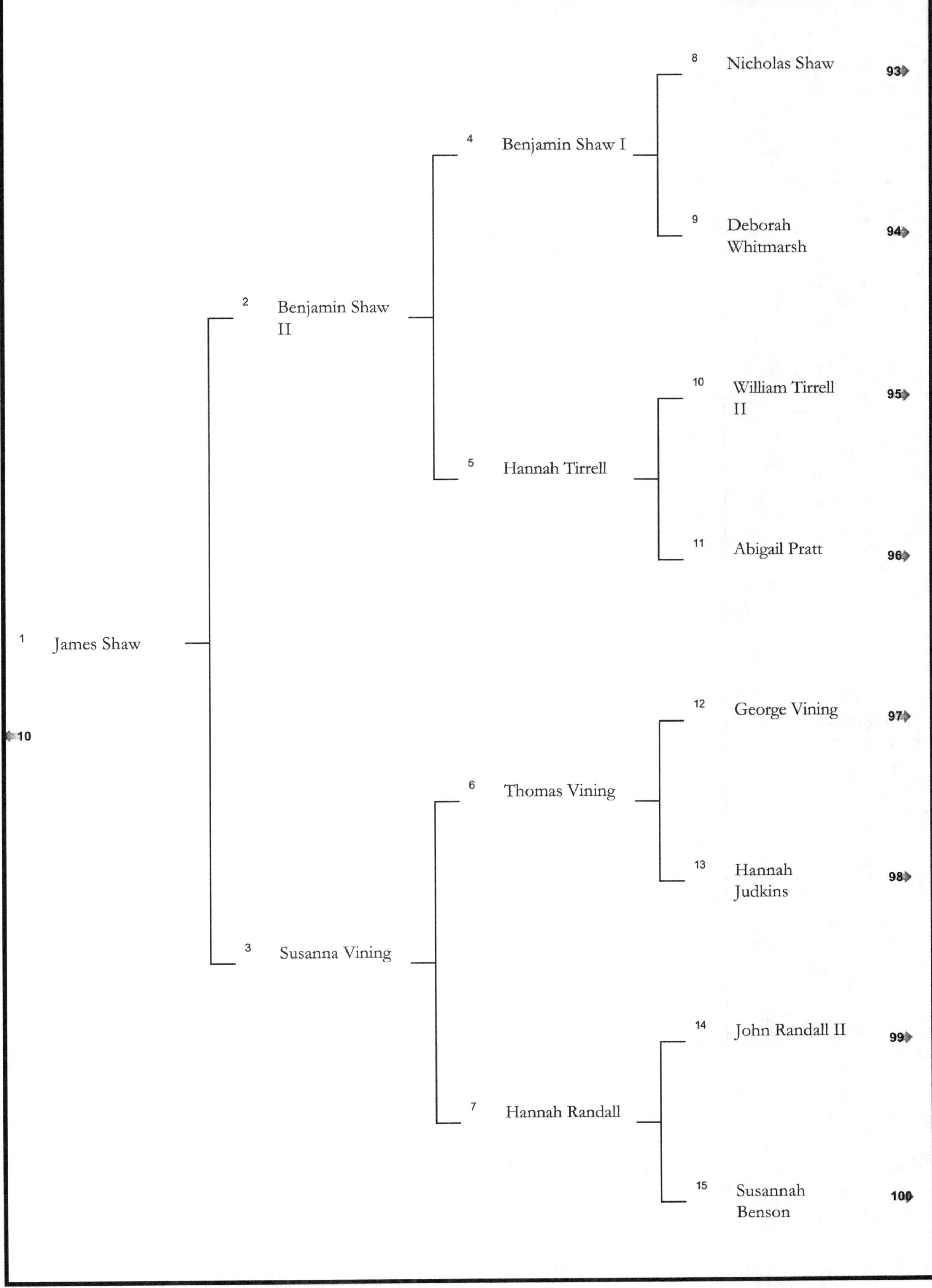

1 James Shaw
2 Benjamin Shaw II
3 Susanna Vining
4 Benjamin Shaw I
5 Hannah Tirrell
6 Thomas Vining
7 Hannah Randall
8 Nicholas Shaw
9 Deborah Whitmarsh
10 William Tirrell II
11 Abigail Pratt
12 George Vining
13 Hannah Judkins
14 John Randall II
15 Susannah Benson
93
94
95
96
97
98
99
100
10

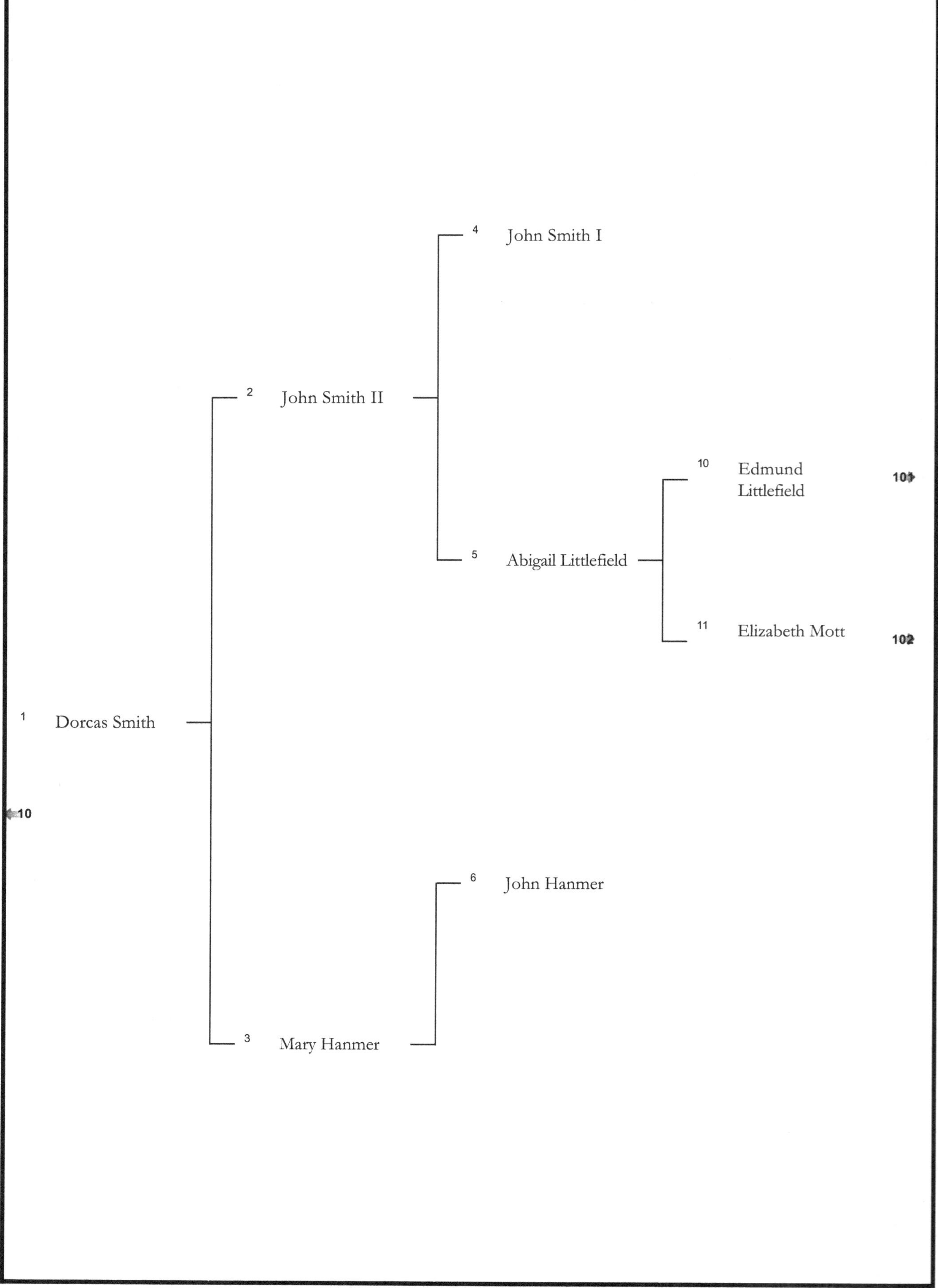

1 Dorcas Smith
2 John Smith II
3 Mary Hanmer
4 John Smith I
5 Abigail Littlefield
6 John Hanmer
10 Edmund Littlefield
11 Elizabeth Mott
101
102
10

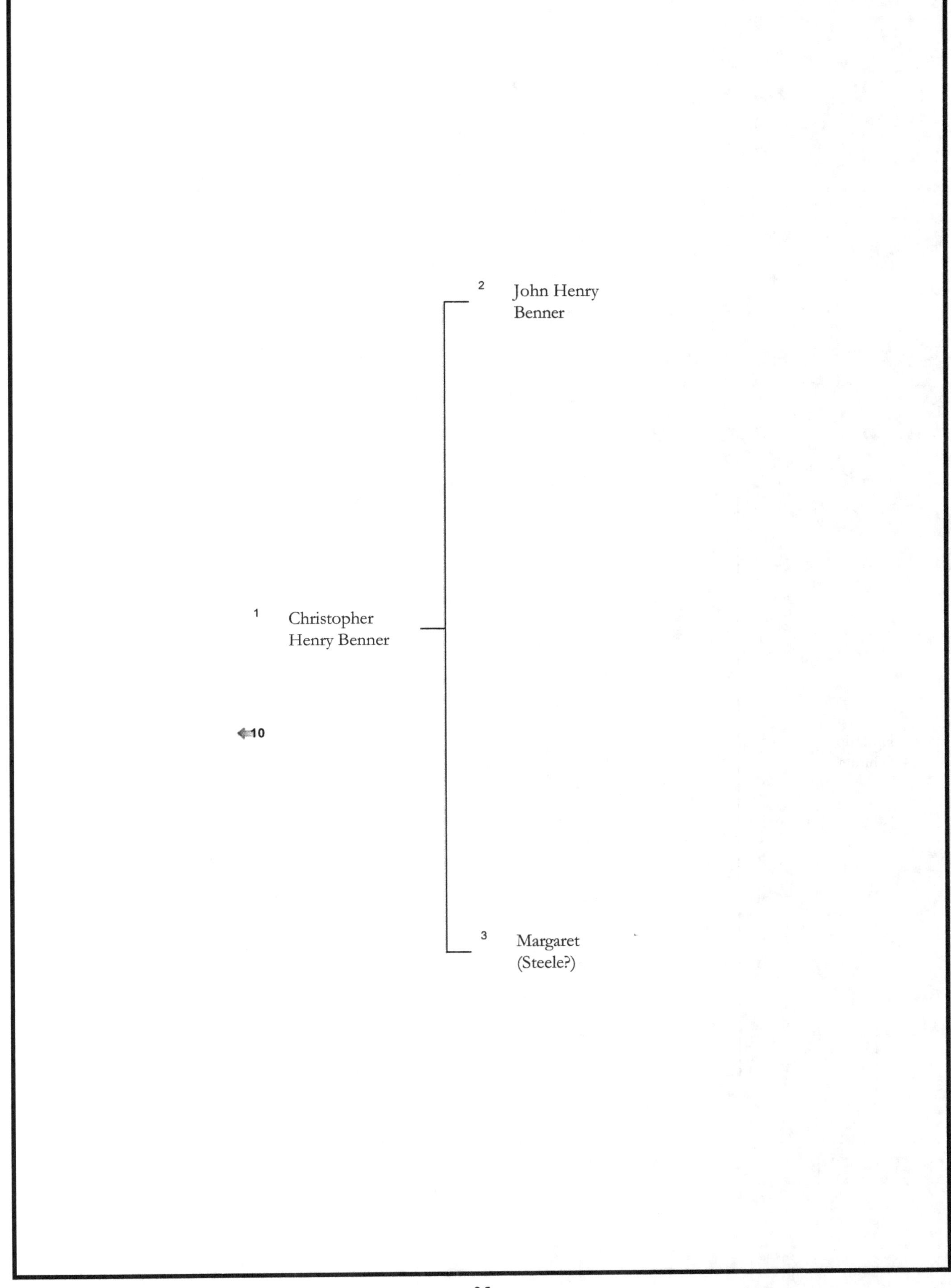

1 Christopher Henry Benner
2 John Henry Benner
3 Margaret (Steele?)
10

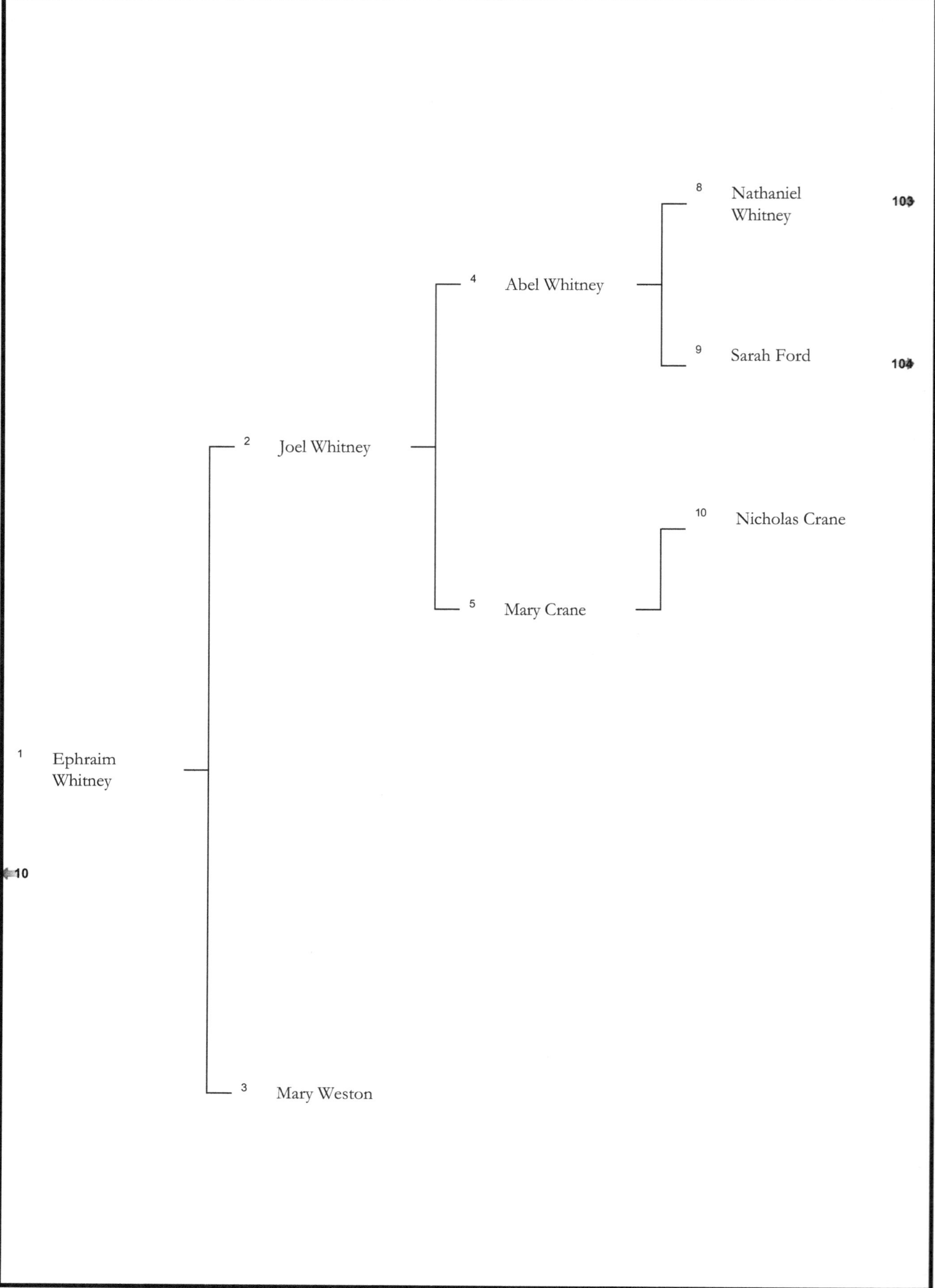

8 Nathaniel Whitney
103
4 Abel Whitney
9 Sarah Ford
104
2 Joel Whitney
10 Nicholas Crane
5 Mary Crane
1 Ephraim Whitney
10
3 Mary Weston

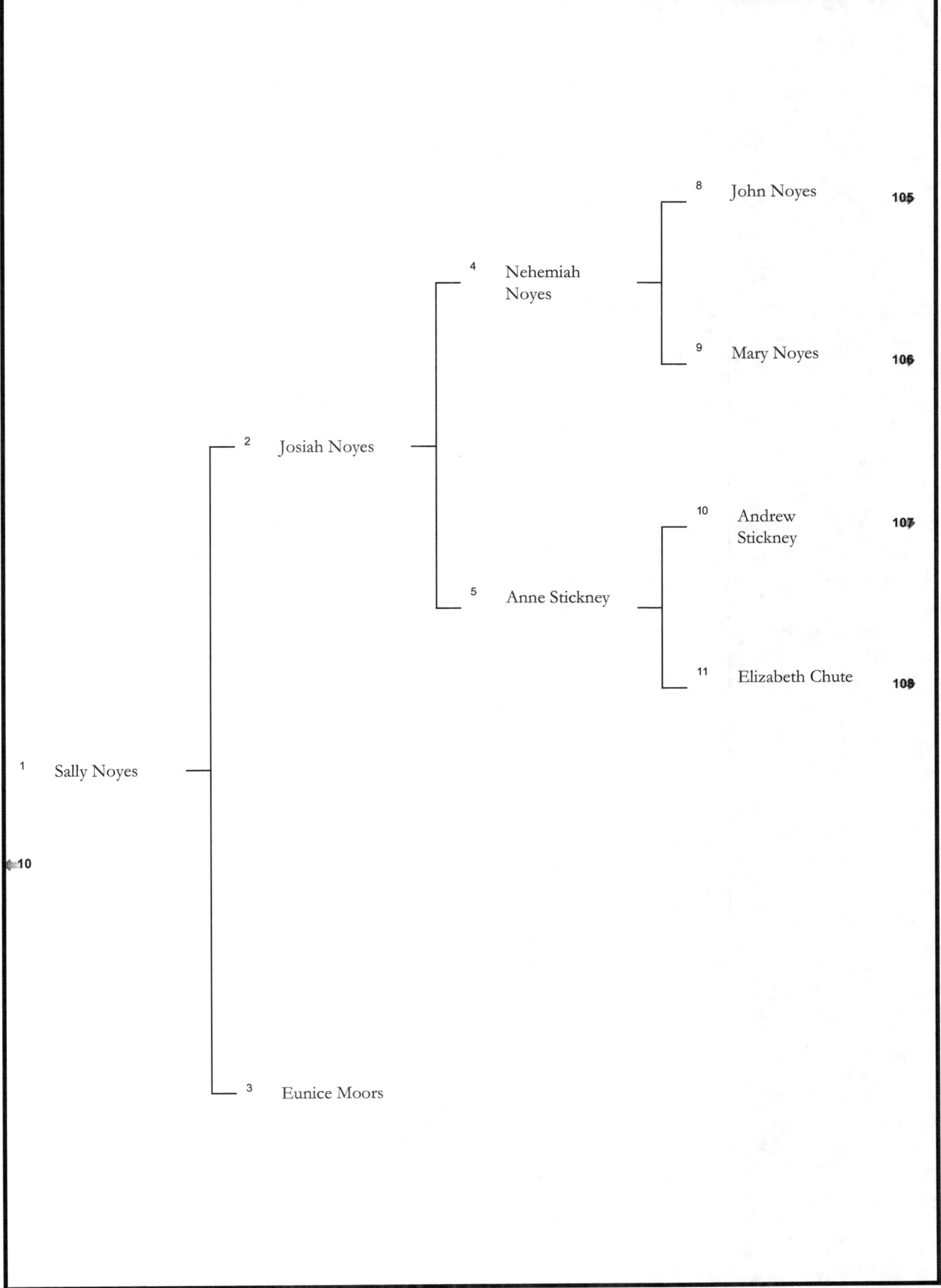

1 Sally Noyes
10
2 Josiah Noyes
3 Eunice Moors
4 Nehemiah Noyes
5 Anne Stickney
8 John Noyes 105
9 Mary Noyes 106
10 Andrew Stickney 107
11 Elizabeth Chute 108

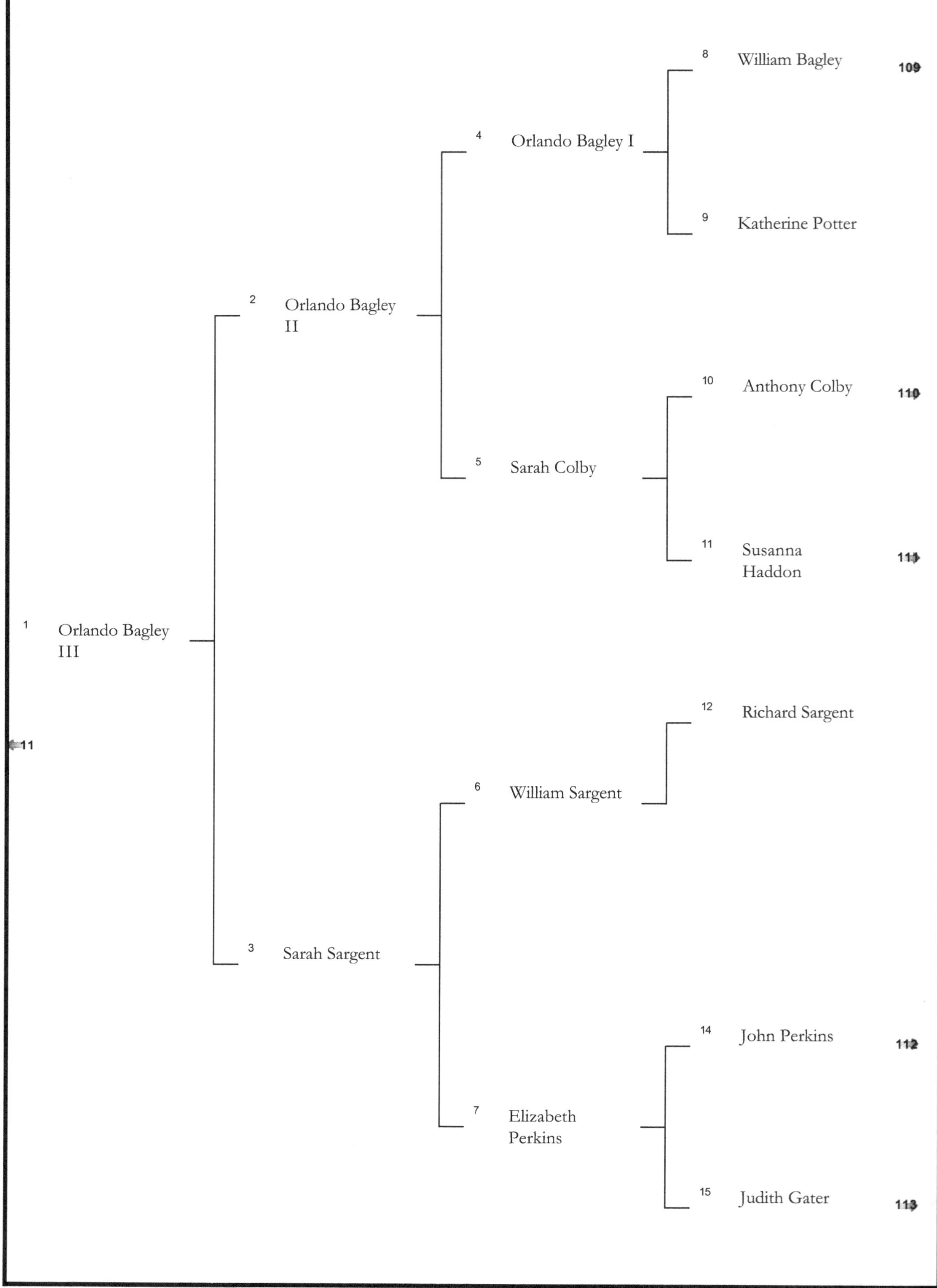

1 Orlando Bagley III
11

2 Orlando Bagley II

3 Sarah Sargent

4 Orlando Bagley I

5 Sarah Colby

6 William Sargent

7 Elizabeth Perkins

8 William Bagley 109

9 Katherine Potter

10 Anthony Colby 110

11 Susanna Haddon 111

12 Richard Sargent

14 John Perkins 112

15 Judith Gater 113

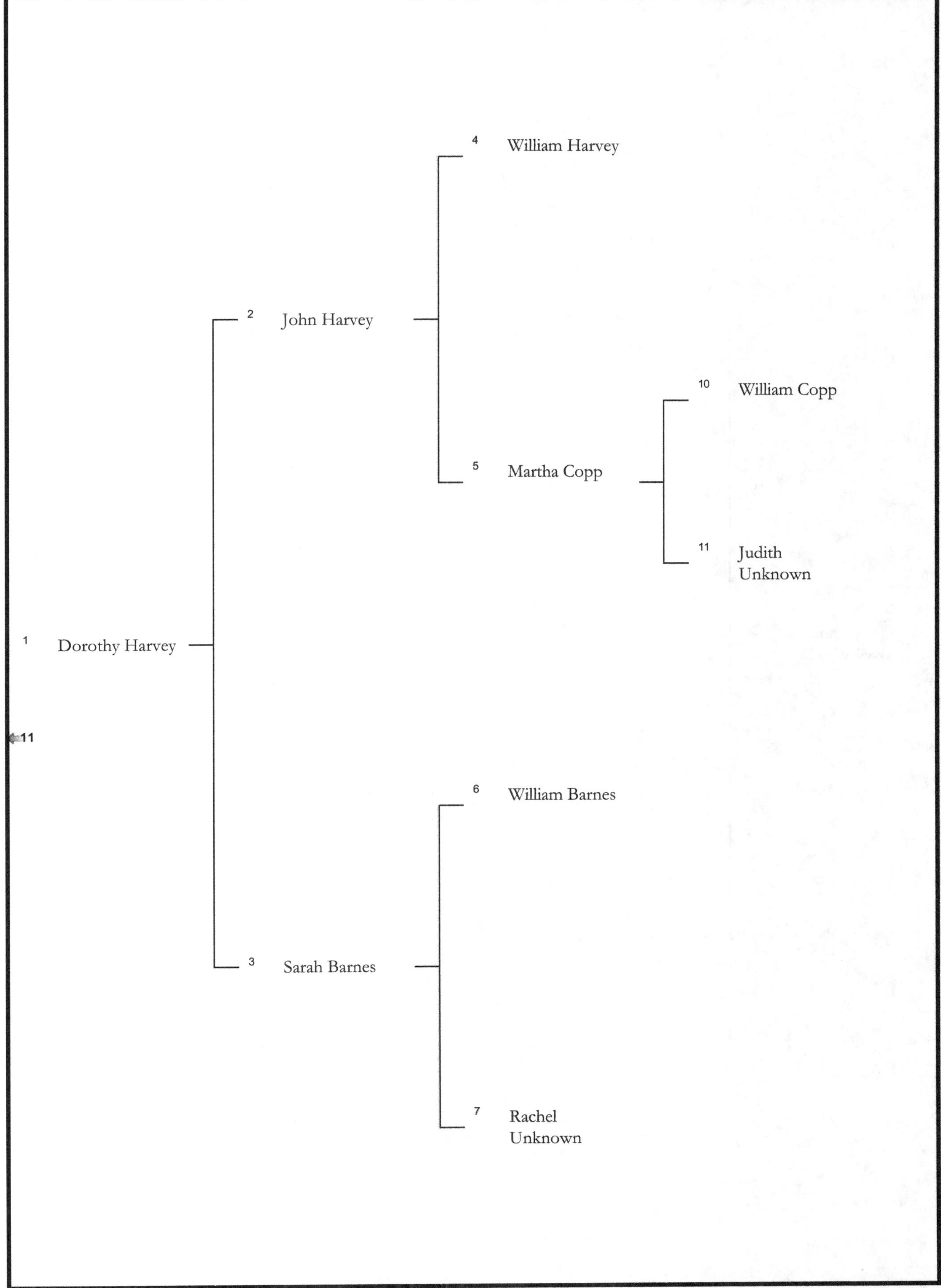

4 William Harvey
2 John Harvey
10 William Copp
5 Martha Copp
11 Judith Unknown
1 Dorothy Harvey
11
6 William Barnes
3 Sarah Barnes
7 Rachel Unknown

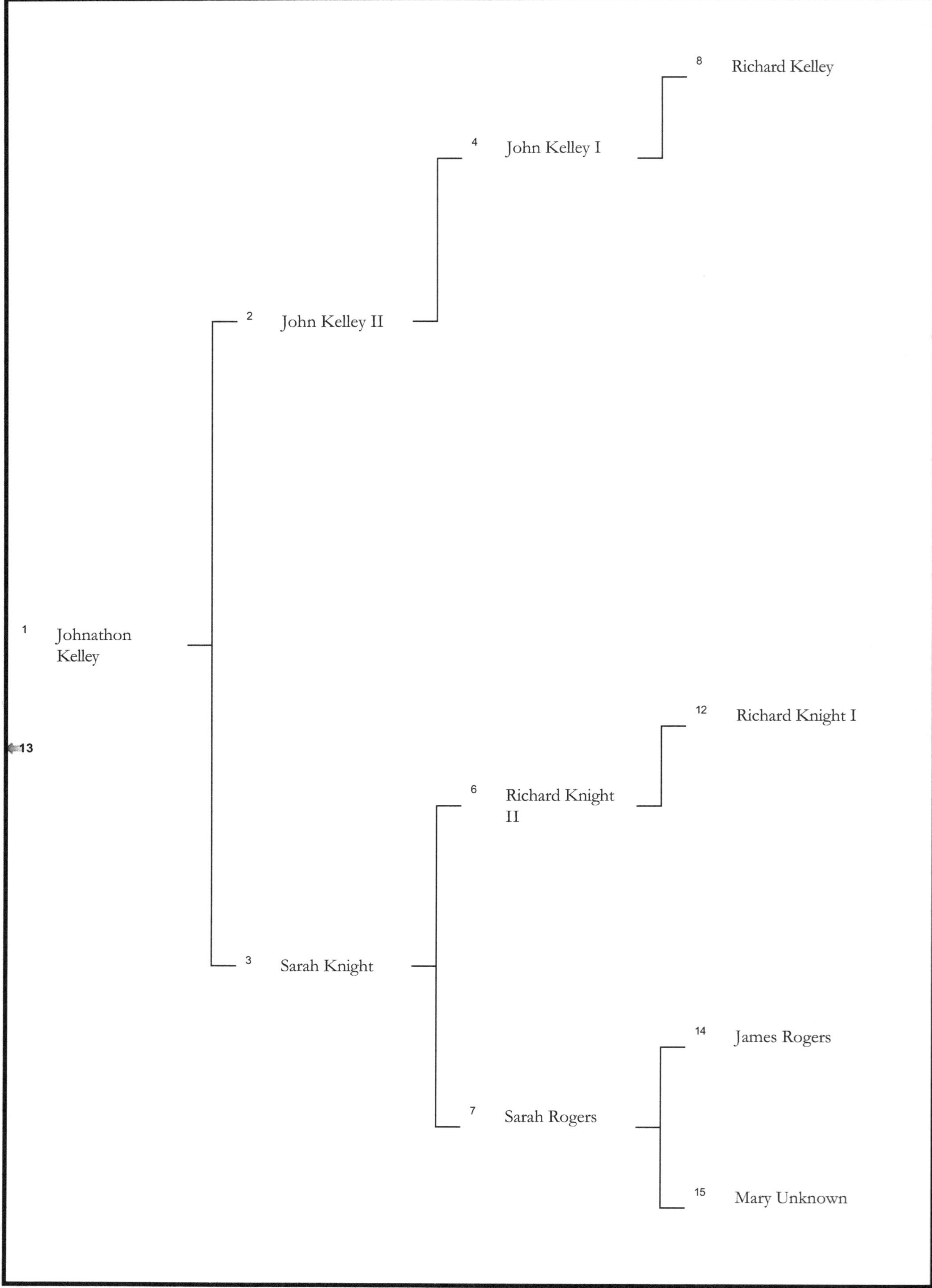

8 Richard Kelley
4 John Kelley I
2 John Kelley II
1 Johnathon Kelley
13
12 Richard Knight I
6 Richard Knight II
3 Sarah Knight
14 James Rogers
7 Sarah Rogers
15 Mary Unknown

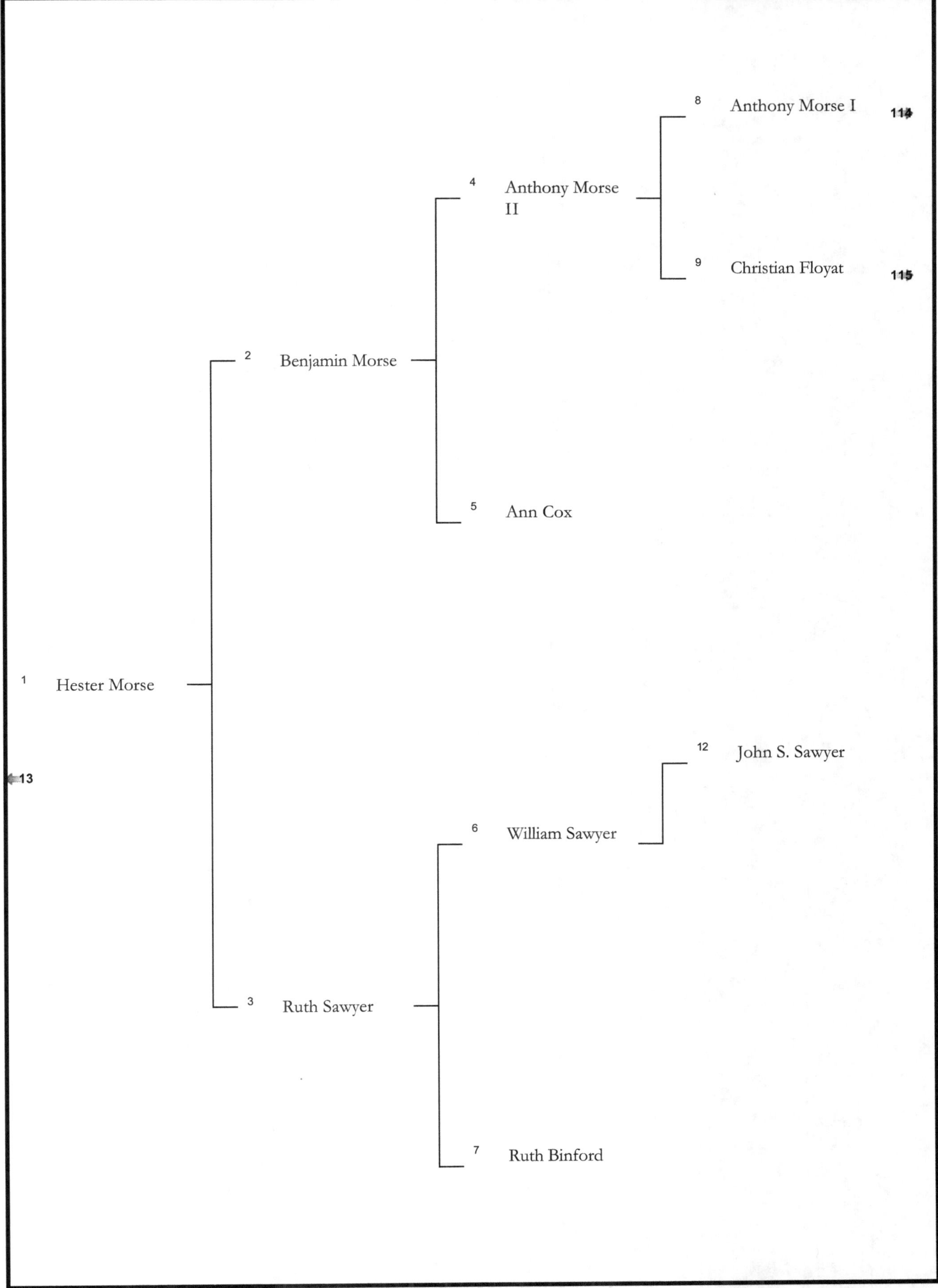

13
1 Hester Morse
2 Benjamin Morse
4 Anthony Morse II
8 Anthony Morse I   114
9 Christian Floyat   115
5 Ann Cox
3 Ruth Sawyer
6 William Sawyer
12 John S. Sawyer
7 Ruth Binford

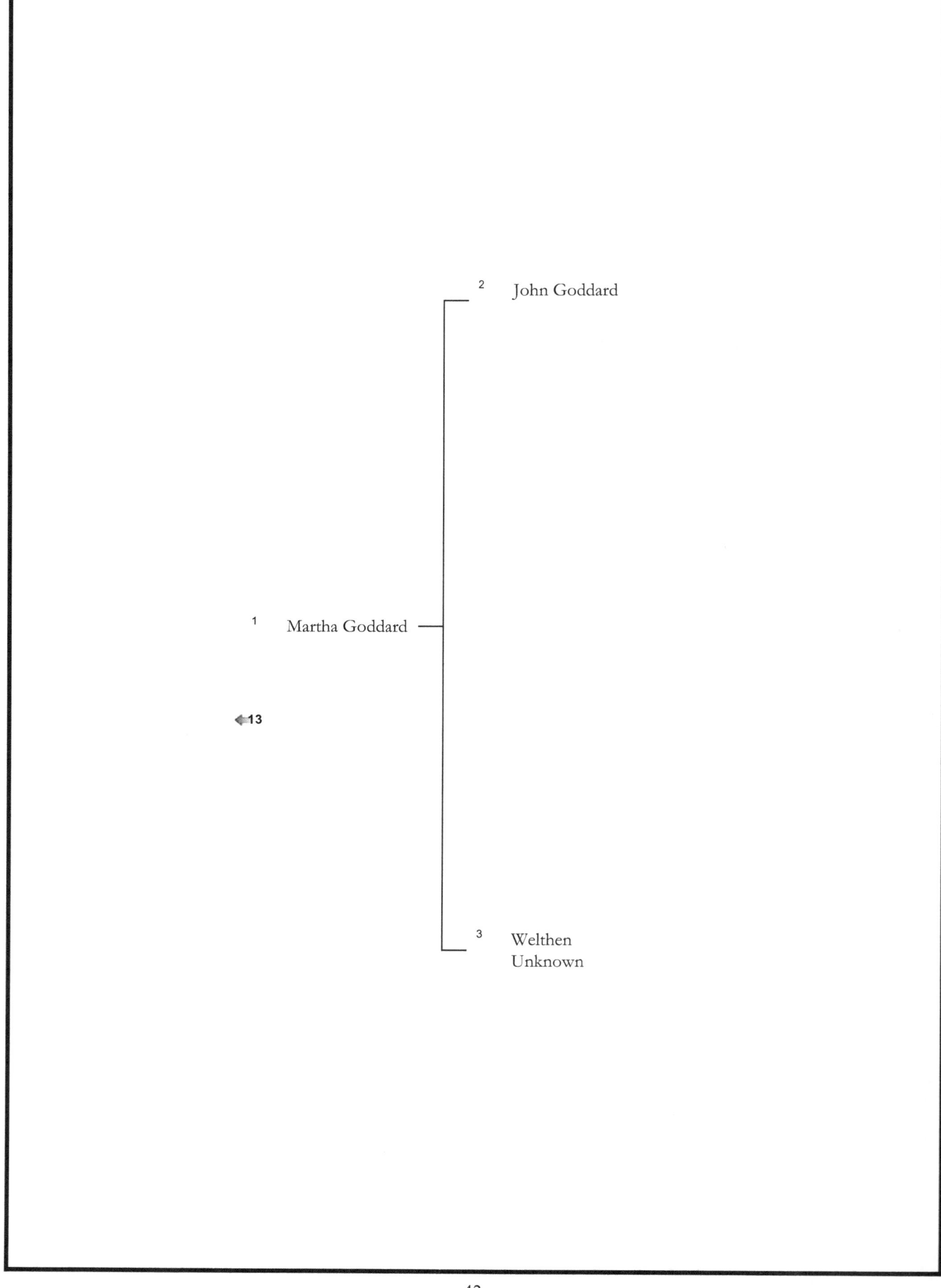

2 John Goddard
1 Martha Goddard
13
3 Welthen
Unknown

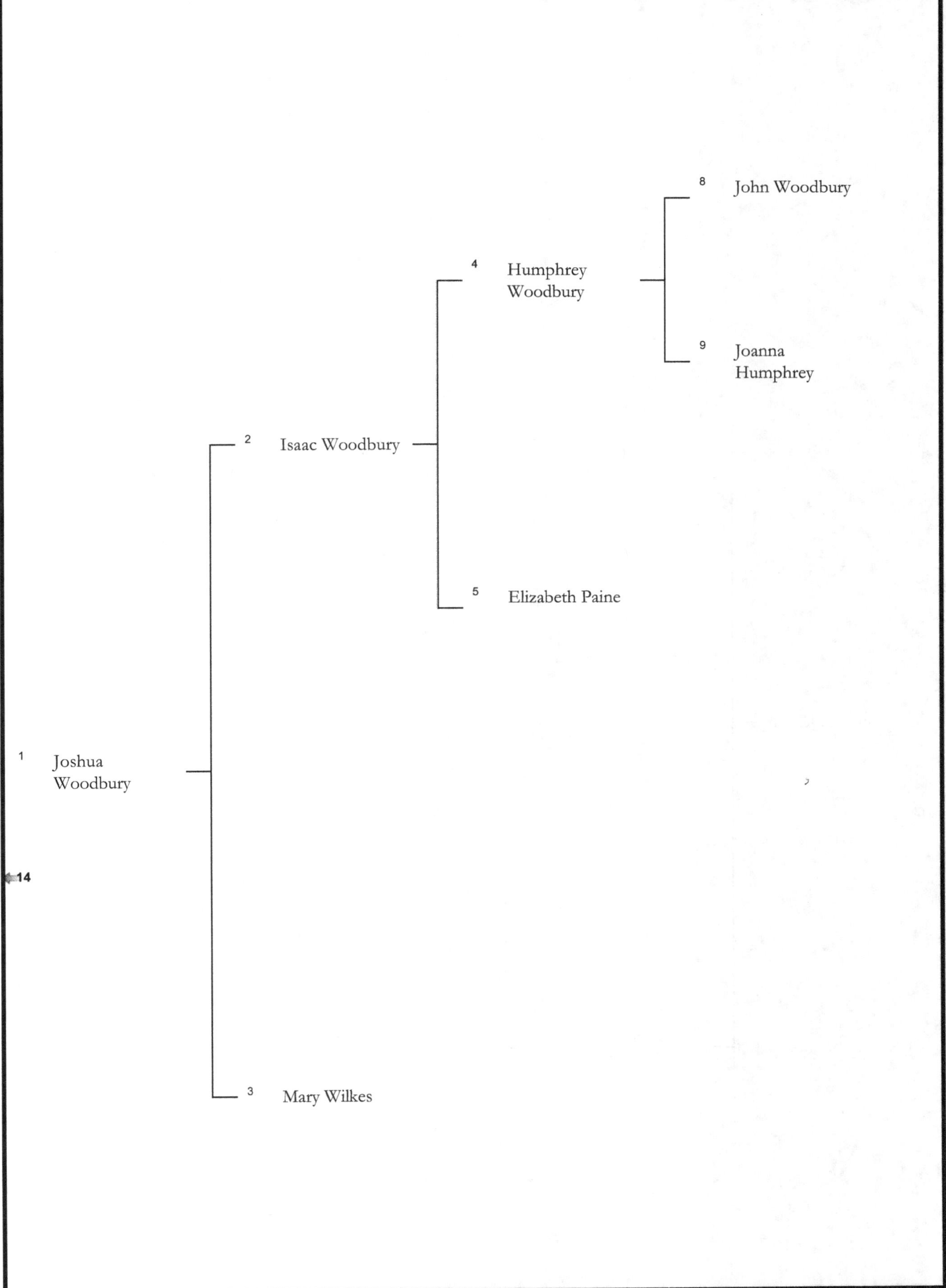

1
Joshua
Woodbury
2
Isaac Woodbury
4
Humphrey
Woodbury
8
John Woodbury
9
Joanna
Humphrey
5
Elizabeth Paine
3
Mary Wilkes
14

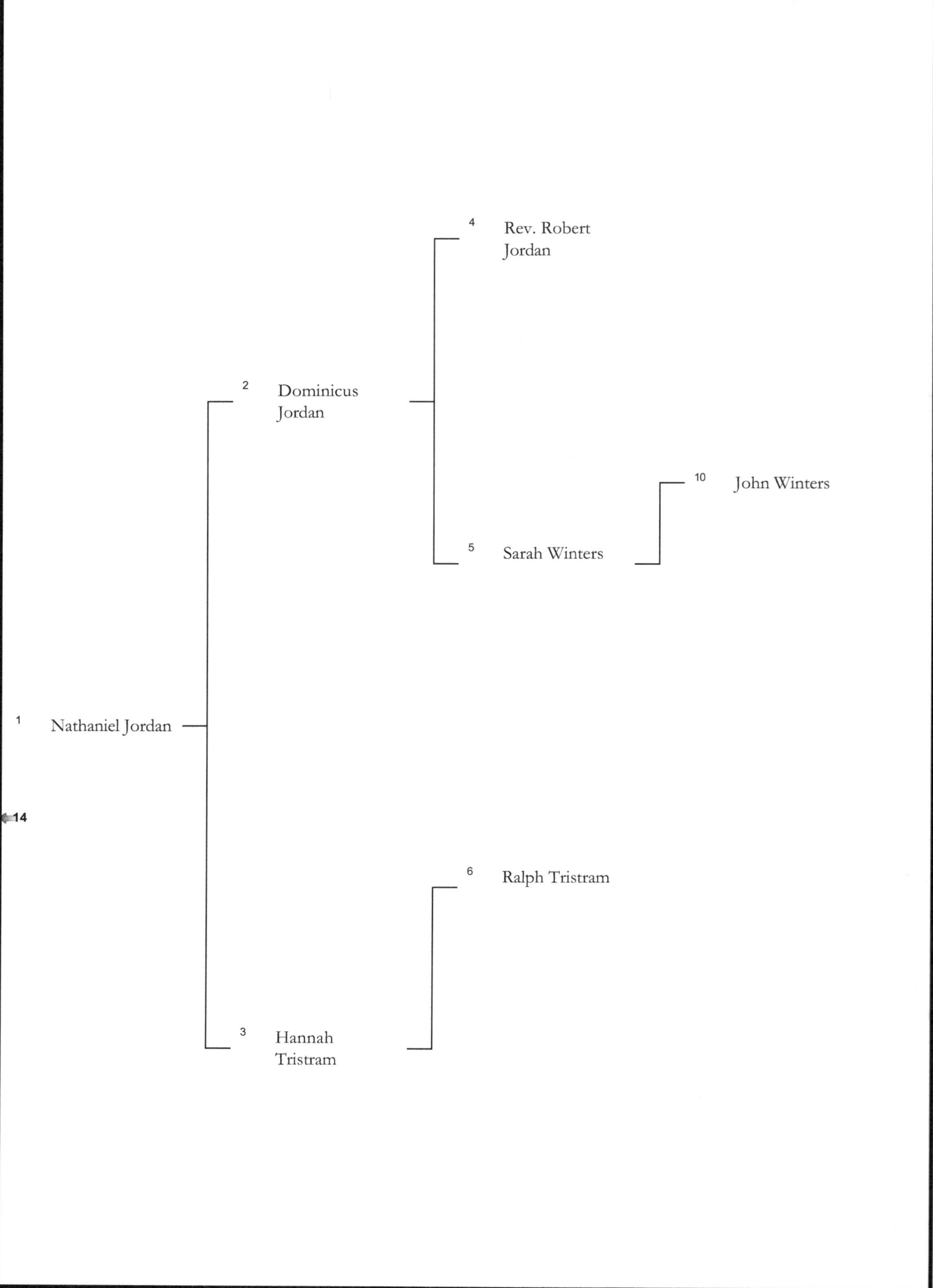

1 Nathaniel Jordan
14
2 Dominicus Jordan
3 Hannah Tristram
4 Rev. Robert Jordan
5 Sarah Winters
6 Ralph Tristram
10 John Winters

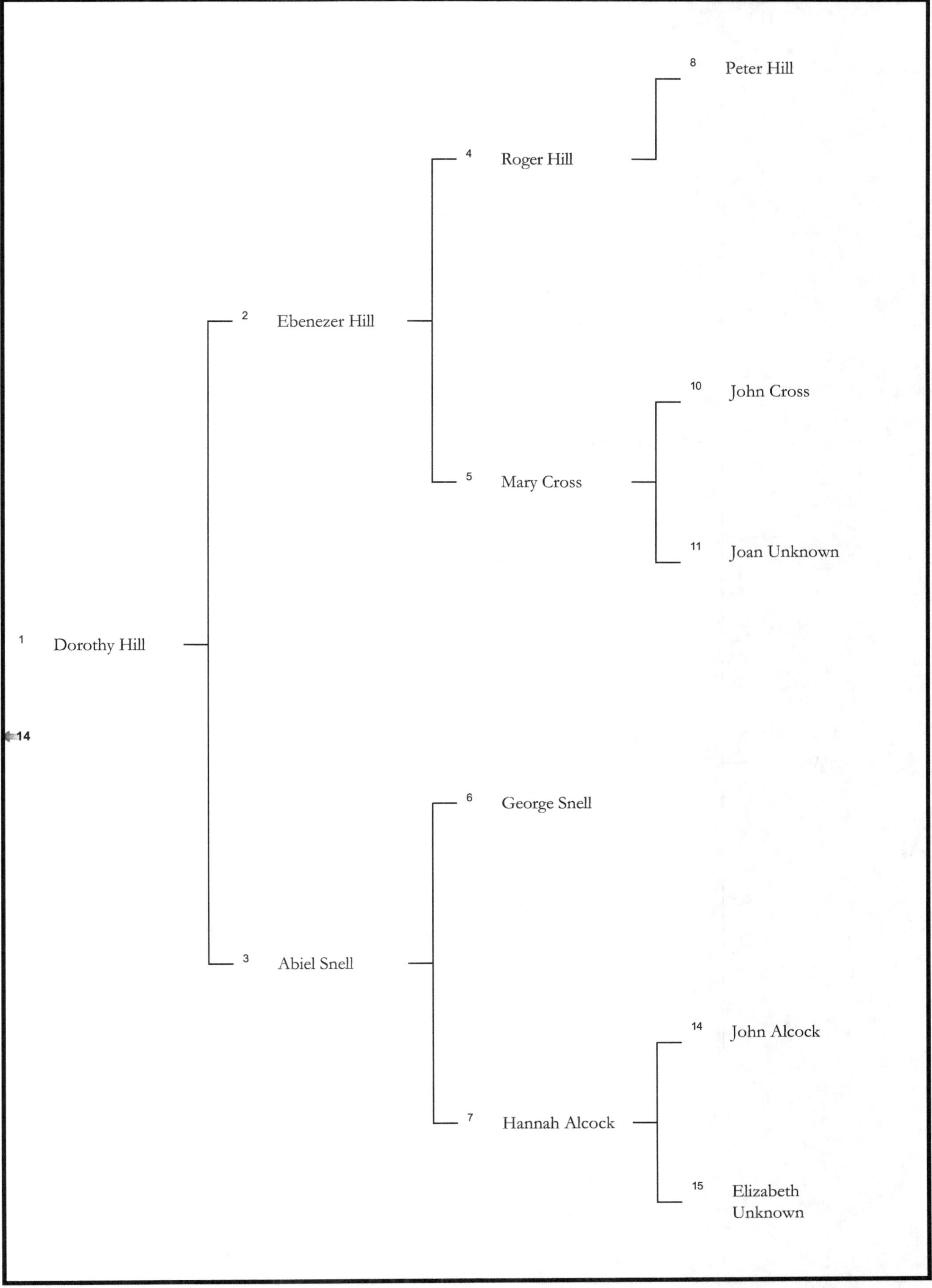

8 Peter Hill
4 Roger Hill
2 Ebenezer Hill
10 John Cross
5 Mary Cross
11 Joan Unknown
1 Dorothy Hill
14
6 George Snell
3 Abiel Snell
14 John Alcock
7 Hannah Alcock
15 Elizabeth Unknown

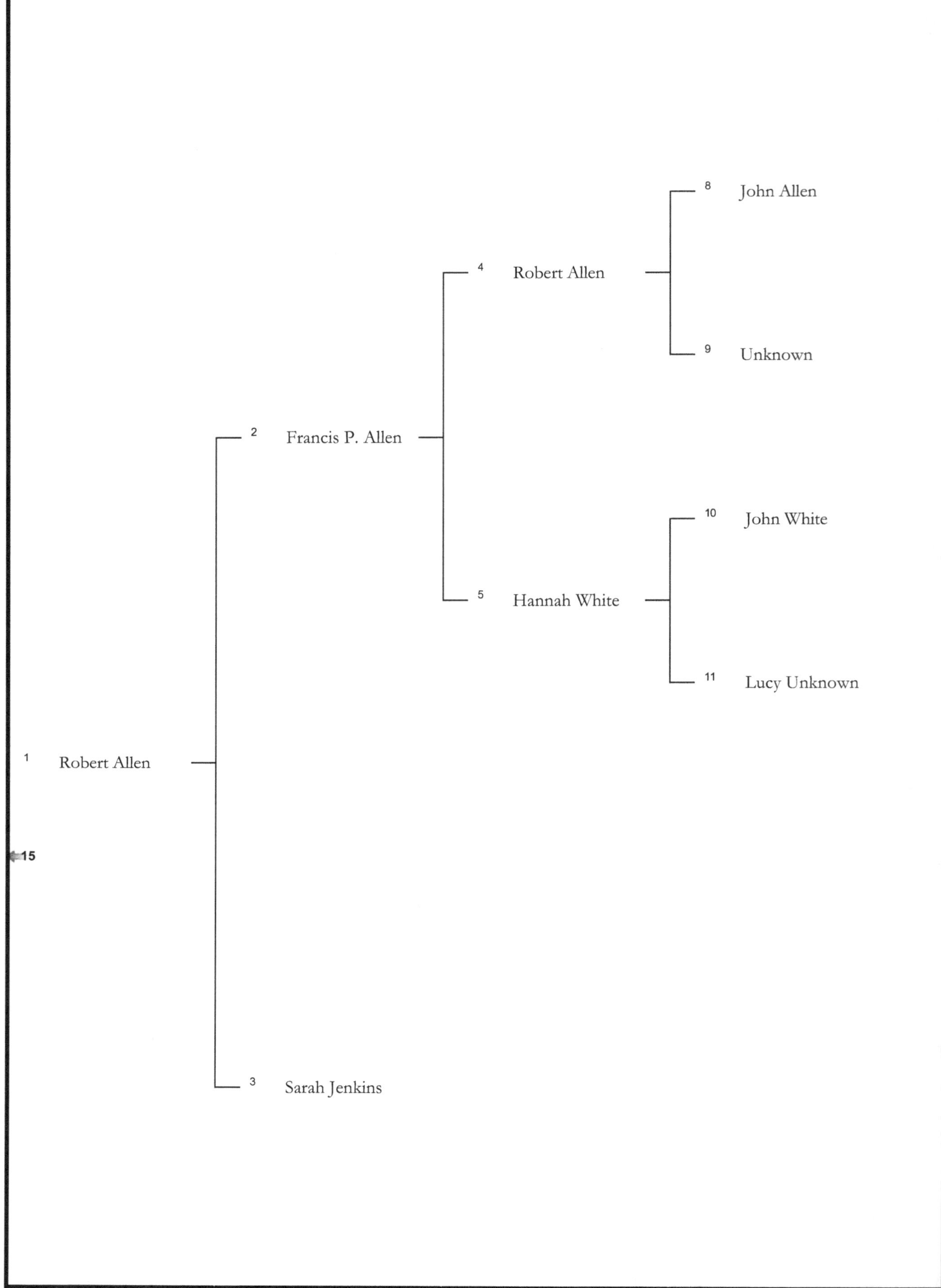

1 Robert Allen
2 Francis P. Allen
3 Sarah Jenkins
4 Robert Allen
5 Hannah White
8 John Allen
9 Unknown
10 John White
11 Lucy Unknown
15

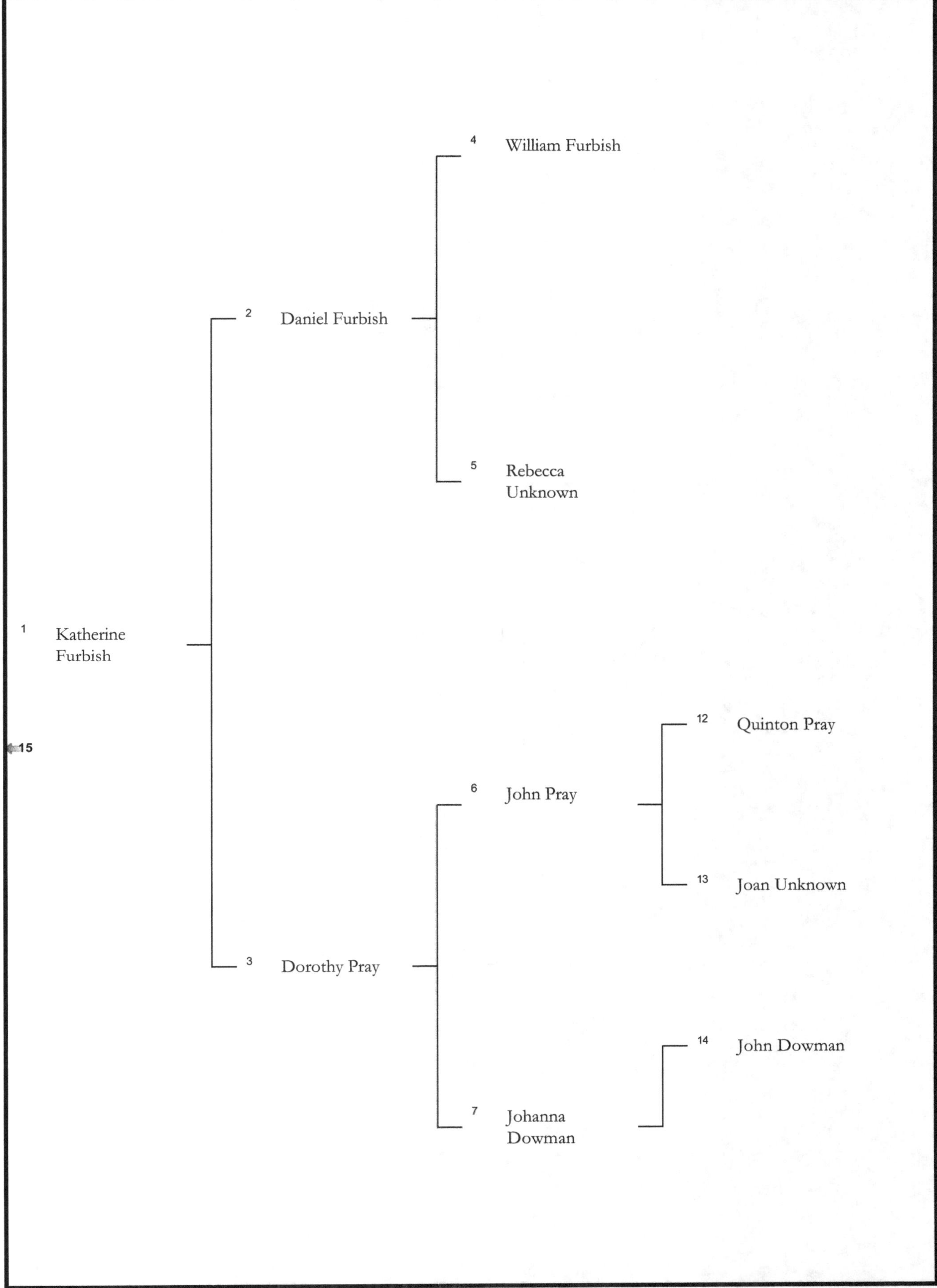

1 Katherine Furbish
2 Daniel Furbish
4 William Furbish
5 Rebecca Unknown
3 Dorothy Pray
6 John Pray
12 Quinton Pray
13 Joan Unknown
7 Johanna Dowman
14 John Dowman
15

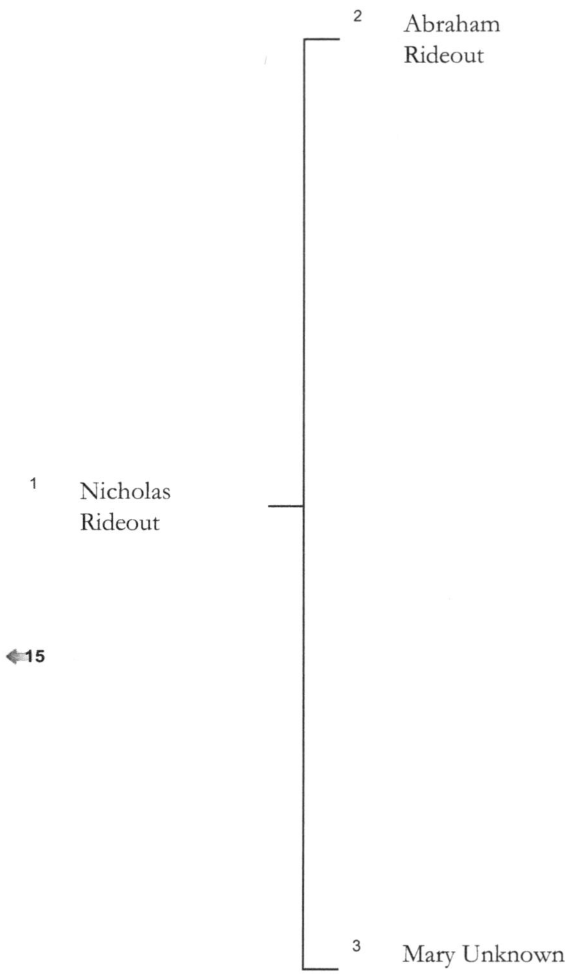

² Abraham
Rideout

¹ Nicholas
Rideout

←15

³ Mary Unknown

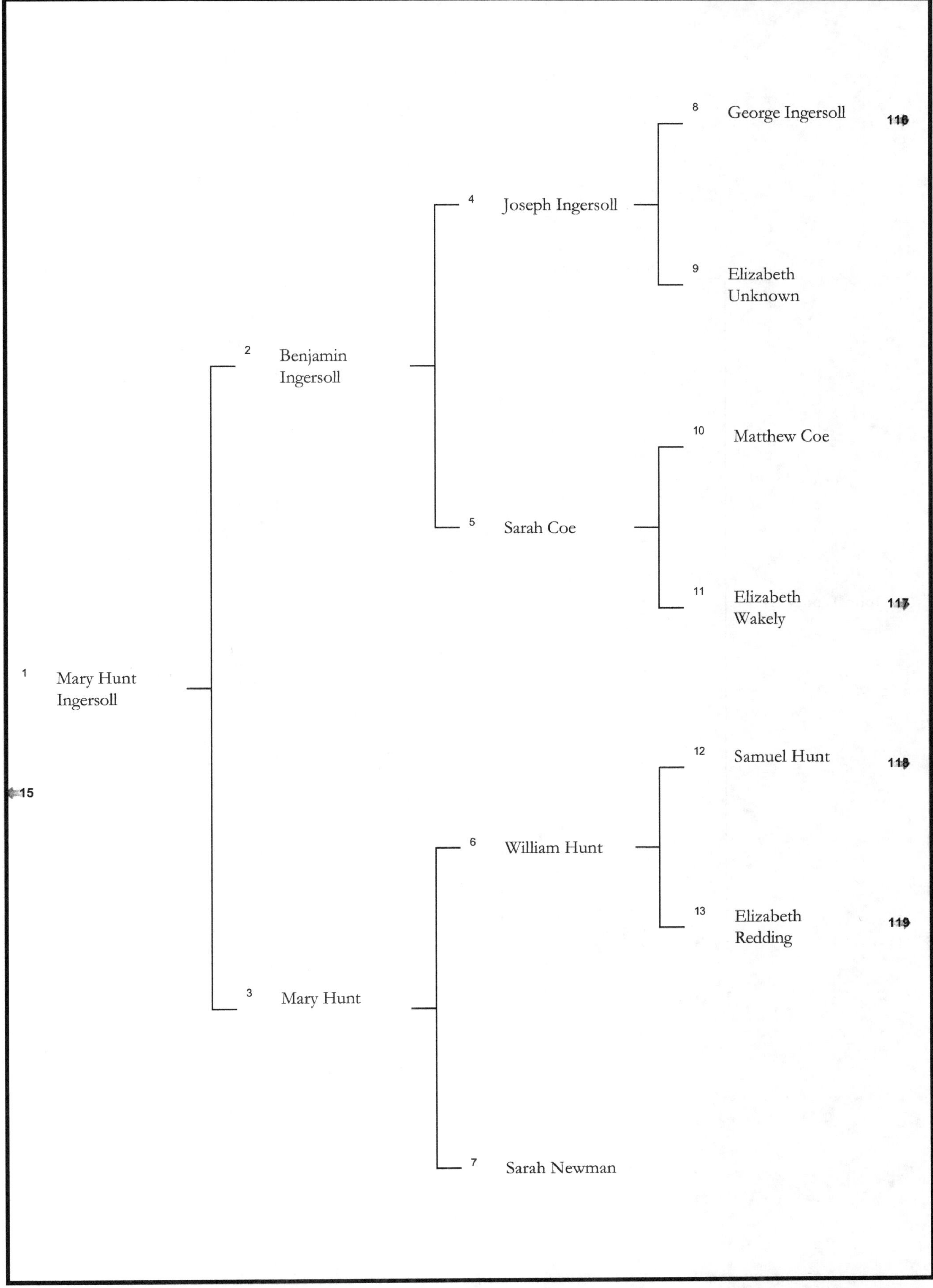

1 Mary Hunt Ingersoll
15
2 Benjamin Ingersoll
3 Mary Hunt
4 Joseph Ingersoll
5 Sarah Coe
6 William Hunt
7 Sarah Newman
8 George Ingersoll 116
9 Elizabeth Unknown
10 Matthew Coe
11 Elizabeth Wakely 117
12 Samuel Hunt 118
13 Elizabeth Redding 119

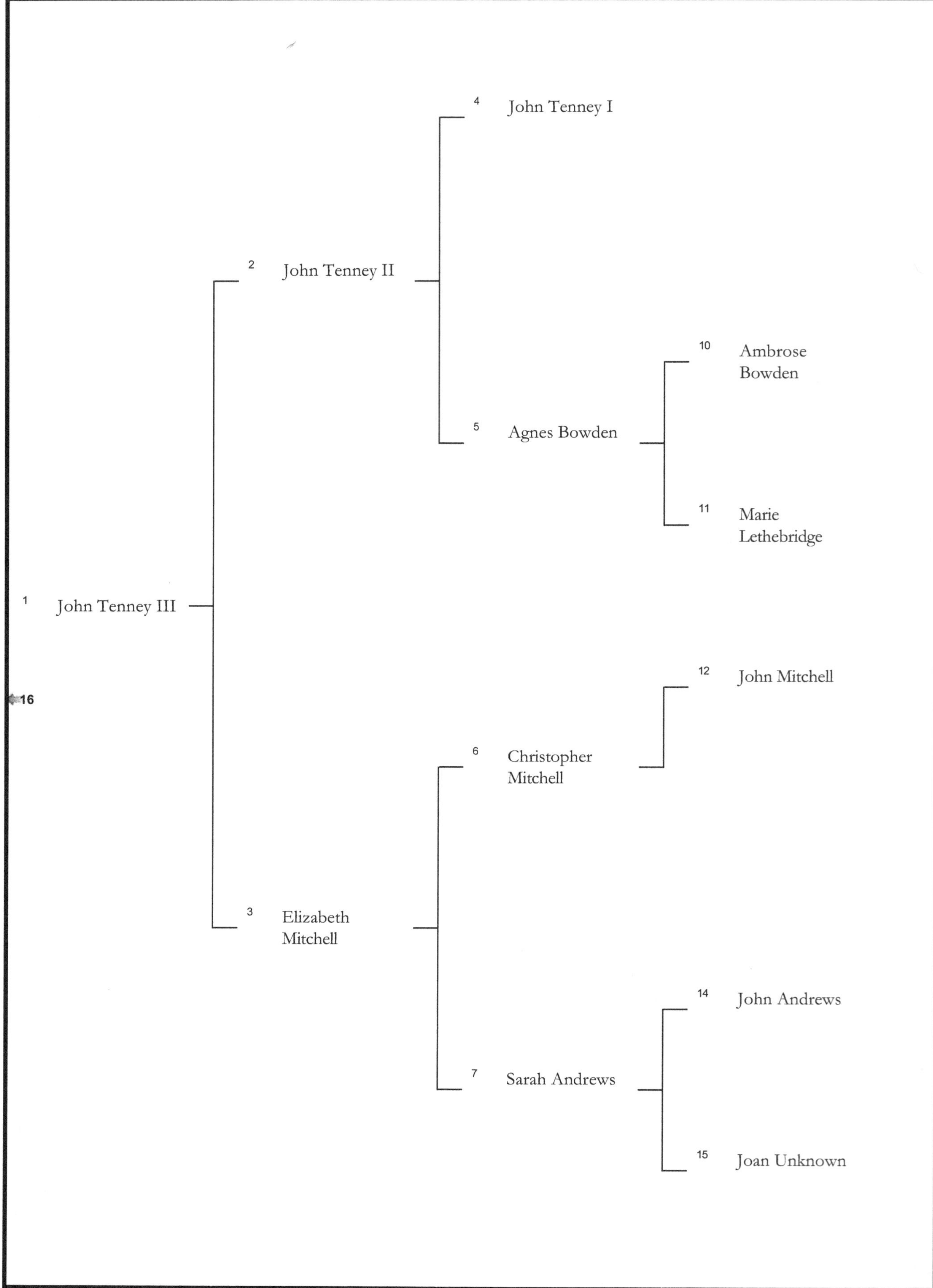

1 John Tenney III
2 John Tenney II
4 John Tenney I
5 Agnes Bowden
10 Ambrose Bowden
11 Marie Lethebridge
3 Elizabeth Mitchell
6 Christopher Mitchell
12 John Mitchell
7 Sarah Andrews
14 John Andrews
15 Joan Unknown
16

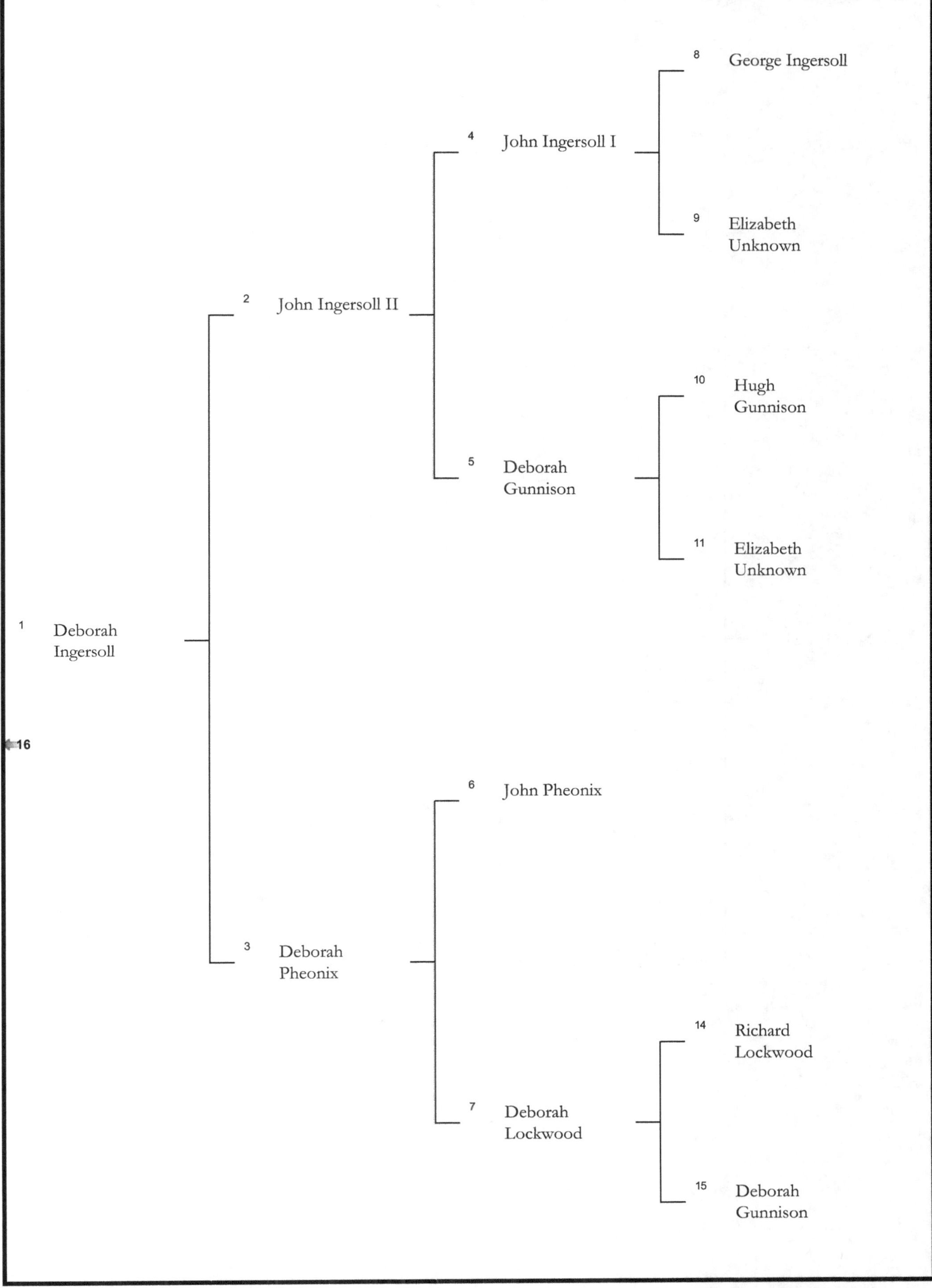

1 Deborah Ingersoll
2 John Ingersoll II
3 Deborah Pheonix
4 John Ingersoll I
5 Deborah Gunnison
6 John Pheonix
7 Deborah Lockwood
8 George Ingersoll
9 Elizabeth Unknown
10 Hugh Gunnison
11 Elizabeth Unknown
14 Richard Lockwood
15 Deborah Gunnison
16

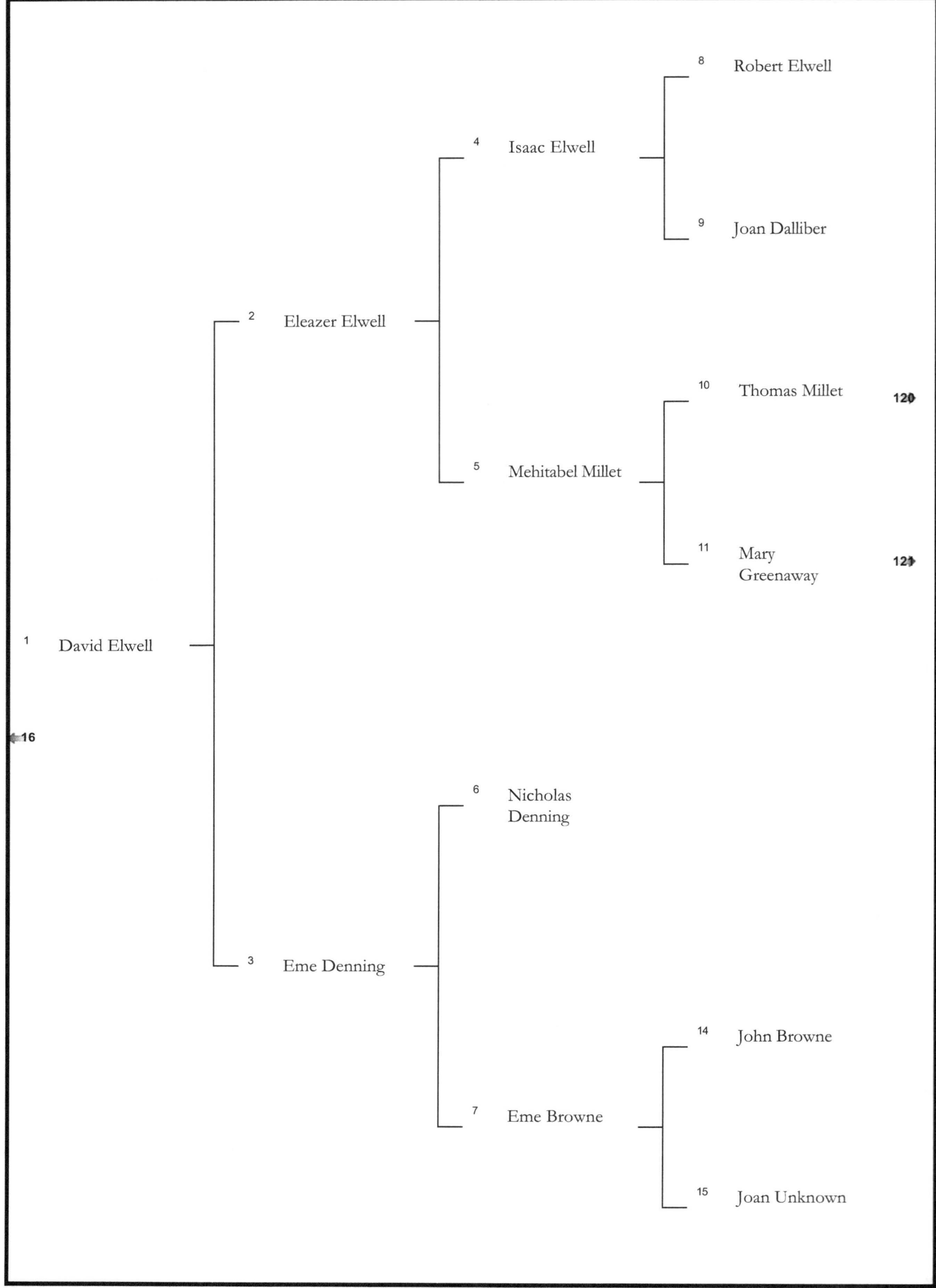

8 Robert Elwell
4 Isaac Elwell
9 Joan Dalliber
2 Eleazer Elwell
10 Thomas Millet 12▸
5 Mehitabel Millet
11 Mary Greenaway 12▸
1 David Elwell
◂16
6 Nicholas Denning
3 Eme Denning
14 John Browne
7 Eme Browne
15 Joan Unknown

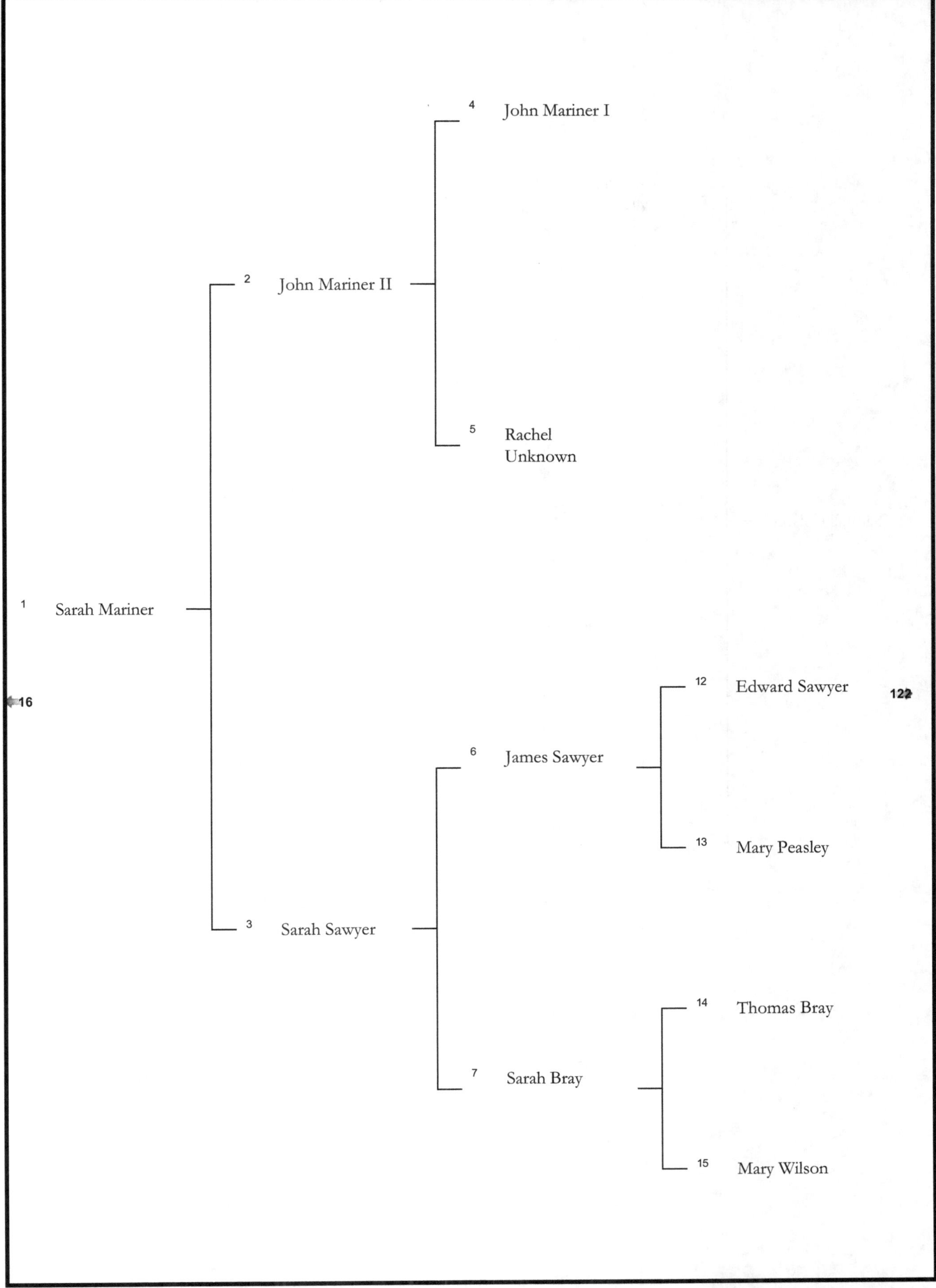

16
1 Sarah Mariner
2 John Mariner II
4 John Mariner I
5 Rachel Unknown
3 Sarah Sawyer
6 James Sawyer
12 Edward Sawyer
13 Mary Peasley
7 Sarah Bray
14 Thomas Bray
15 Mary Wilson
122

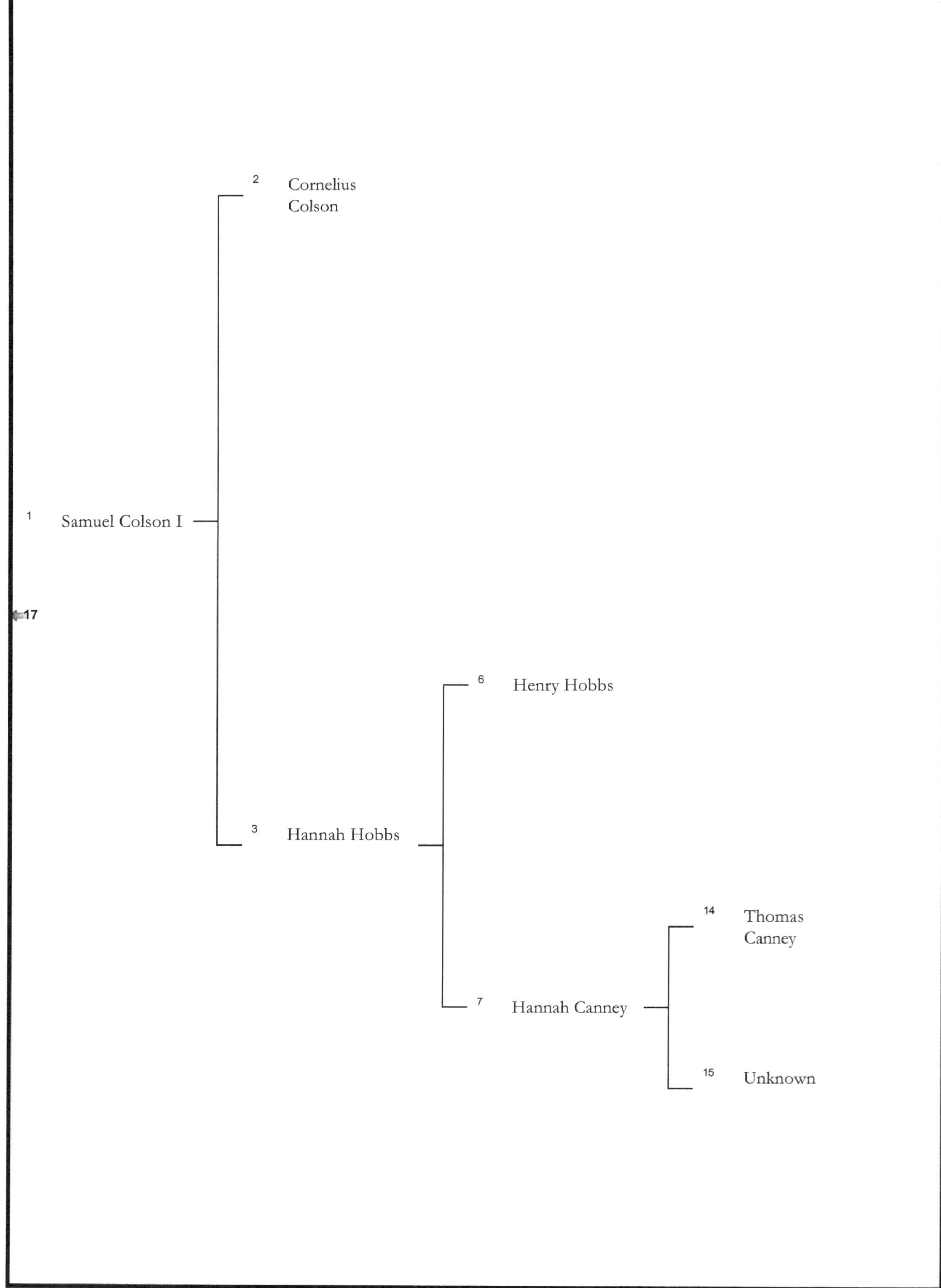

1 Samuel Colson I
2 Cornelius Colson
3 Hannah Hobbs
6 Henry Hobbs
7 Hannah Canney
14 Thomas Canney
15 Unknown
17

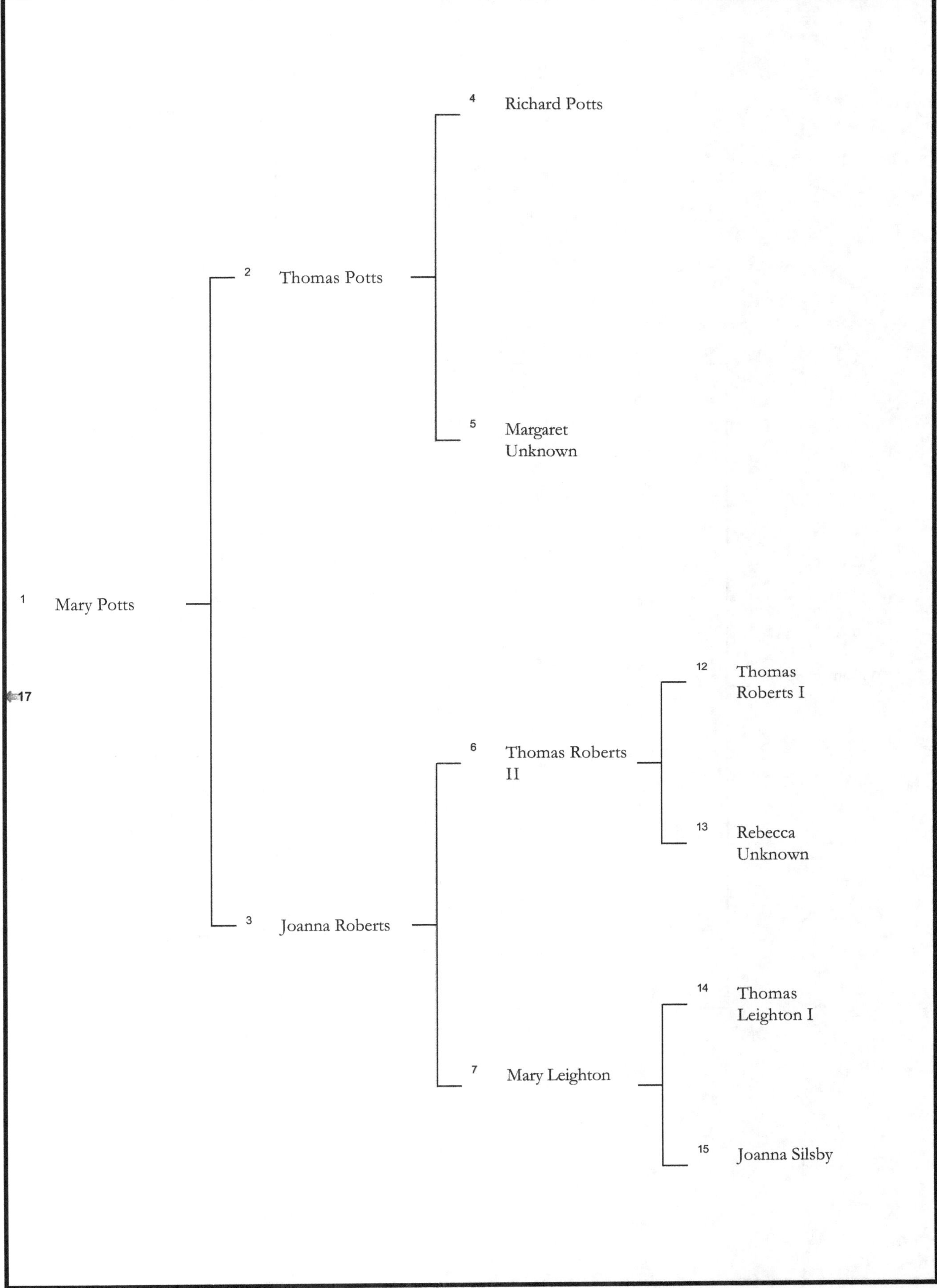

4 Richard Potts
2 Thomas Potts
5 Margaret Unknown
1 Mary Potts
17
12 Thomas Roberts I
6 Thomas Roberts II
13 Rebecca Unknown
3 Joanna Roberts
14 Thomas Leighton I
7 Mary Leighton
15 Joanna Silsby

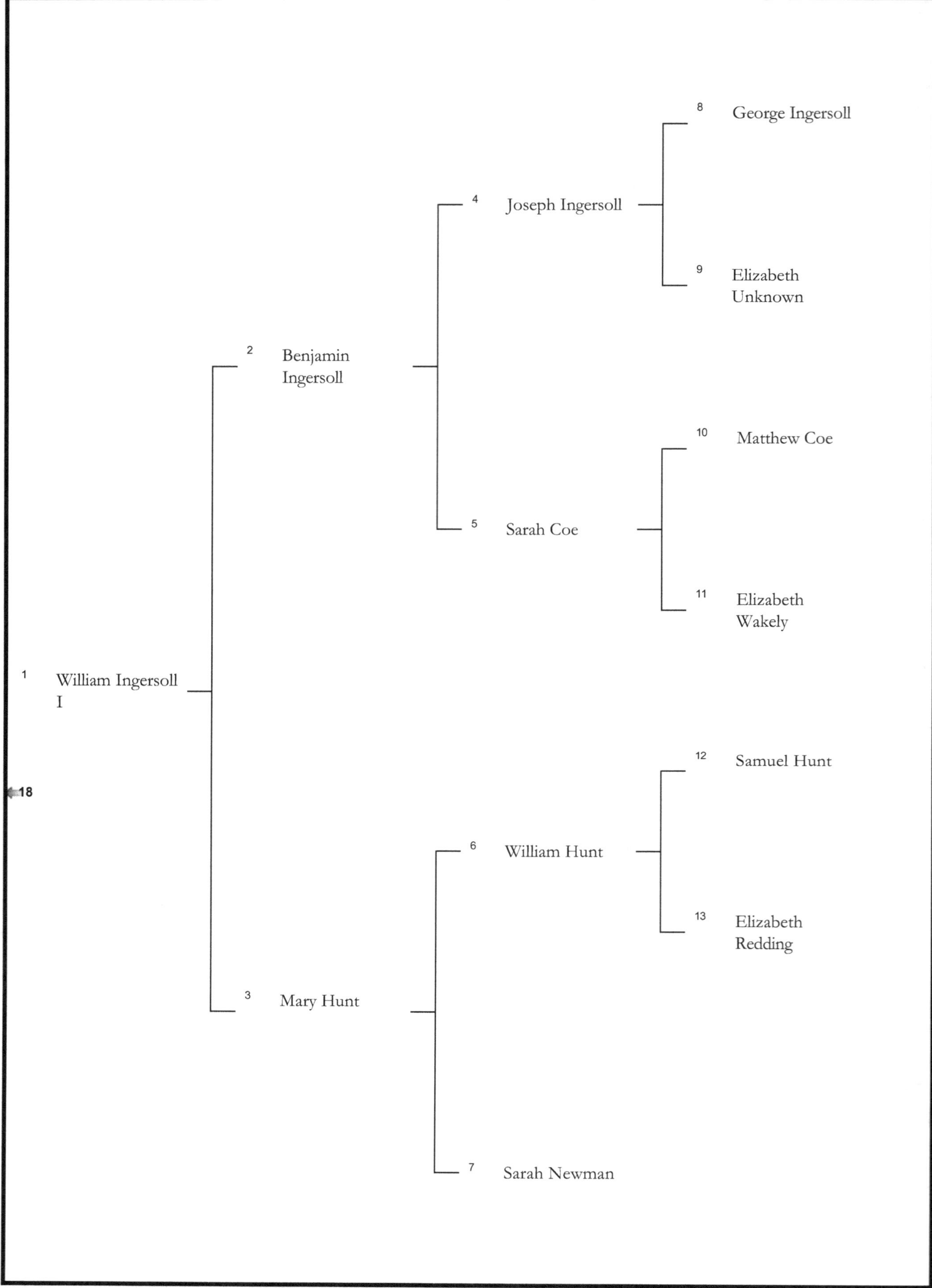

1 William Ingersoll I
18
2 Benjamin Ingersoll
3 Mary Hunt
4 Joseph Ingersoll
5 Sarah Coe
6 William Hunt
7 Sarah Newman
8 George Ingersoll
9 Elizabeth Unknown
10 Matthew Coe
11 Elizabeth Wakely
12 Samuel Hunt
13 Elizabeth Redding

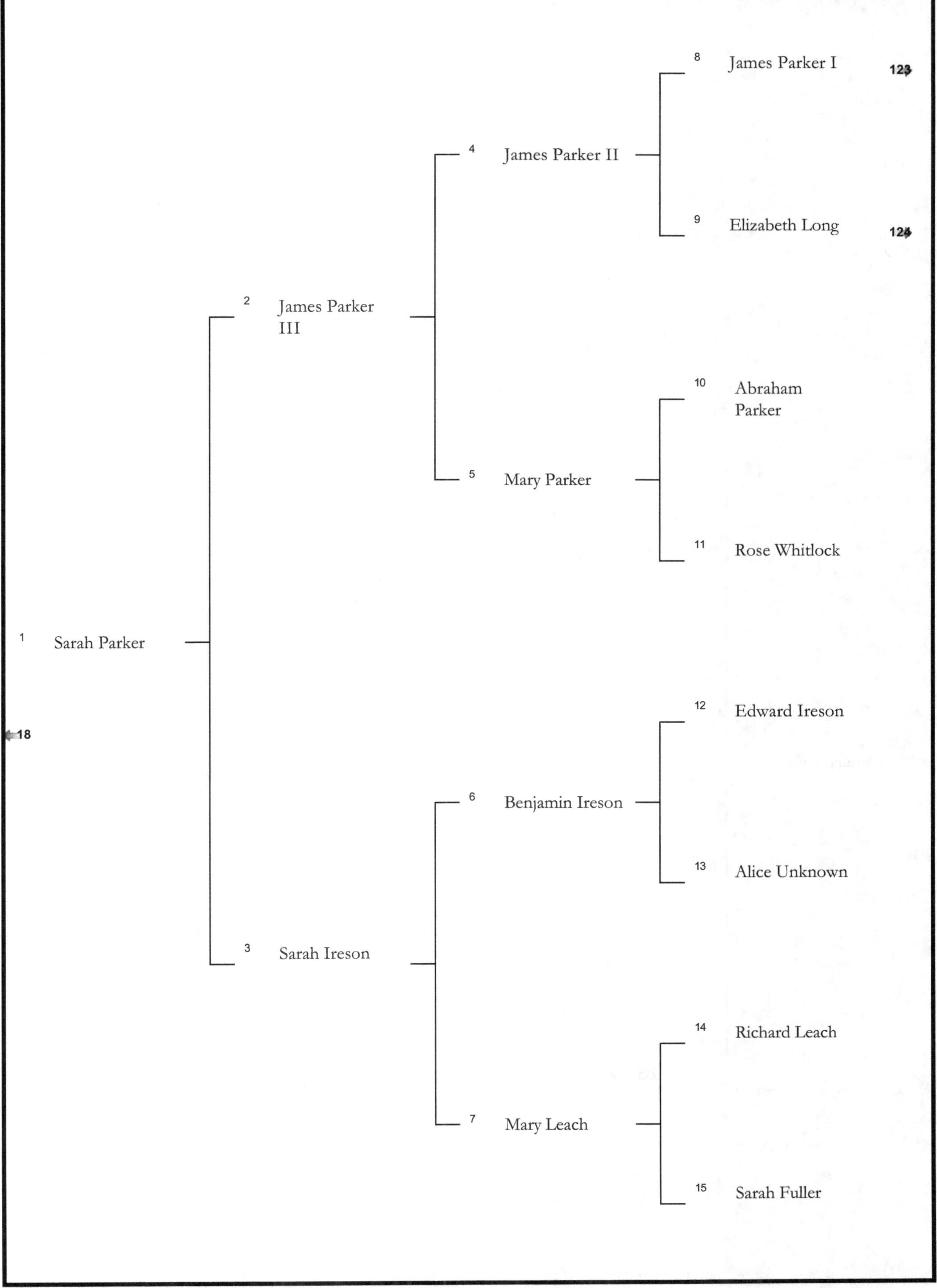

8 James Parker I 123
4 James Parker II
9 Elizabeth Long 124
2 James Parker III
10 Abraham Parker
5 Mary Parker
11 Rose Whitlock
1 Sarah Parker
18
12 Edward Ireson
6 Benjamin Ireson
13 Alice Unknown
3 Sarah Ireson
14 Richard Leach
7 Mary Leach
15 Sarah Fuller

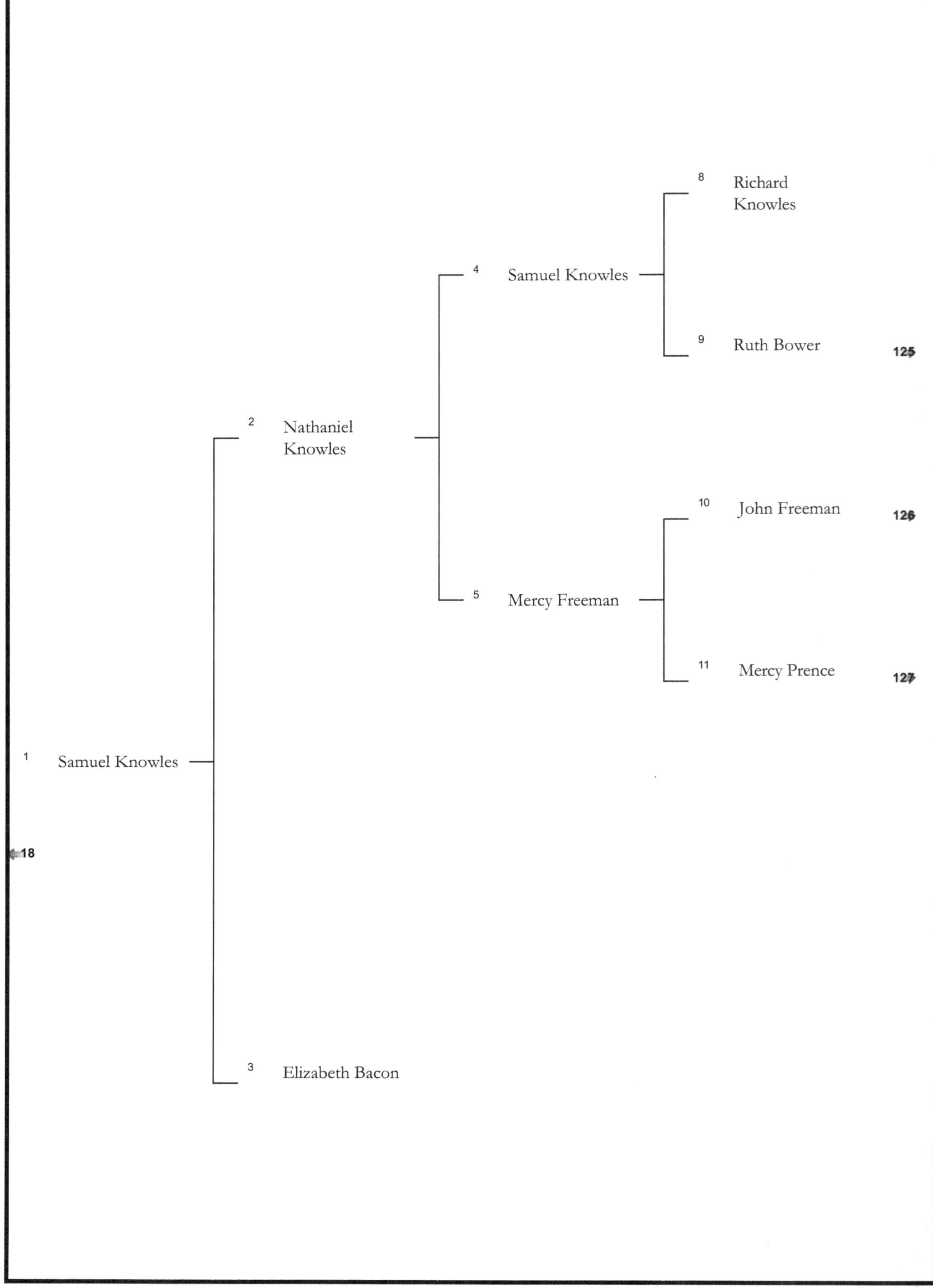

8 Richard Knowles
4 Samuel Knowles
9 Ruth Bower
125
2 Nathaniel Knowles
10 John Freeman
126
5 Mercy Freeman
11 Mercy Prence
127
1 Samuel Knowles
18
3 Elizabeth Bacon

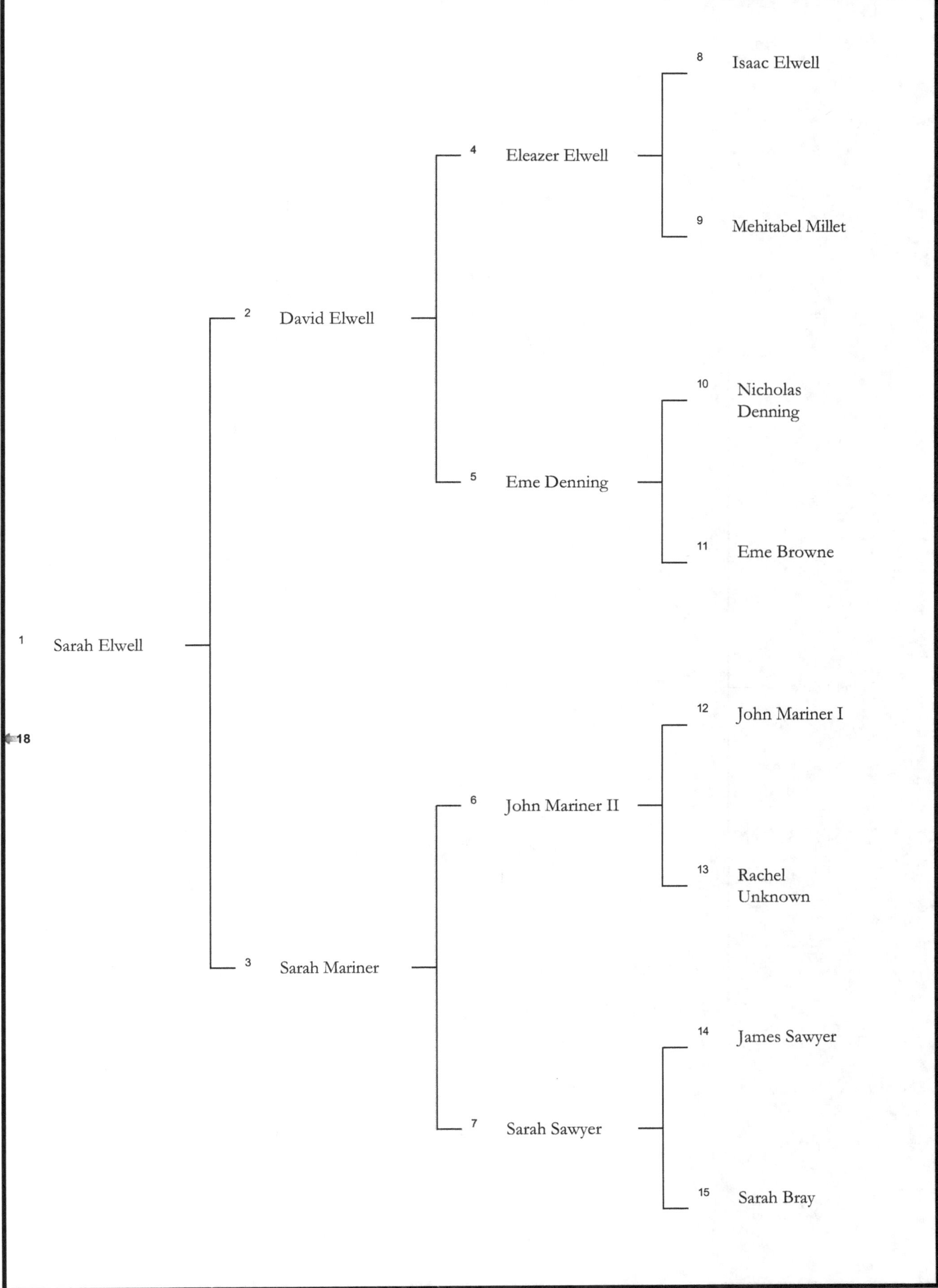

1 Sarah Elwell
18
2 David Elwell
3 Sarah Mariner
4 Eleazer Elwell
5 Eme Denning
6 John Mariner II
7 Sarah Sawyer
8 Isaac Elwell
9 Mehitabel Millet
10 Nicholas Denning
11 Eme Browne
12 John Mariner I
13 Rachel Unknown
14 James Sawyer
15 Sarah Bray

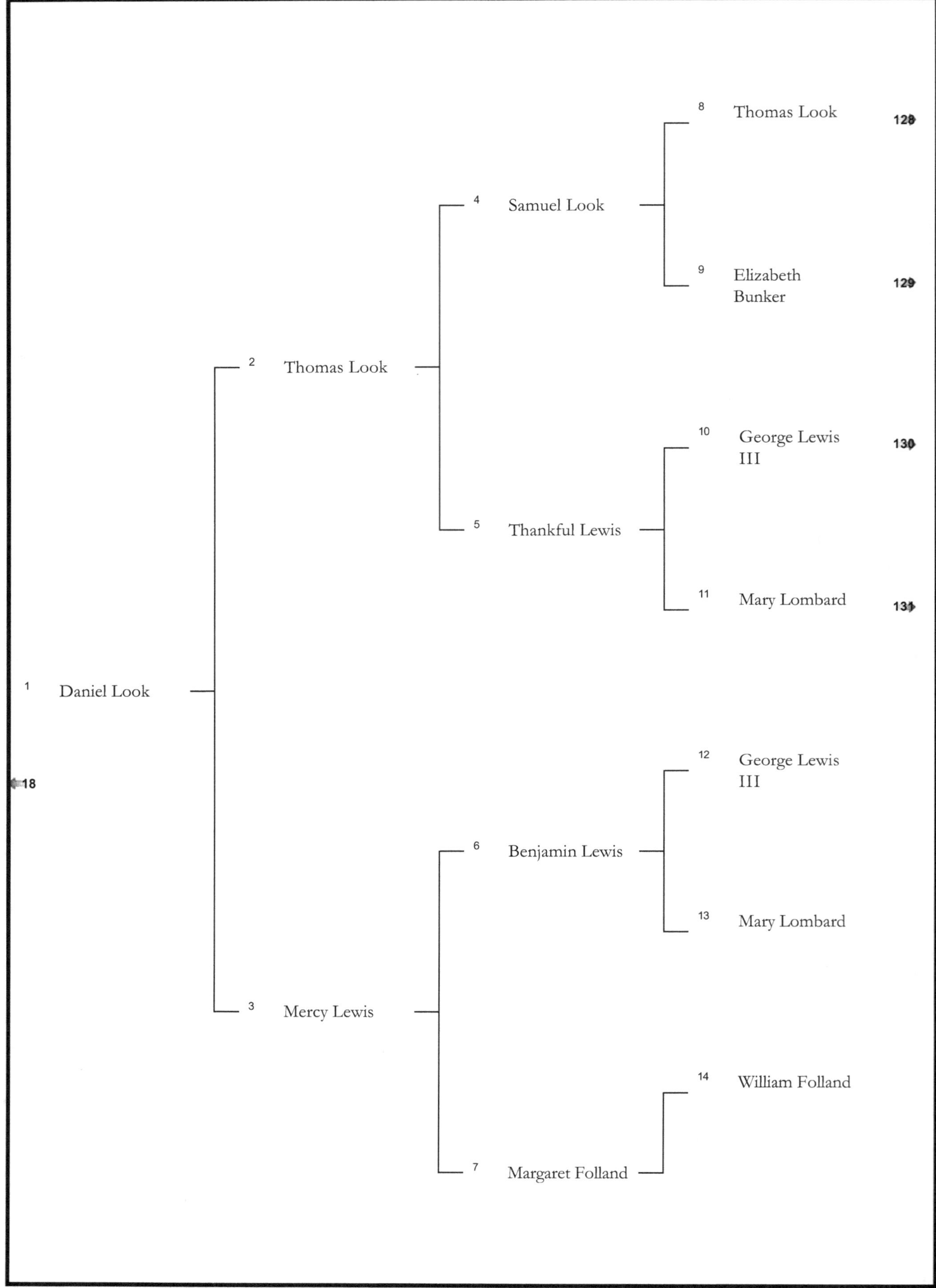

1 Daniel Look
18
2 Thomas Look
3 Mercy Lewis
4 Samuel Look
5 Thankful Lewis
6 Benjamin Lewis
7 Margaret Folland
8 Thomas Look 128
9 Elizabeth Bunker 129
10 George Lewis III 130
11 Mary Lombard 131
12 George Lewis III
13 Mary Lombard
14 William Folland

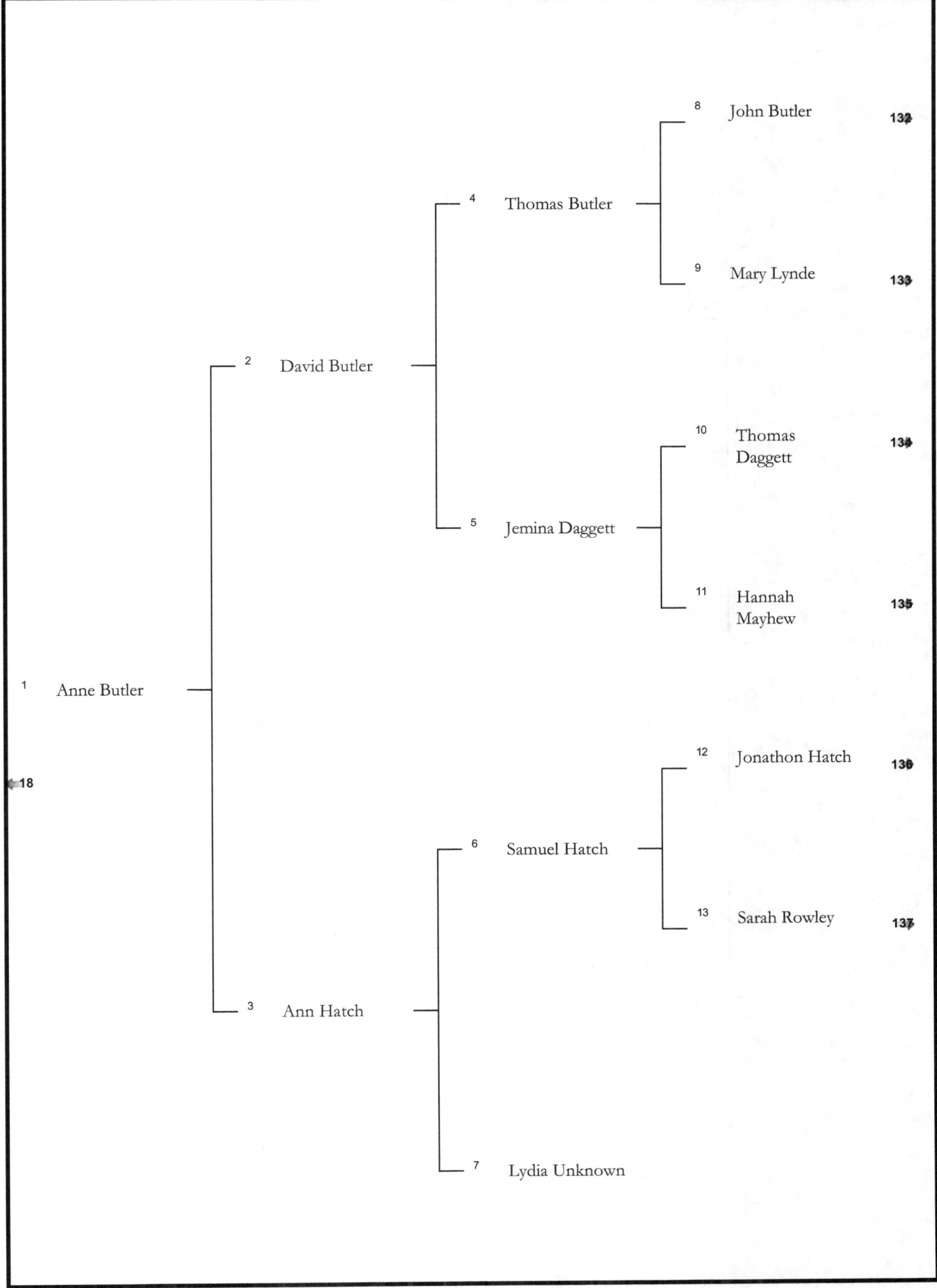

1 Anne Butler
18
2 David Butler
3 Ann Hatch
4 Thomas Butler
5 Jemina Daggett
6 Samuel Hatch
7 Lydia Unknown
8 John Butler 132
9 Mary Lynde 133
10 Thomas Daggett 134
11 Hannah Mayhew 135
12 Jonathon Hatch 136
13 Sarah Rowley 137

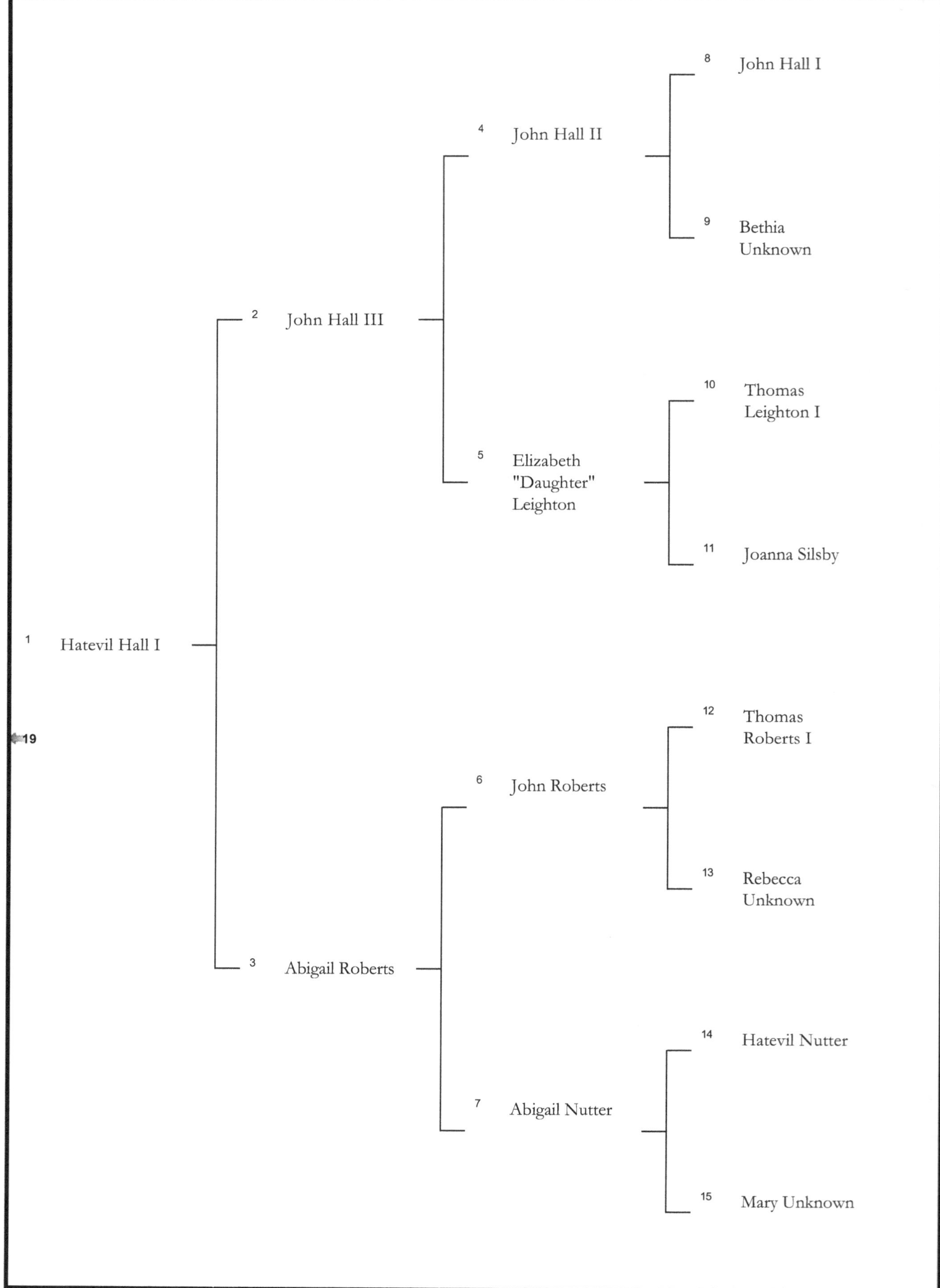

8 John Hall I
4 John Hall II
9 Bethia Unknown
2 John Hall III
10 Thomas Leighton I
5 Elizabeth "Daughter" Leighton
11 Joanna Silsby
1 Hatevil Hall I
19
12 Thomas Roberts I
6 John Roberts
13 Rebecca Unknown
3 Abigail Roberts
14 Hatevil Nutter
7 Abigail Nutter
15 Mary Unknown

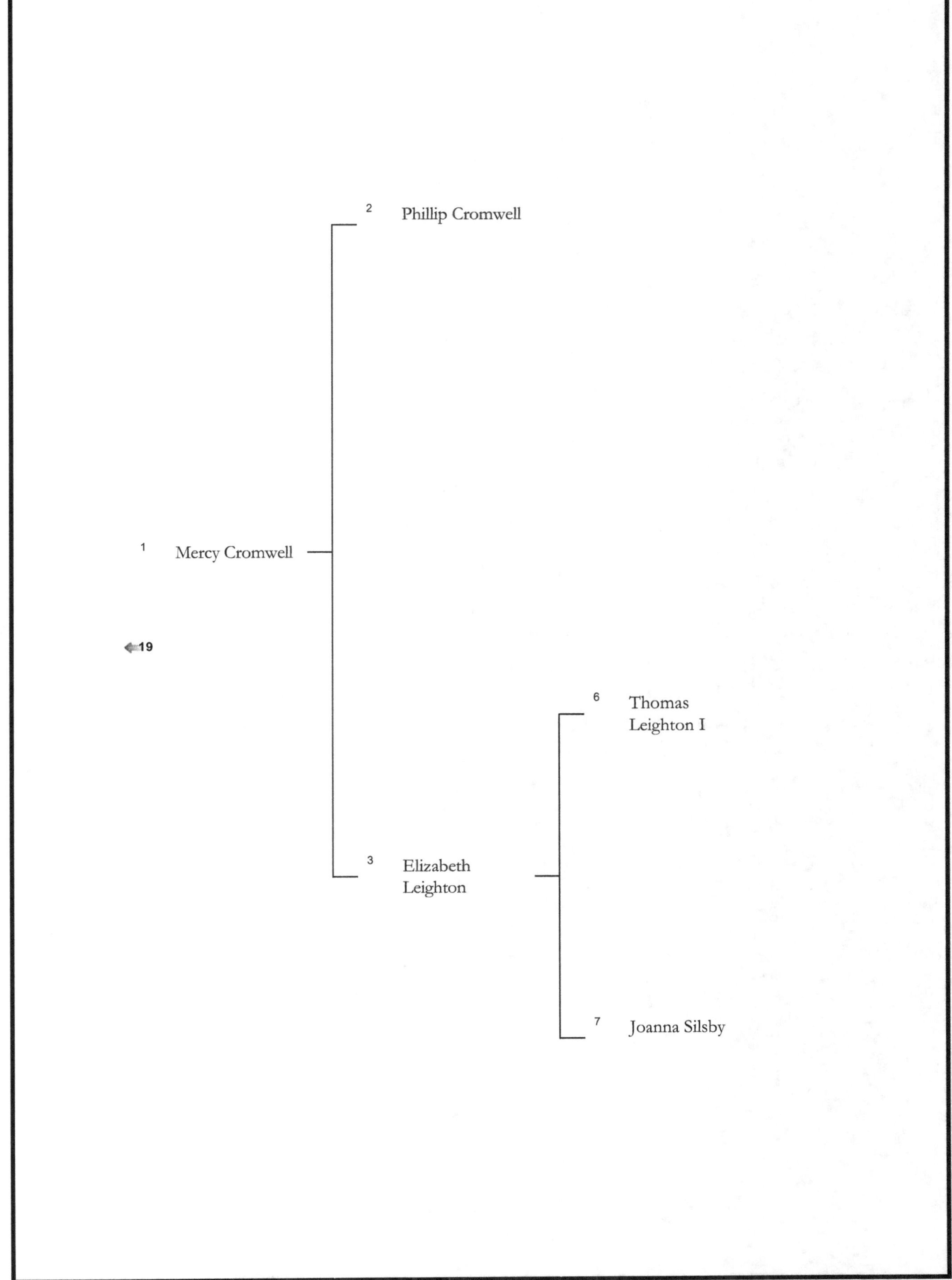

2 Phillip Cromwell
1 Mercy Cromwell
19
6 Thomas Leighton I
3 Elizabeth Leighton
7 Joanna Silsby

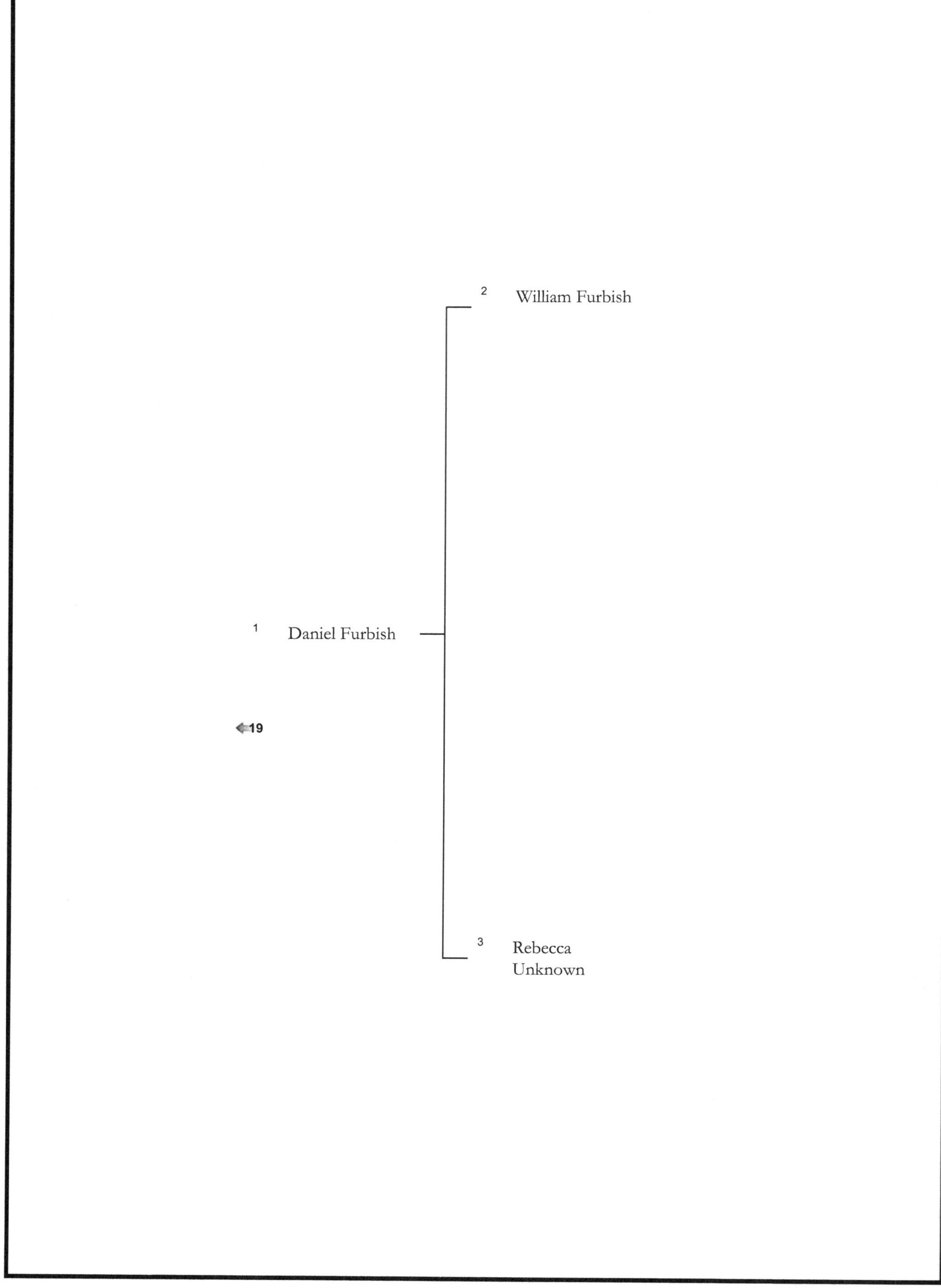

2 William Furbish
1 Daniel Furbish
19
3 Rebecca
Unknown

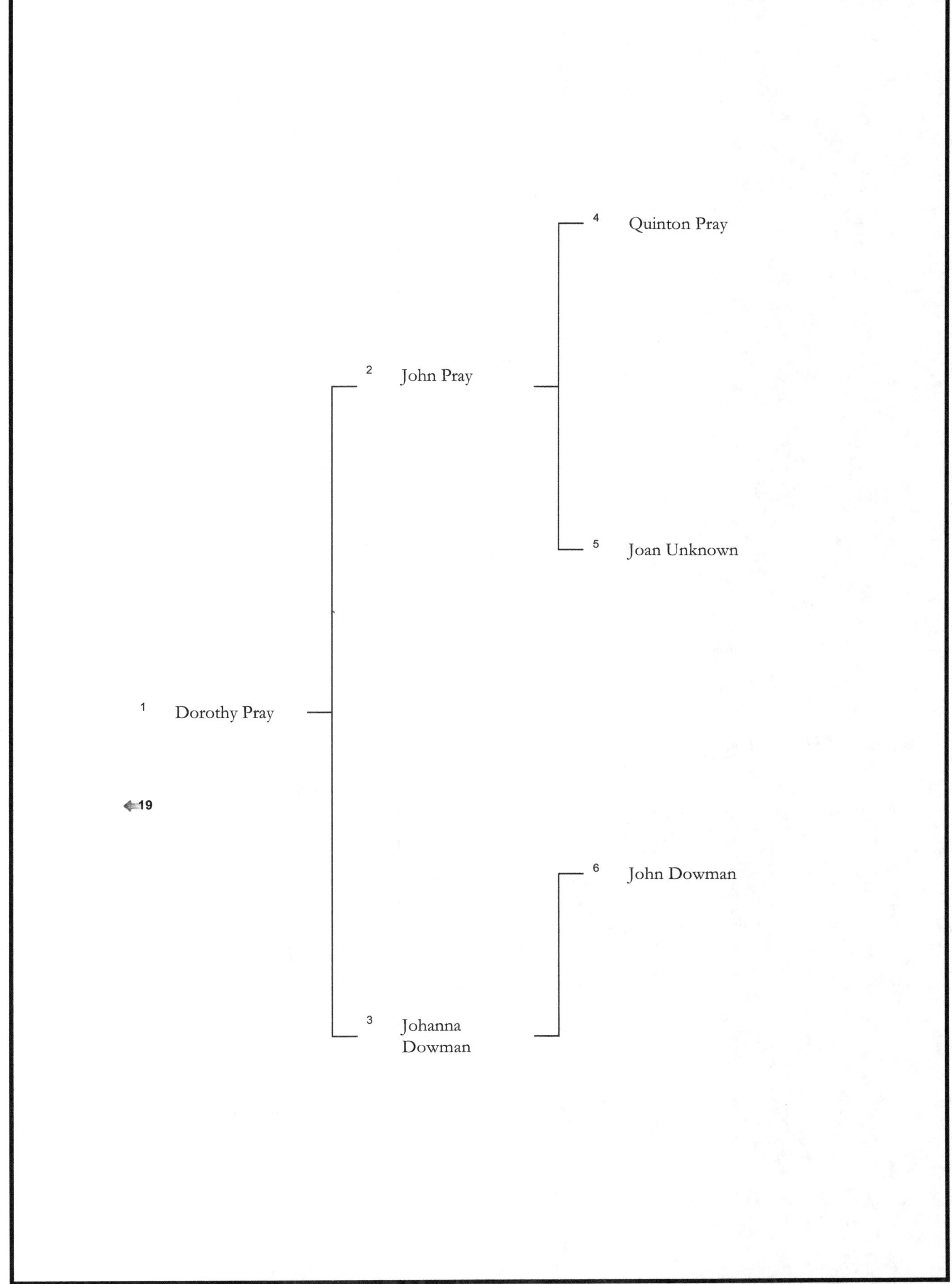

4 Quinton Pray
2 John Pray
5 Joan Unknown
1 Dorothy Pray
19
6 John Dowman
3 Johanna Dowman

4
Thomas
Philbrook I

2
Thomas
Philbrook II

5
Elizabeth
Unknown

1
William
Philbrook

22

6
Edward French

3
Hannah French

7
Ann Unknown

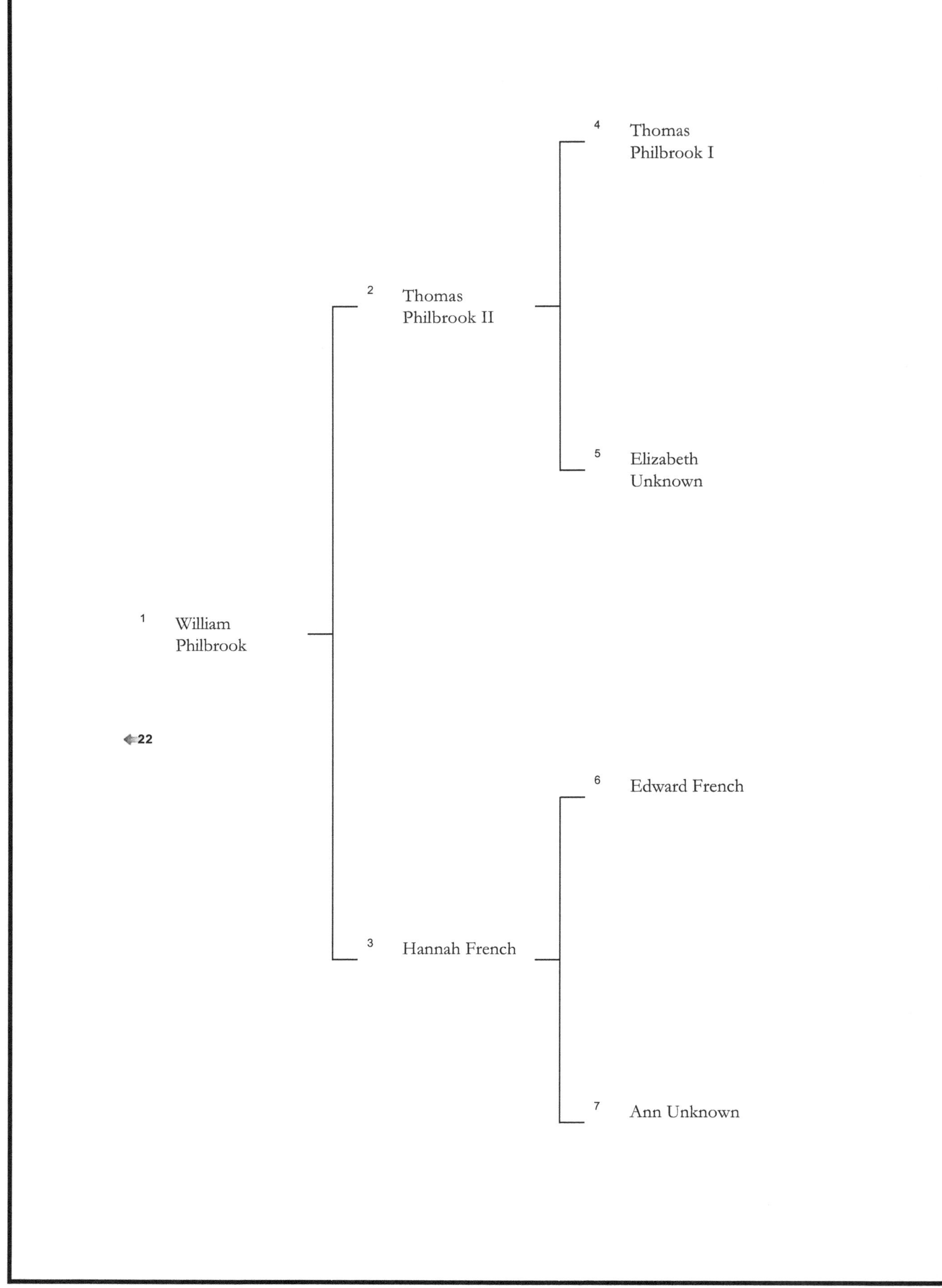

66

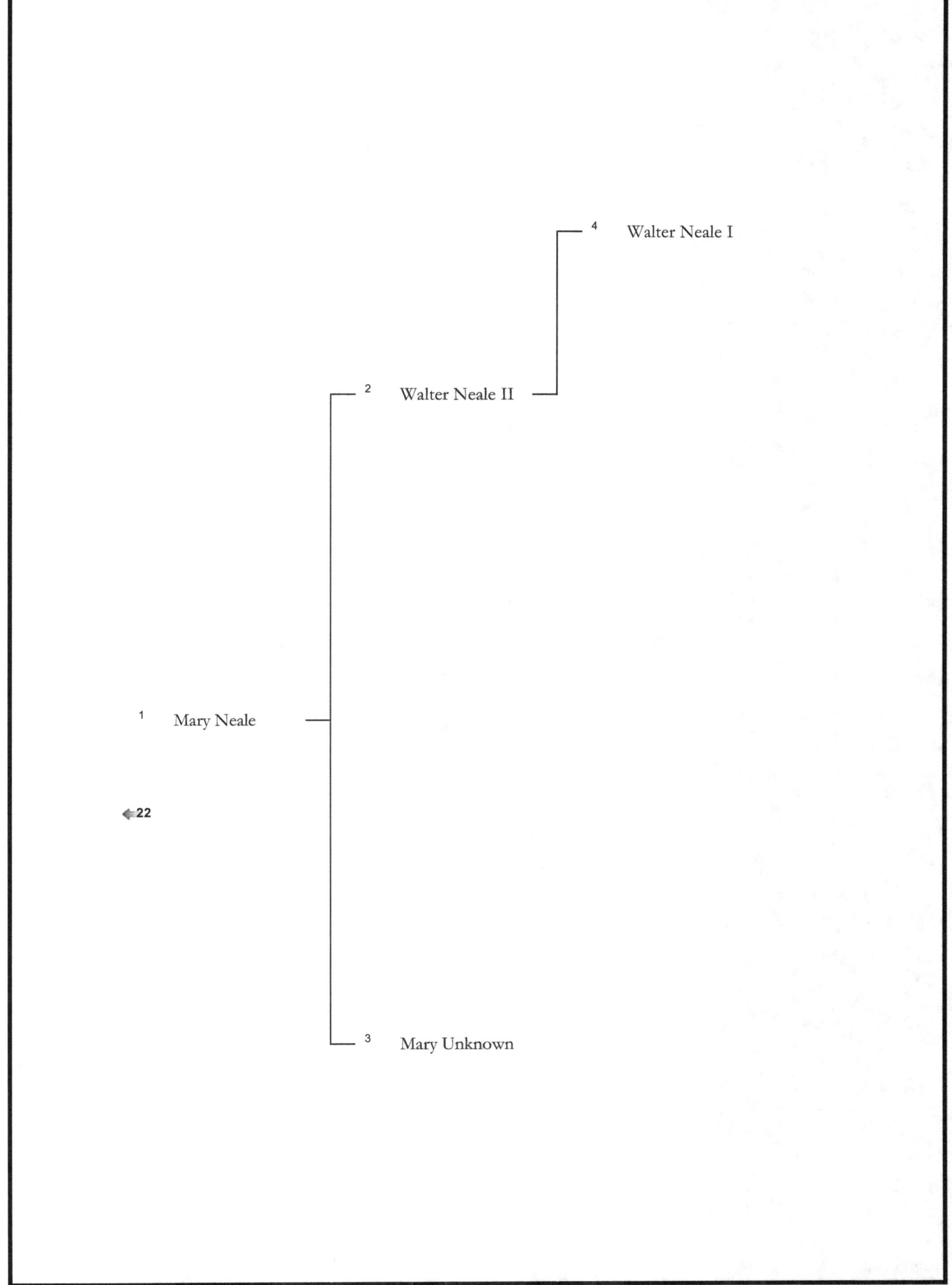

4 Walter Neale I
2 Walter Neale II
1 Mary Neale
22
3 Mary Unknown

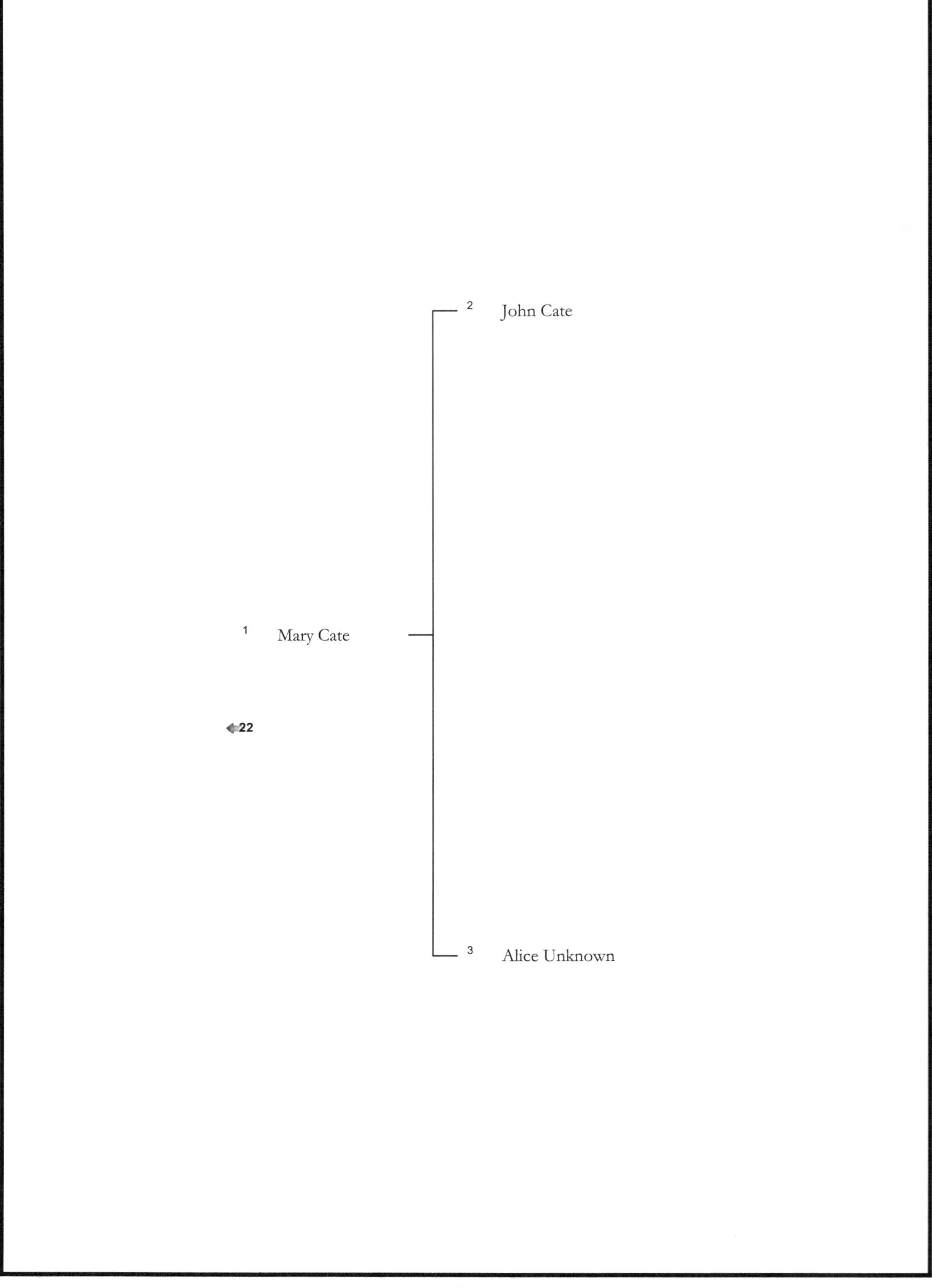

1   Mary Cate
2   John Cate
3   Alice Unknown
22

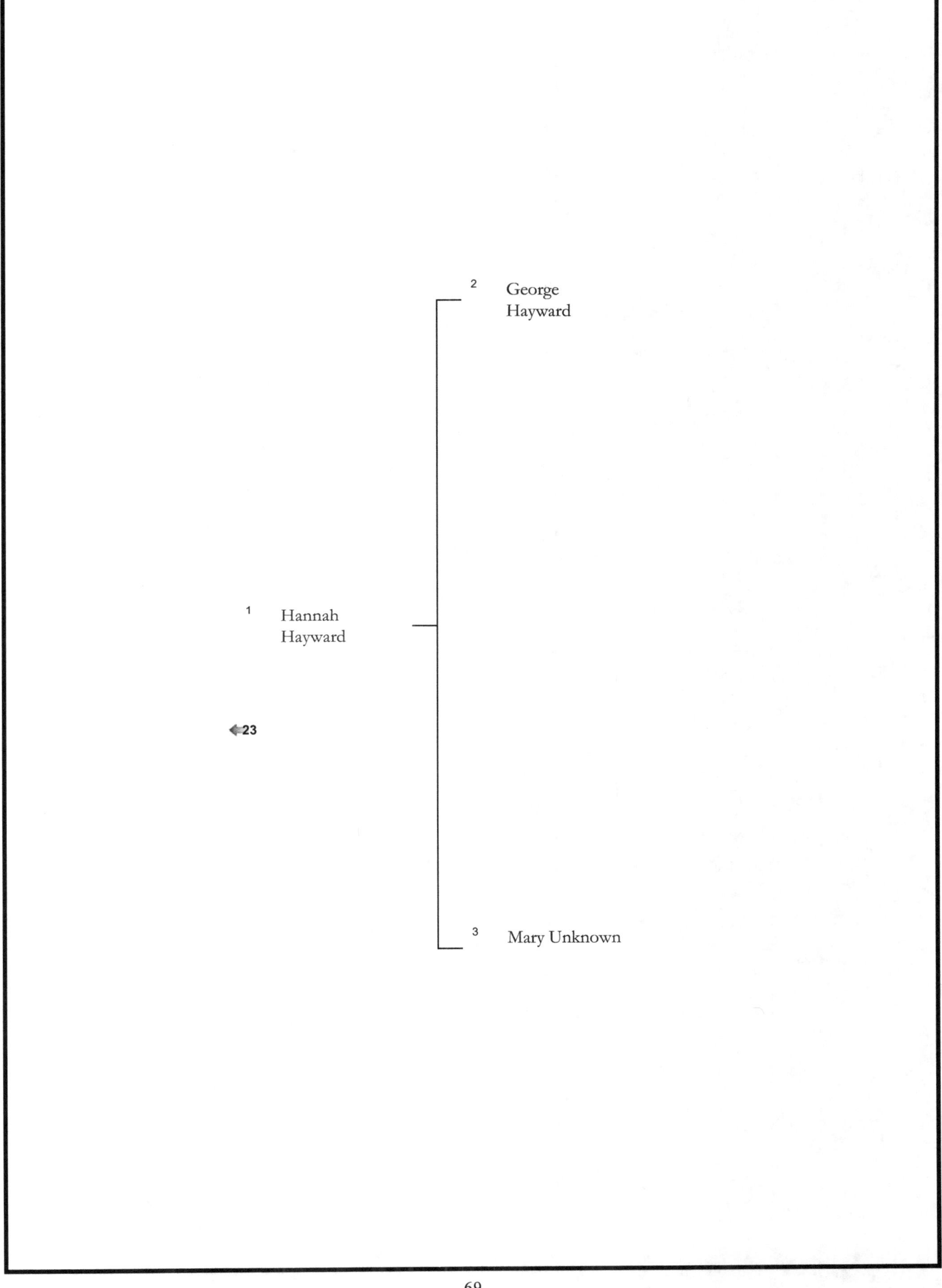
2 George
Hayward

1 Hannah
Hayward

23

3 Mary Unknown

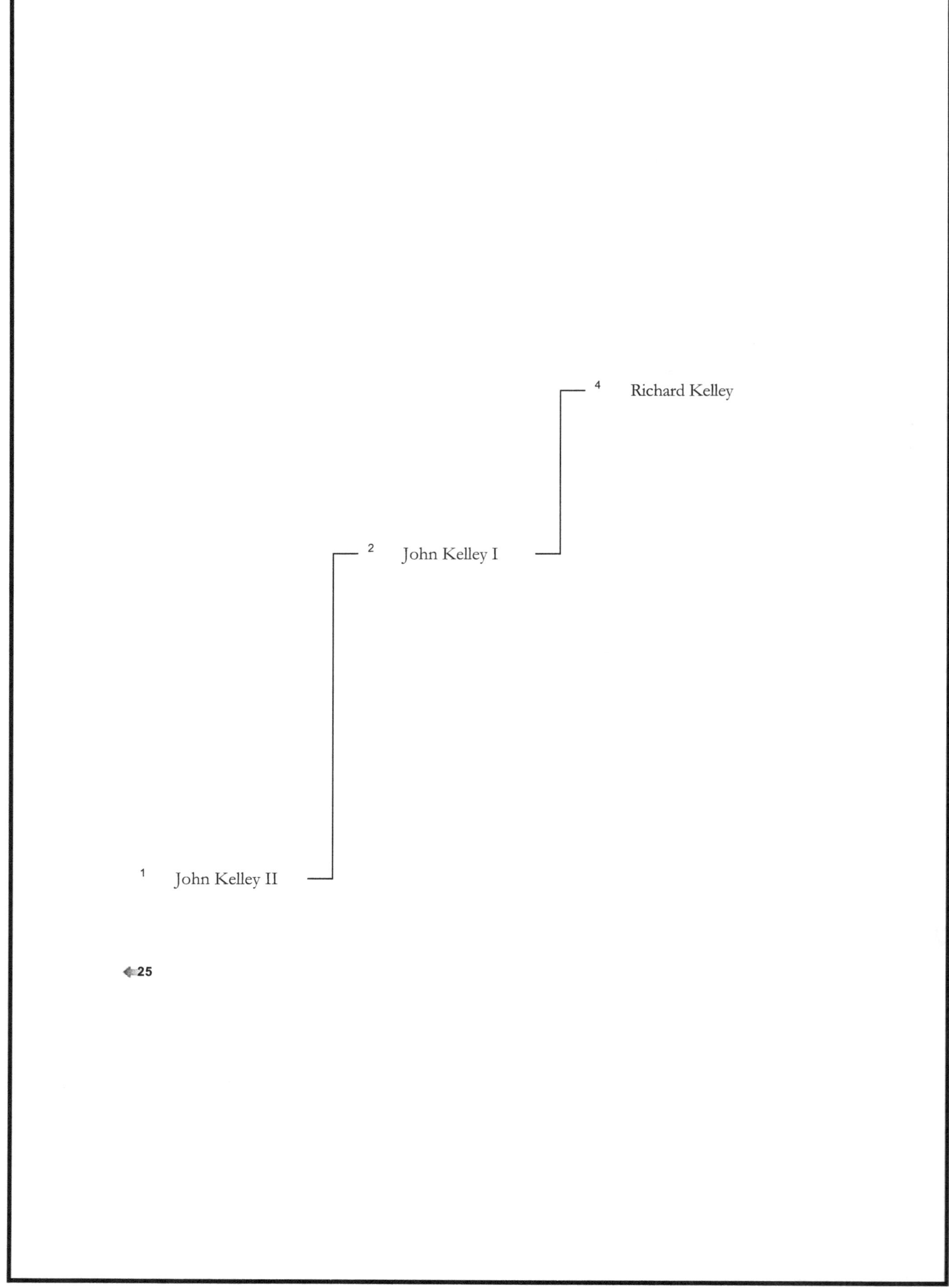

25

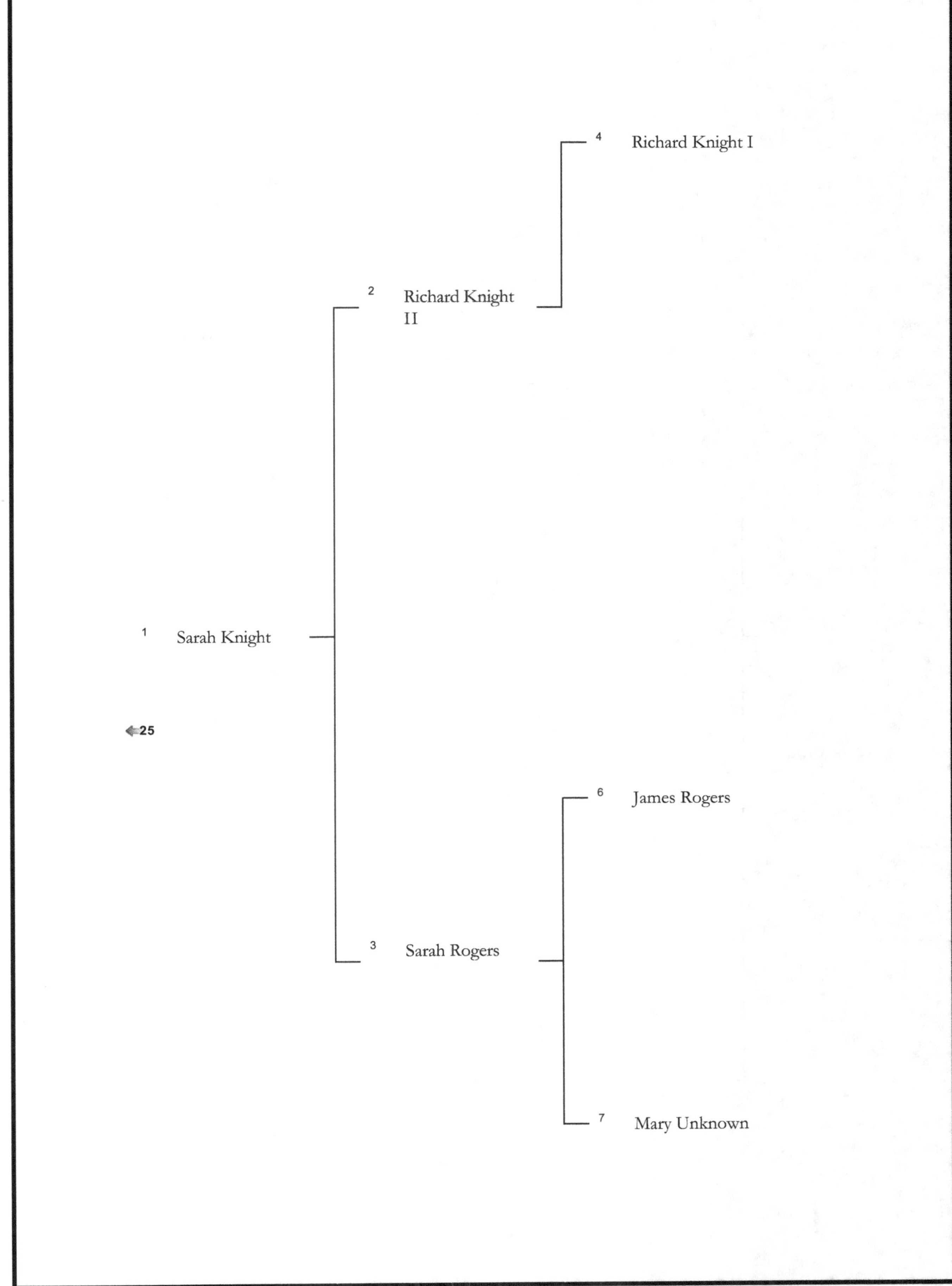

4 Richard Knight I
2 Richard Knight II
1 Sarah Knight
25
6 James Rogers
3 Sarah Rogers
7 Mary Unknown

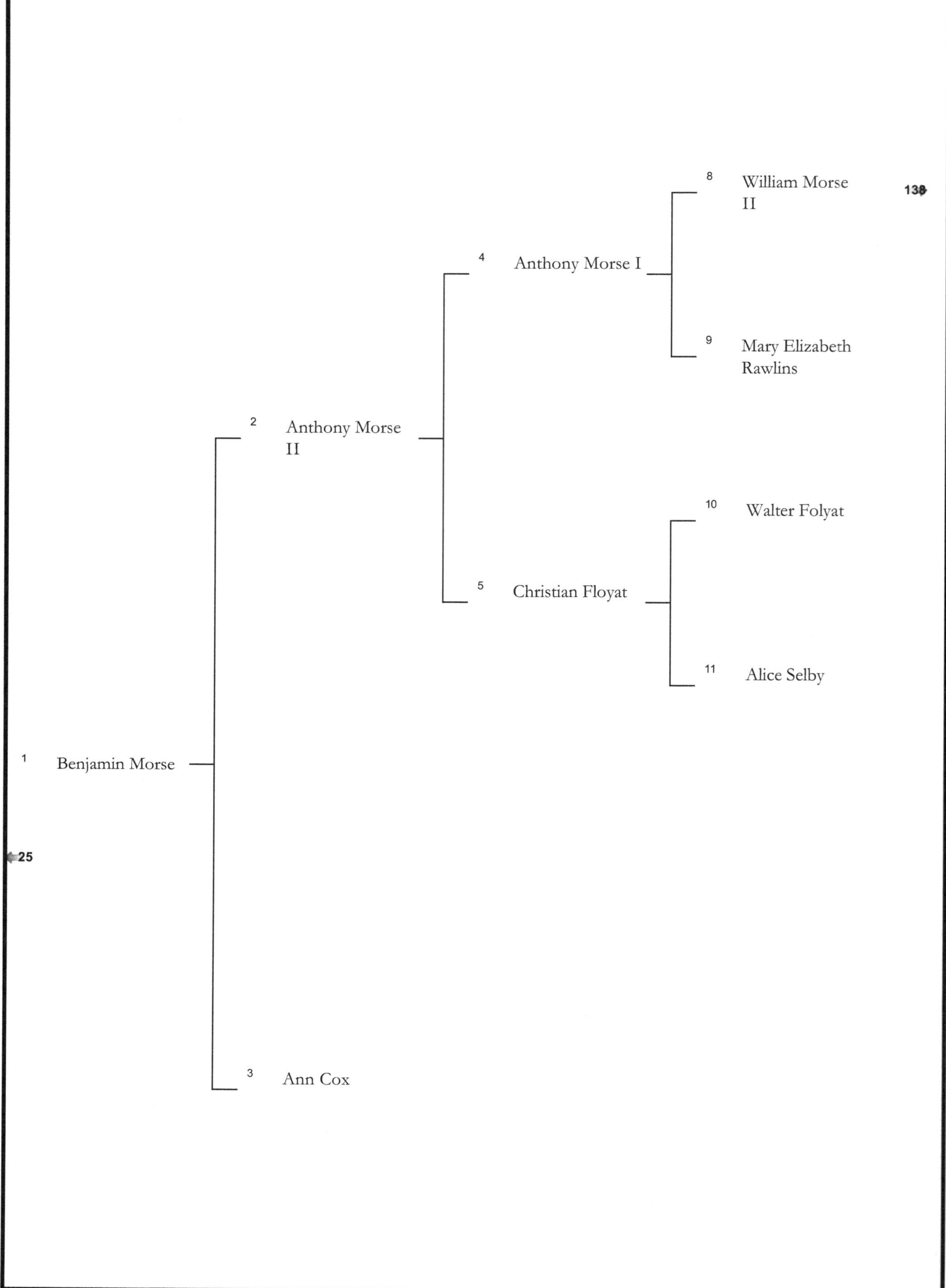

1 Benjamin Morse
2 Anthony Morse II
3 Ann Cox
4 Anthony Morse I
5 Christian Floyat
8 William Morse II
9 Mary Elizabeth Rawlins
10 Walter Folyat
11 Alice Selby
25
138

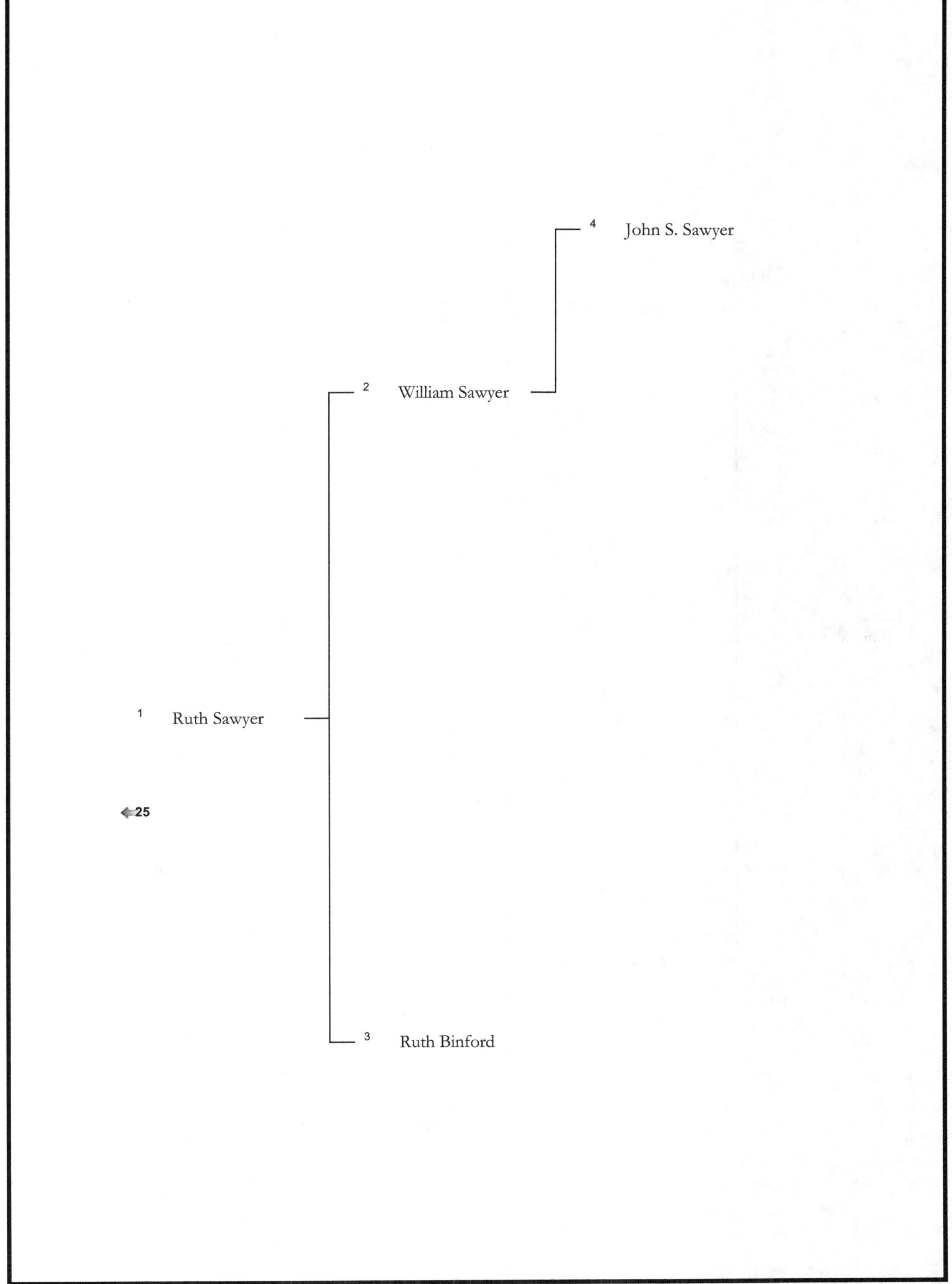

4 John S. Sawyer
2 William Sawyer
1 Ruth Sawyer
25
3 Ruth Binford

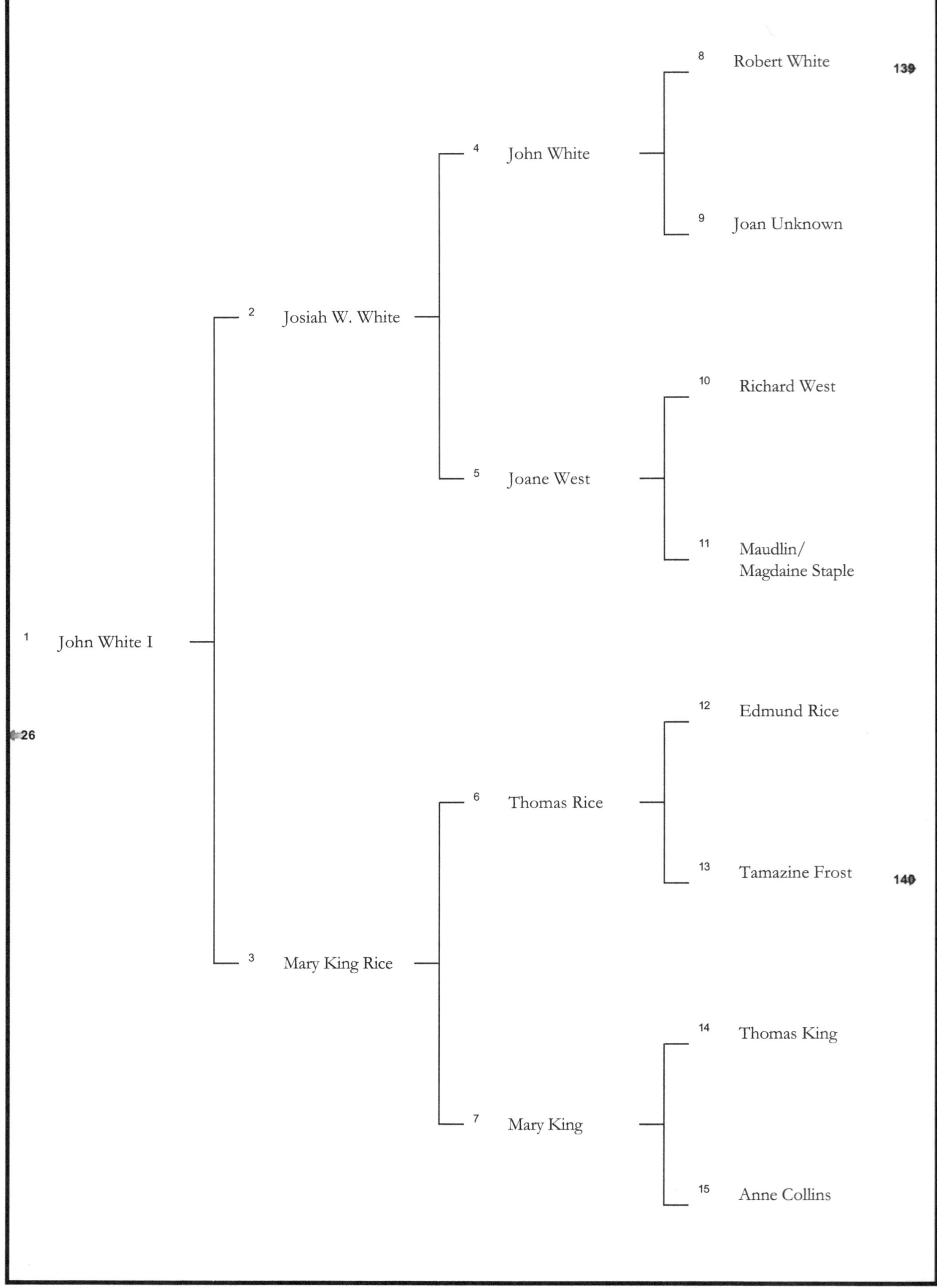

8 Robert White
139
4 John White
9 Joan Unknown
2 Josiah W. White
10 Richard West
5 Joane West
11 Maudlin/ Magdaine Staple
1 John White I
26
12 Edmund Rice
6 Thomas Rice
13 Tamazine Frost
140
3 Mary King Rice
14 Thomas King
7 Mary King
15 Anne Collins

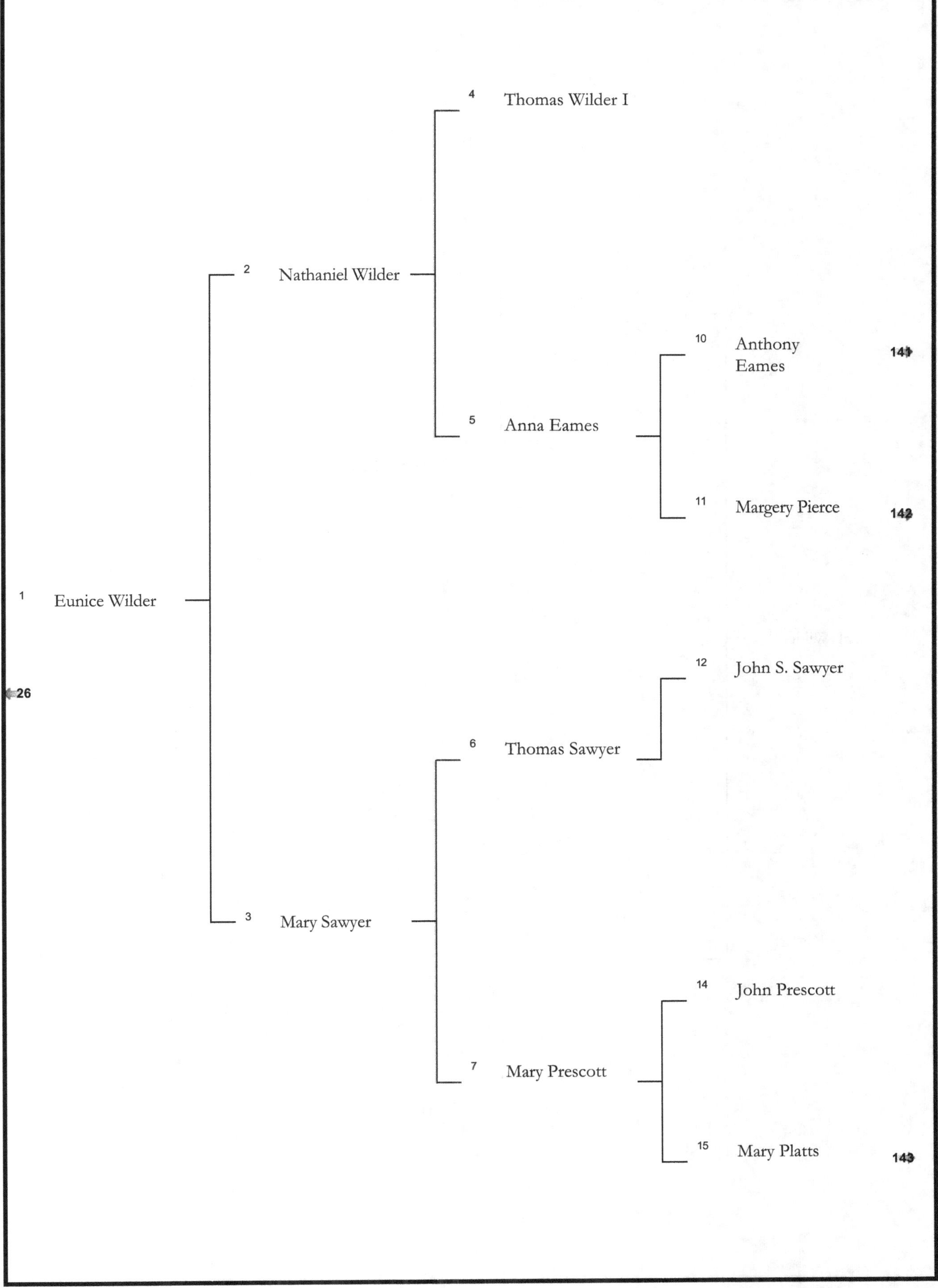

1 Eunice Wilder
26
2 Nathaniel Wilder
4 Thomas Wilder I
5 Anna Eames
10 Anthony Eames
141
11 Margery Pierce
142
3 Mary Sawyer
6 Thomas Sawyer
12 John S. Sawyer
7 Mary Prescott
14 John Prescott
15 Mary Platts
143

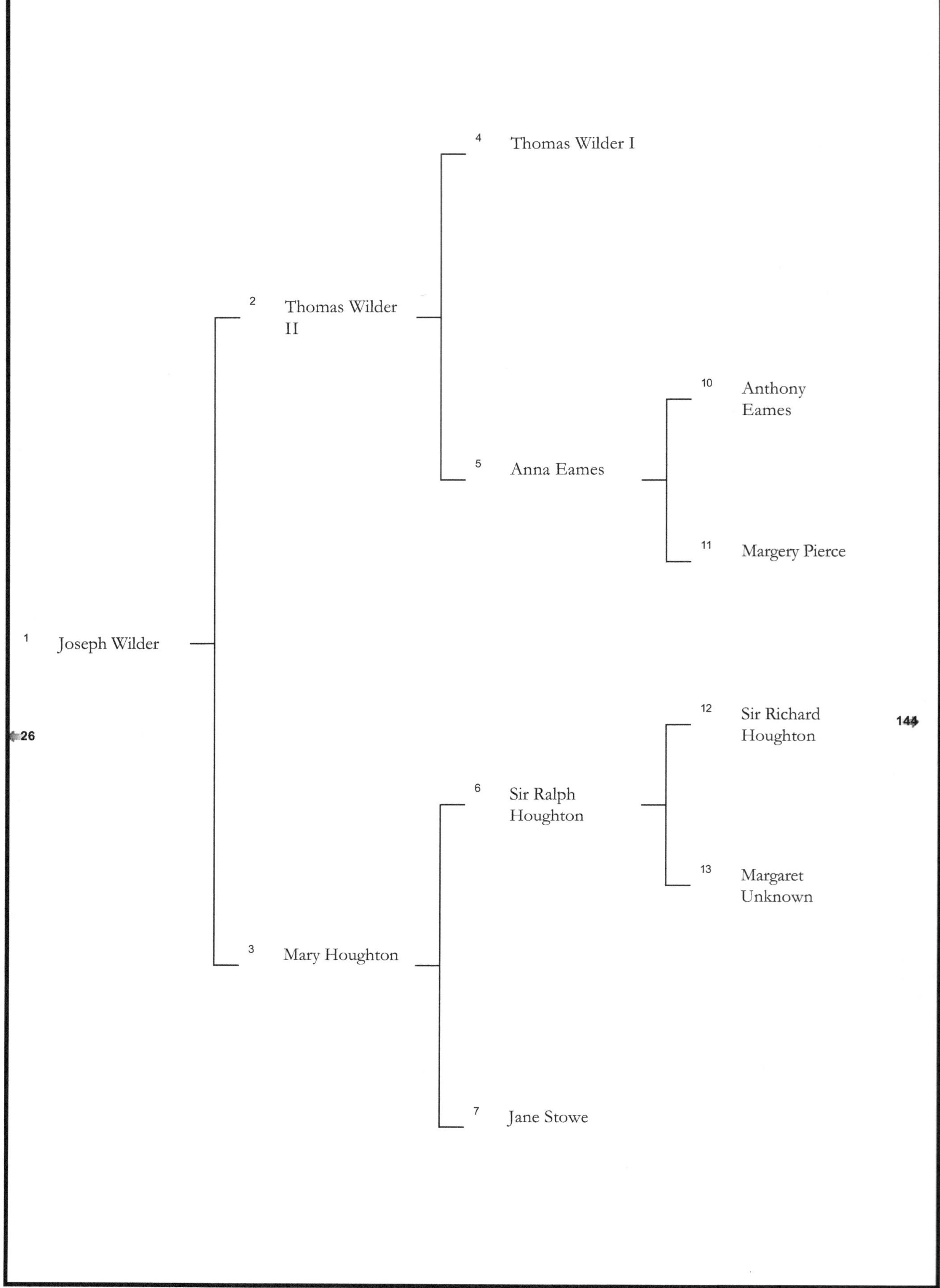

4 Thomas Wilder I
2 Thomas Wilder II
10 Anthony Eames
5 Anna Eames
11 Margery Pierce
1 Joseph Wilder
26
12 Sir Richard Houghton
14
6 Sir Ralph Houghton
13 Margaret Unknown
3 Mary Houghton
7 Jane Stowe

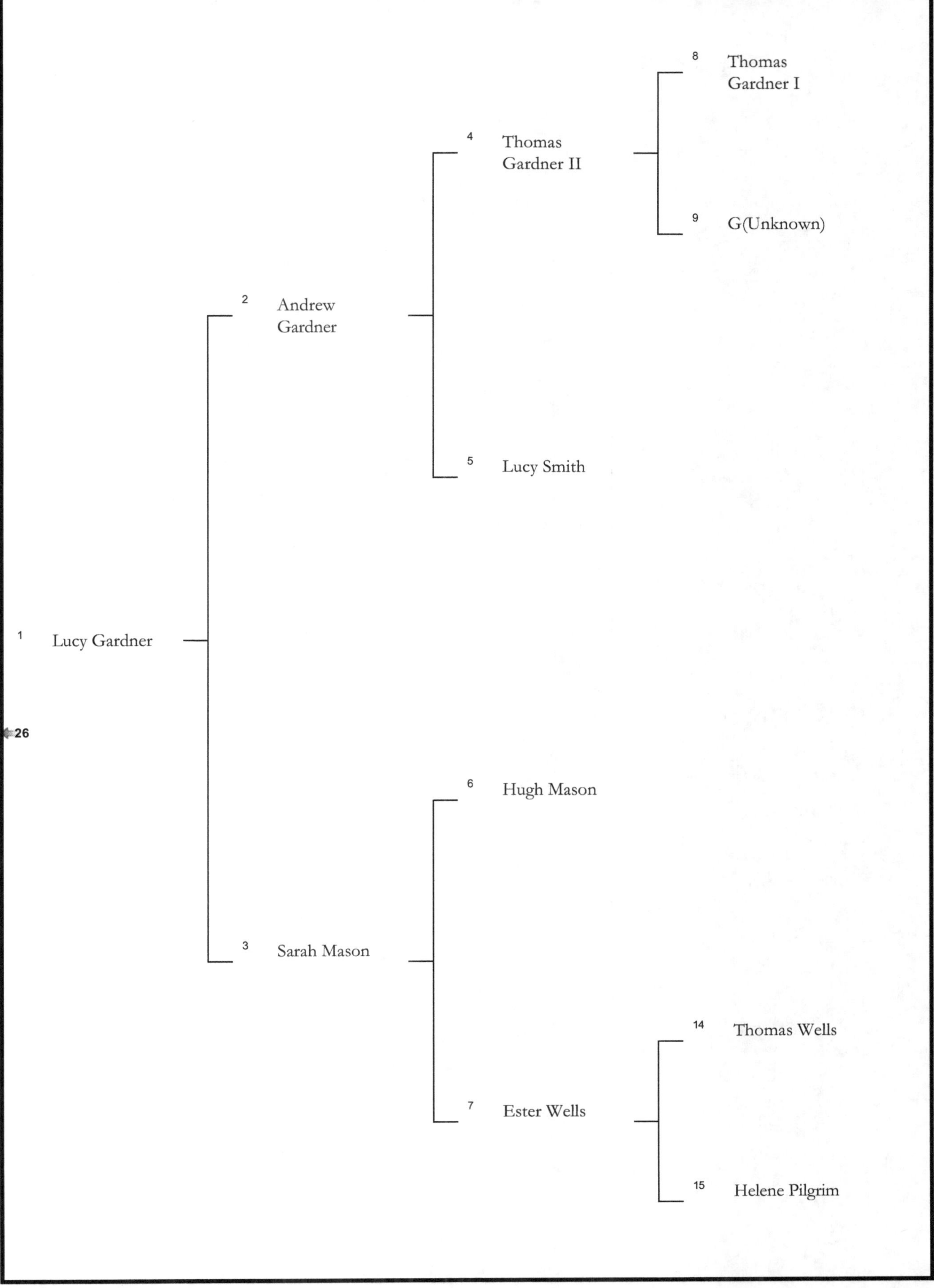

1 Lucy Gardner
2 Andrew Gardner
3 Sarah Mason
4 Thomas Gardner II
5 Lucy Smith
6 Hugh Mason
7 Ester Wells
8 Thomas Gardner I
9 G(Unknown)
14 Thomas Wells
15 Helene Pilgrim
26

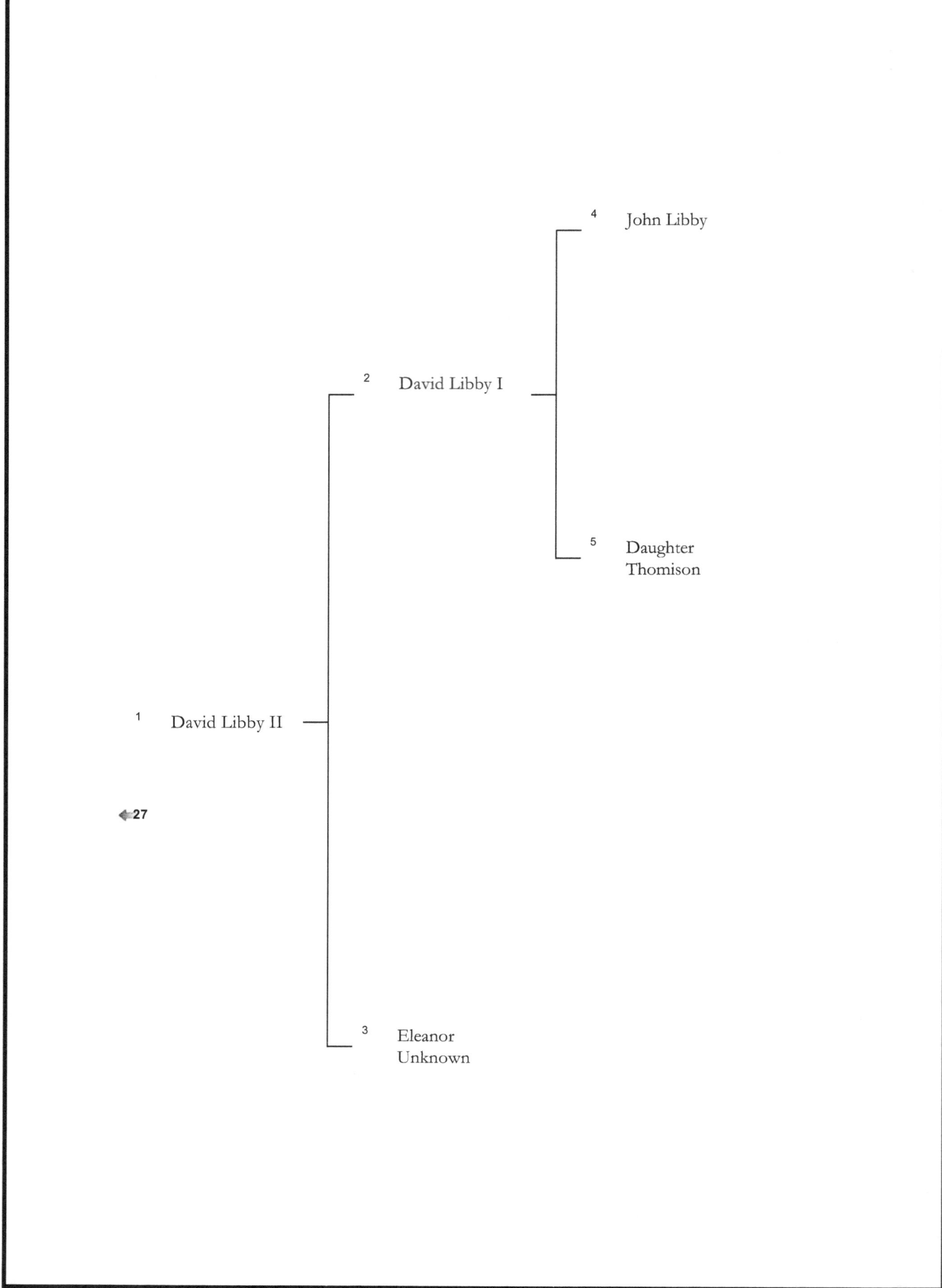

4 John Libby
2 David Libby I
5 Daughter Thomison
1 David Libby II
27
3 Eleanor Unknown

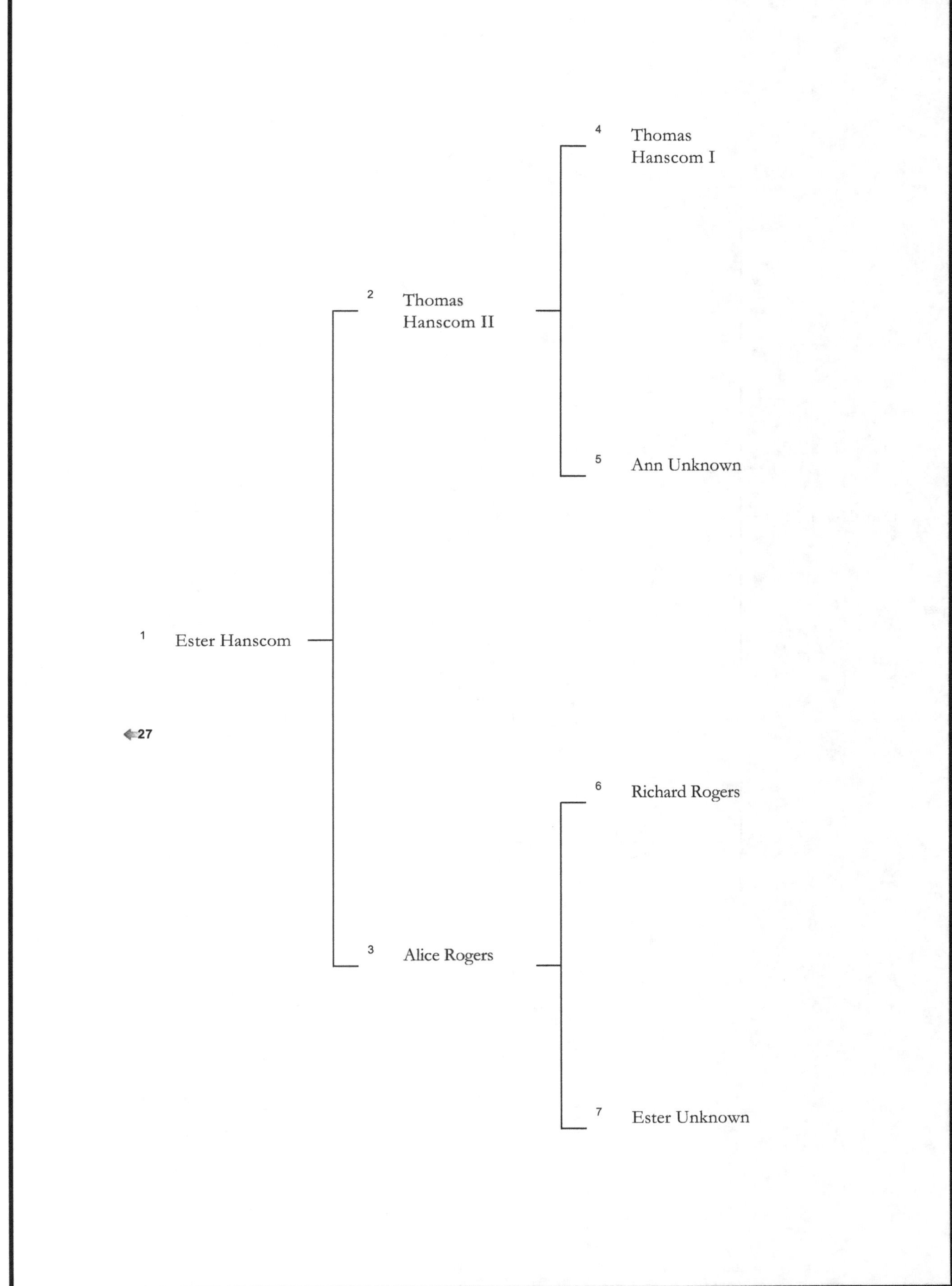

4 Thomas Hanscom I
2 Thomas Hanscom II
5 Ann Unknown
1 Ester Hanscom
27
6 Richard Rogers
3 Alice Rogers
7 Ester Unknown

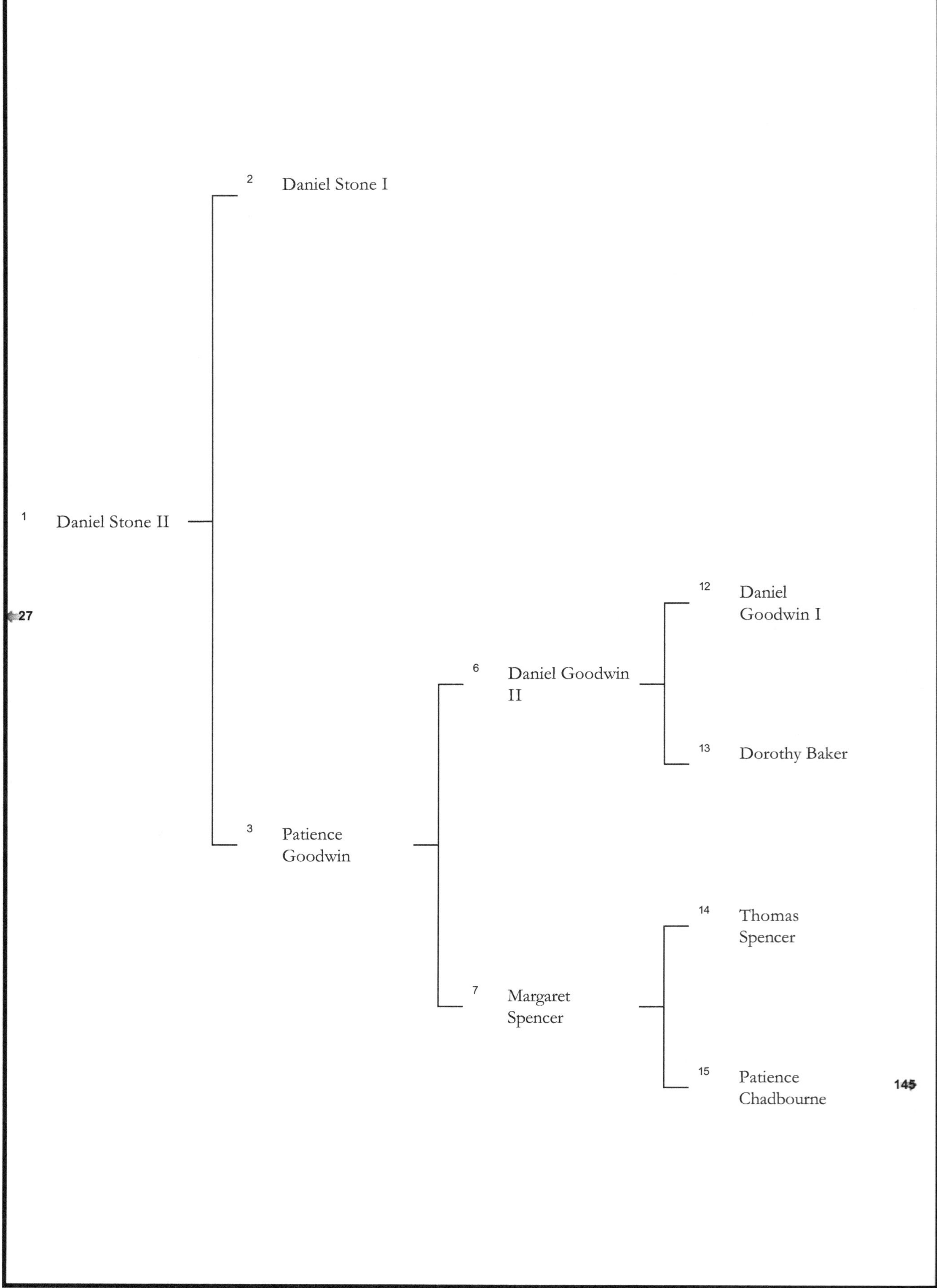

27
1 Daniel Stone II
2 Daniel Stone I
3 Patience Goodwin
6 Daniel Goodwin II
7 Margaret Spencer
12 Daniel Goodwin I
13 Dorothy Baker
14 Thomas Spencer
15 Patience Chadbourne
145

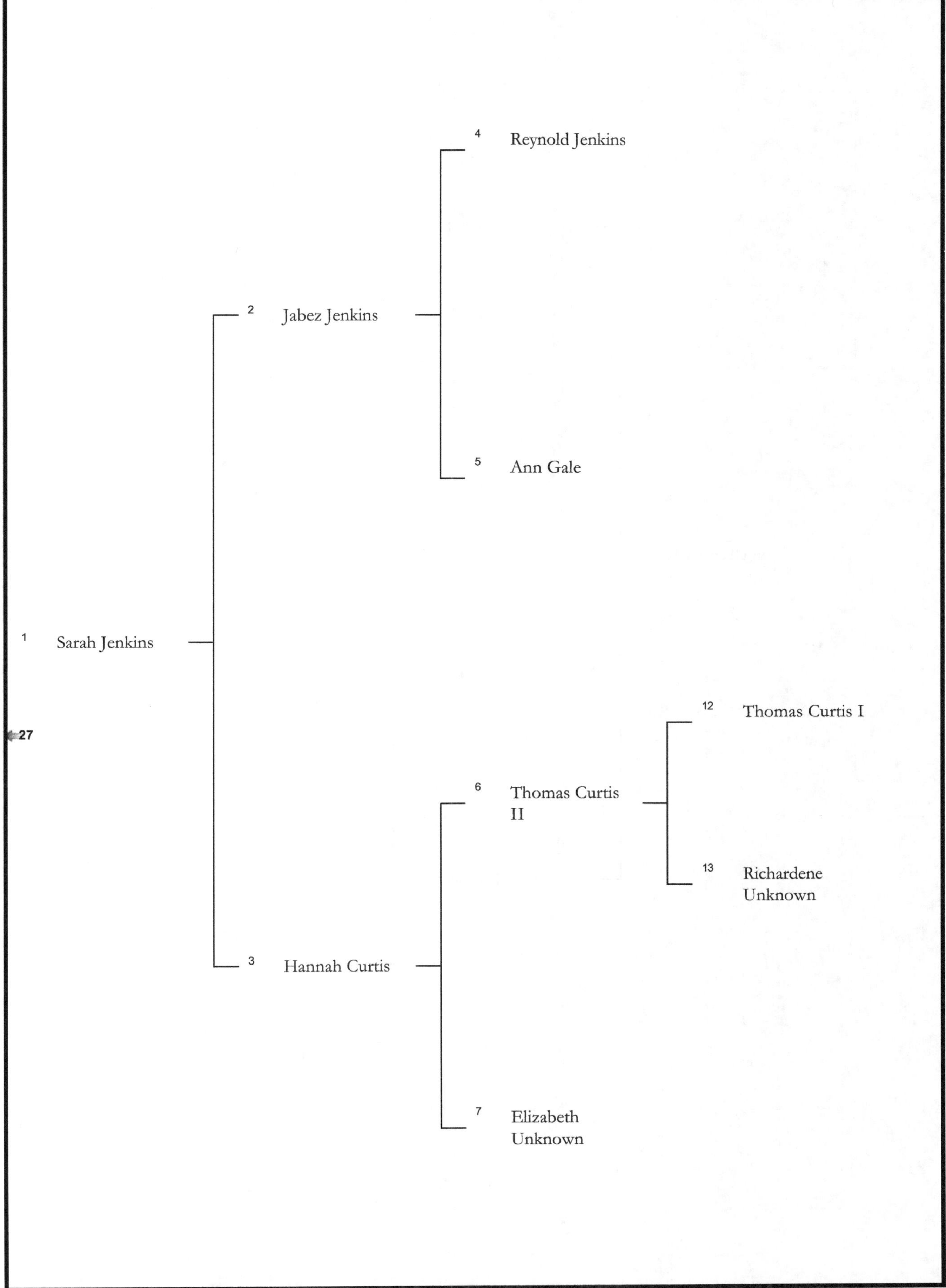

1 Sarah Jenkins
27
2 Jabez Jenkins
4 Reynold Jenkins
5 Ann Gale
3 Hannah Curtis
6 Thomas Curtis II
7 Elizabeth Unknown
12 Thomas Curtis I
13 Richardene Unknown

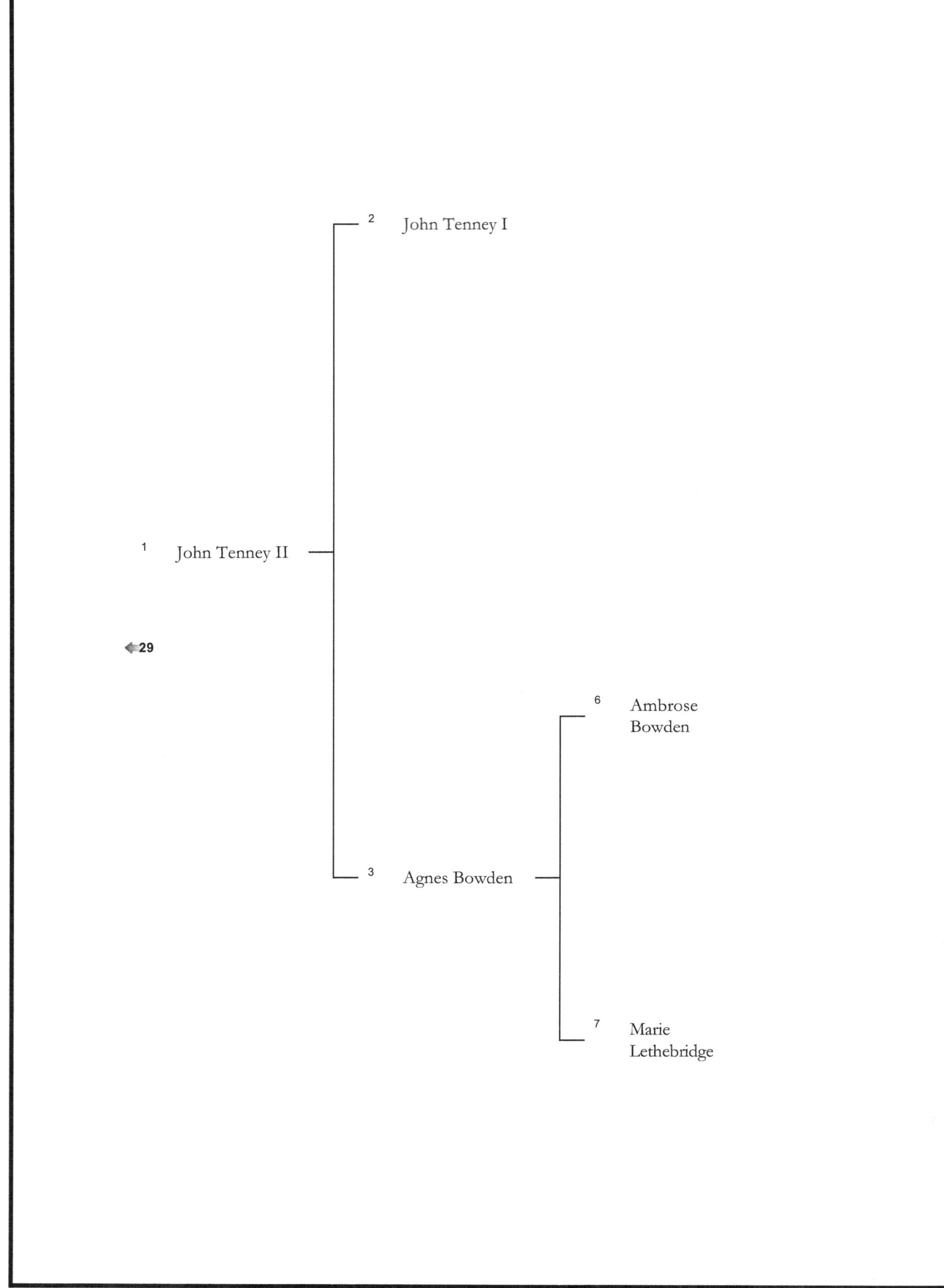

2 John Tenney I
1 John Tenney II
29
6 Ambrose Bowden
3 Agnes Bowden
7 Marie Lethebridge

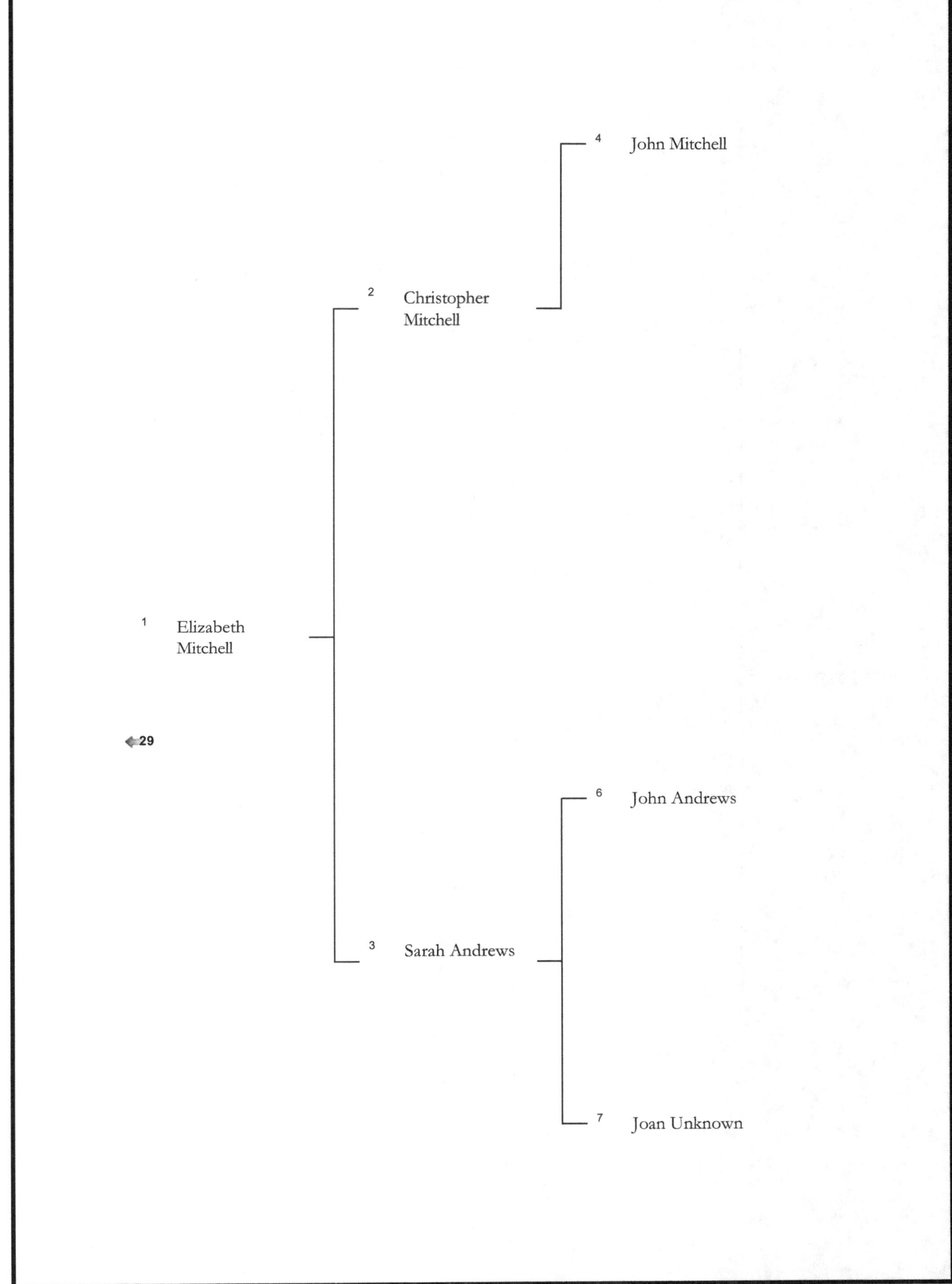

1 Elizabeth Mitchell
2 Christopher Mitchell
4 John Mitchell
3 Sarah Andrews
6 John Andrews
7 Joan Unknown
29

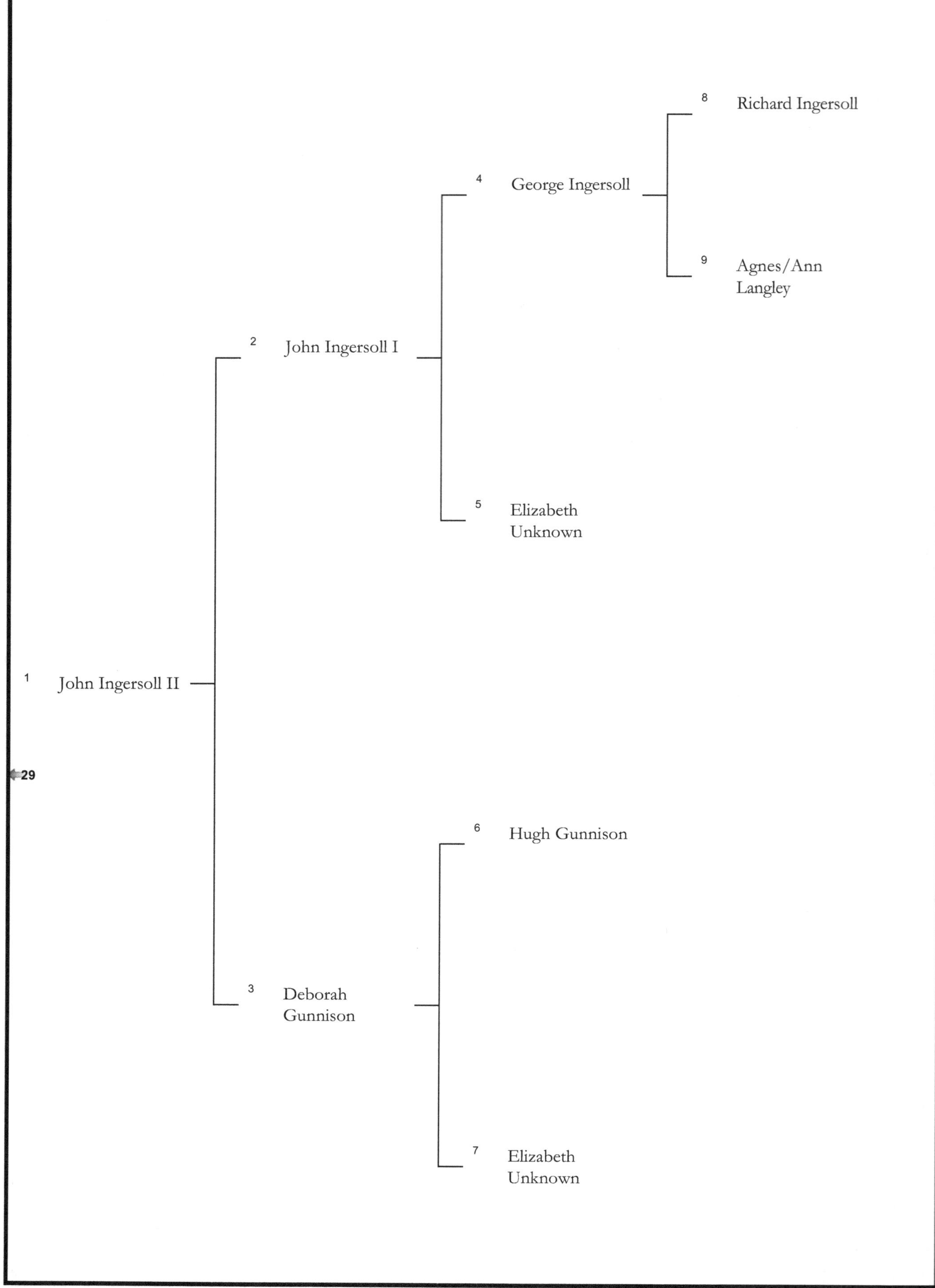

8 Richard Ingersoll
4 George Ingersoll
9 Agnes/Ann Langley
2 John Ingersoll I
5 Elizabeth Unknown
1 John Ingersoll II
29
6 Hugh Gunnison
3 Deborah Gunnison
7 Elizabeth Unknown

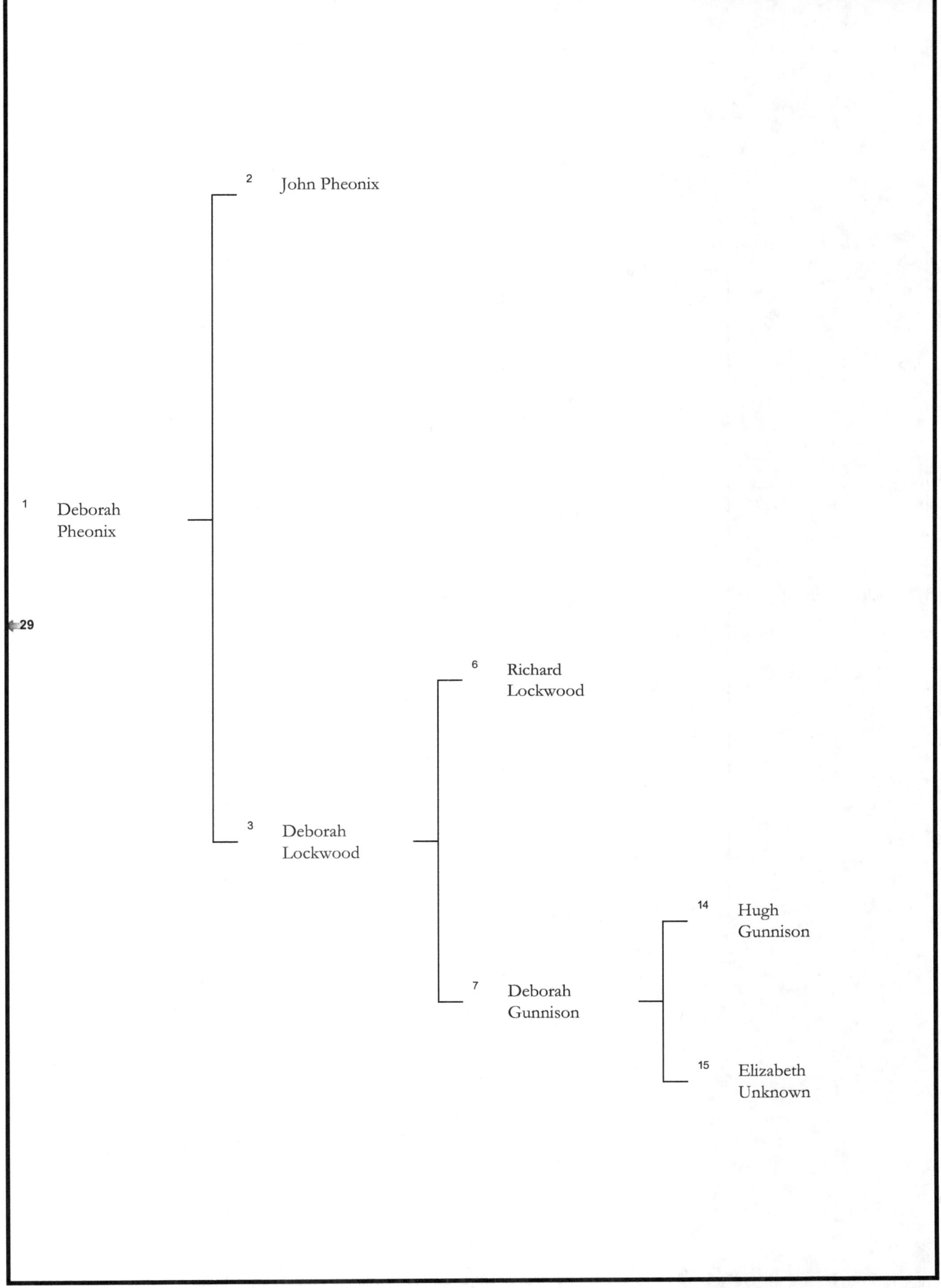

1 Deborah Pheonix
29
2 John Pheonix
3 Deborah Lockwood
6 Richard Lockwood
7 Deborah Gunnison
14 Hugh Gunnison
15 Elizabeth Unknown

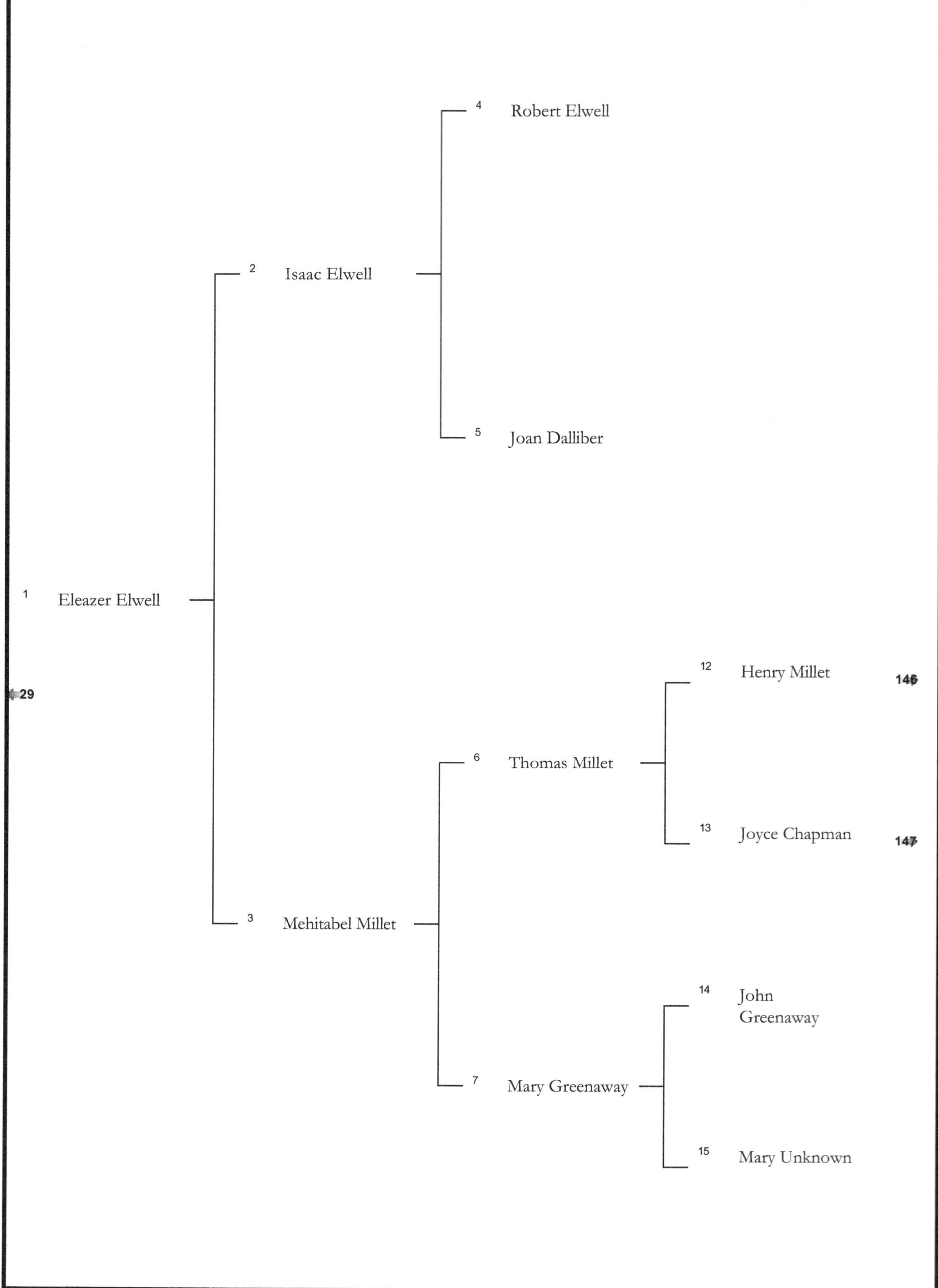

4 Robert Elwell
2 Isaac Elwell
5 Joan Dalliber
1 Eleazer Elwell
29
12 Henry Millet 146
6 Thomas Millet
13 Joyce Chapman 147
3 Mehitabel Millet
14 John Greenaway
7 Mary Greenaway
15 Mary Unknown

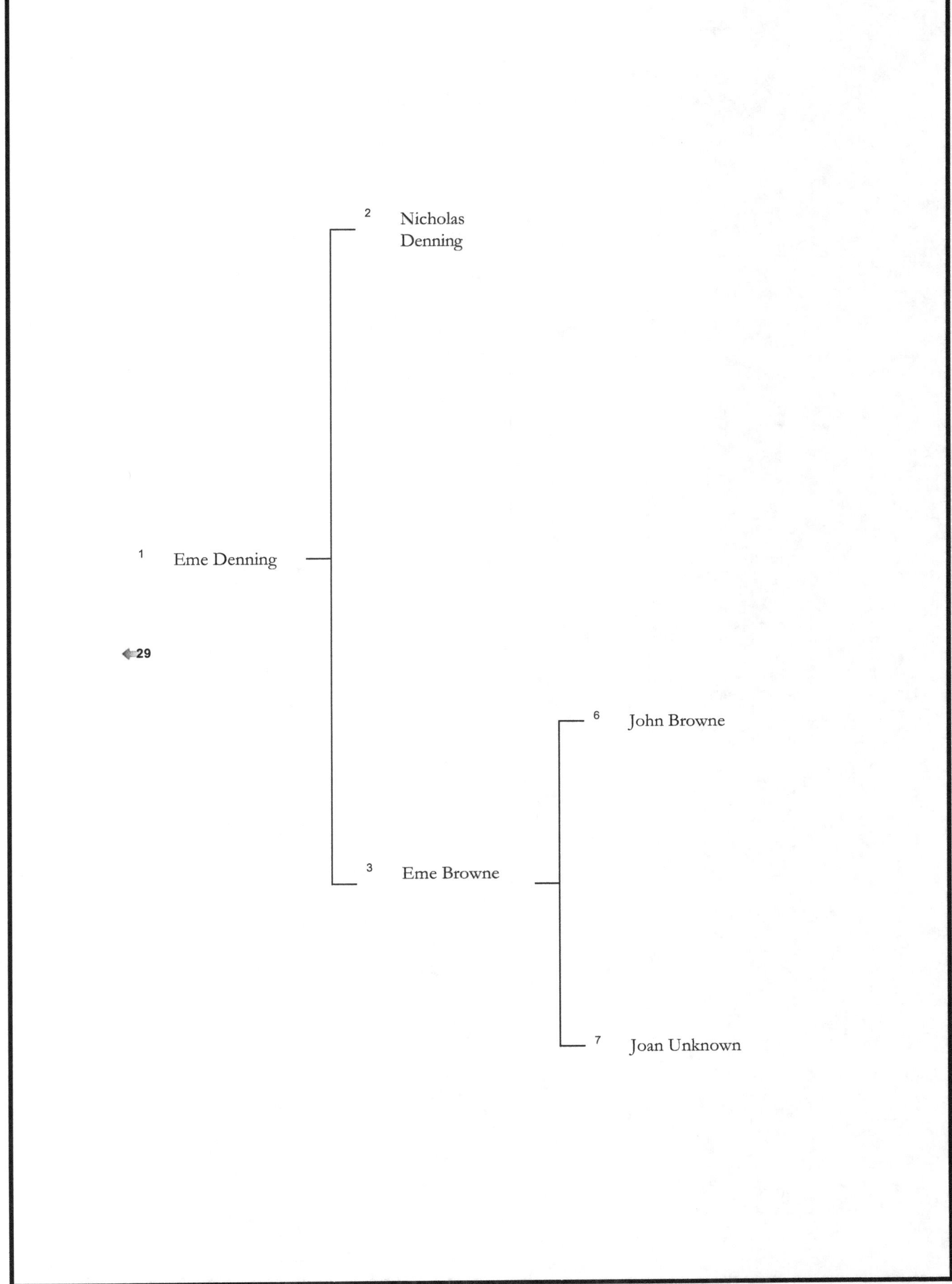

2 Nicholas Denning
1 Eme Denning
29
6 John Browne
3 Eme Browne
7 Joan Unknown

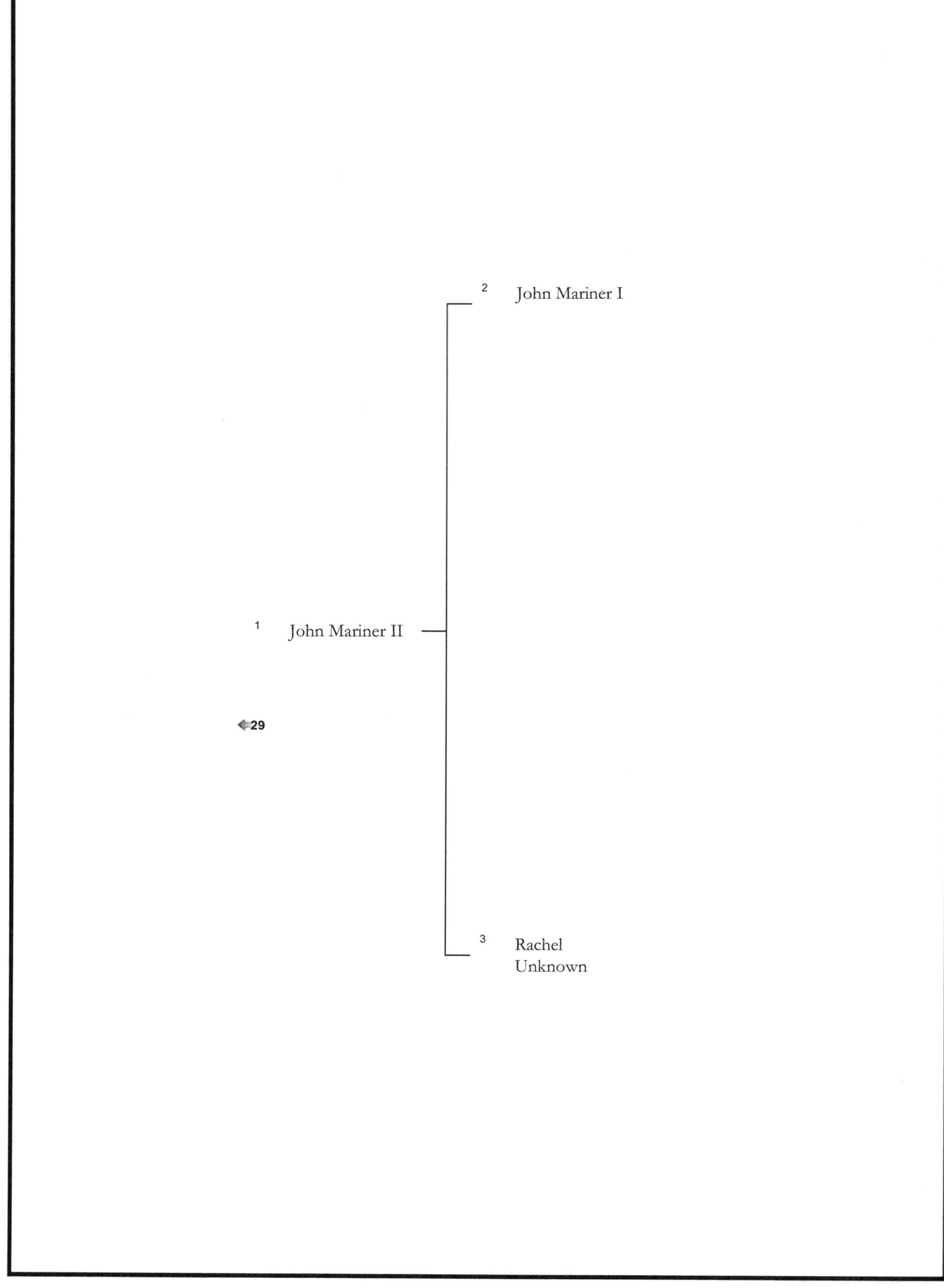

2 John Mariner I
1 John Mariner II
29
3 Rachel
Unknown

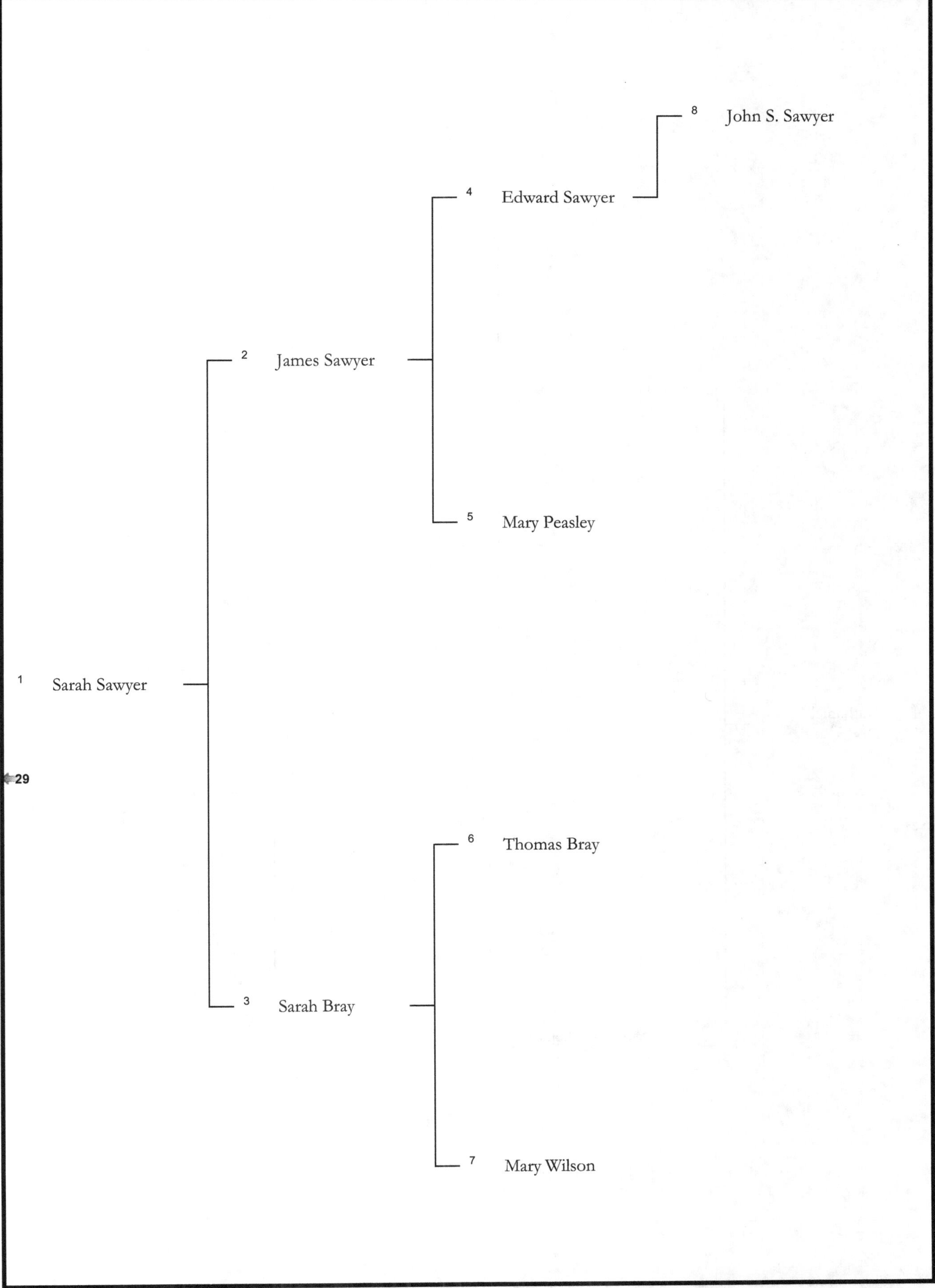

1 Sarah Sawyer
2 James Sawyer
3 Sarah Bray
4 Edward Sawyer
5 Mary Peasley
6 Thomas Bray
7 Mary Wilson
8 John S. Sawyer
29

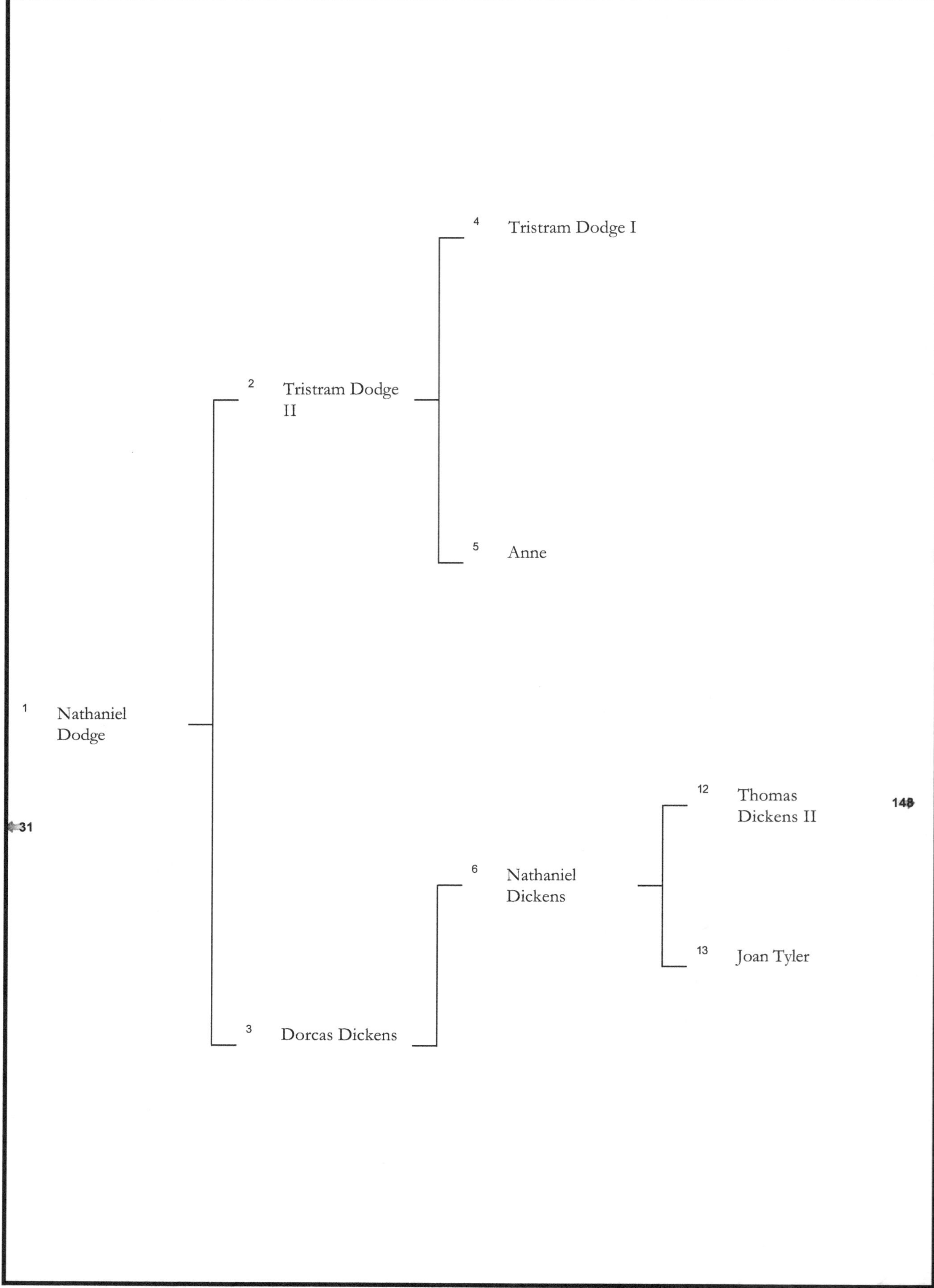

1 Nathaniel Dodge
2 Tristram Dodge II
4 Tristram Dodge I
5 Anne
3 Dorcas Dickens
6 Nathaniel Dickens
12 Thomas Dickens II
13 Joan Tyler
31
148

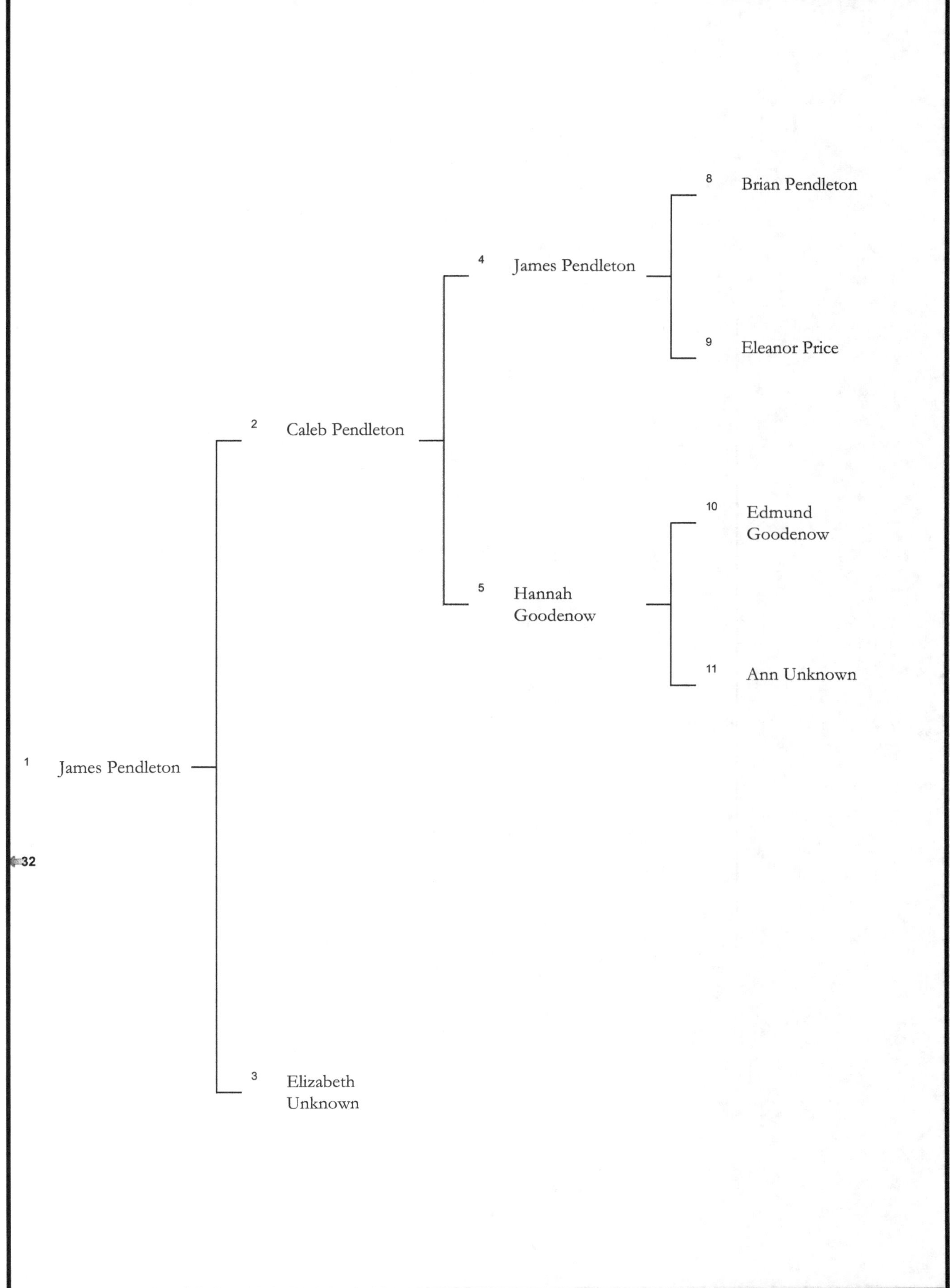

1 James Pendleton
32
2 Caleb Pendleton
3 Elizabeth Unknown
4 James Pendleton
5 Hannah Goodenow
8 Brian Pendleton
9 Eleanor Price
10 Edmund Goodenow
11 Ann Unknown

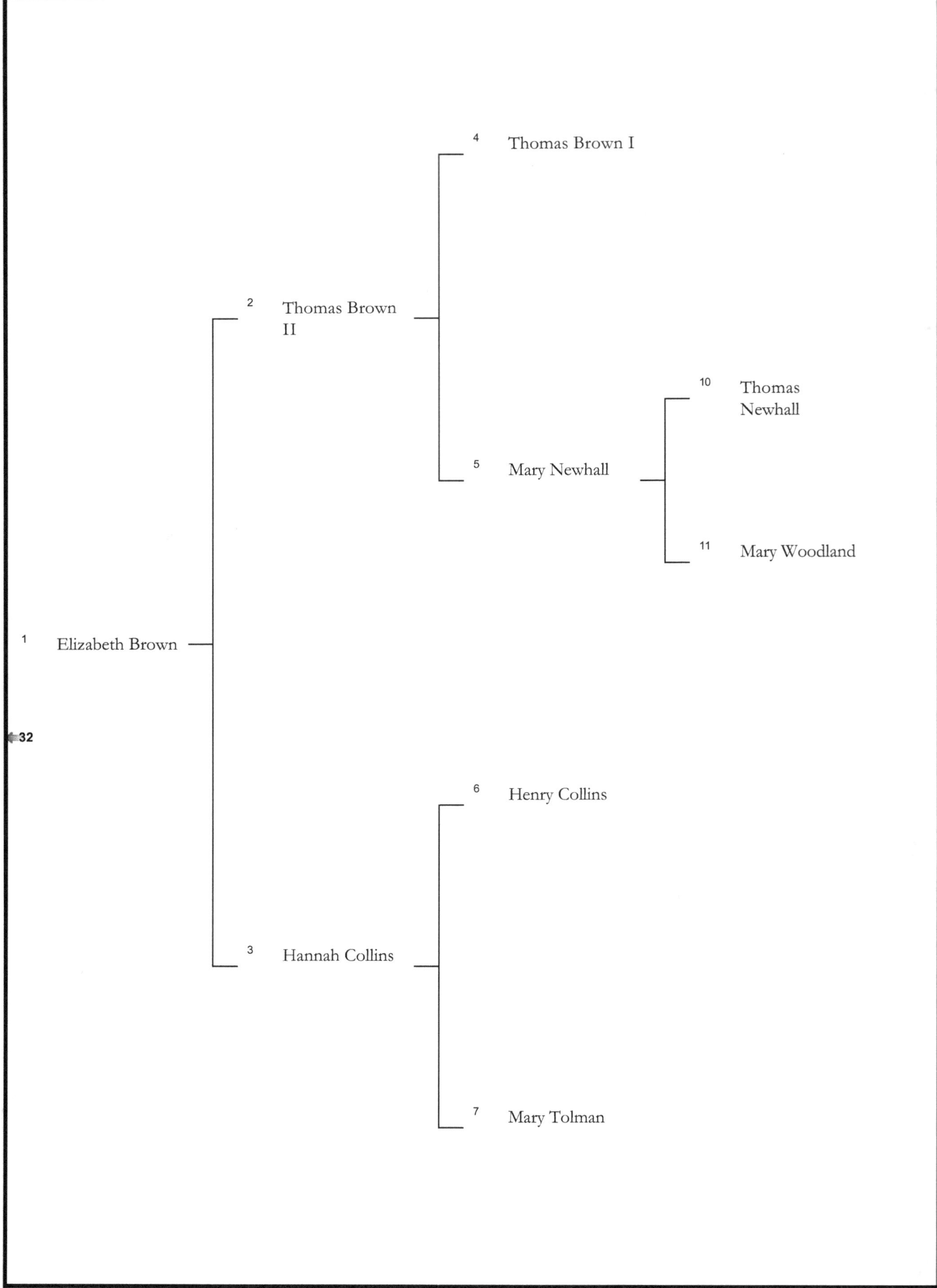

1 Elizabeth Brown
2 Thomas Brown II
3 Hannah Collins
4 Thomas Brown I
5 Mary Newhall
6 Henry Collins
7 Mary Tolman
10 Thomas Newhall
11 Mary Woodland
32

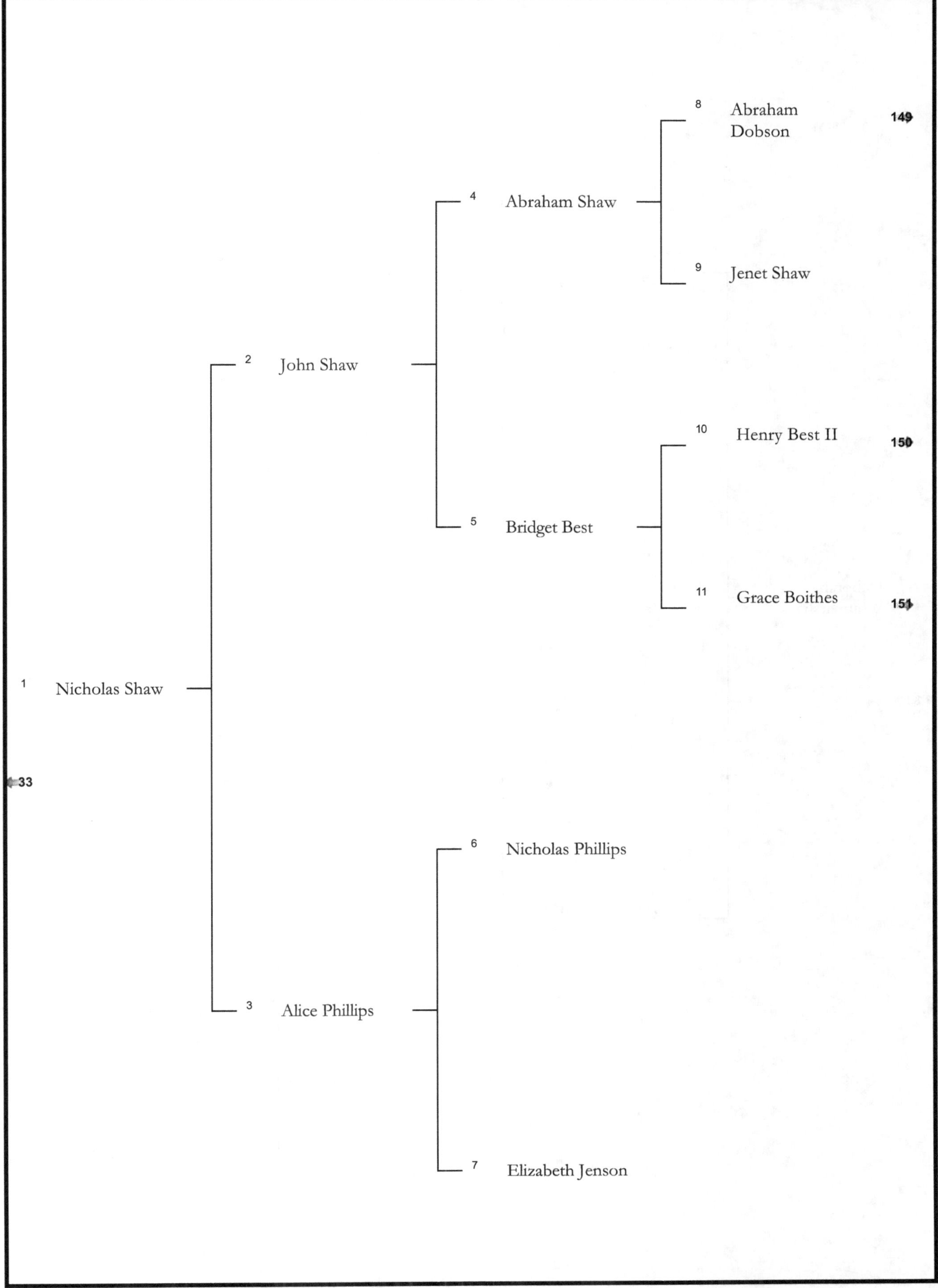

8 Abraham Dobson 149
4 Abraham Shaw
9 Jenet Shaw
2 John Shaw
10 Henry Best II 150
5 Bridget Best
11 Grace Boithes 151
1 Nicholas Shaw
33
6 Nicholas Phillips
3 Alice Phillips
7 Elizabeth Jenson

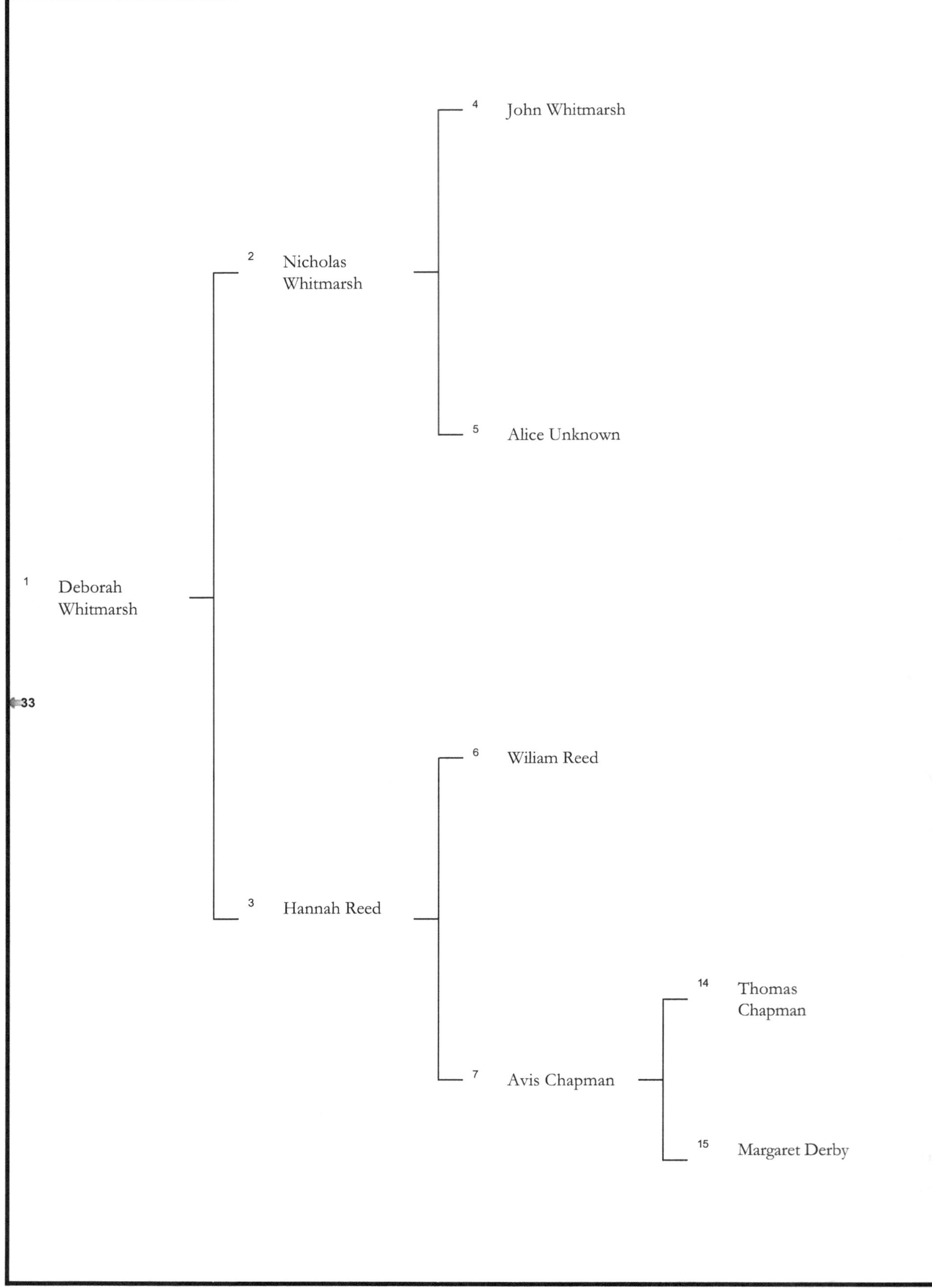

1 Deborah Whitmarsh
33
2 Nicholas Whitmarsh
3 Hannah Reed
4 John Whitmarsh
5 Alice Unknown
6 Wiliam Reed
7 Avis Chapman
14 Thomas Chapman
15 Margaret Derby

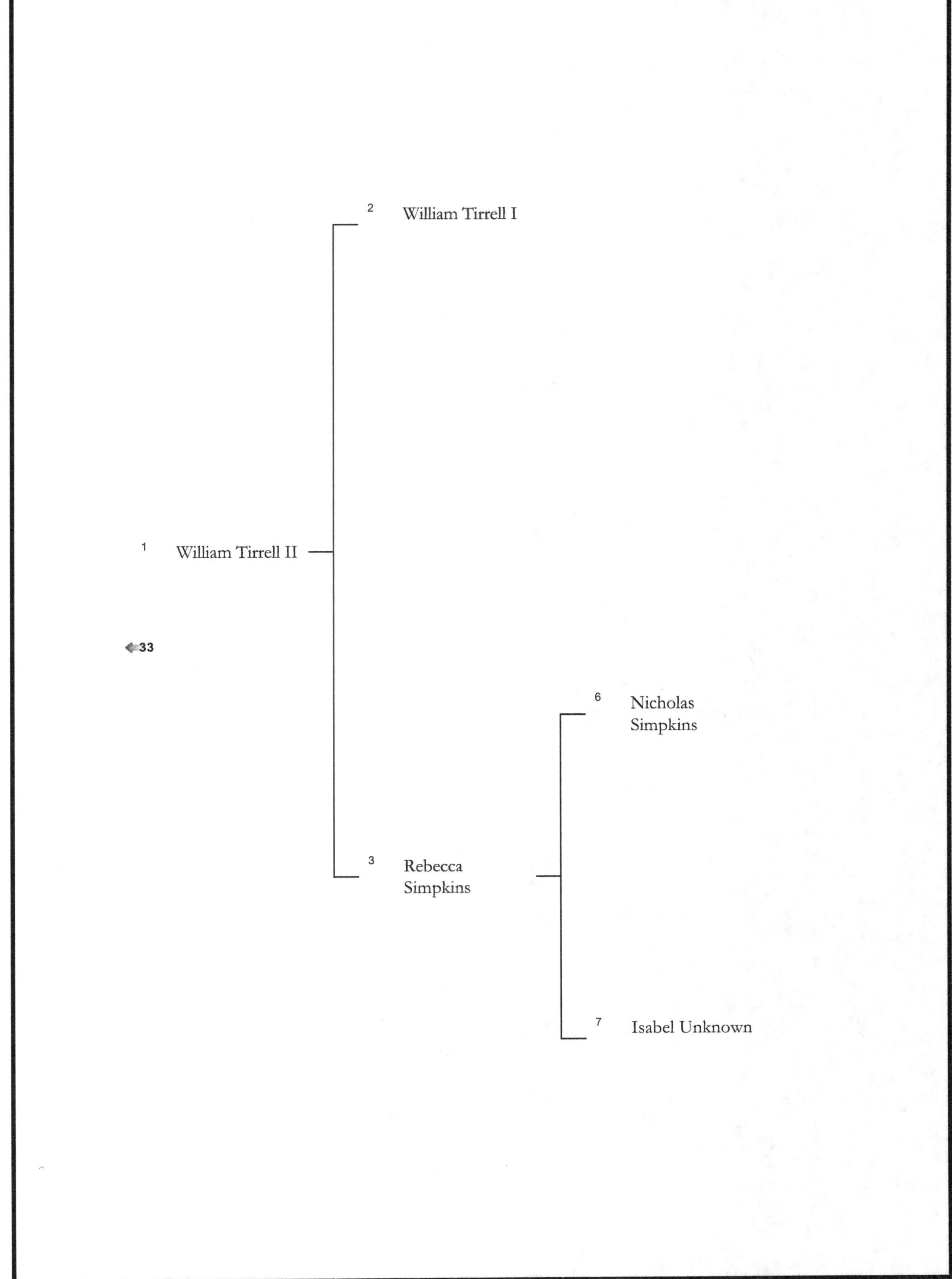

2 William Tirrell I
1 William Tirrell II
33
6 Nicholas Simpkins
3 Rebecca Simpkins
7 Isabel Unknown

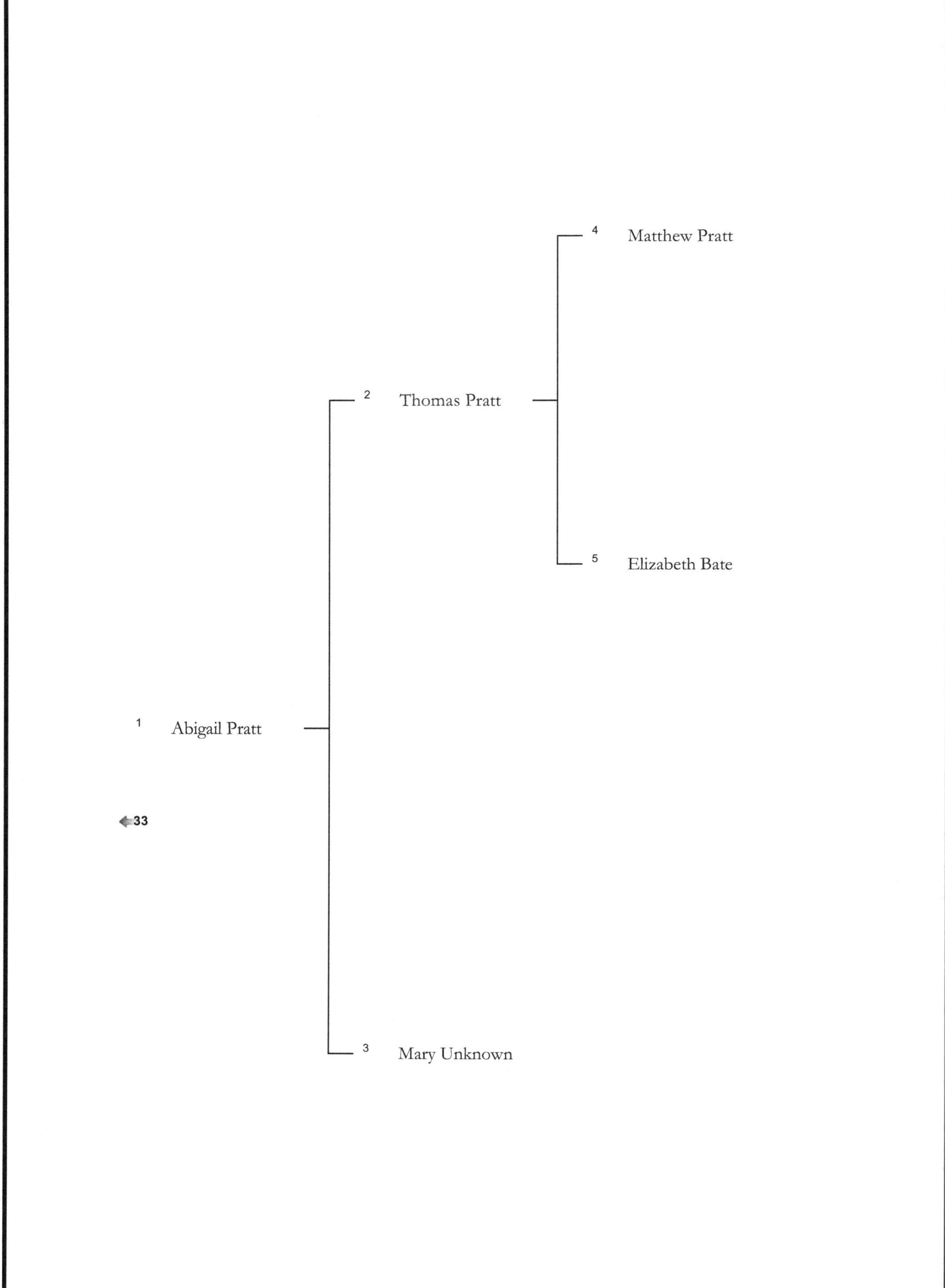

4 Matthew Pratt

2 Thomas Pratt

5 Elizabeth Bate

1 Abigail Pratt

33

3 Mary Unknown

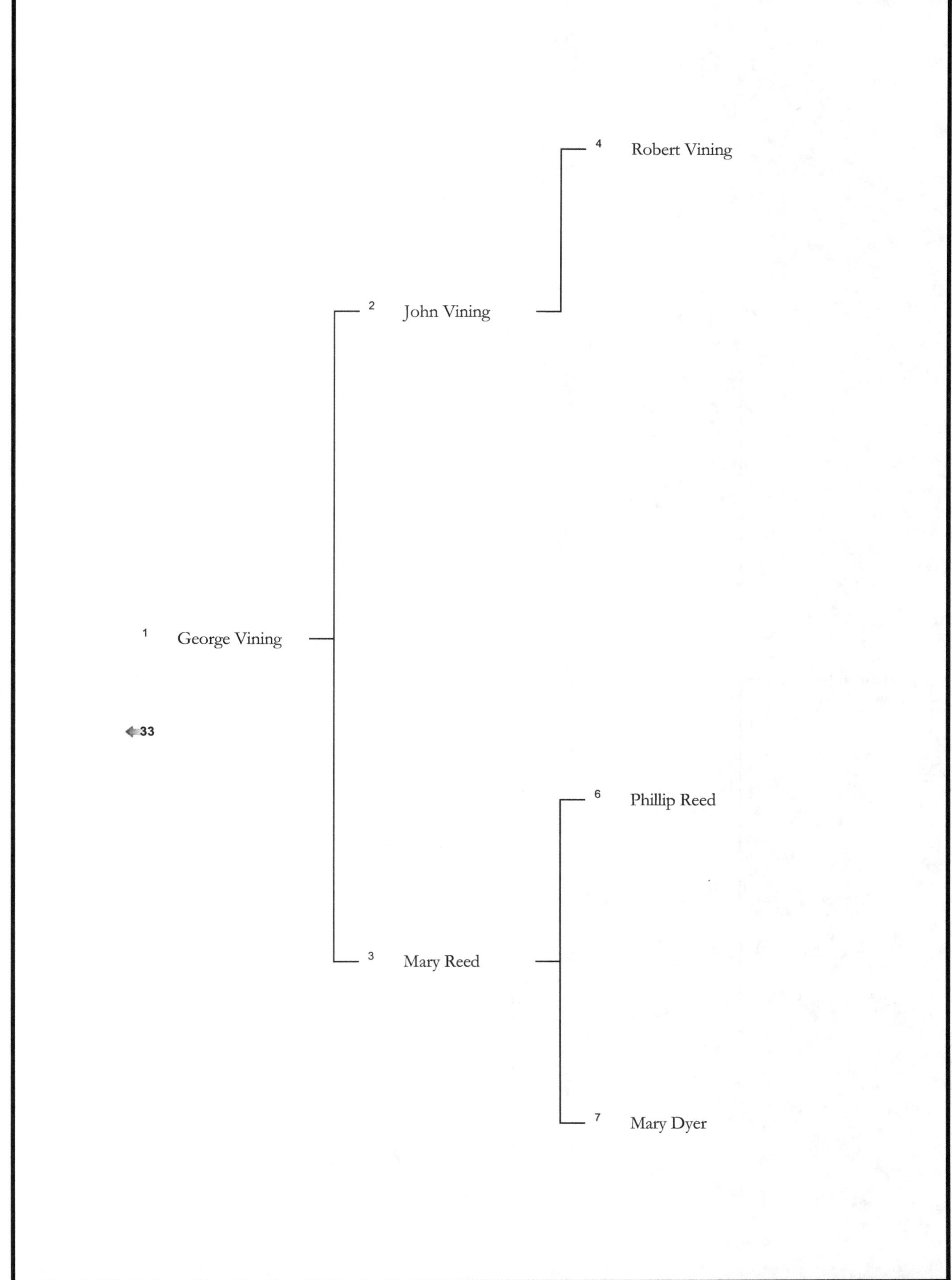

4 Robert Vining
2 John Vining
1 George Vining
33
6 Phillip Reed
3 Mary Reed
7 Mary Dyer

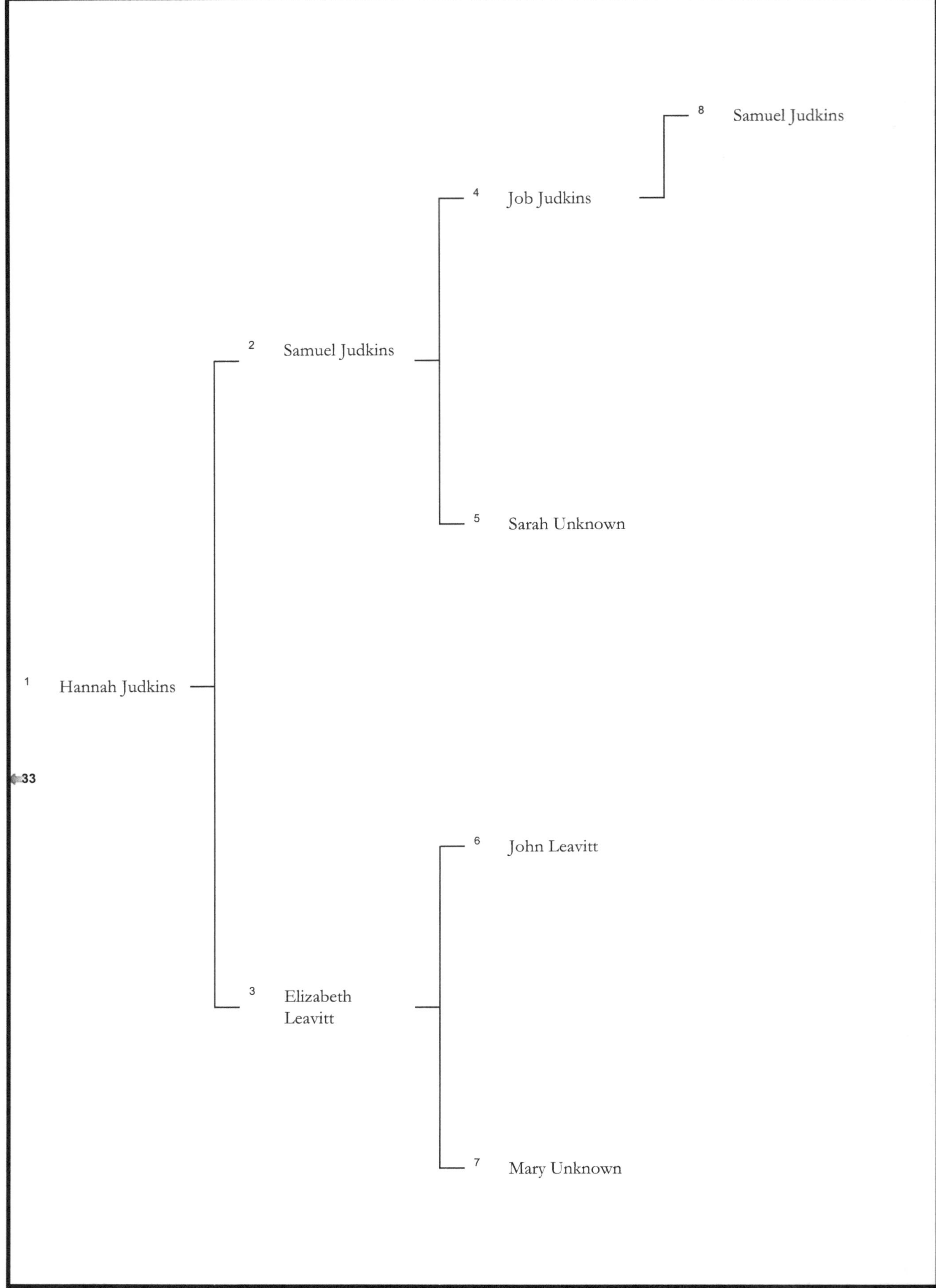

1 Hannah Judkins
33
2 Samuel Judkins
3 Elizabeth Leavitt
4 Job Judkins
5 Sarah Unknown
6 John Leavitt
7 Mary Unknown
8 Samuel Judkins

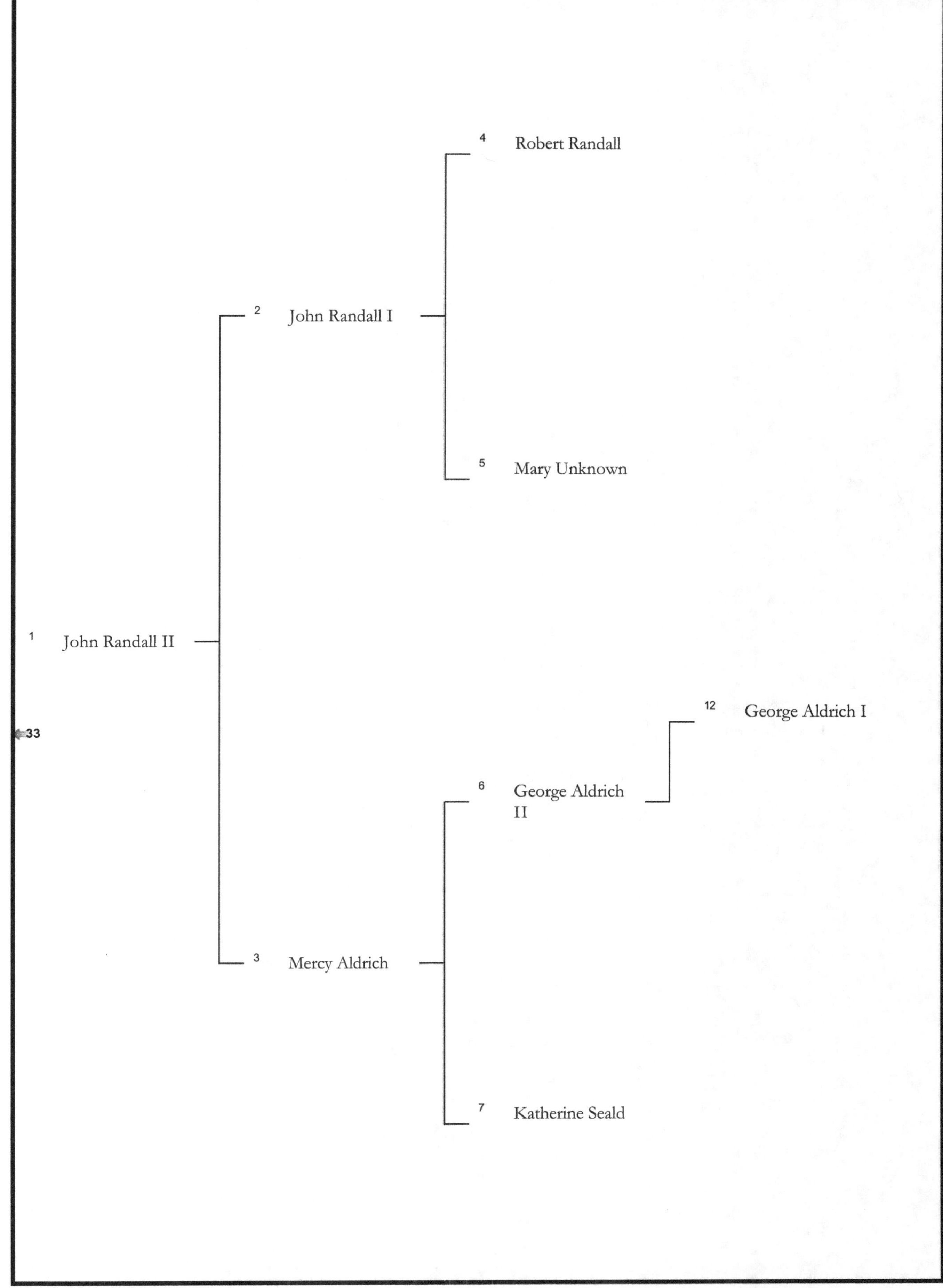

4 Robert Randall
2 John Randall I
5 Mary Unknown
1 John Randall II
33
12 George Aldrich I
6 George Aldrich II
3 Mercy Aldrich
7 Katherine Seald

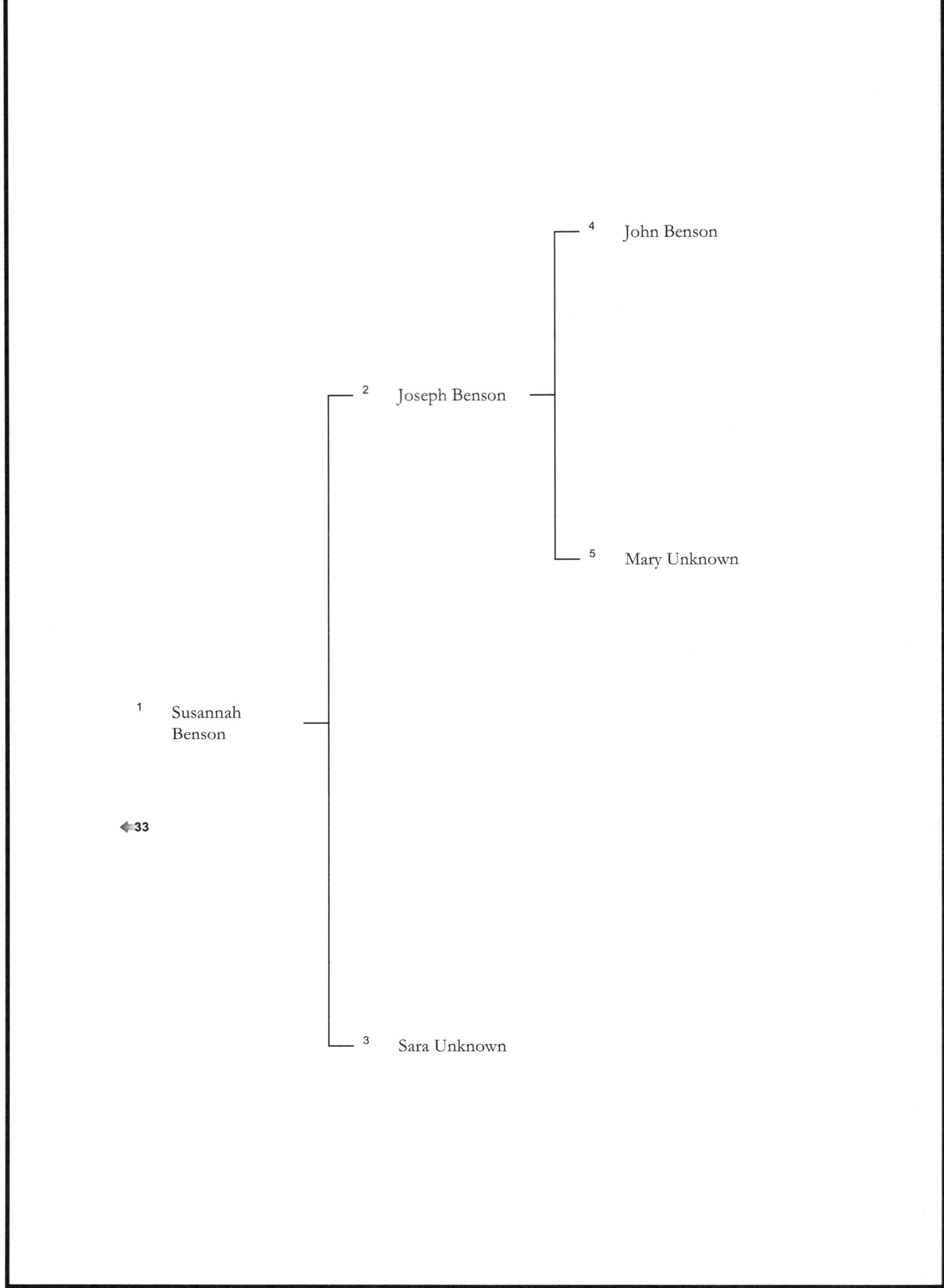

1
Susannah
Benson

2
Joseph Benson

3
Sara Unknown

4
John Benson

5
Mary Unknown

33

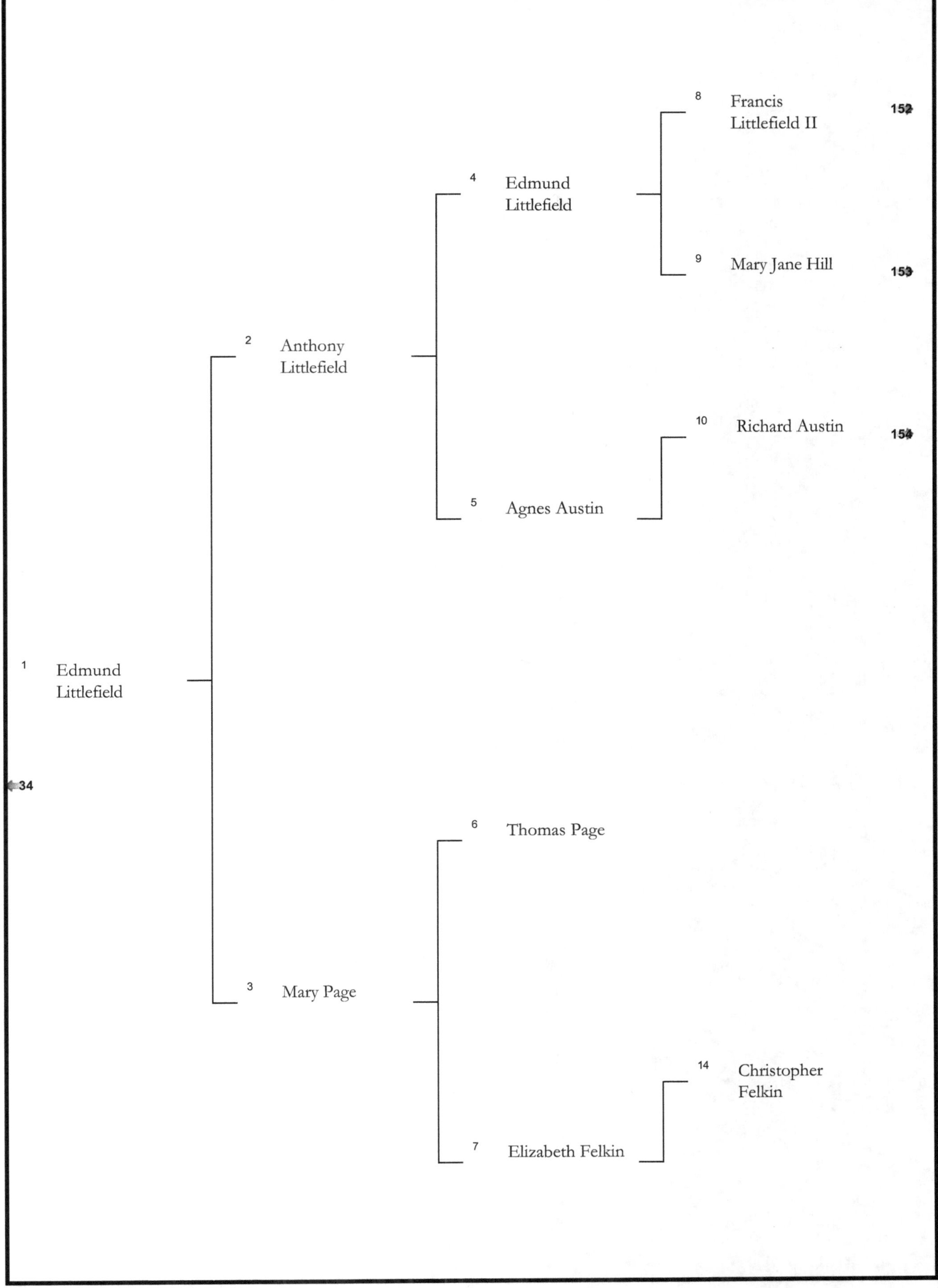

1 Edmund Littlefield
34
2 Anthony Littlefield
3 Mary Page
4 Edmund Littlefield
5 Agnes Austin
6 Thomas Page
7 Elizabeth Felkin
8 Francis Littlefield II
152
9 Mary Jane Hill
153
10 Richard Austin
154
14 Christopher Felkin

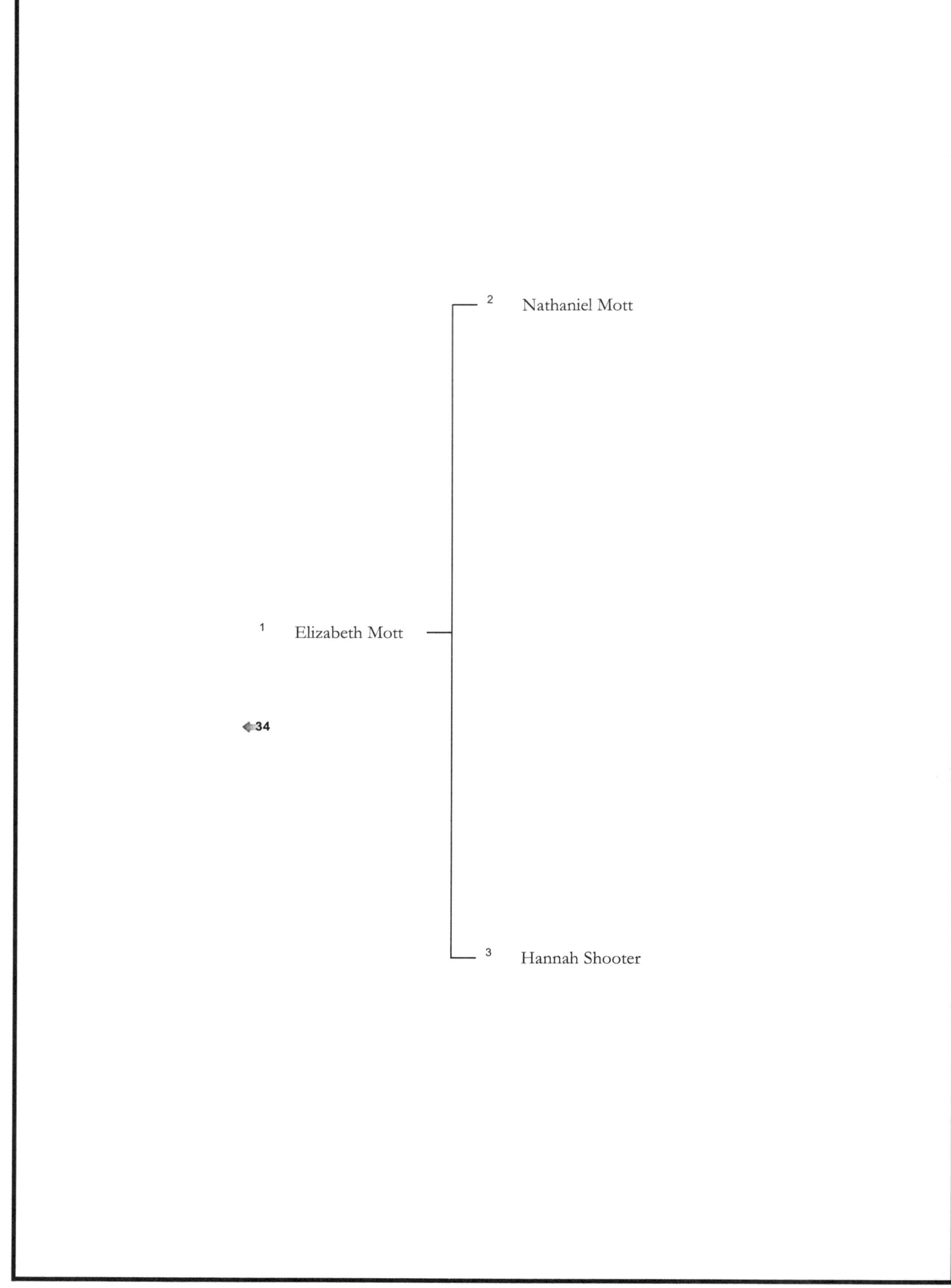

2 Nathaniel Mott
1 Elizabeth Mott
34
3 Hannah Shooter

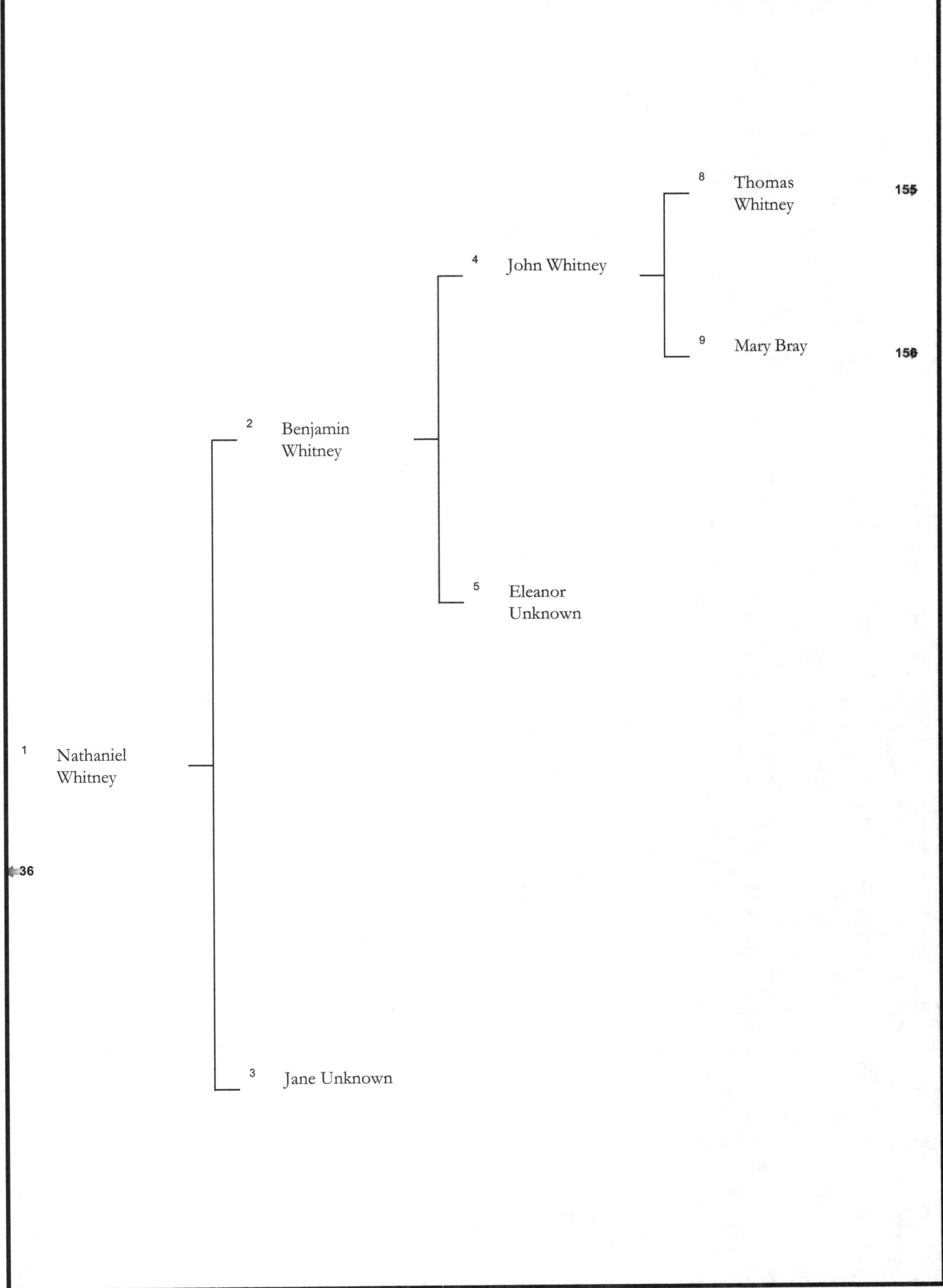

8 Thomas Whitney 155
4 John Whitney
9 Mary Bray 156
2 Benjamin Whitney
5 Eleanor Unknown
1 Nathaniel Whitney
36
3 Jane Unknown

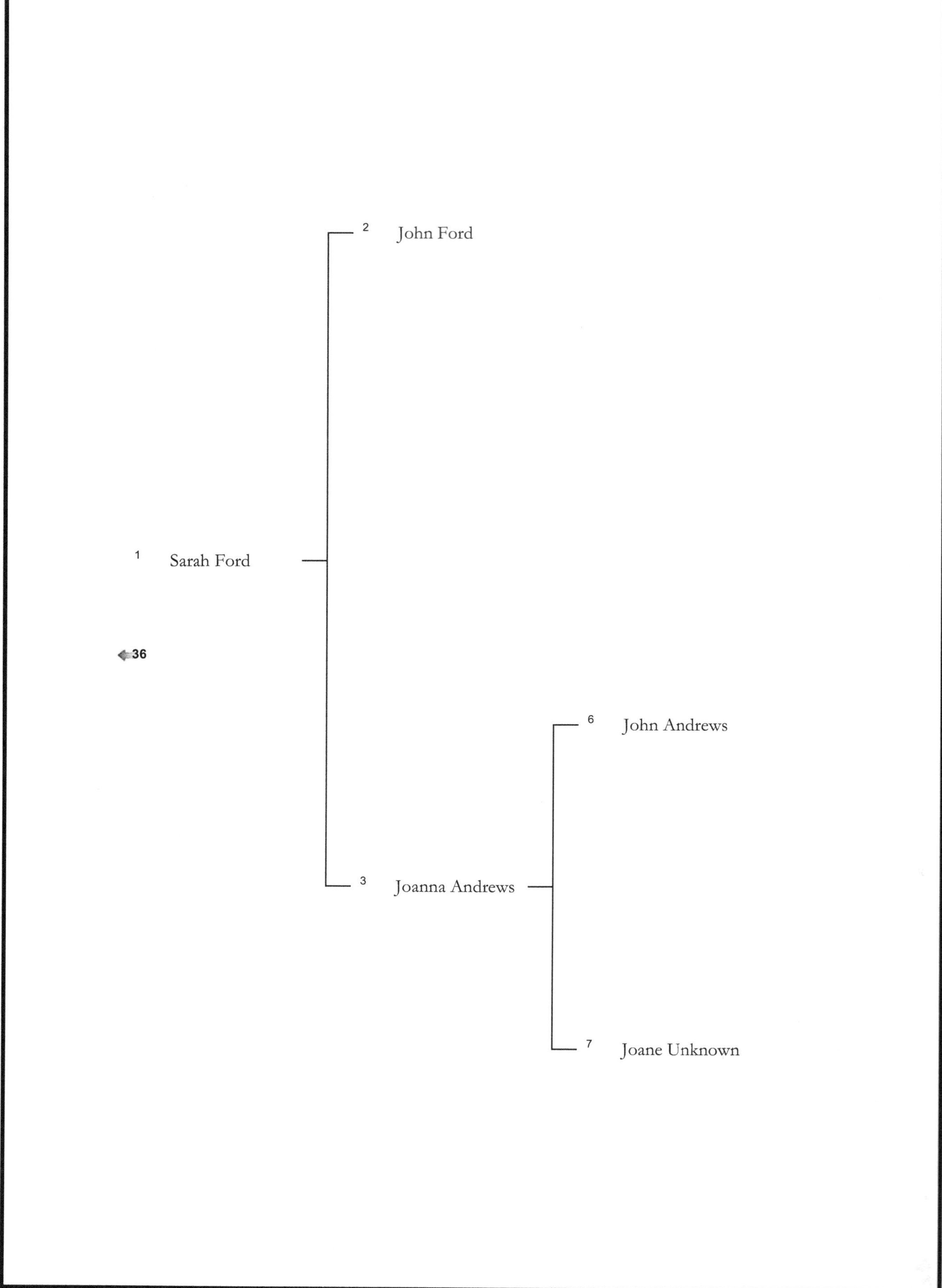

2 John Ford
1 Sarah Ford
6 John Andrews
3 Joanna Andrews
7 Joane Unknown

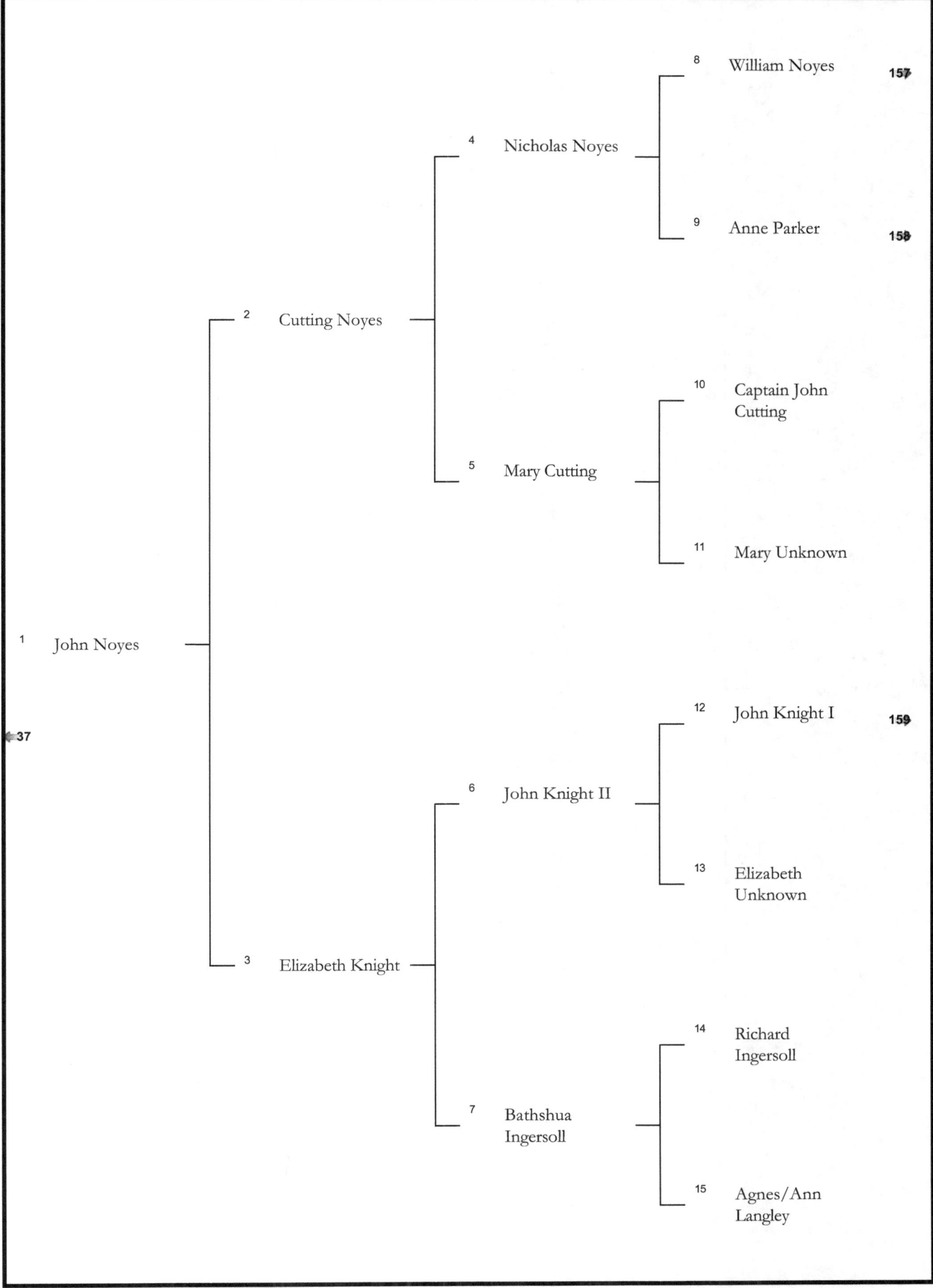

1 John Noyes
37
2 Cutting Noyes
3 Elizabeth Knight
4 Nicholas Noyes
5 Mary Cutting
6 John Knight II
7 Bathshua Ingersoll
8 William Noyes 157
9 Anne Parker 158
10 Captain John Cutting
11 Mary Unknown
12 John Knight I 159
13 Elizabeth Unknown
14 Richard Ingersoll
15 Agnes/Ann Langley

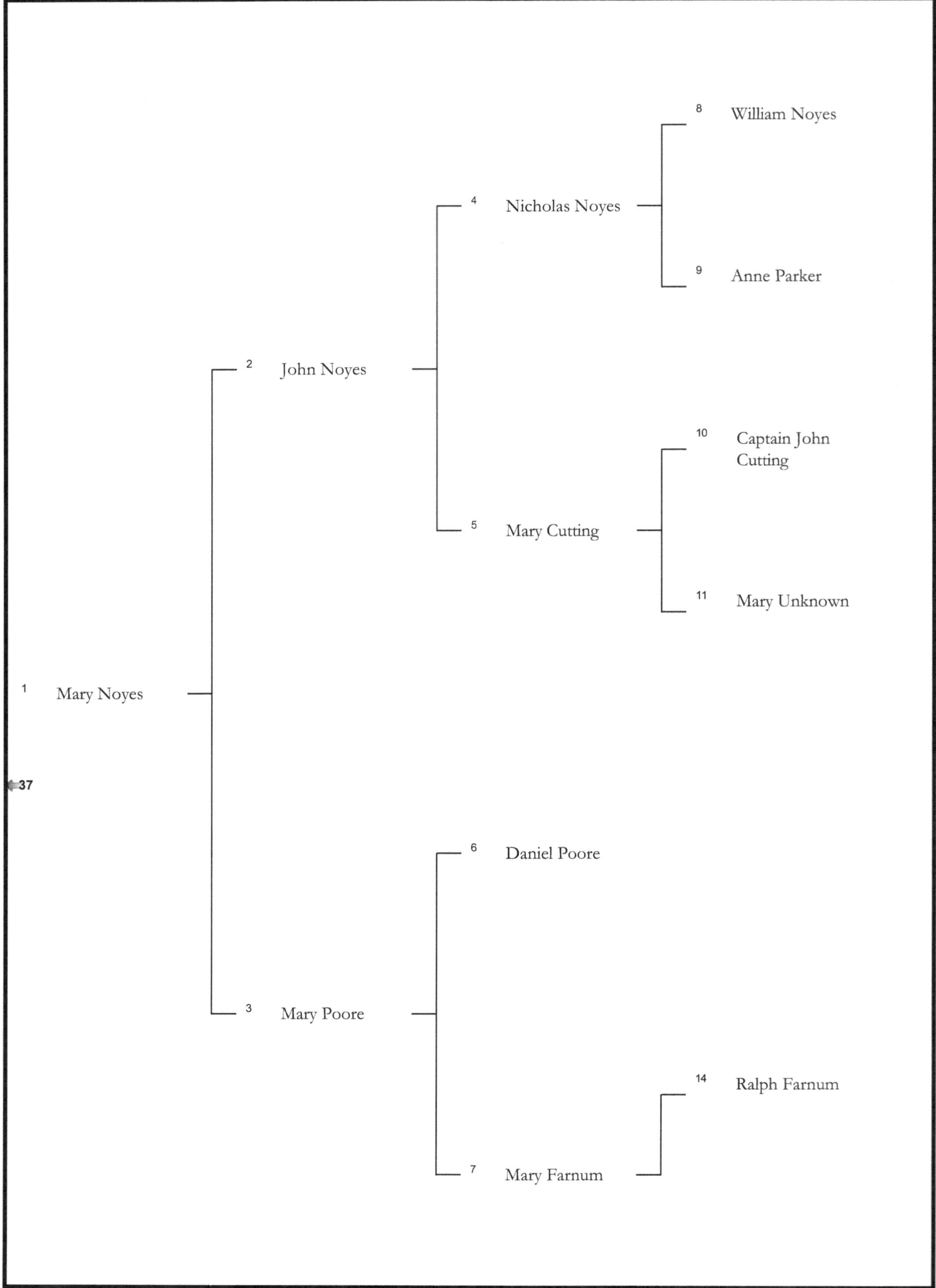

8 William Noyes
4 Nicholas Noyes
9 Anne Parker
2 John Noyes
10 Captain John Cutting
5 Mary Cutting
11 Mary Unknown
1 Mary Noyes
37
6 Daniel Poore
3 Mary Poore
14 Ralph Farnum
7 Mary Farnum

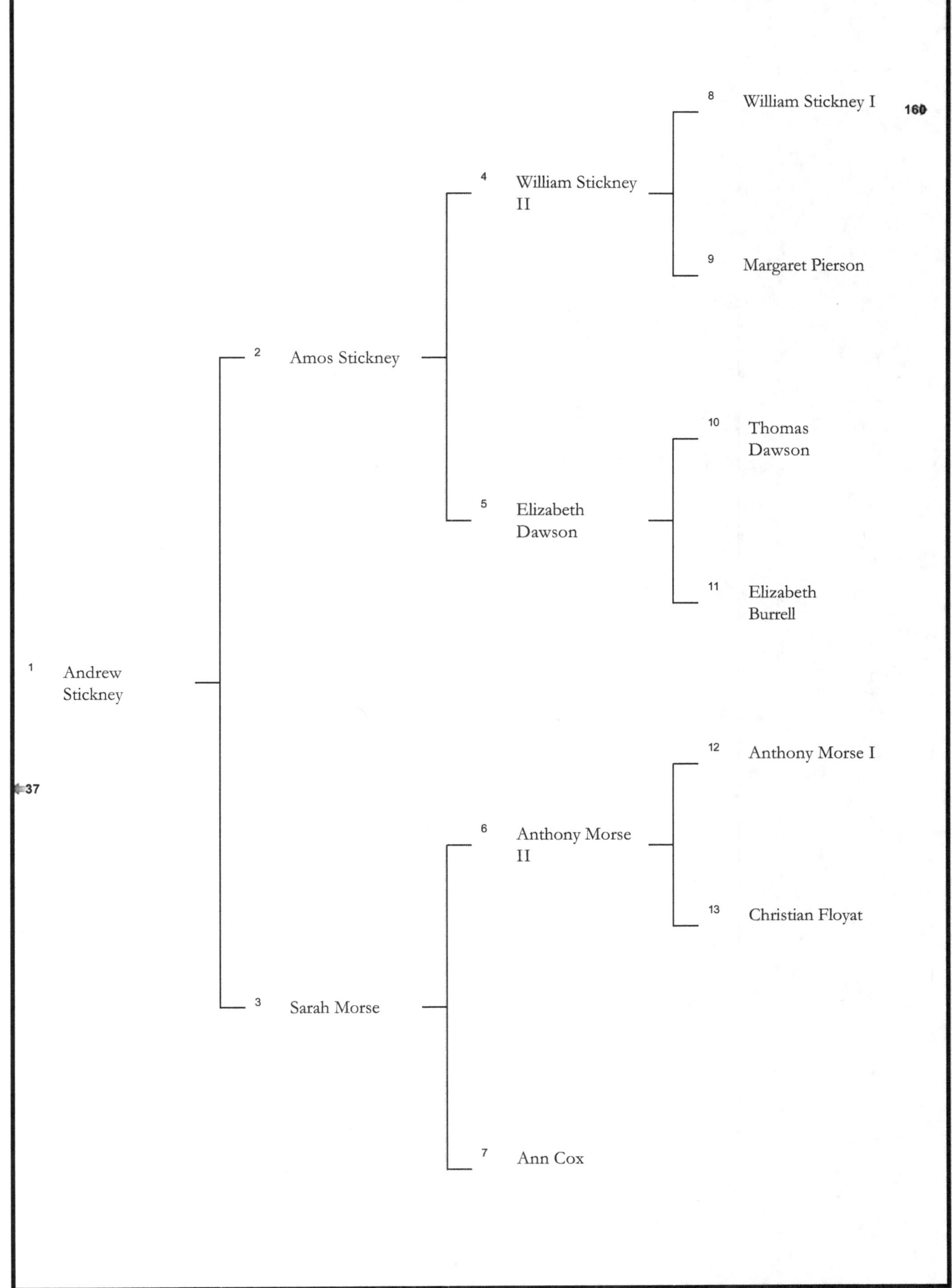

1 Andrew Stickney
2 Amos Stickney
3 Sarah Morse
4 William Stickney II
5 Elizabeth Dawson
6 Anthony Morse II
7 Ann Cox
8 William Stickney I
9 Margaret Pierson
10 Thomas Dawson
11 Elizabeth Burrell
12 Anthony Morse I
13 Christian Floyat
37
160

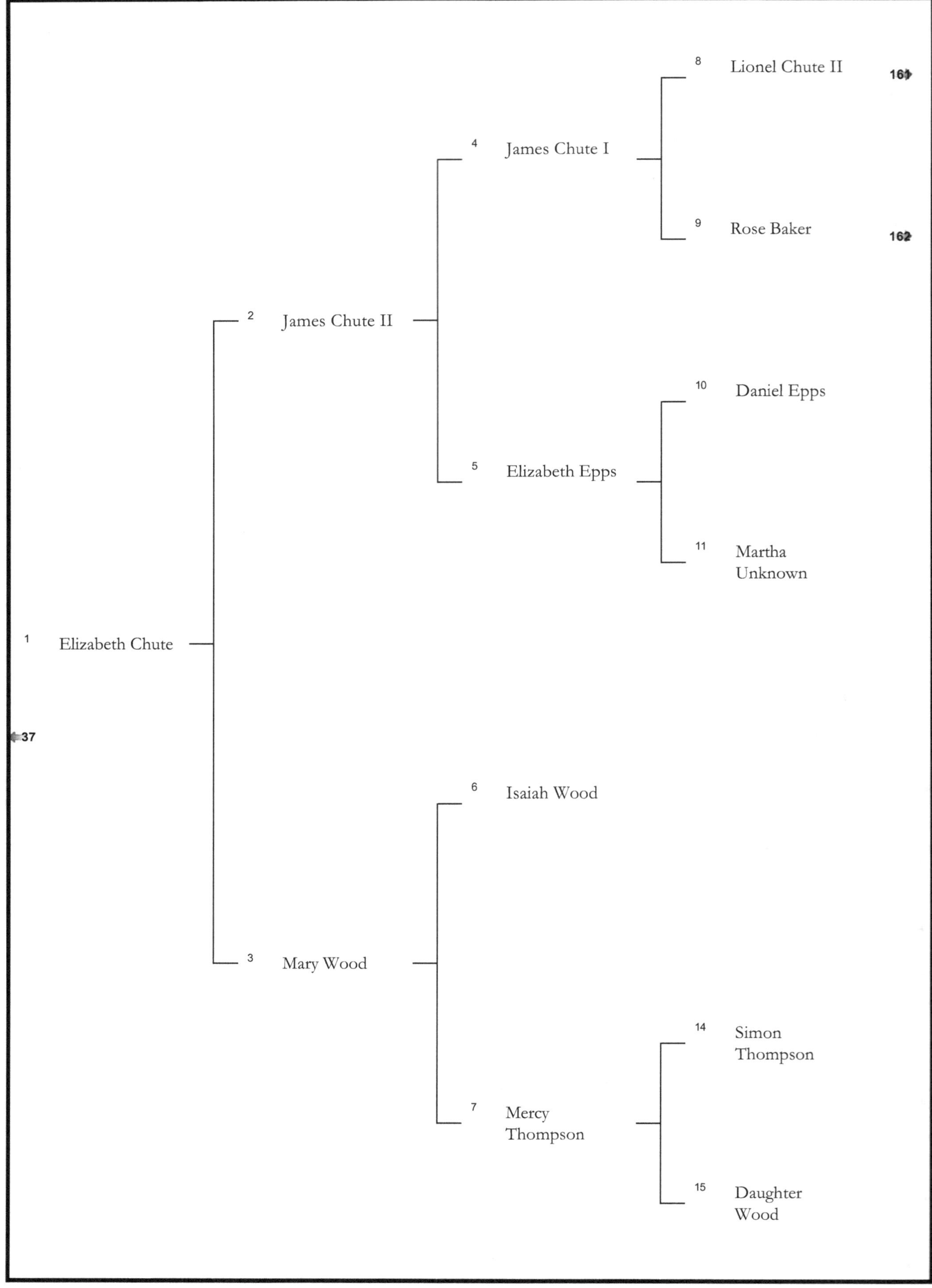

1 Elizabeth Chute
37
2 James Chute II
3 Mary Wood
4 James Chute I
5 Elizabeth Epps
6 Isaiah Wood
7 Mercy Thompson
8 Lionel Chute II
161
9 Rose Baker
162
10 Daniel Epps
11 Martha Unknown
14 Simon Thompson
15 Daughter Wood

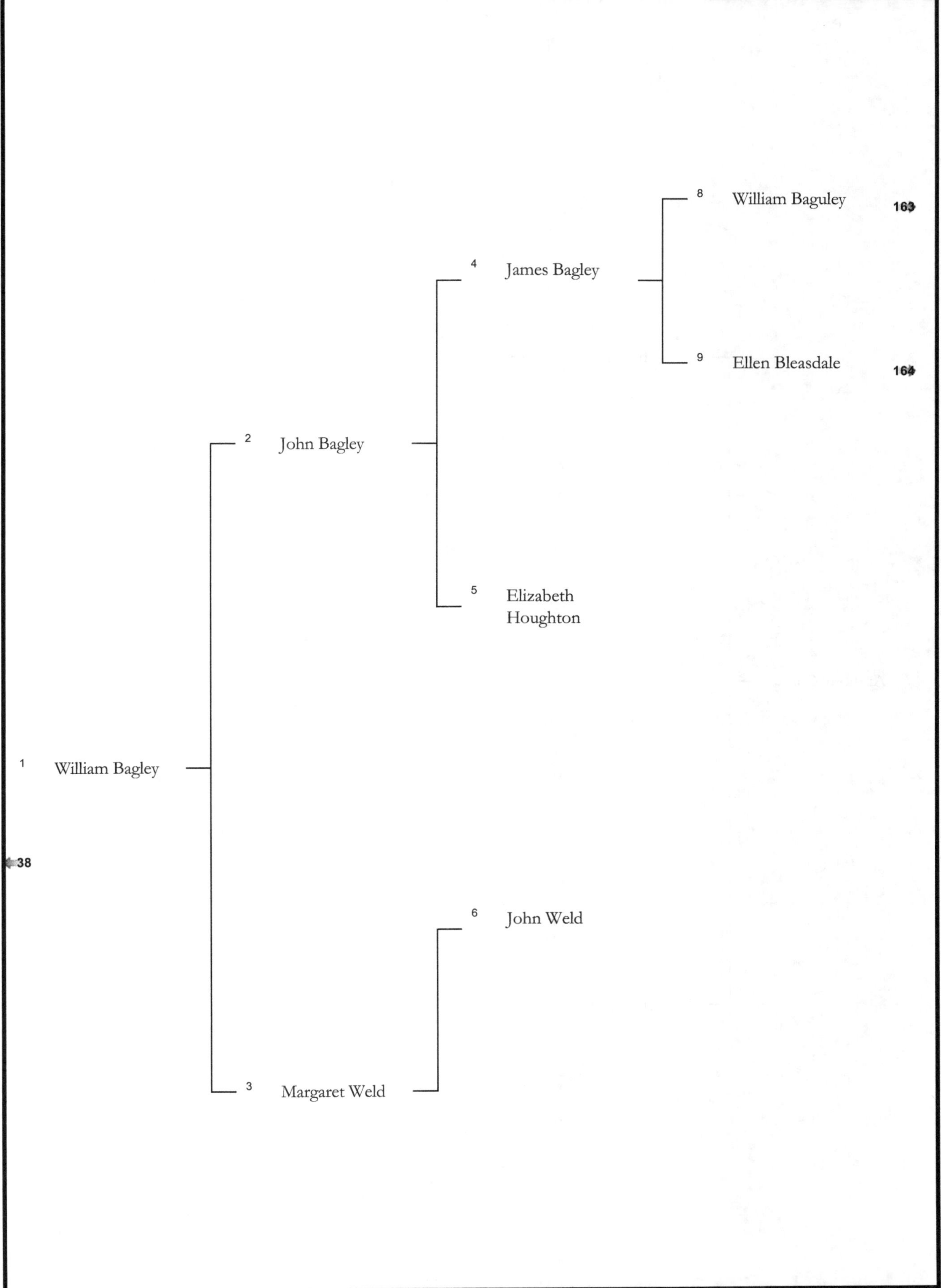

1 William Bagley
38
2 John Bagley
3 Margaret Weld
4 James Bagley
5 Elizabeth Houghton
6 John Weld
8 William Baguley 163
9 Ellen Bleasdale 164

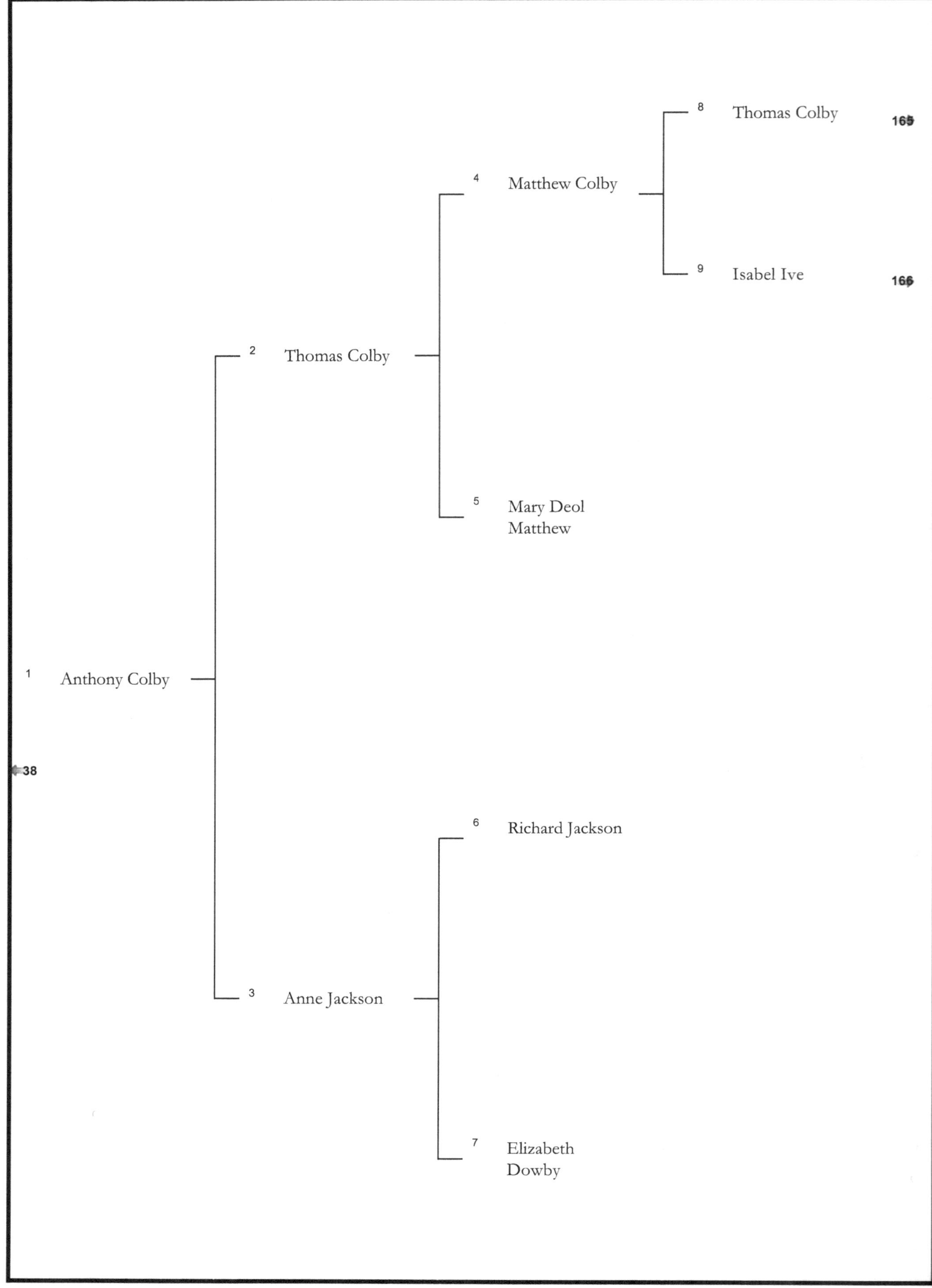

1 Anthony Colby
38
2 Thomas Colby
3 Anne Jackson
4 Matthew Colby
5 Mary Deol Matthew
6 Richard Jackson
7 Elizabeth Dowby
8 Thomas Colby
165
9 Isabel Ive
166

[2] William Haddon

[1] Susanna
Haddon

◄ **38**

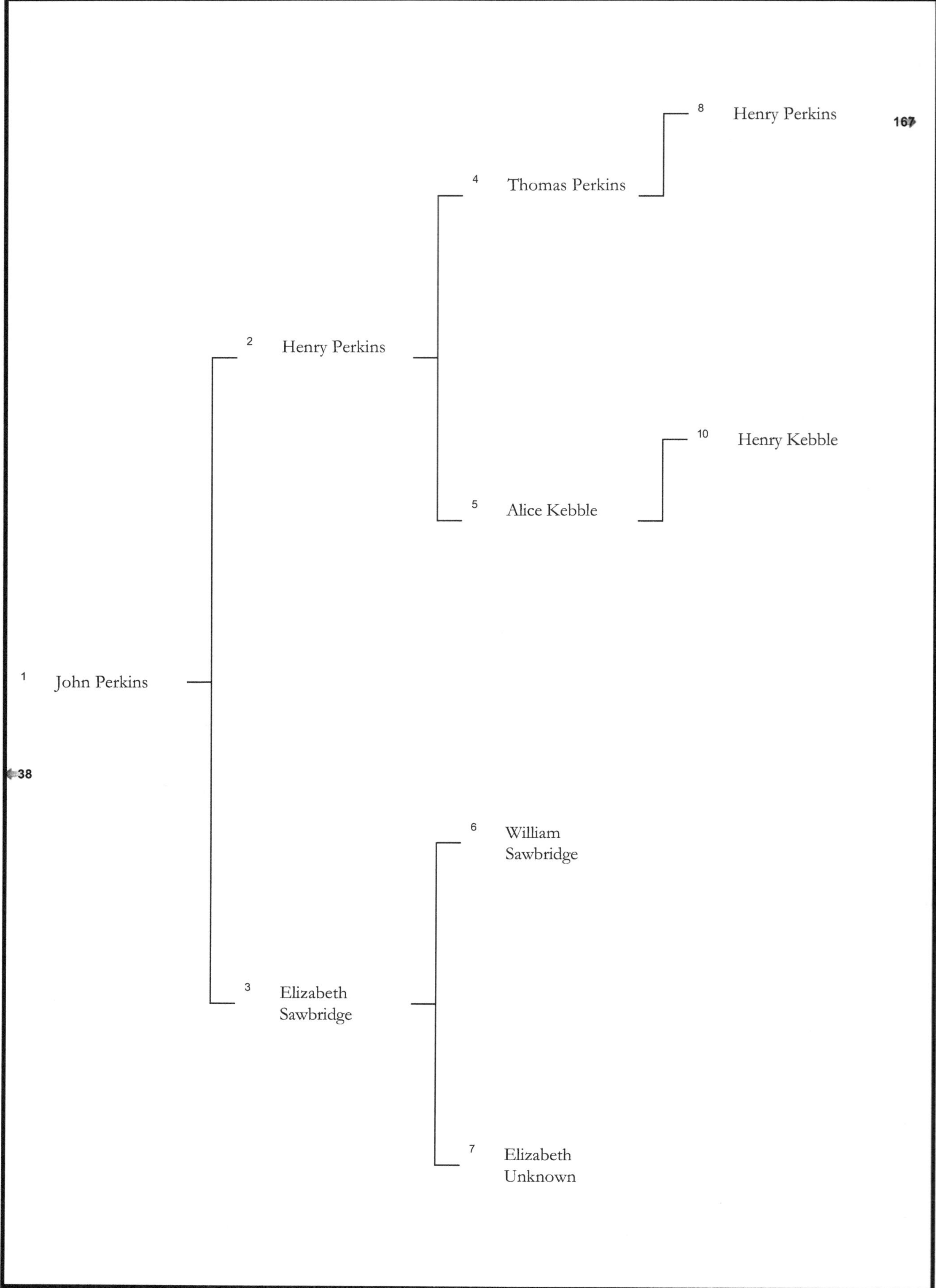

167
8 Henry Perkins
4 Thomas Perkins
2 Henry Perkins
10 Henry Kebble
5 Alice Kebble
1 John Perkins
38
6 William Sawbridge
3 Elizabeth Sawbridge
7 Elizabeth Unknown

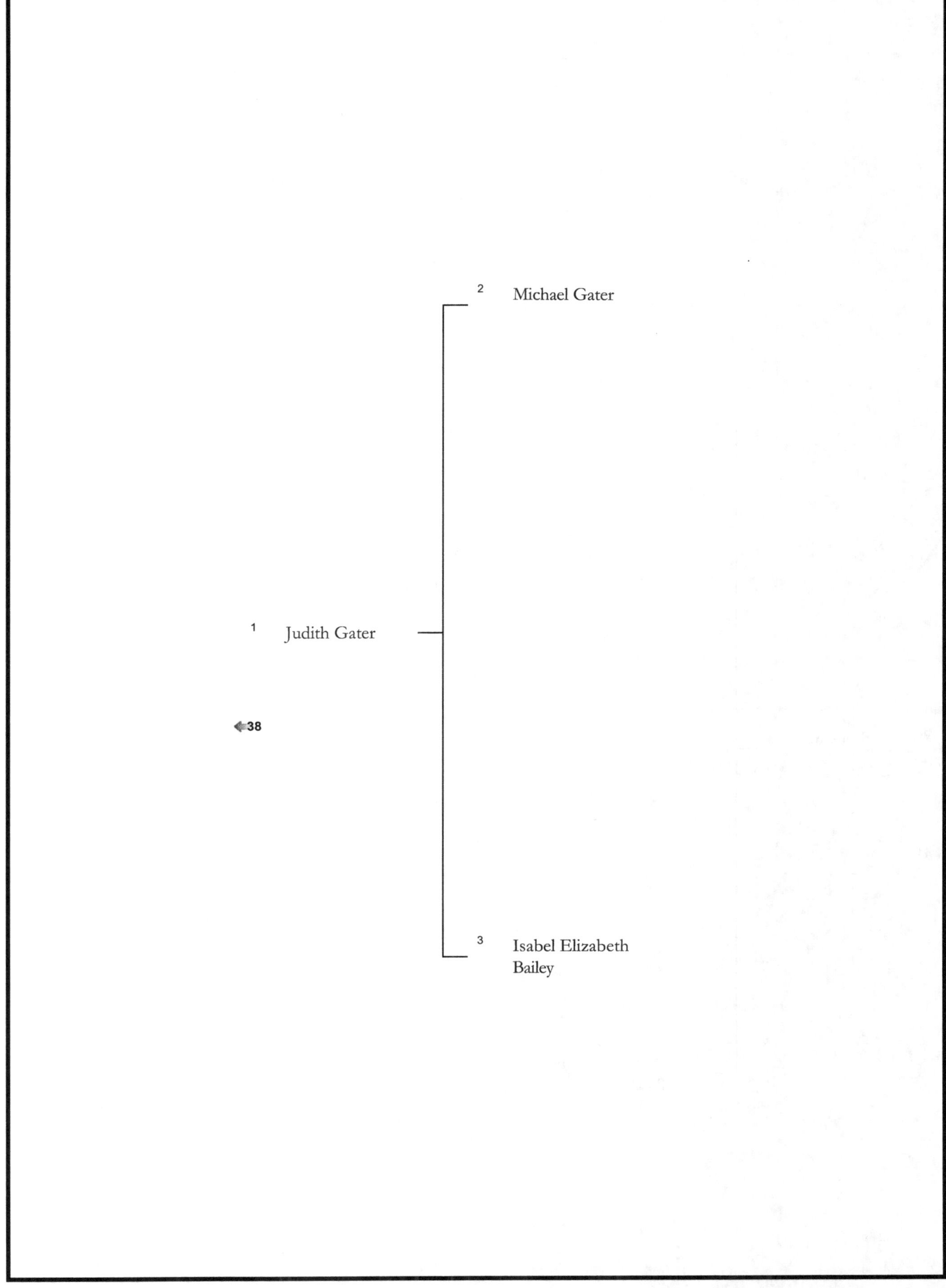

2 Michael Gater
1 Judith Gater
38
3 Isabel Elizabeth Bailey

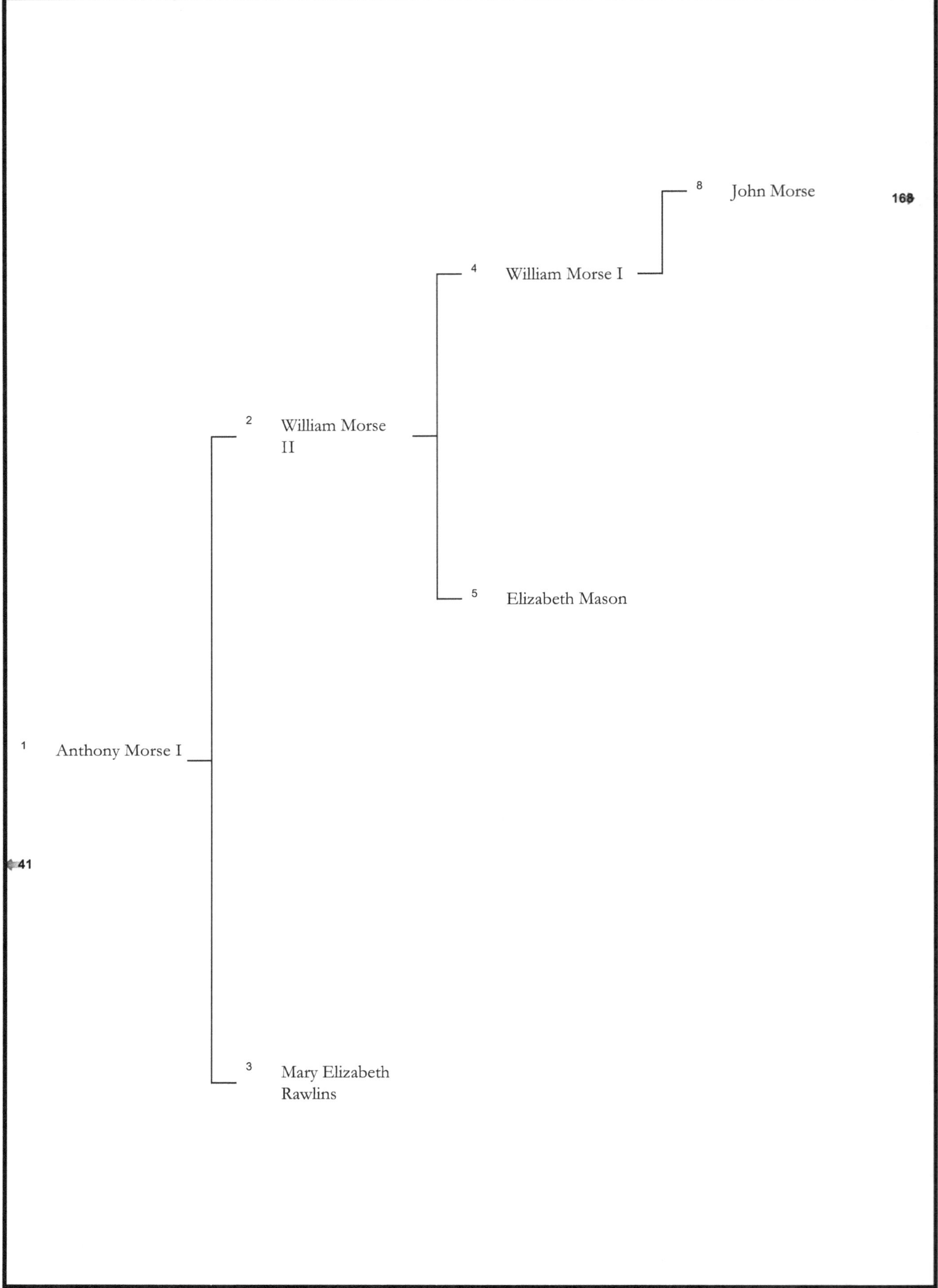

1 Anthony Morse I
2 William Morse II
3 Mary Elizabeth Rawlins
4 William Morse I
5 Elizabeth Mason
8 John Morse
41
168

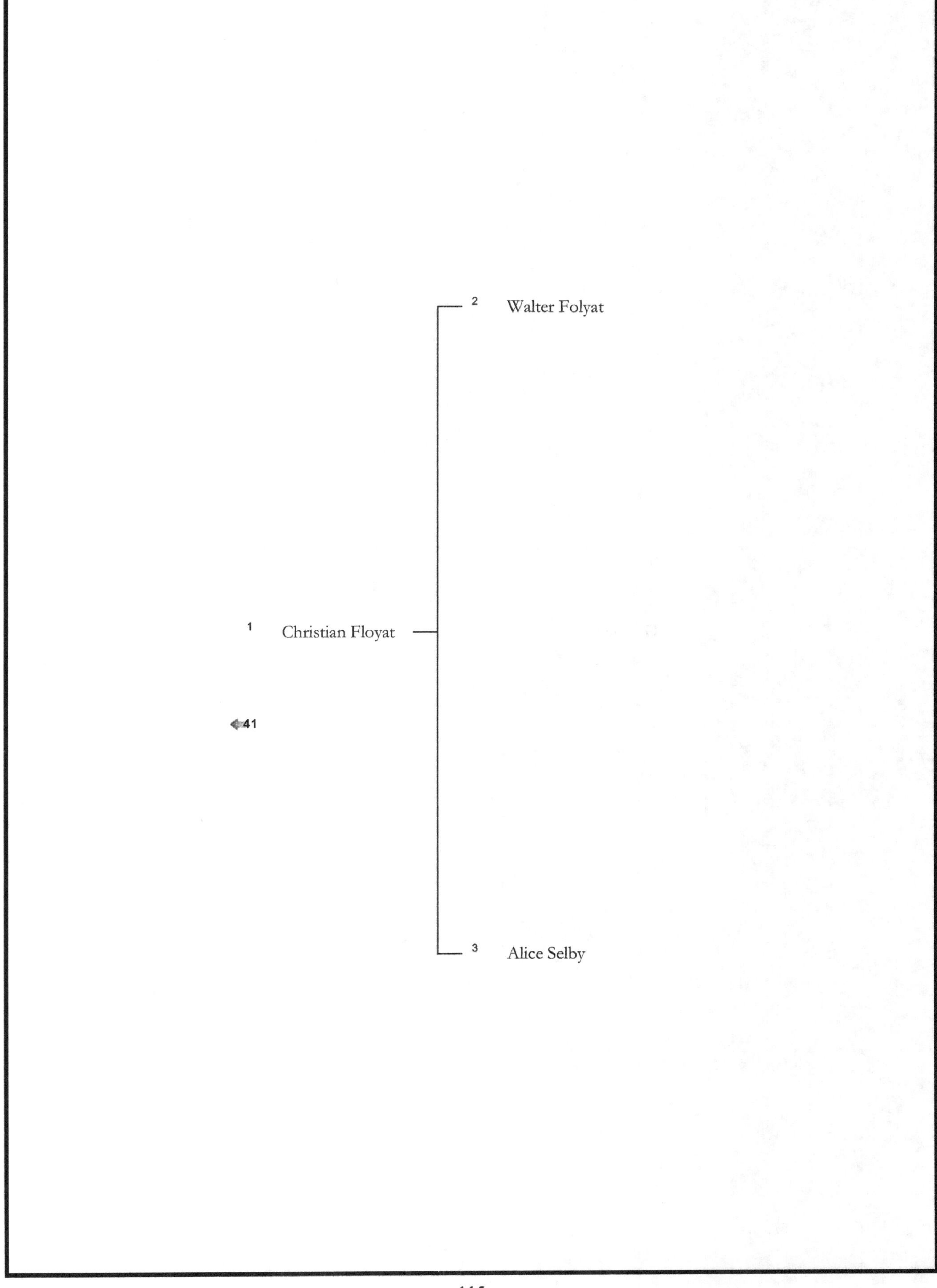

2 Walter Folyat
1 Christian Floyat
41
3 Alice Selby

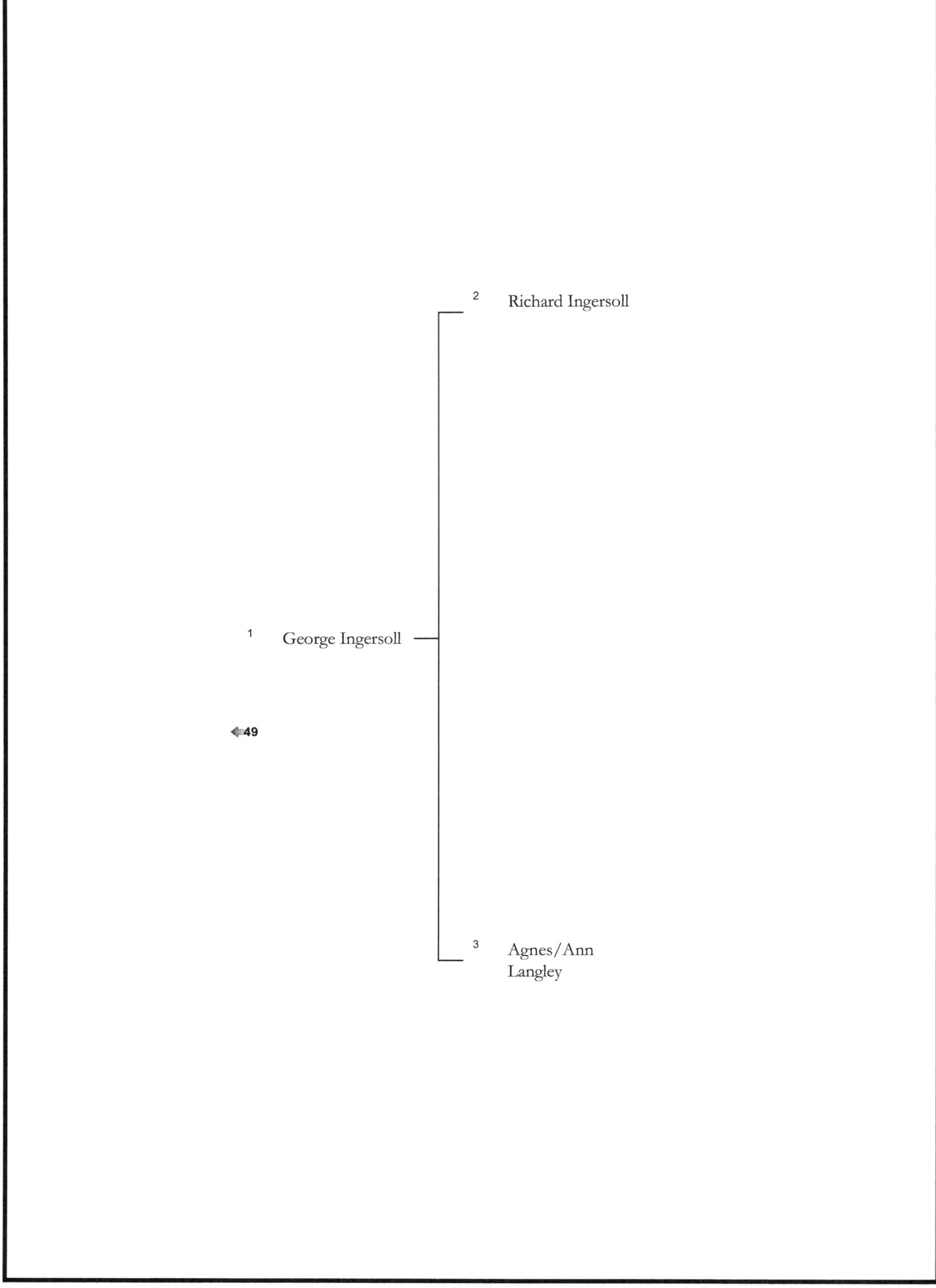

2   Richard Ingersoll
1   George Ingersoll
49
3   Agnes/Ann
Langley

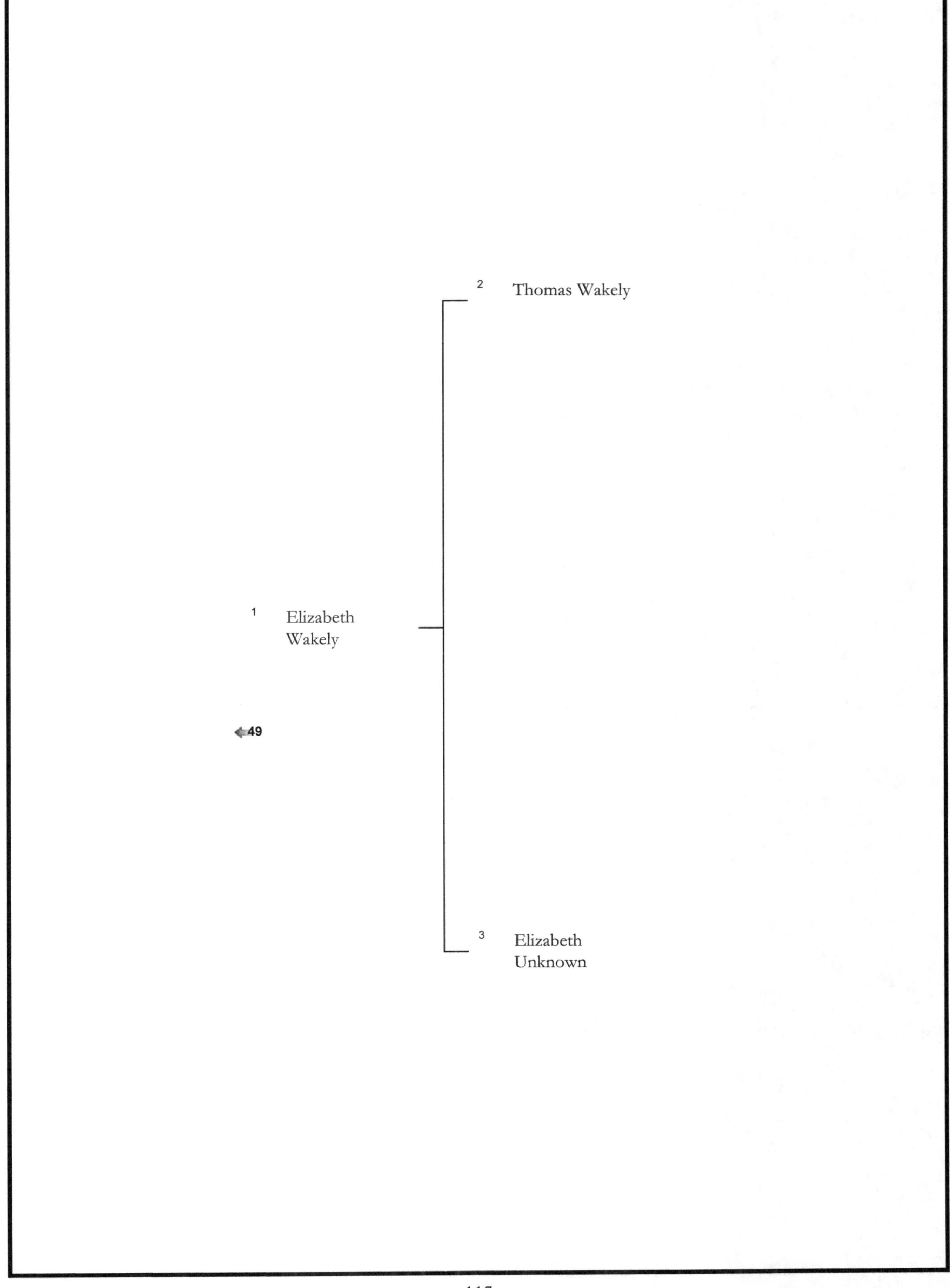

2 Thomas Wakely
1 Elizabeth Wakely
49
3 Elizabeth Unknown

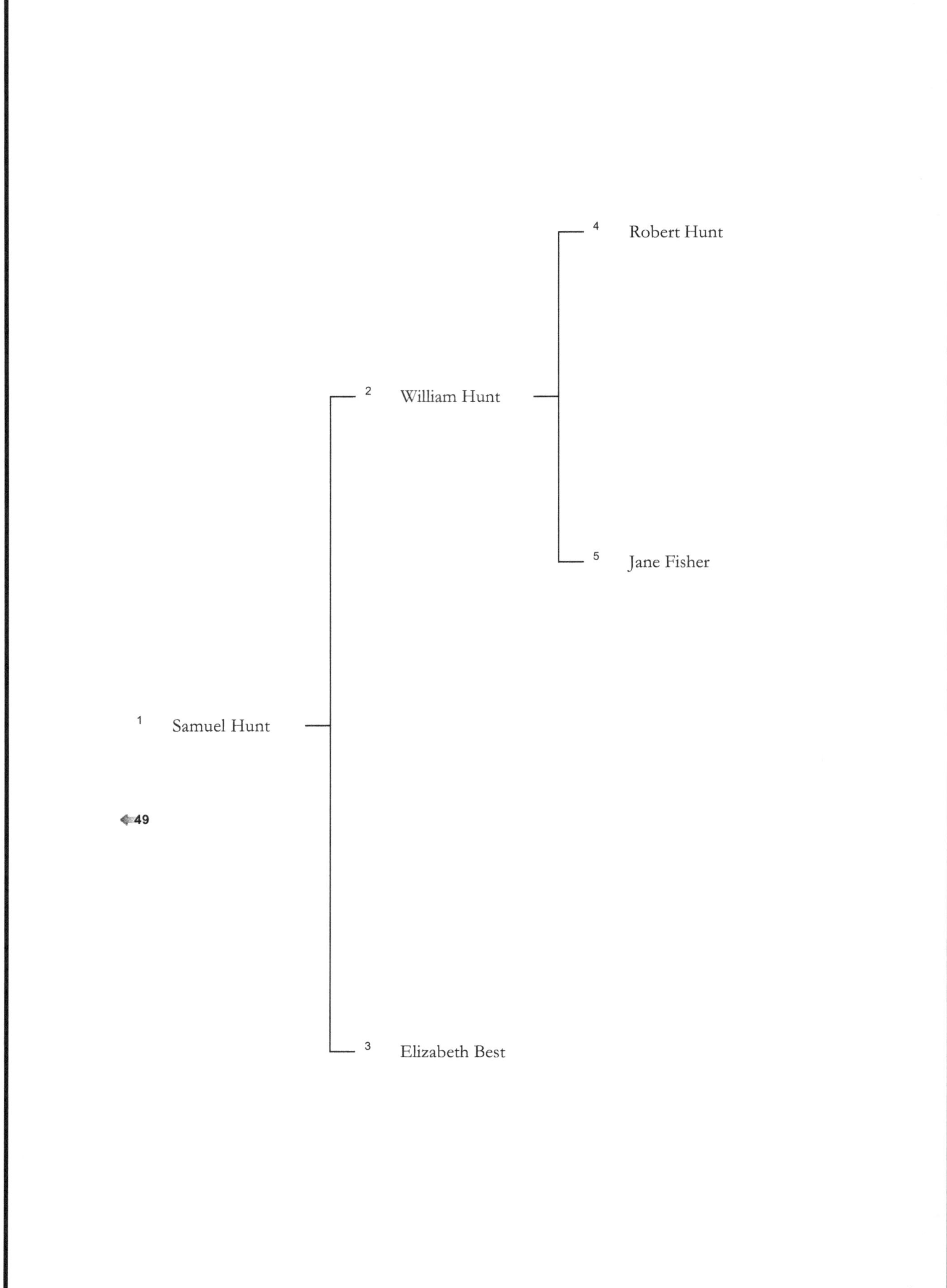

4 Robert Hunt
2 William Hunt
5 Jane Fisher
1 Samuel Hunt
49
3 Elizabeth Best

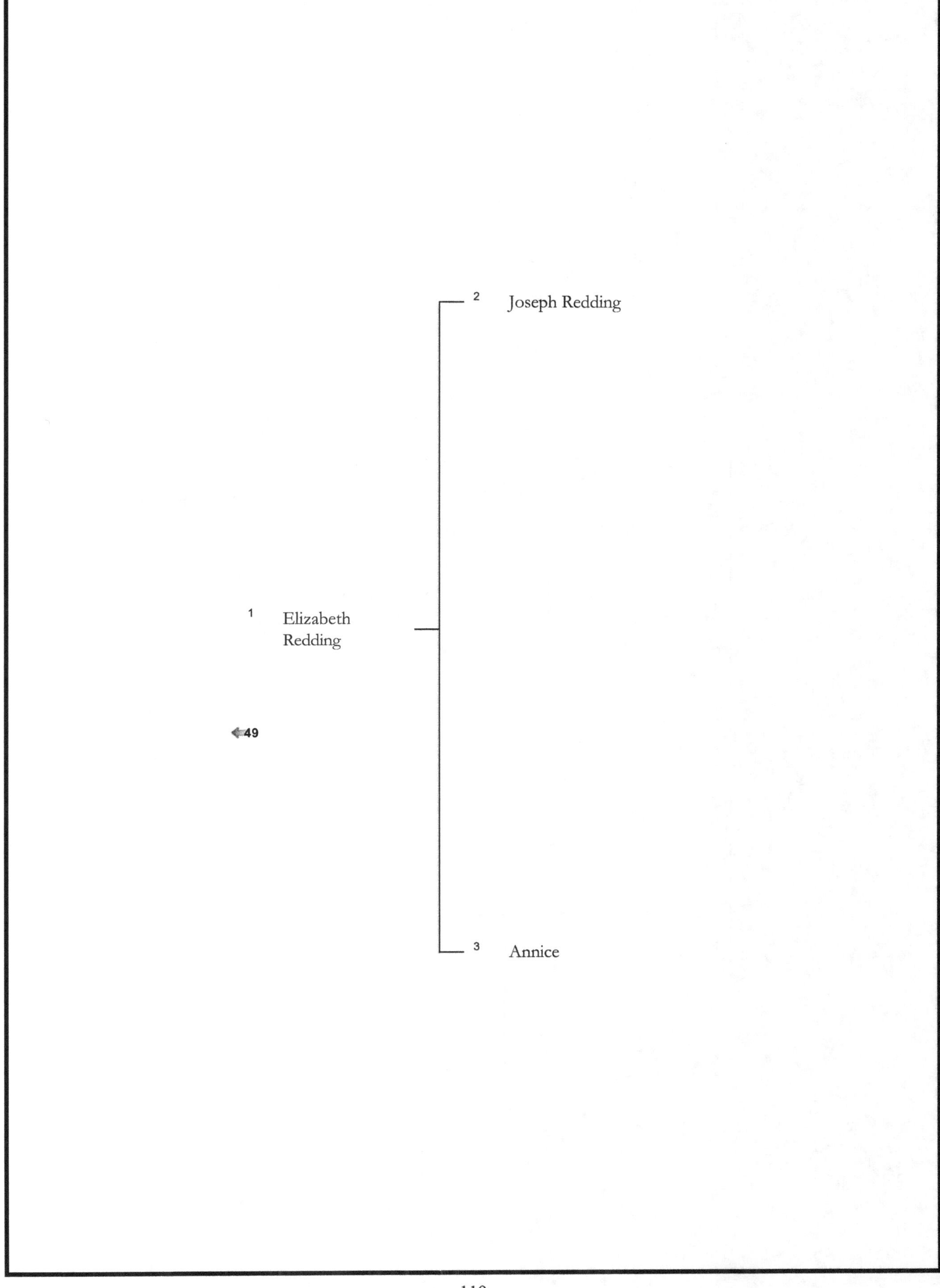

2 Joseph Redding
1 Elizabeth Redding
49
3 Annice

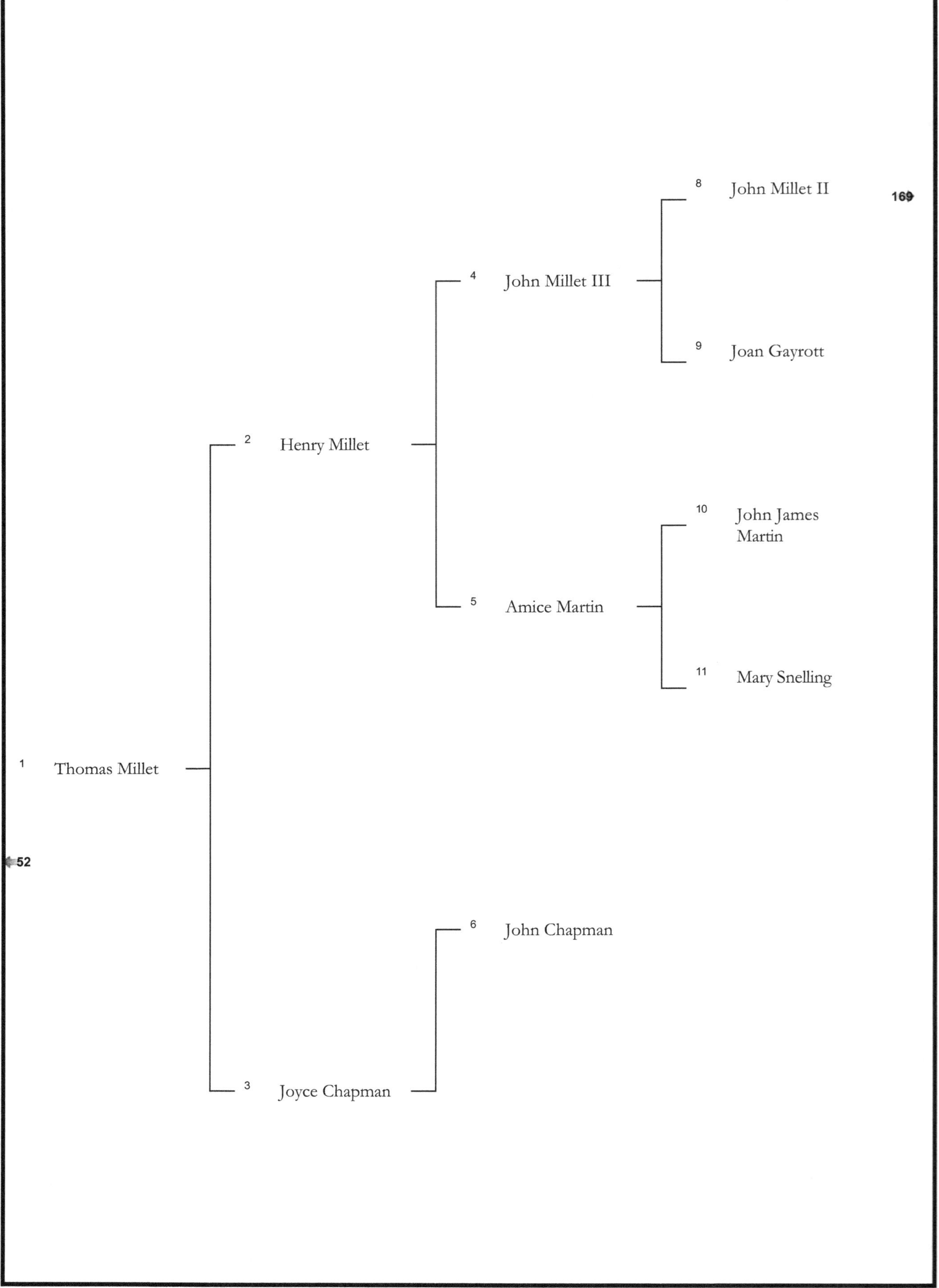
169
8 John Millet II
4 John Millet III
9 Joan Gayrott
2 Henry Millet
10 John James
Martin
5 Amice Martin
11 Mary Snelling
1 Thomas Millet
52
6 John Chapman
3 Joyce Chapman

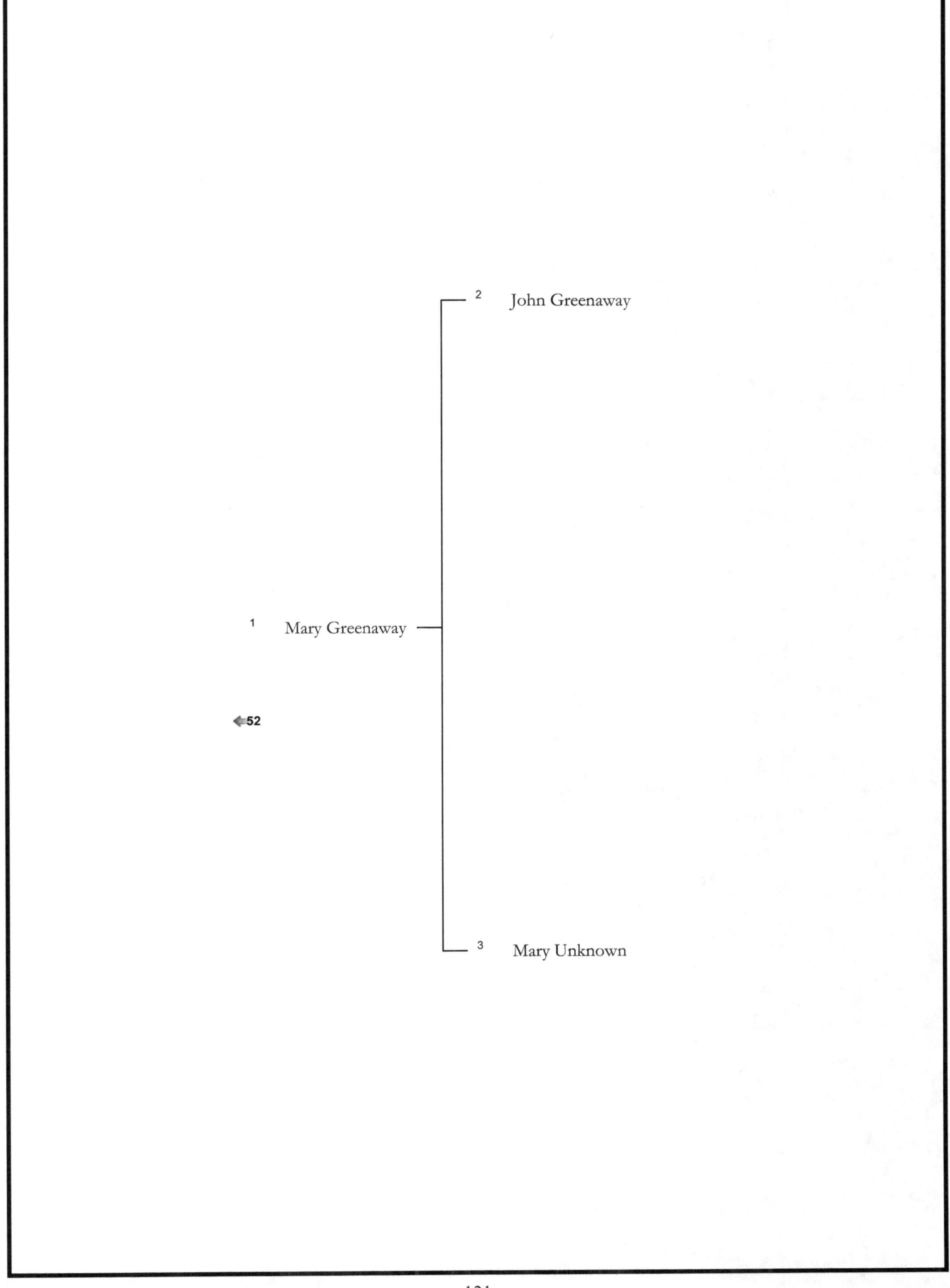

1 Mary Greenaway
2 John Greenaway
3 Mary Unknown
52

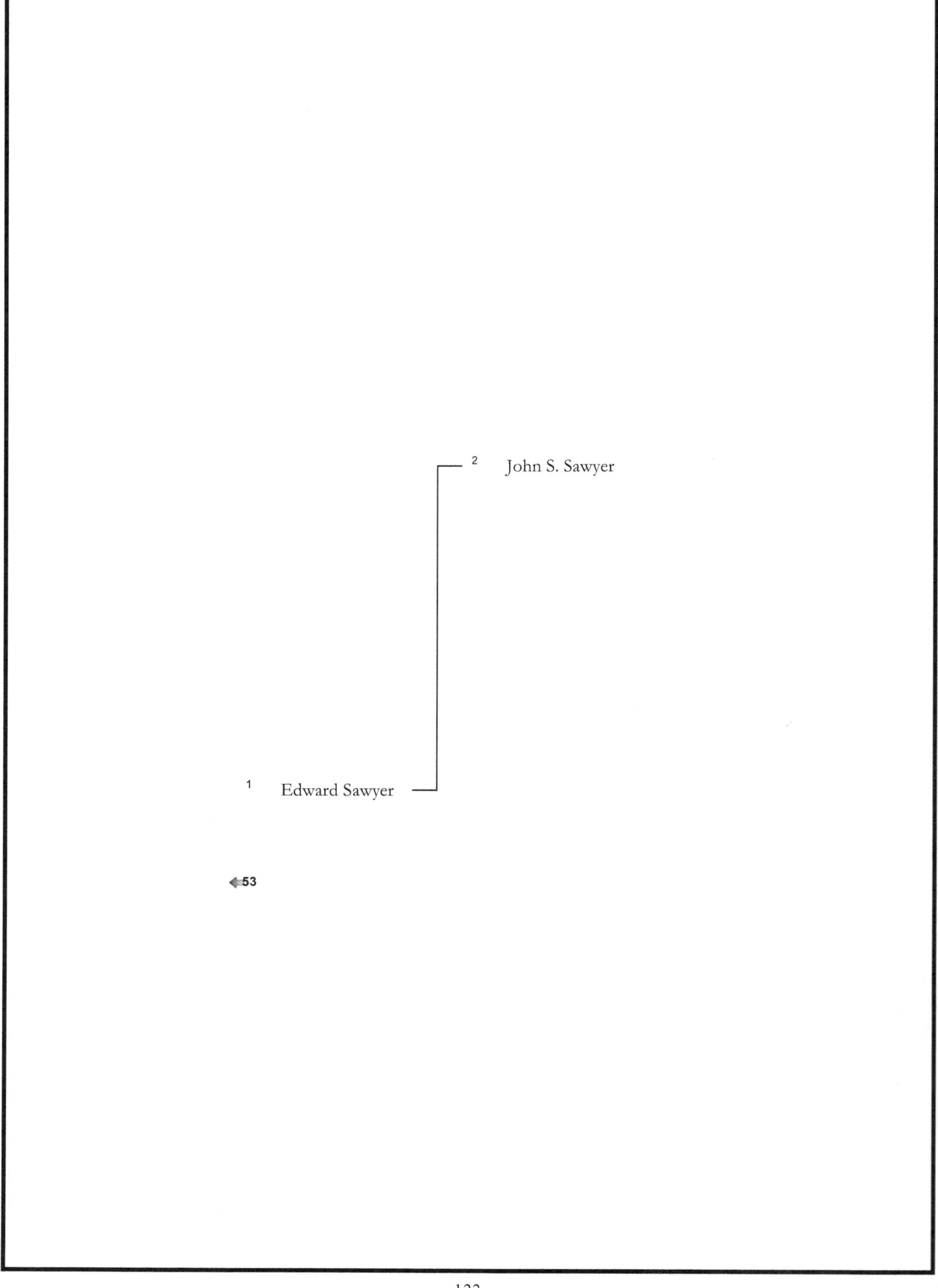

2 John S. Sawyer
1 Edward Sawyer
53

[2] Unknown
Parker

[1] James Parker I

◄57

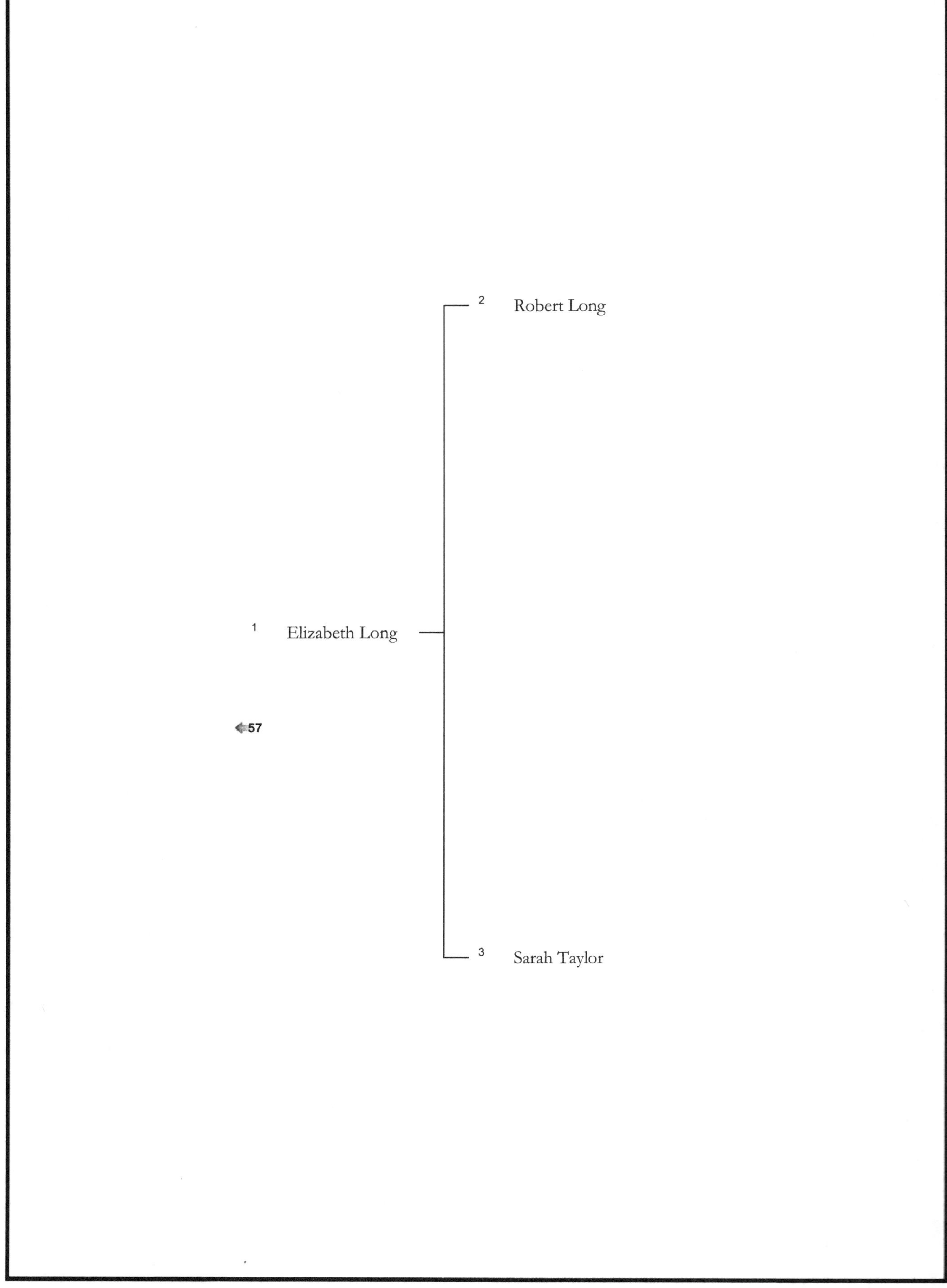

2 Robert Long
1 Elizabeth Long
57
3 Sarah Taylor

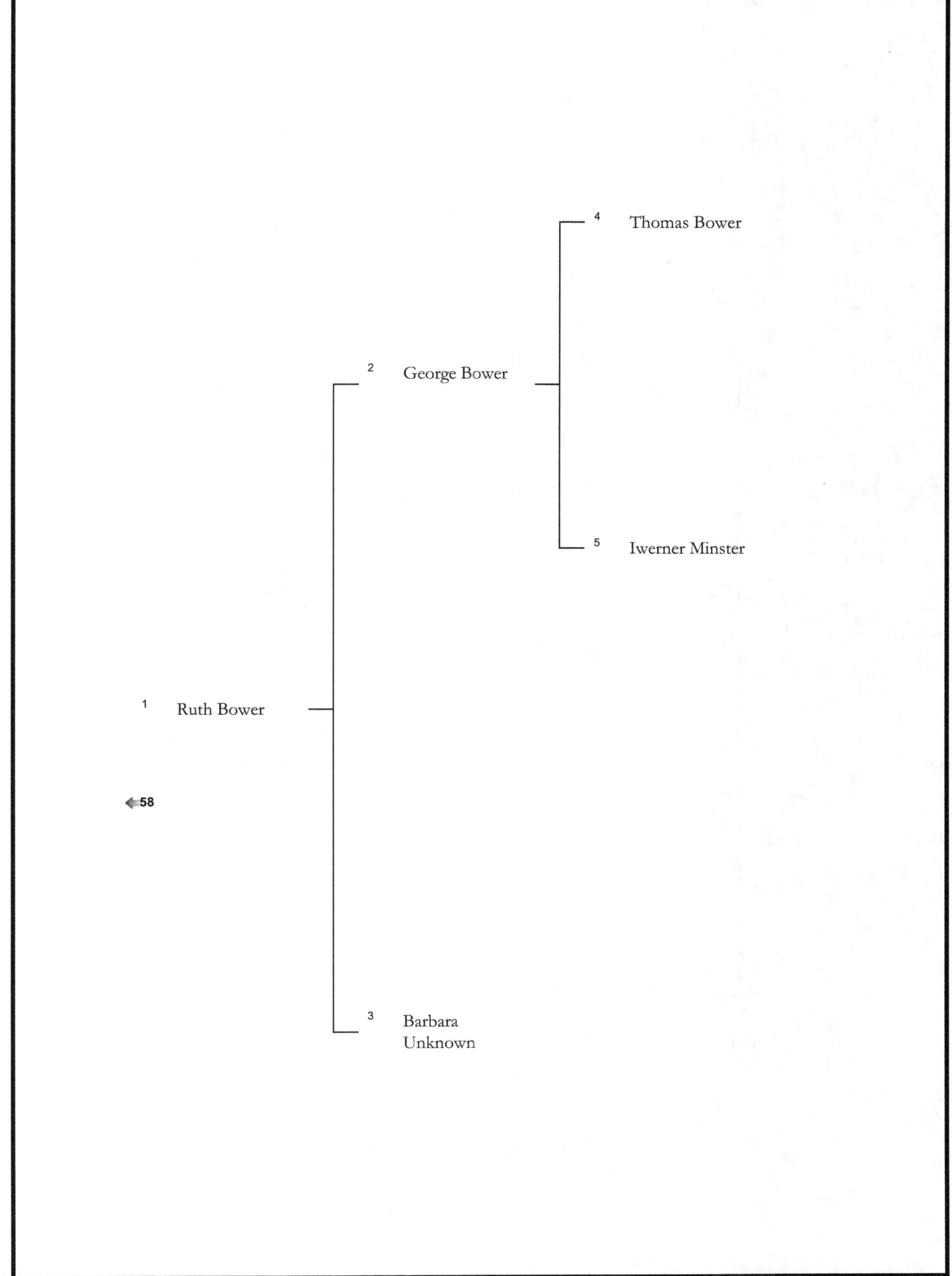

4 Thomas Bower
2 George Bower
5 Iwerner Minster
1 Ruth Bower
58
3 Barbara
Unknown

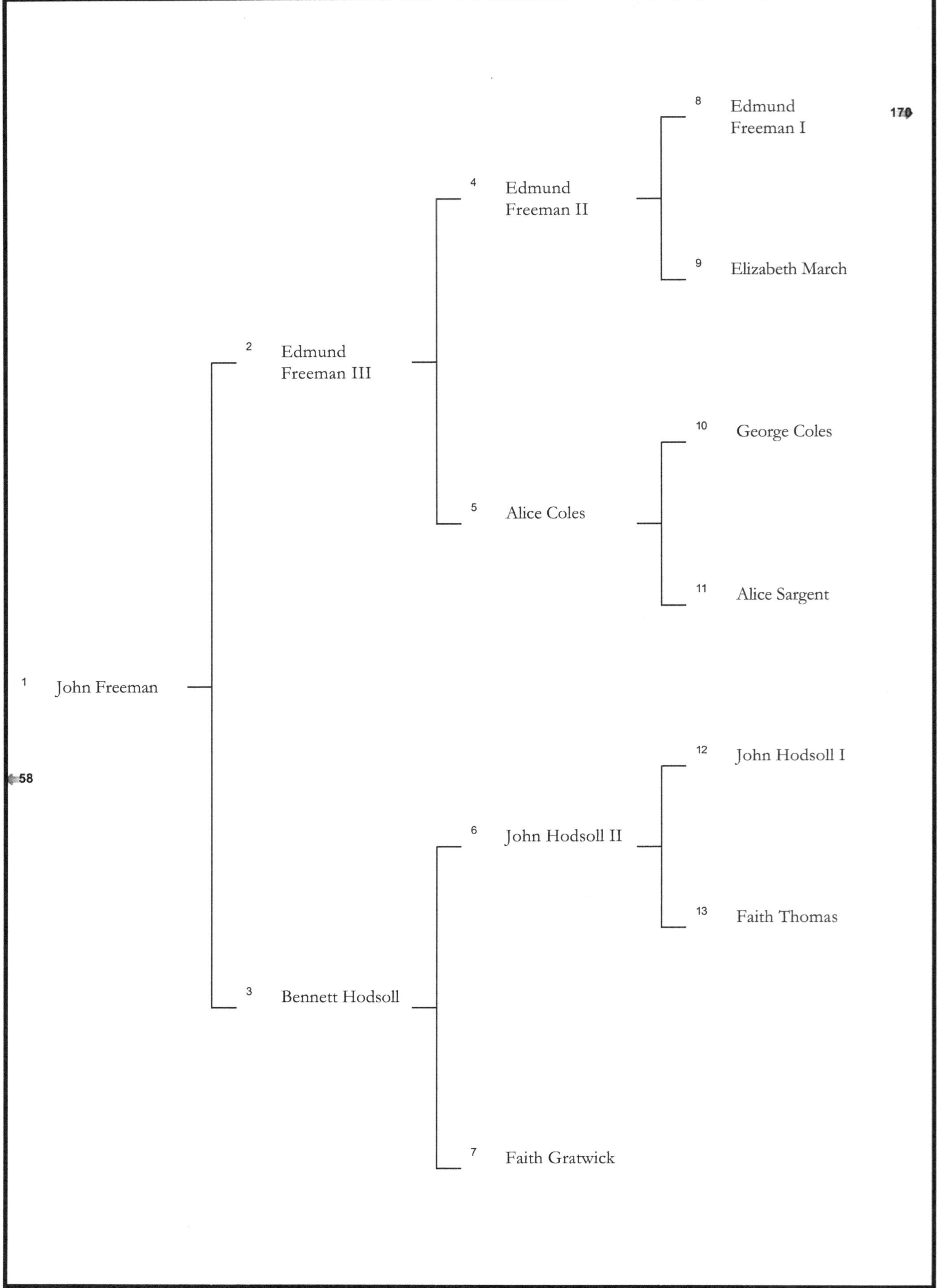

1 John Freeman
2 Edmund Freeman III
3 Bennett Hodsoll
4 Edmund Freeman II
5 Alice Coles
6 John Hodsoll II
7 Faith Gratwick
8 Edmund Freeman I
9 Elizabeth March
10 George Coles
11 Alice Sargent
12 John Hodsoll I
13 Faith Thomas
58
170

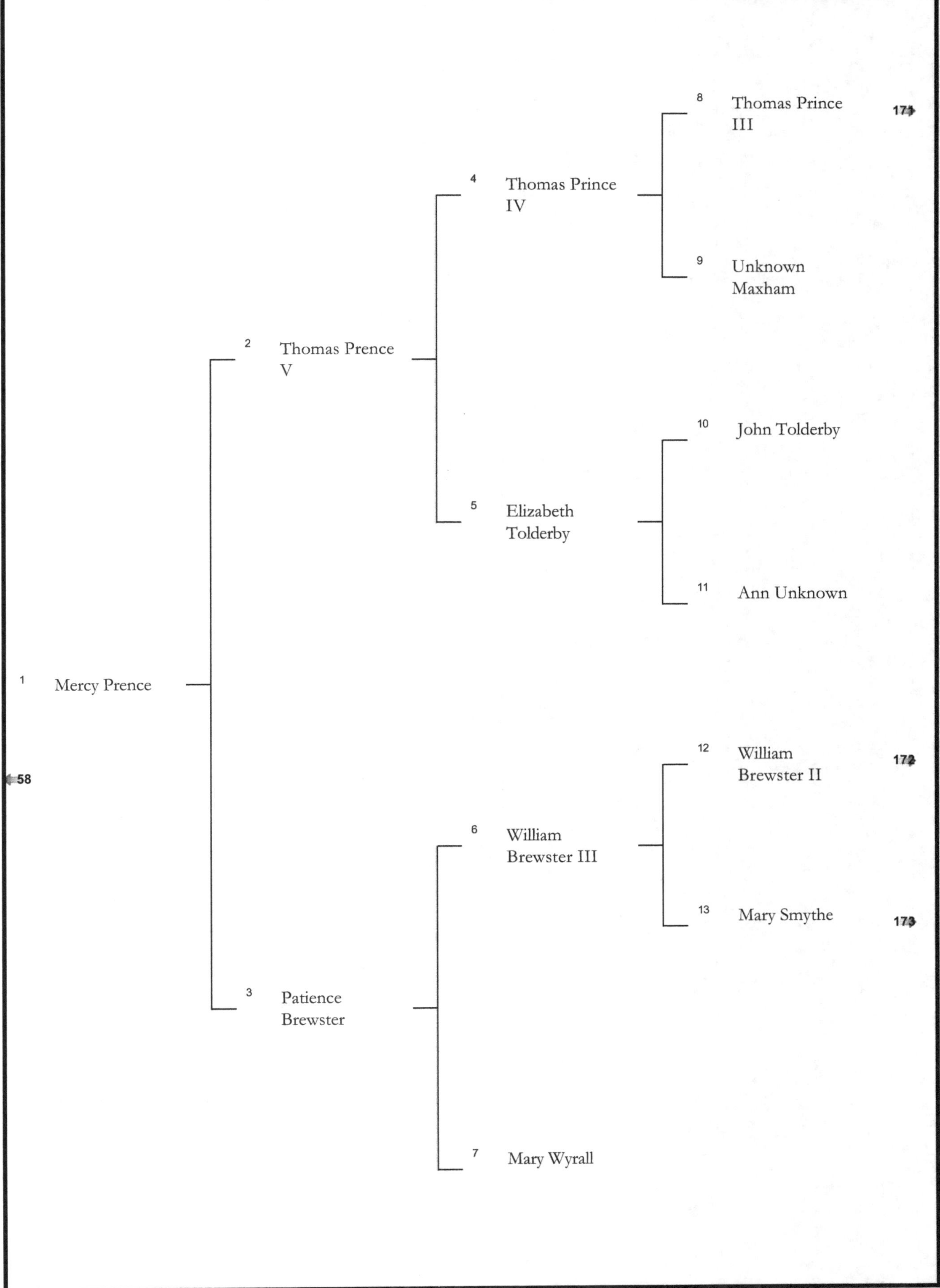

1 Mercy Prence
58
2 Thomas Prence V
3 Patience Brewster
4 Thomas Prince IV
5 Elizabeth Tolderby
6 William Brewster III
7 Mary Wyrall
8 Thomas Prince III — 174
9 Unknown Maxham
10 John Tolderby
11 Ann Unknown
12 William Brewster II — 172
13 Mary Smythe — 173

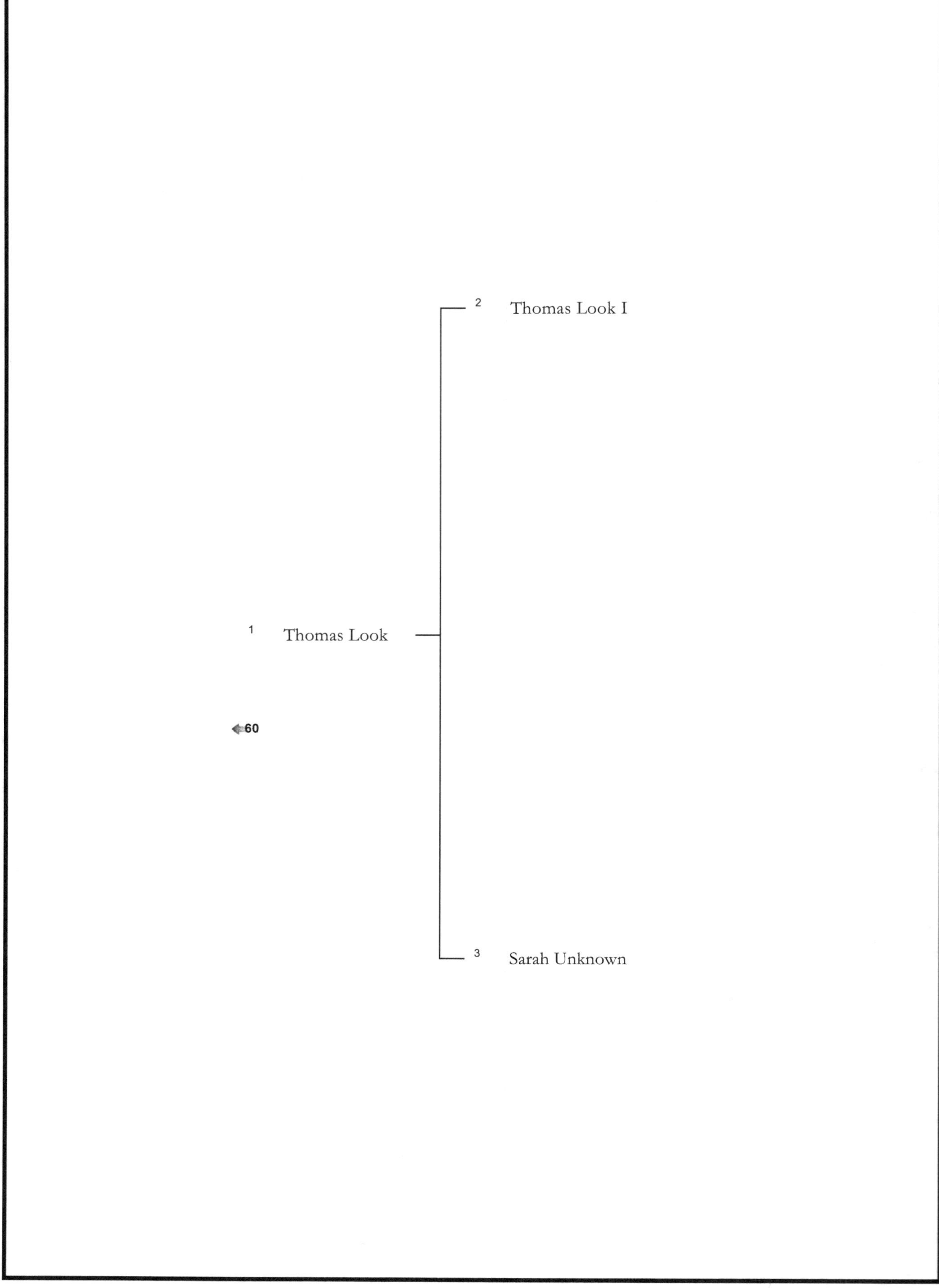

2 Thomas Look I
1 Thomas Look
60
3 Sarah Unknown

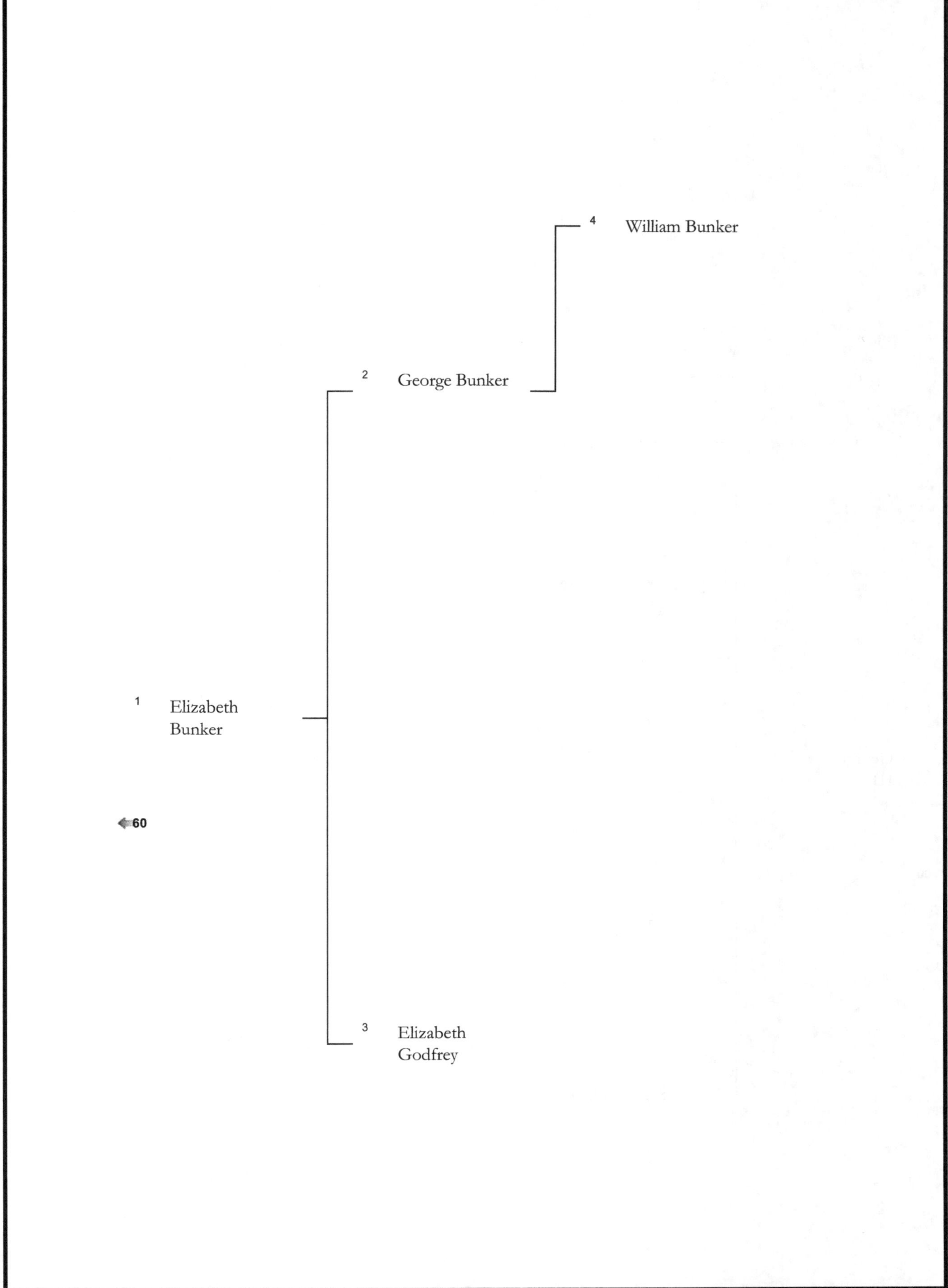

4 William Bunker
2 George Bunker
1 Elizabeth Bunker
60
3 Elizabeth Godfrey

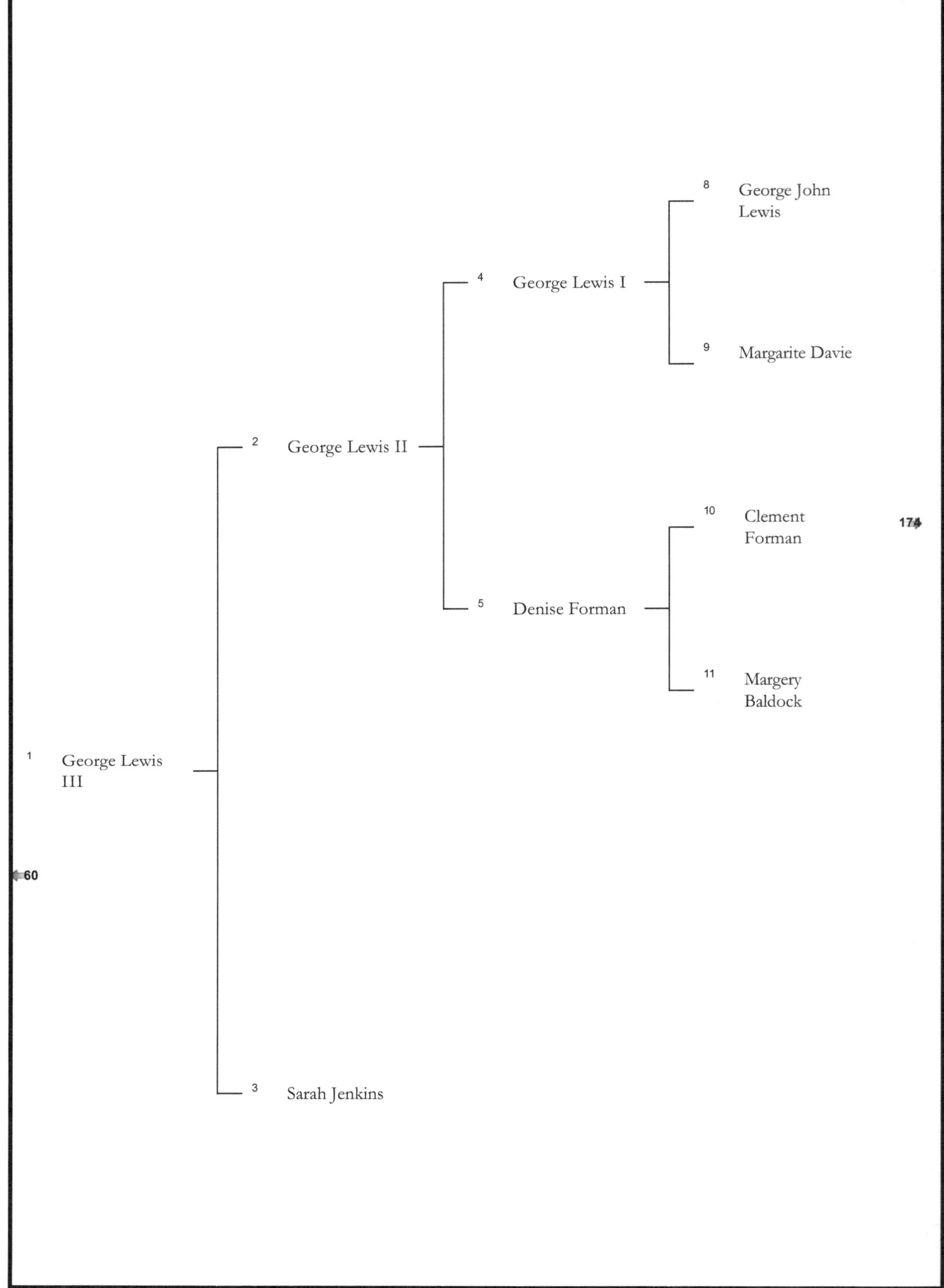
1
George Lewis
III
60
2
George Lewis II
3
Sarah Jenkins
4
George Lewis I
5
Denise Forman
8
George John
Lewis
9
Margarite Davie
10
Clement
Forman
11
Margery
Baldock
174

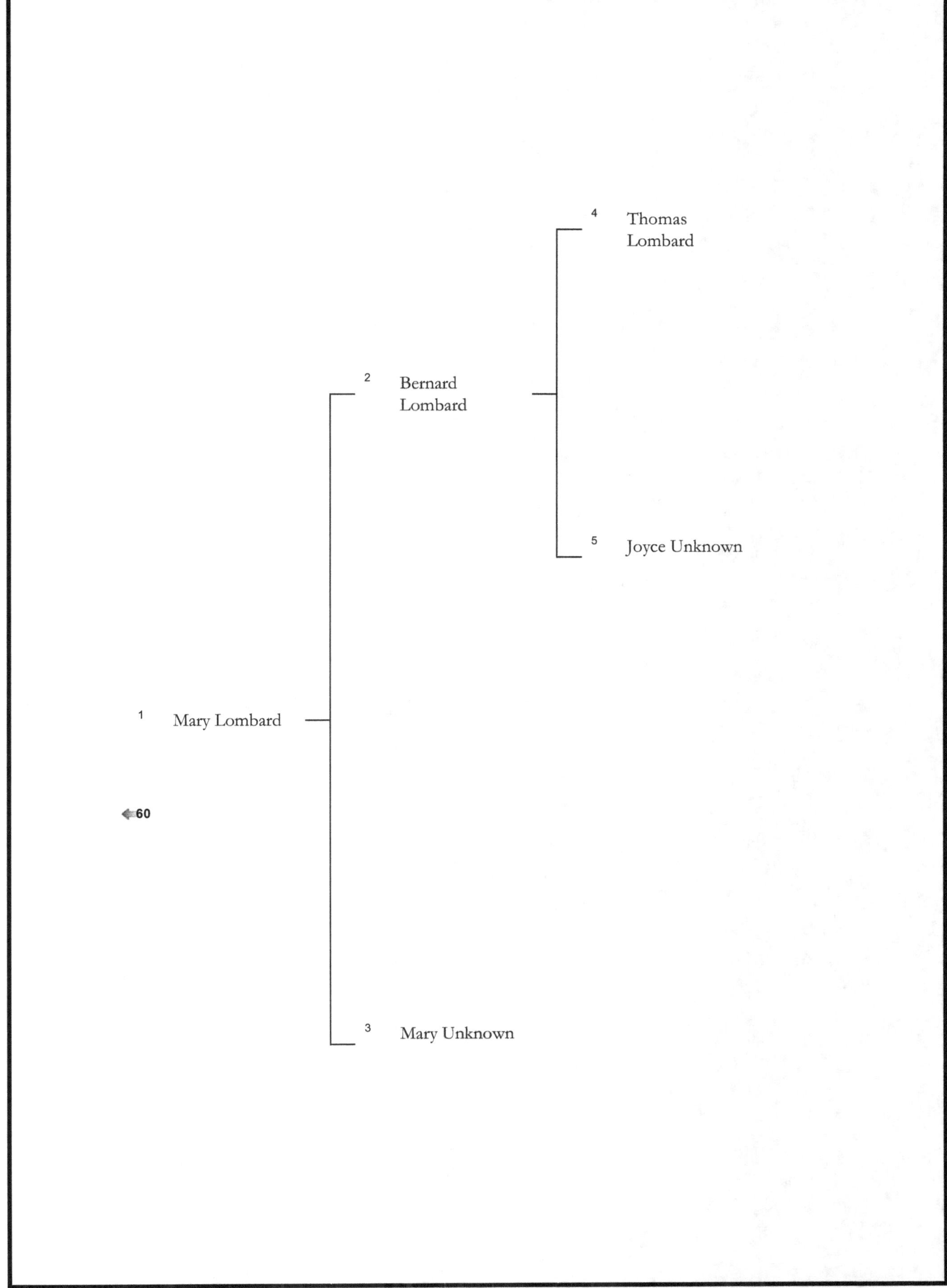

4
Thomas
Lombard

2
Bernard
Lombard

5
Joyce Unknown

1
Mary Lombard

60

3
Mary Unknown

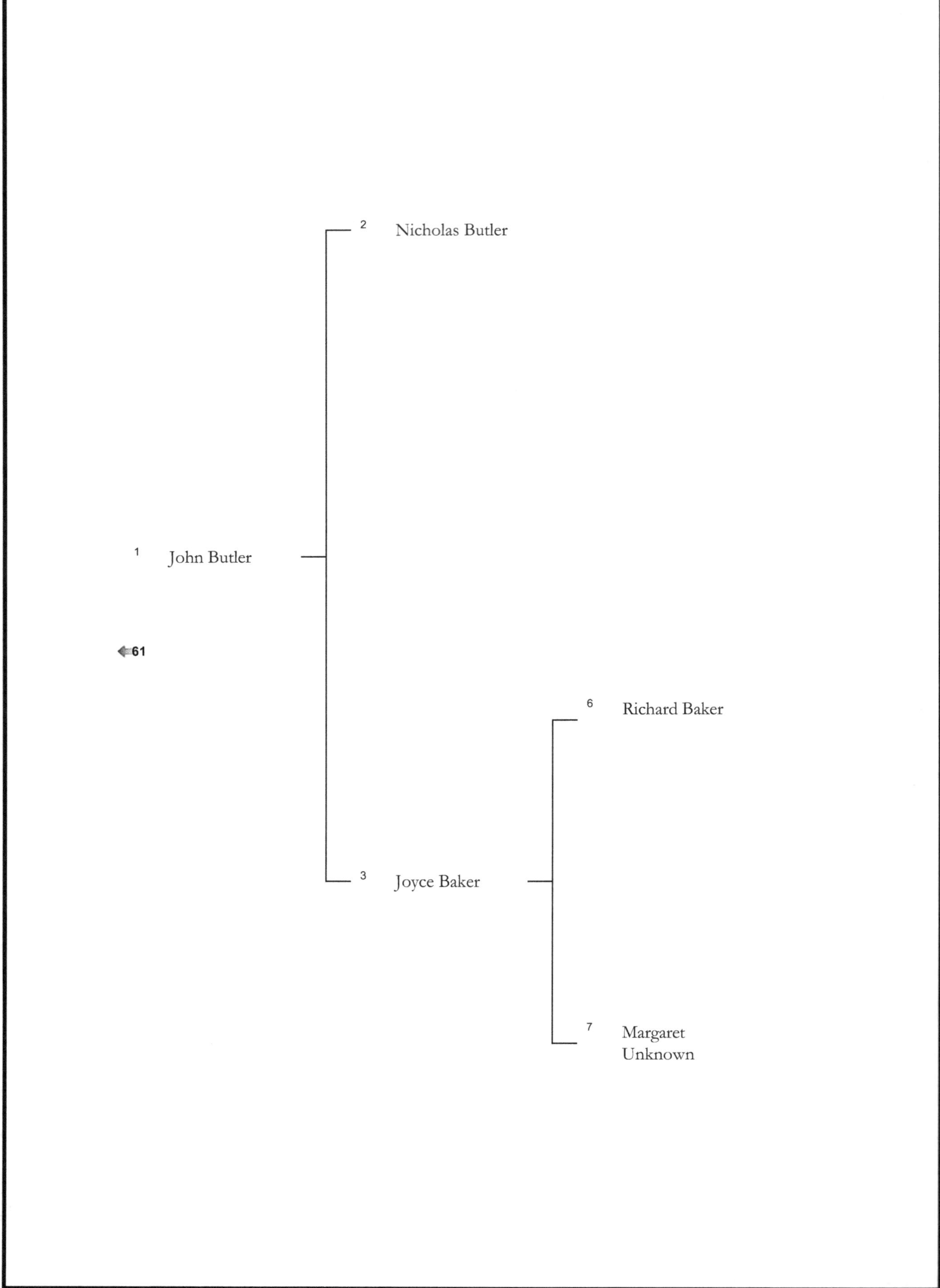

2   Nicholas Butler
1   John Butler
61
6   Richard Baker
3   Joyce Baker
7   Margaret
Unknown

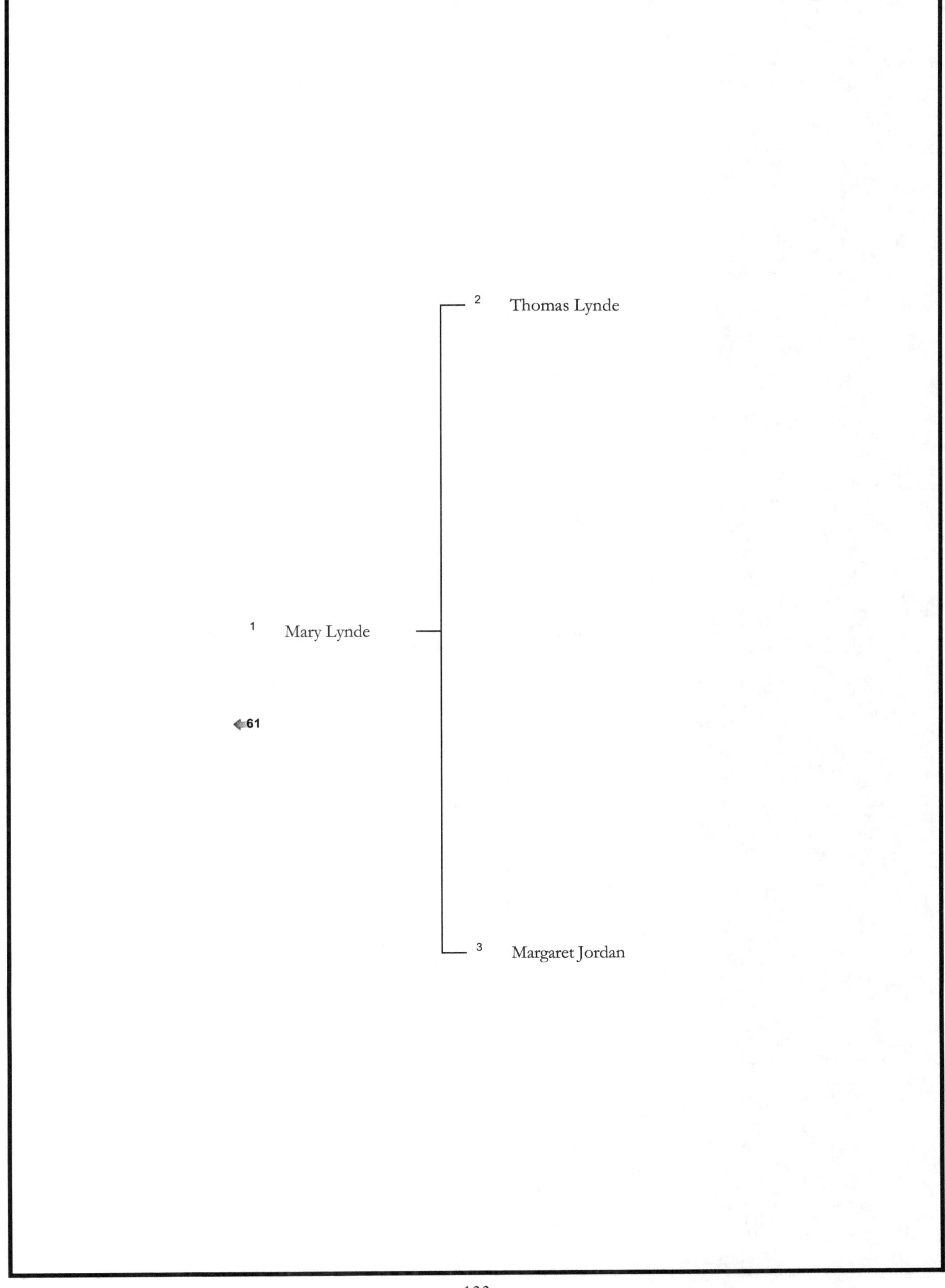

2 Thomas Lynde
1 Mary Lynde
61
3 Margaret Jordan

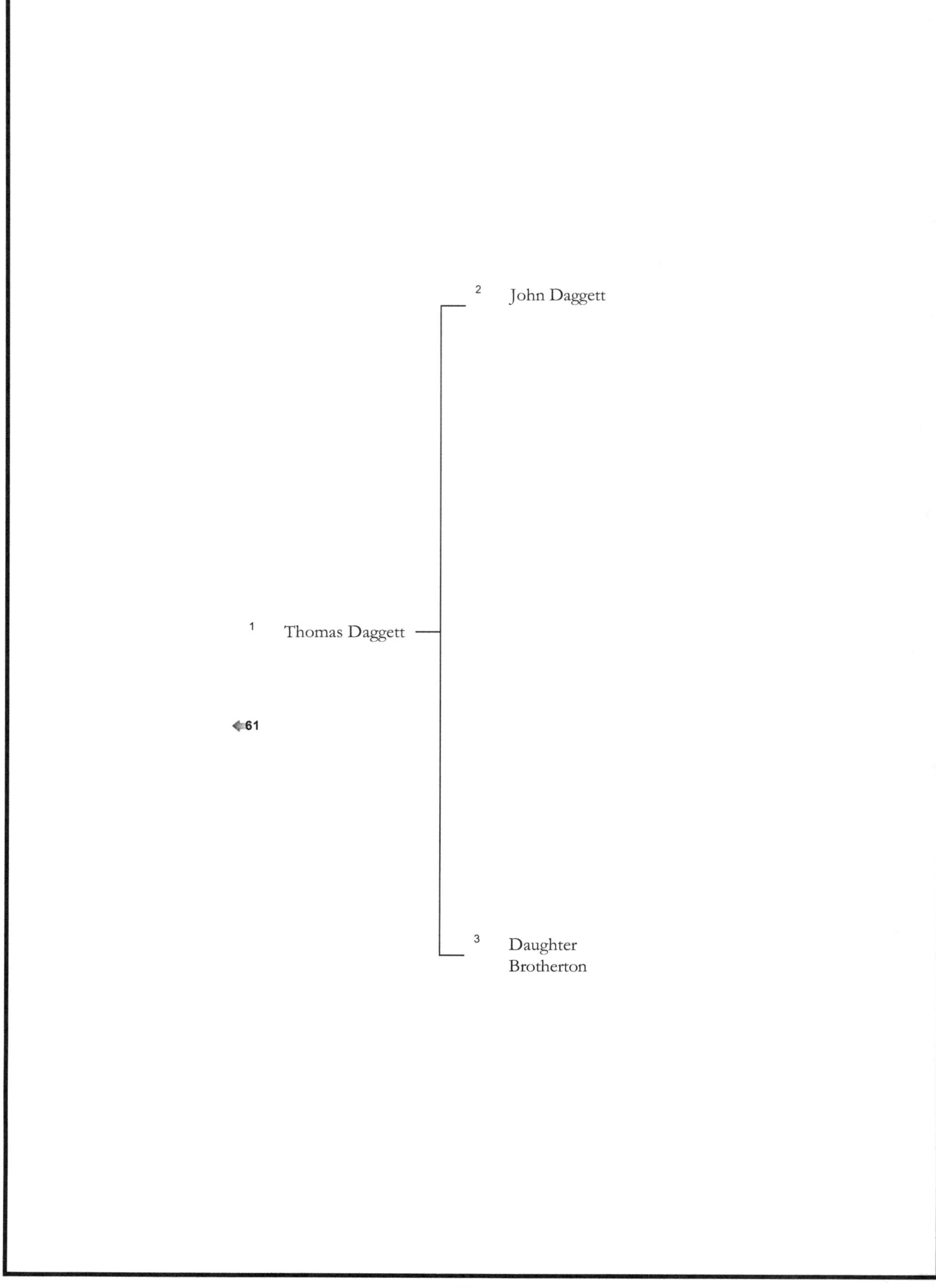

2 John Daggett
1 Thomas Daggett
61
3 Daughter
Brotherton

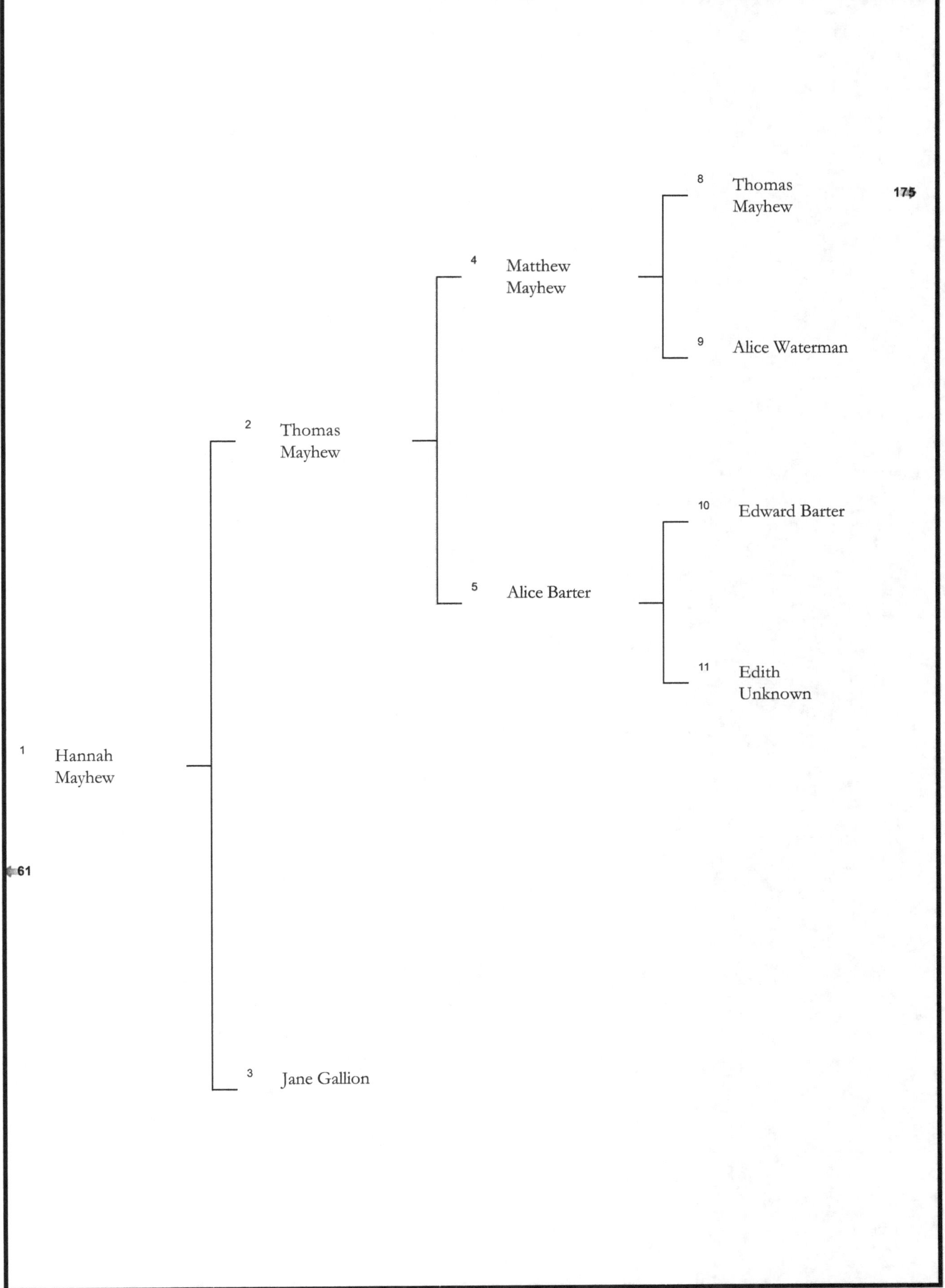

8 Thomas Mayhew
4 Matthew Mayhew
9 Alice Waterman
2 Thomas Mayhew
10 Edward Barter
5 Alice Barter
11 Edith Unknown
1 Hannah Mayhew
61
3 Jane Gallion

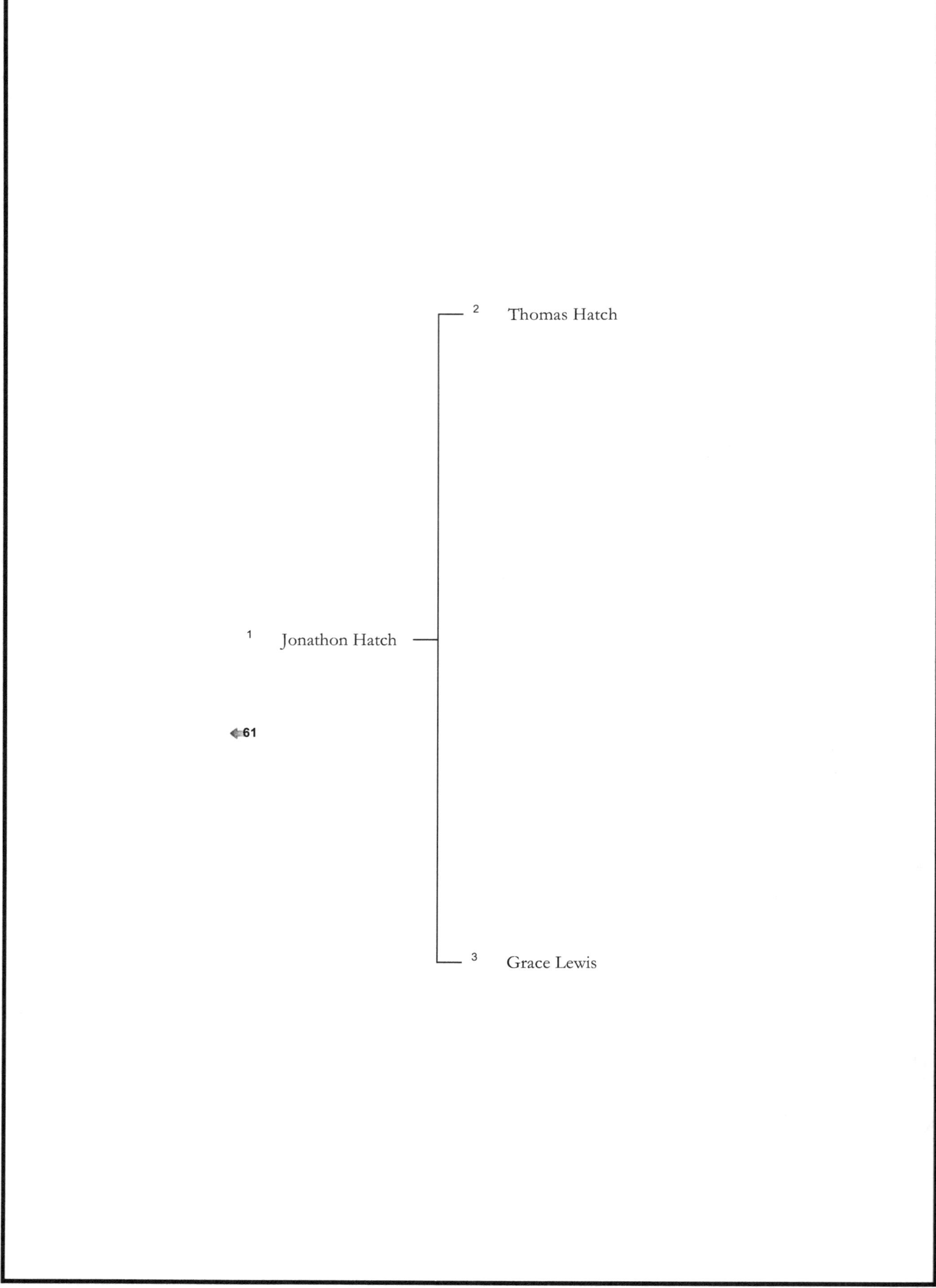

2 Thomas Hatch
1 Jonathon Hatch
61
3 Grace Lewis

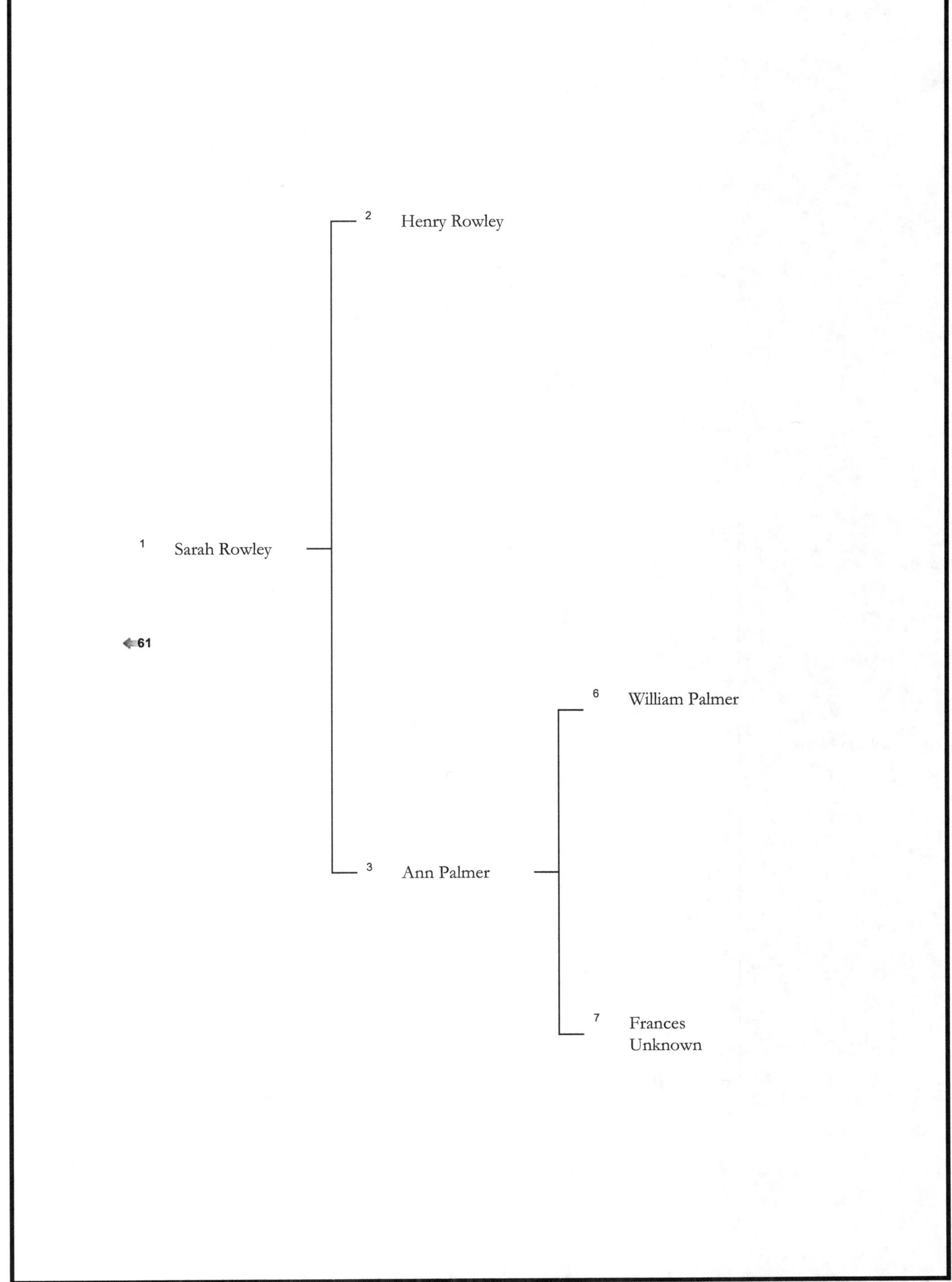

2 Henry Rowley
1 Sarah Rowley
61
6 William Palmer
3 Ann Palmer
7 Frances
Unknown

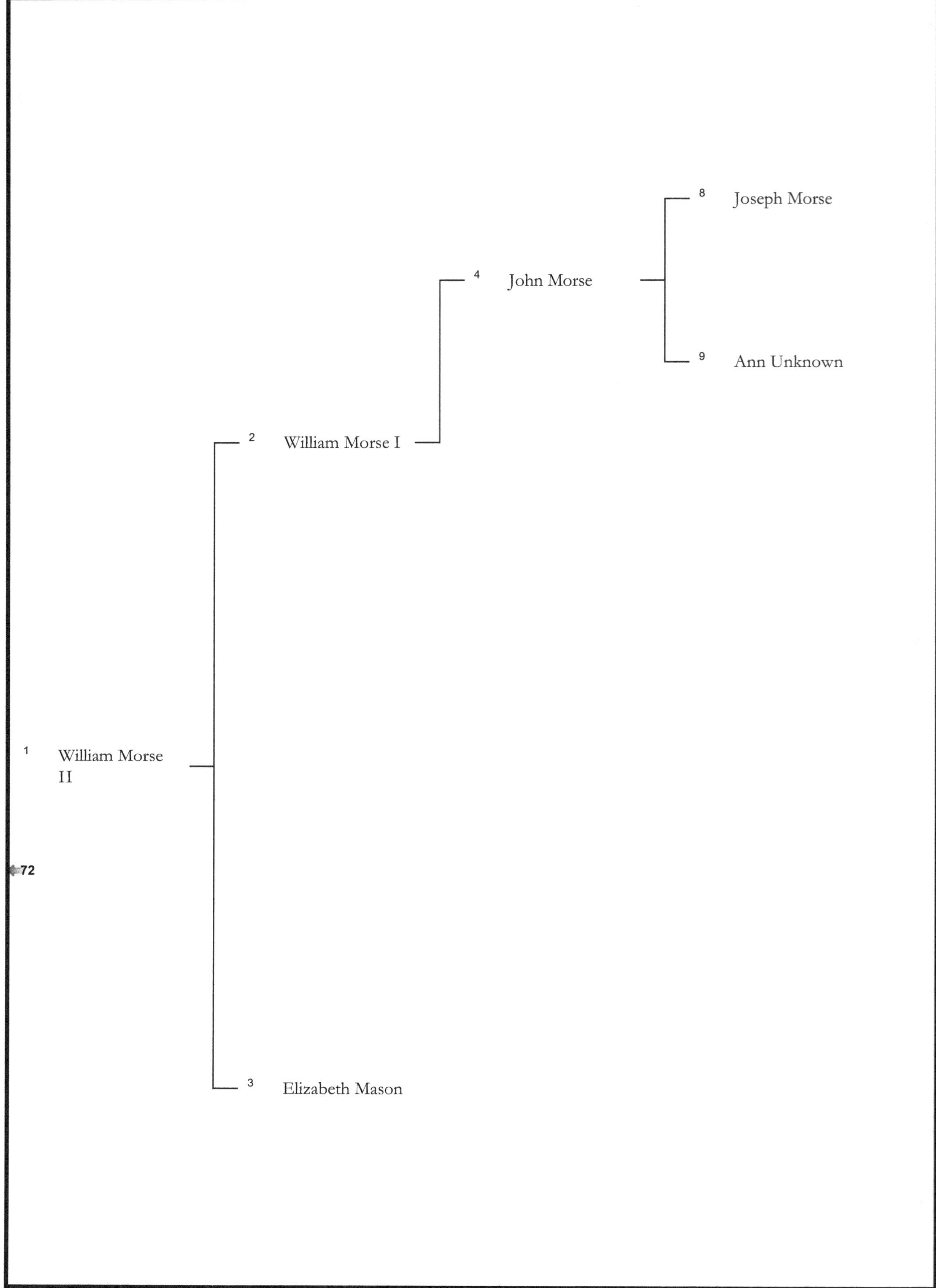

8 Joseph Morse
4 John Morse
9 Ann Unknown
2 William Morse I
1 William Morse II
72
3 Elizabeth Mason

2 Robert W.
White

1 Robert White

74

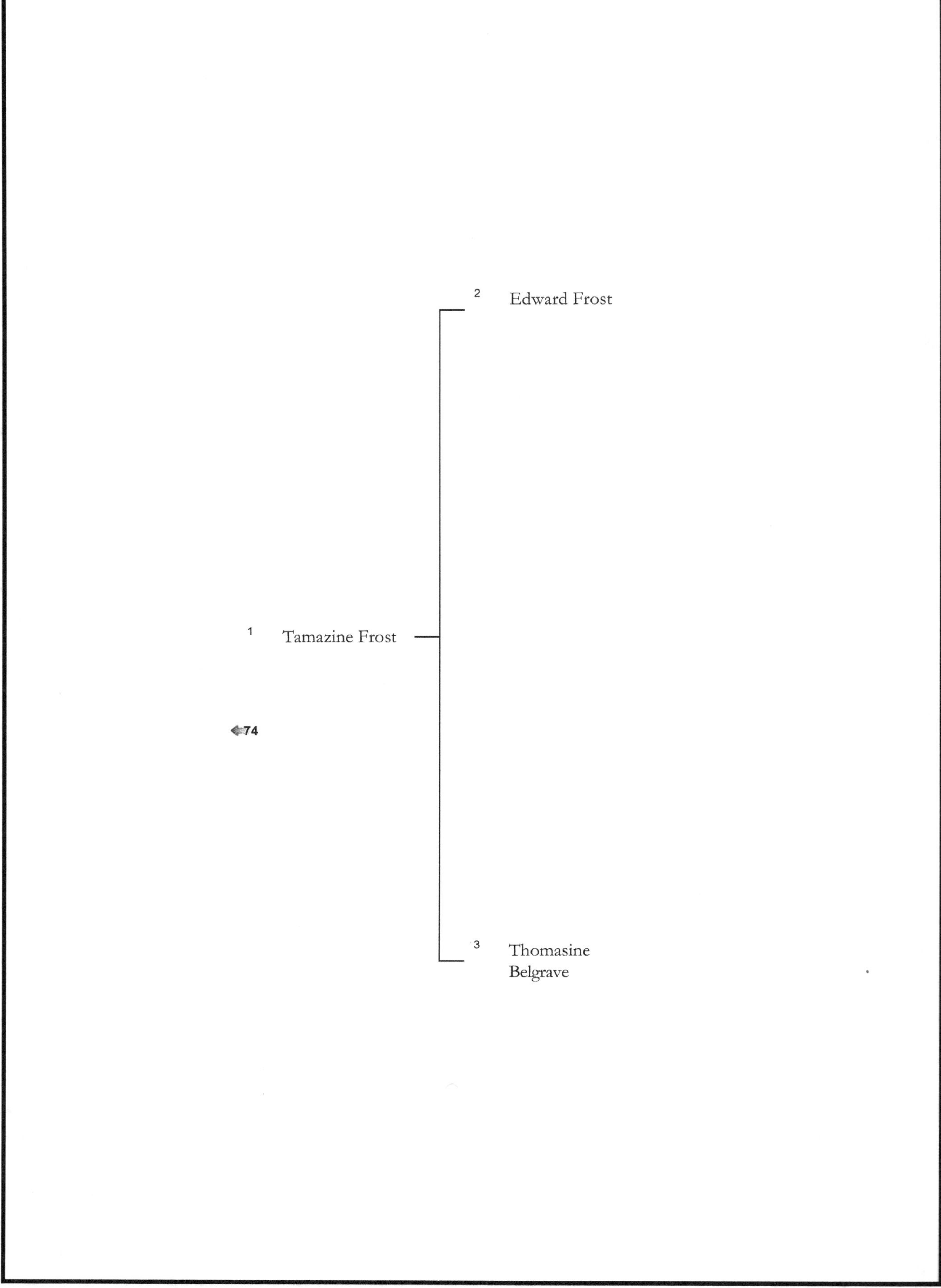

2 Edward Frost
1 Tamazine Frost
74
3 Thomasine Belgrave

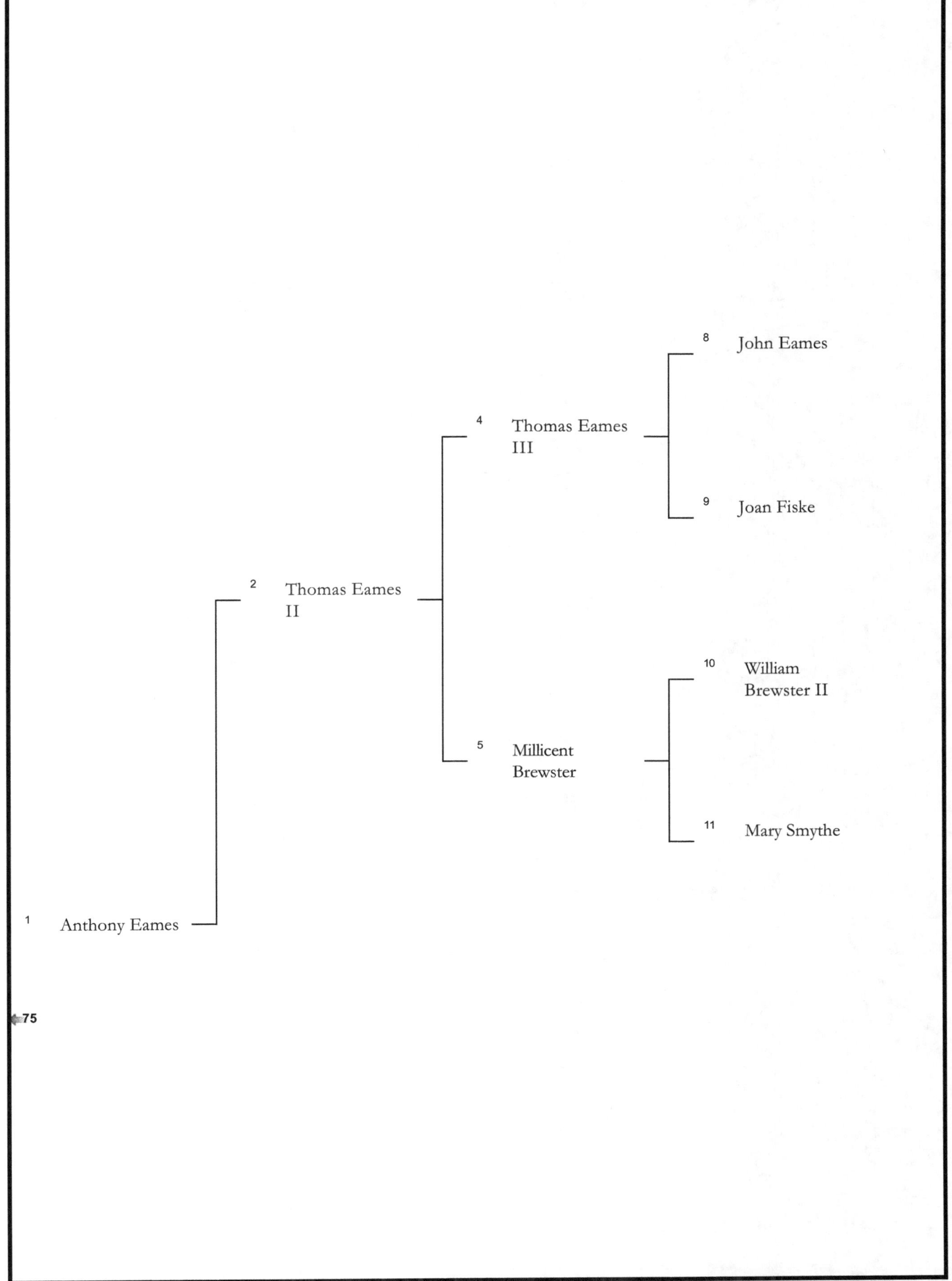

1 Anthony Eames
2 Thomas Eames II
4 Thomas Eames III
8 John Eames
9 Joan Fiske
5 Millicent Brewster
10 William Brewster II
11 Mary Smythe
75

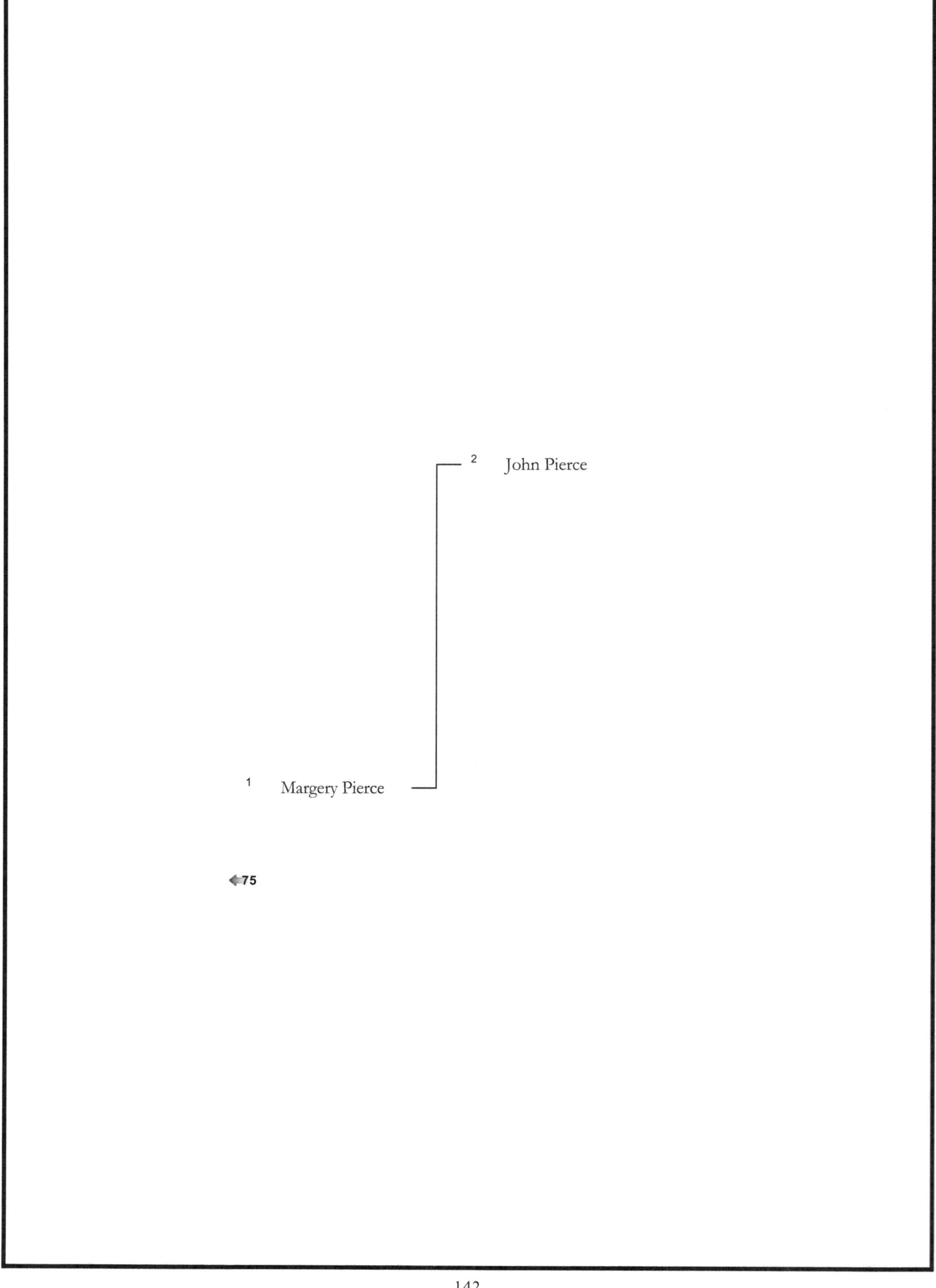

75

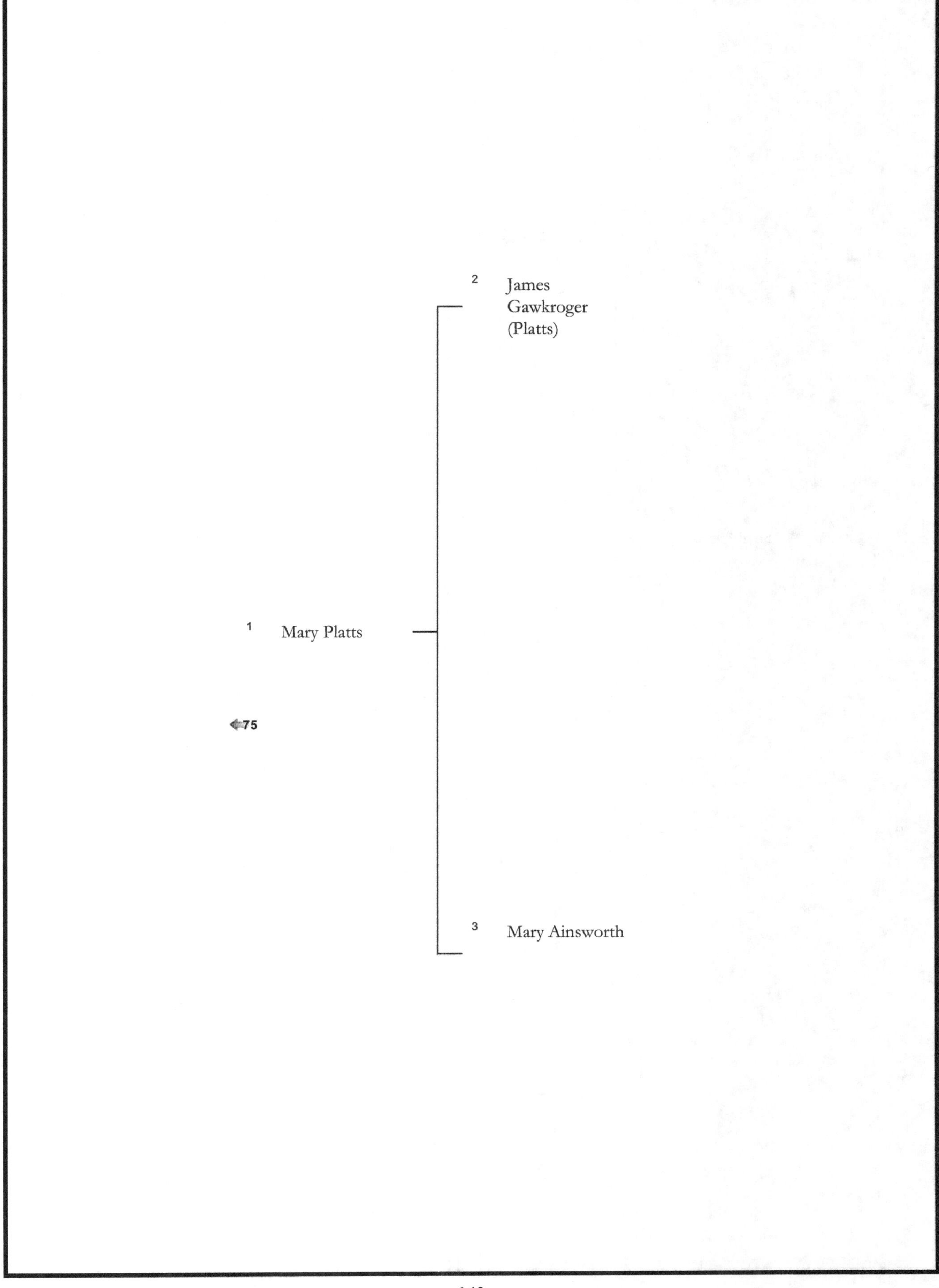

2 James Gawkroger (Platts)
1 Mary Platts
75
3 Mary Ainsworth

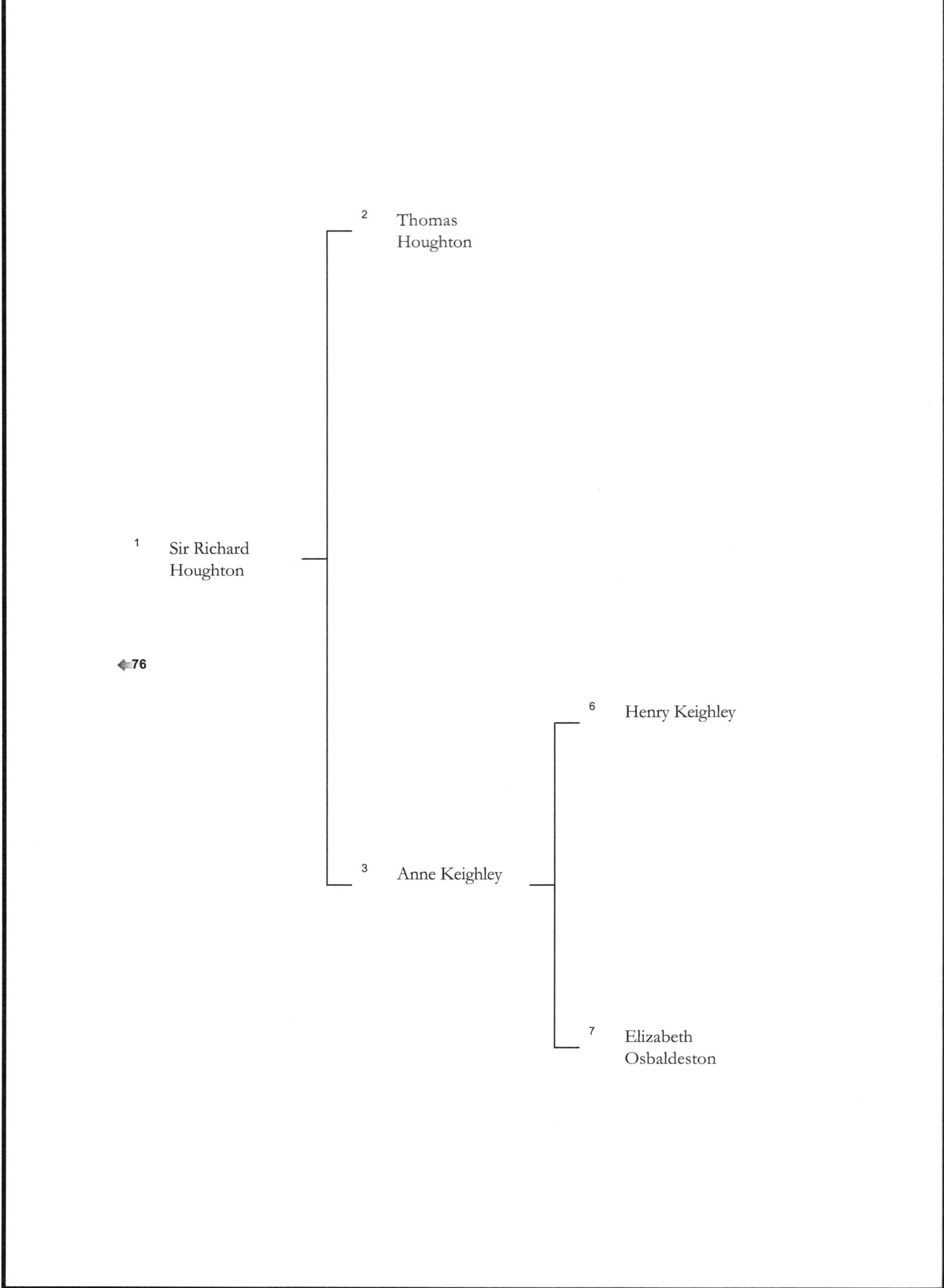

2 Thomas Houghton
1 Sir Richard Houghton
76
6 Henry Keighley
3 Anne Keighley
7 Elizabeth Osbaldeston

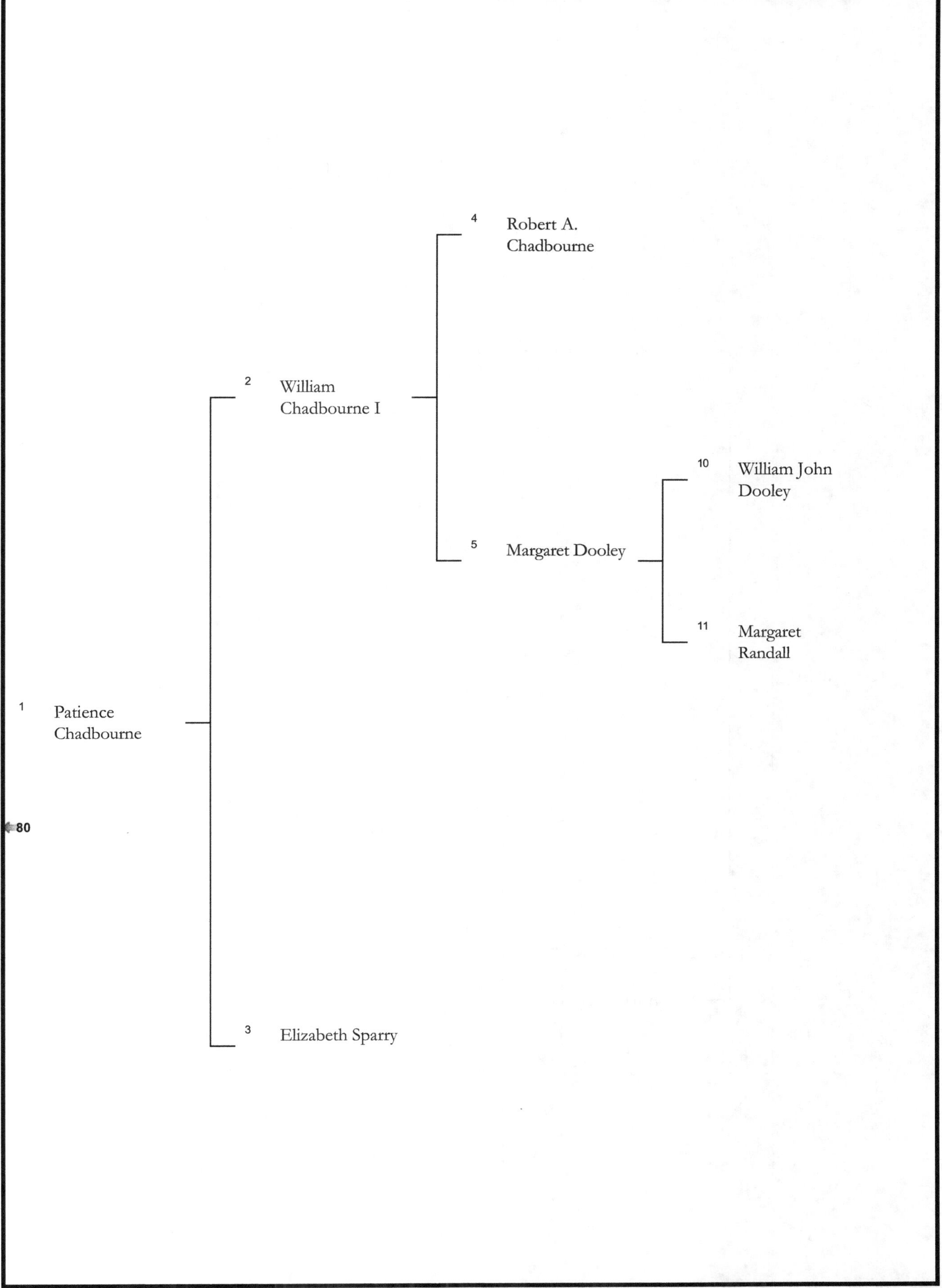

1 Patience Chadbourne
2 William Chadbourne I
3 Elizabeth Sparry
4 Robert A. Chadbourne
5 Margaret Dooley
10 William John Dooley
11 Margaret Randall
80

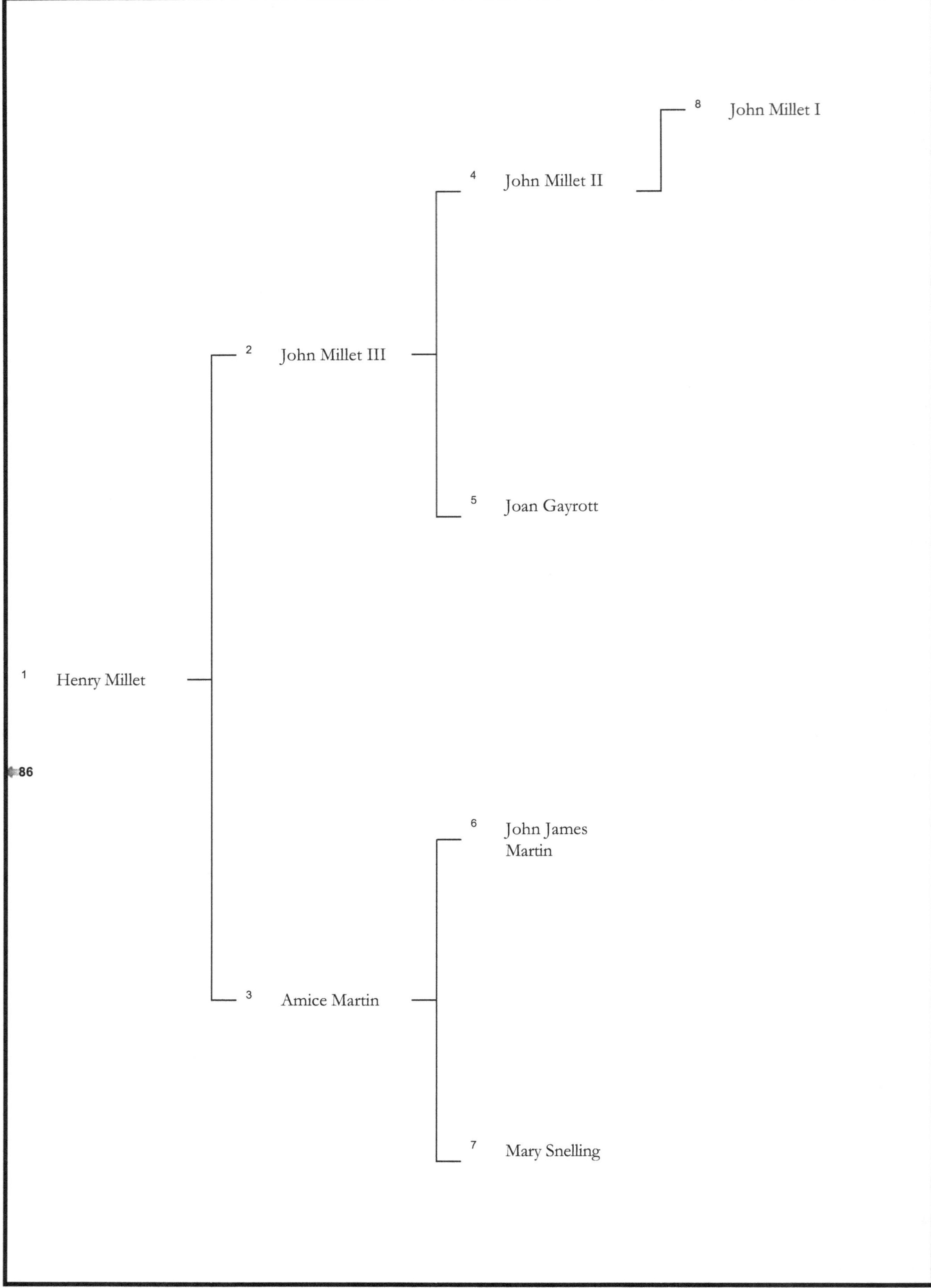

8 John Millet I
4 John Millet II
2 John Millet III
5 Joan Gayrott
1 Henry Millet
86
6 John James Martin
3 Amice Martin
7 Mary Snelling

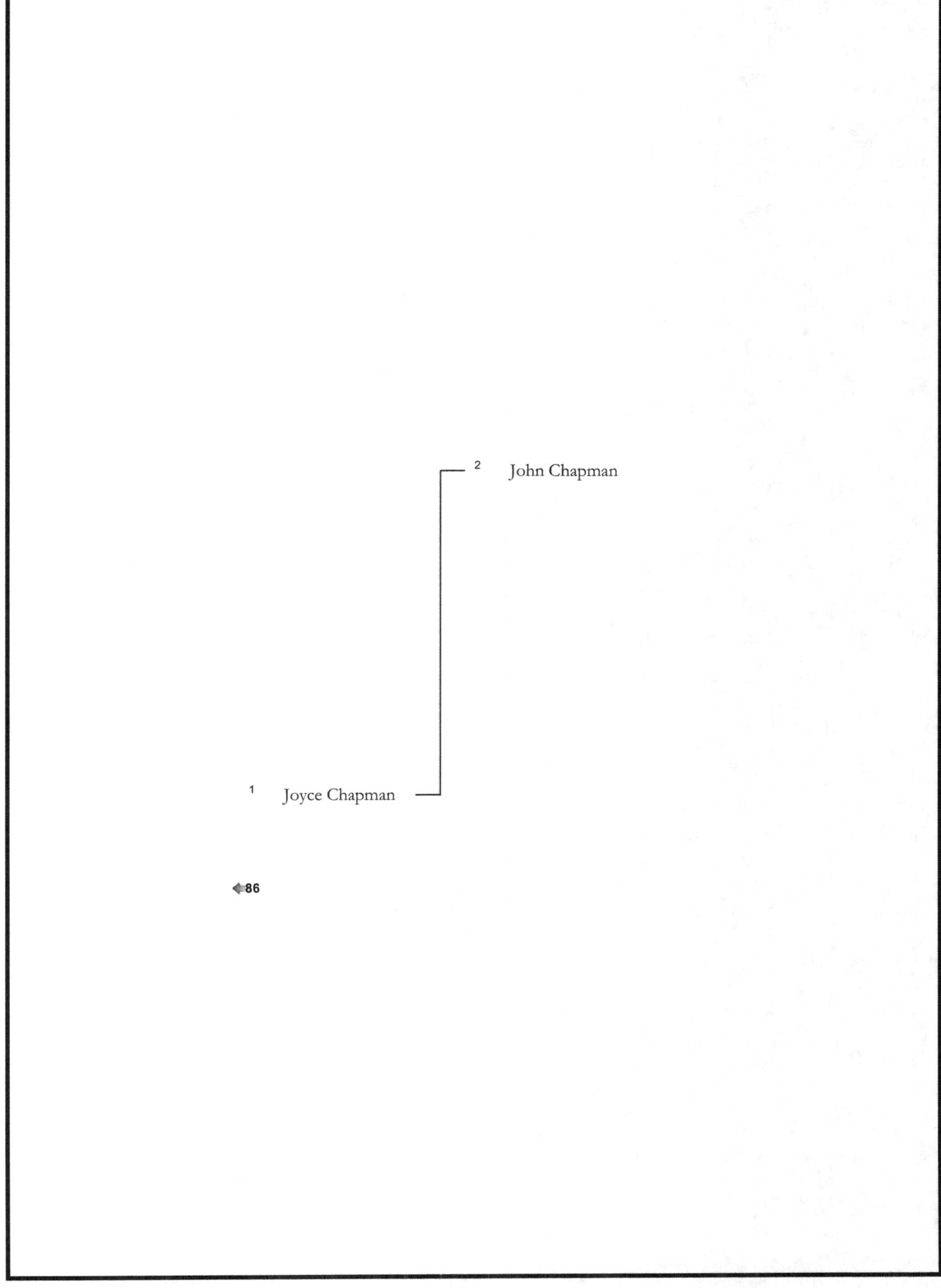

2 John Chapman
1 Joyce Chapman
86

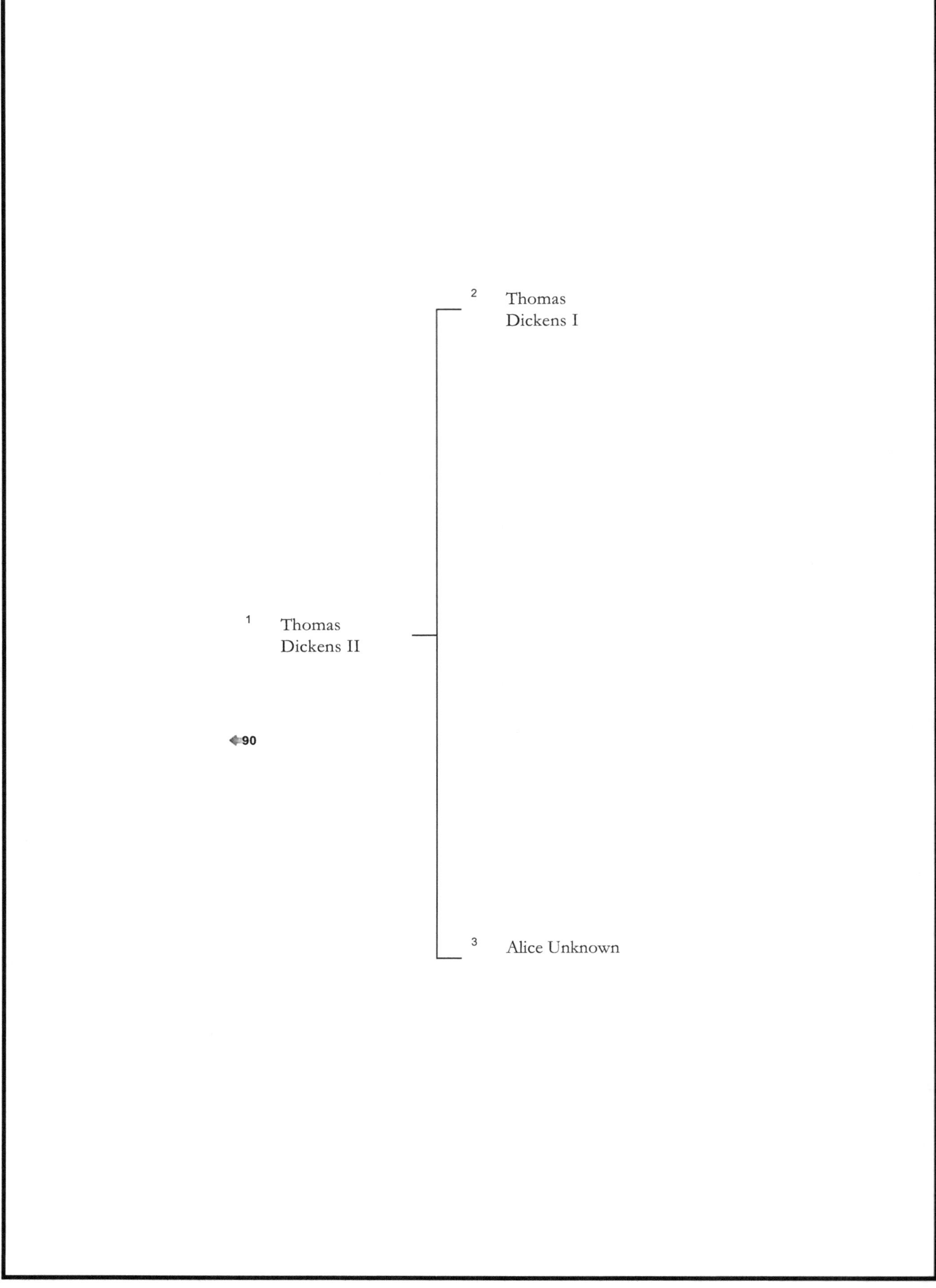

1 Thomas Dickens II
2 Thomas Dickens I
3 Alice Unknown
90

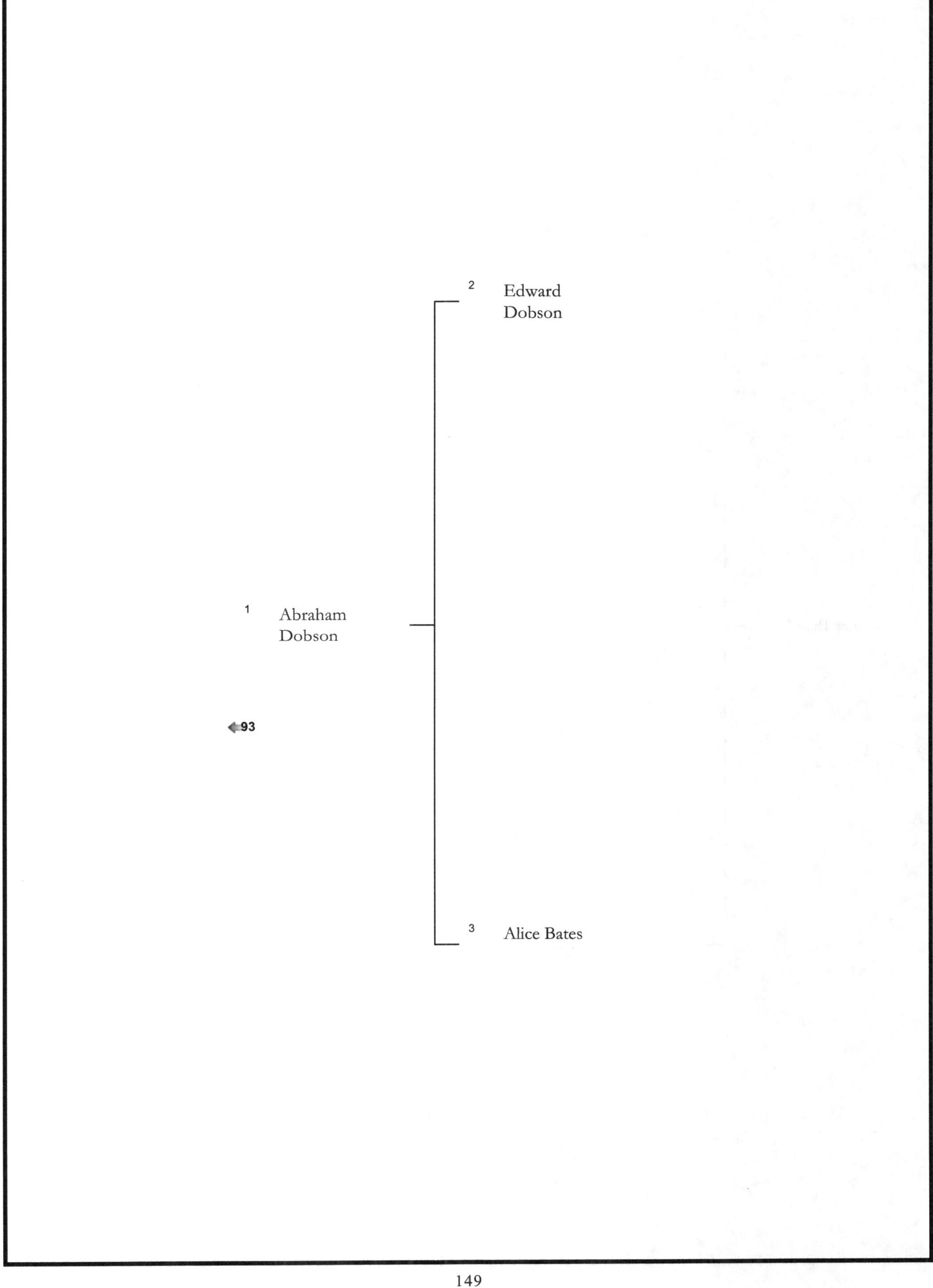

2 Edward Dobson
1 Abraham Dobson
93
3 Alice Bates

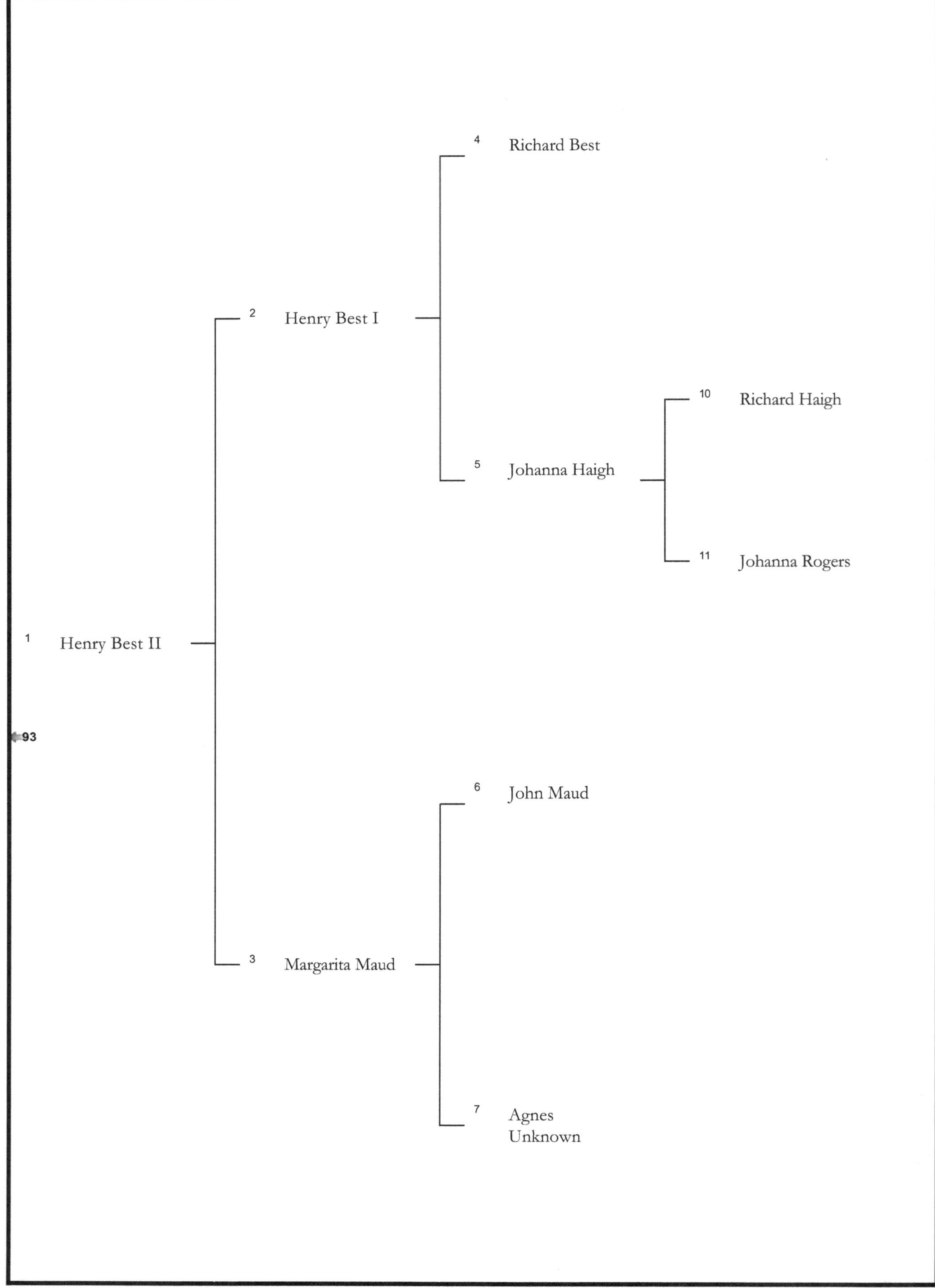

4 Richard Best
2 Henry Best I
10 Richard Haigh
5 Johanna Haigh
11 Johanna Rogers
1 Henry Best II
93
6 John Maud
3 Margarita Maud
7 Agnes
Unknown

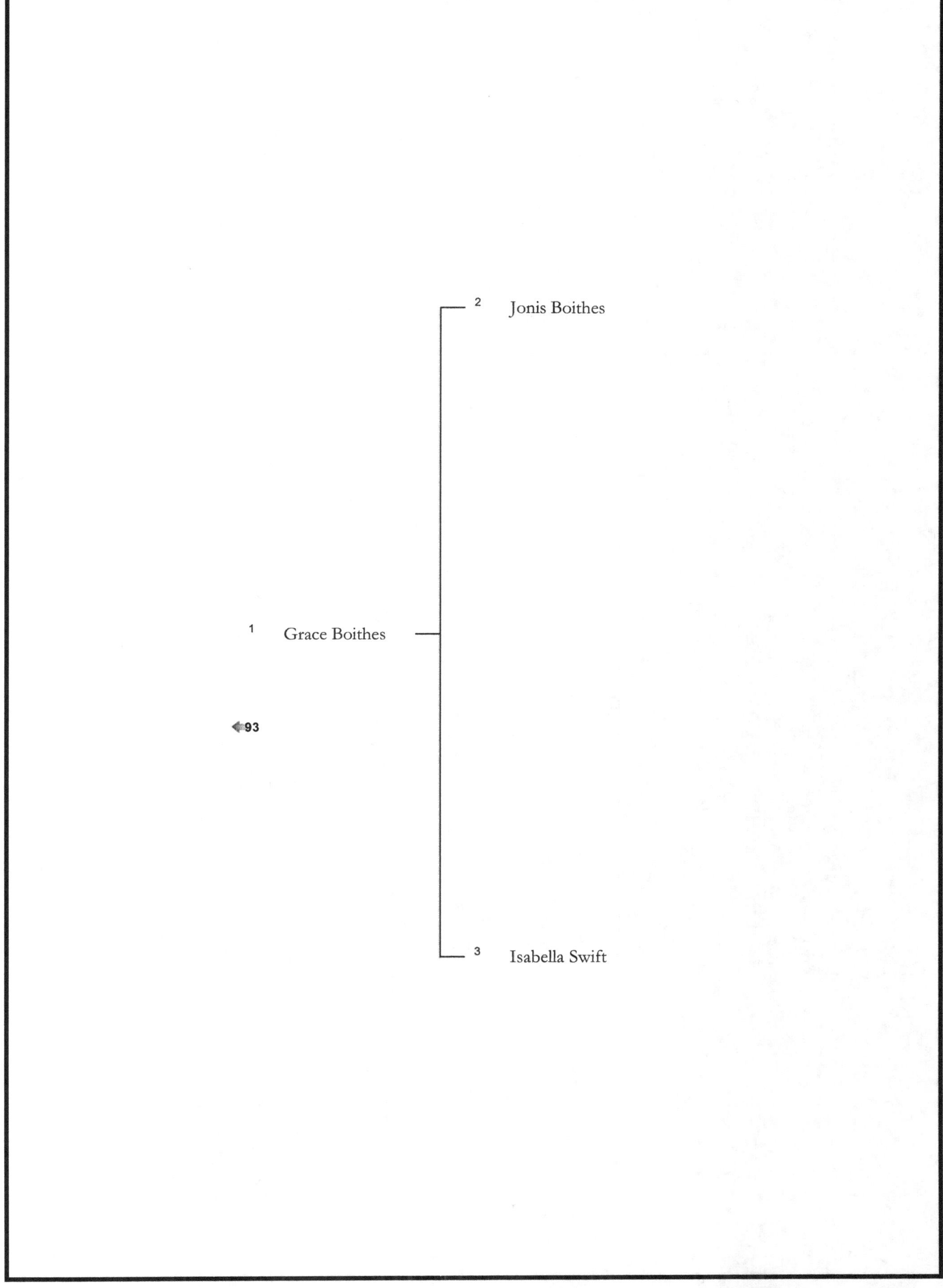

1 Grace Boithes
2 Jonis Boithes
3 Isabella Swift
93

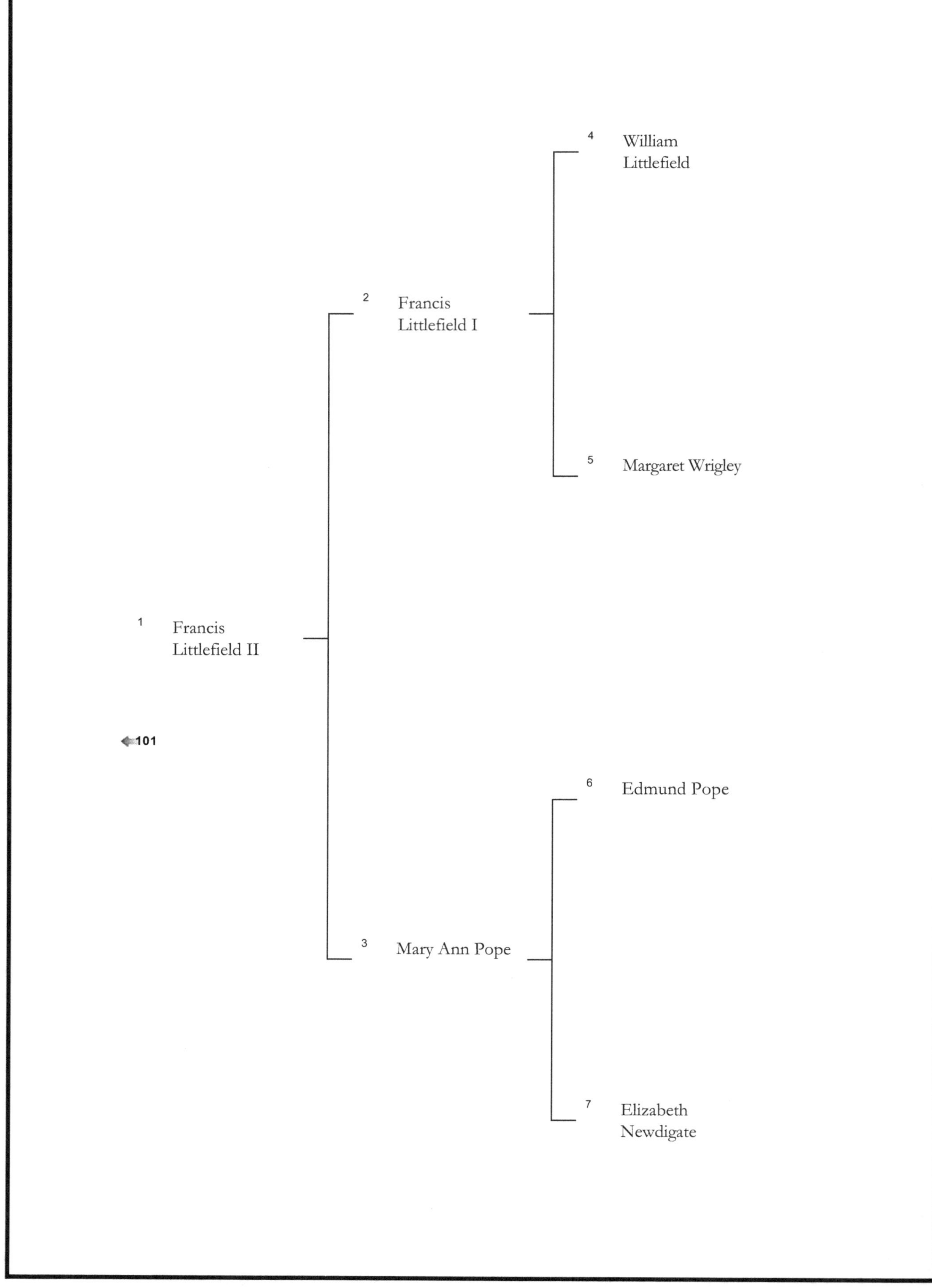

4 William Littlefield
2 Francis Littlefield I
5 Margaret Wrigley
1 Francis Littlefield II
101
6 Edmund Pope
3 Mary Ann Pope
7 Elizabeth Newdigate

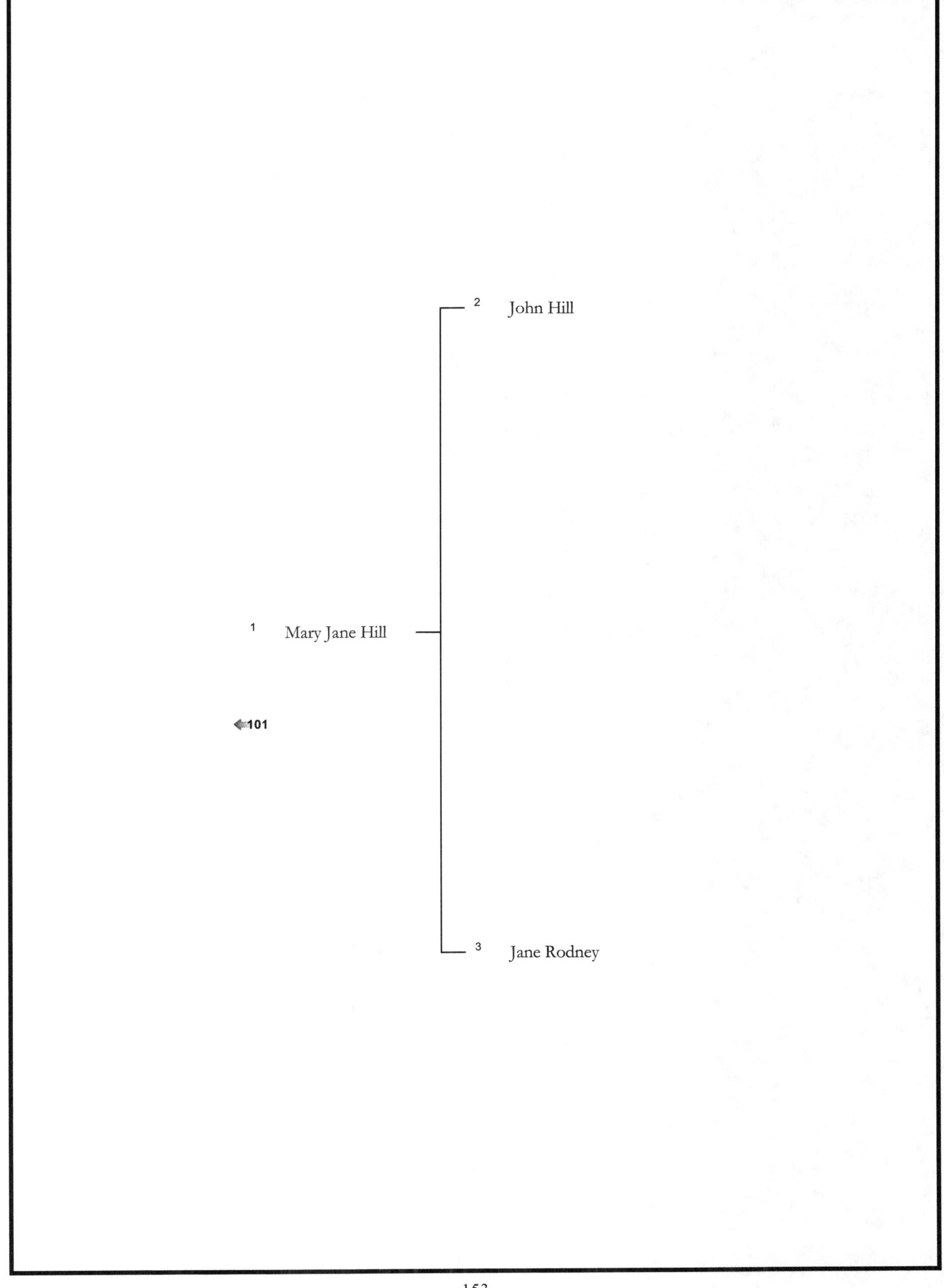

1   Mary Jane Hill
2   John Hill
3   Jane Rodney
101

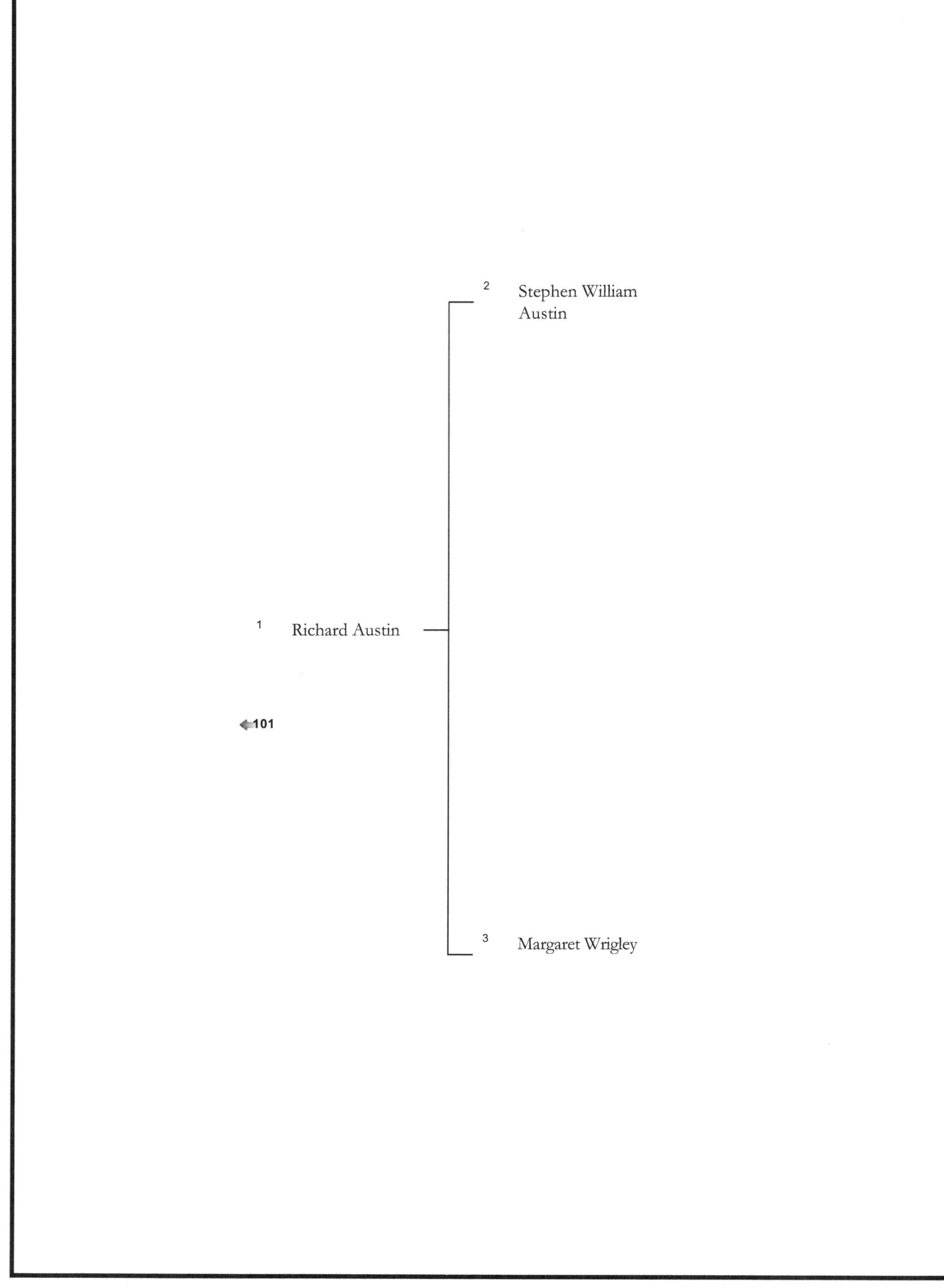

2 Stephen William Austin
1 Richard Austin
101
3 Margaret Wrigley

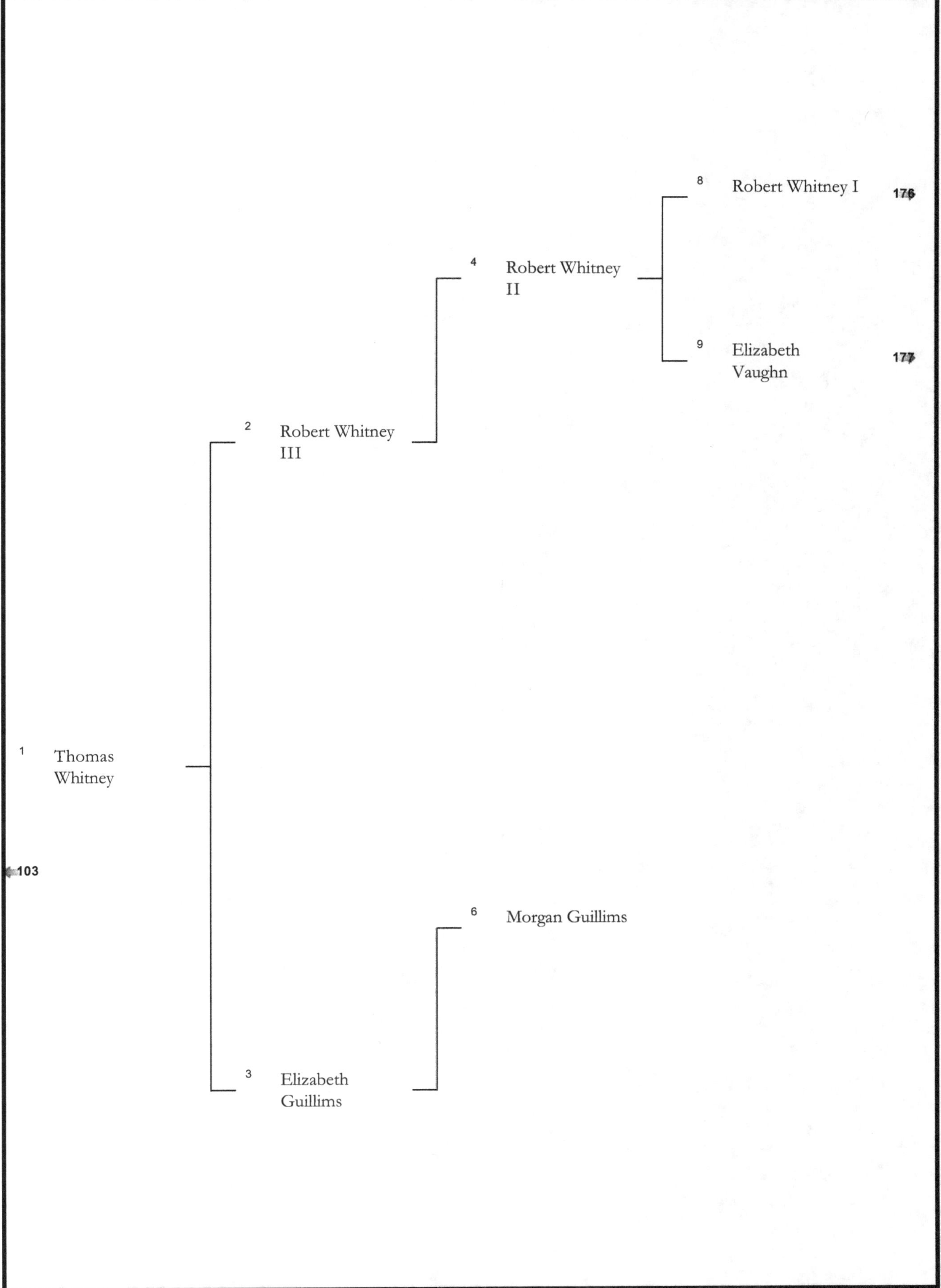

8 Robert Whitney I
176
4 Robert Whitney II
9 Elizabeth Vaughn
177
2 Robert Whitney III
1 Thomas Whitney
103
6 Morgan Guillims
3 Elizabeth Guillims

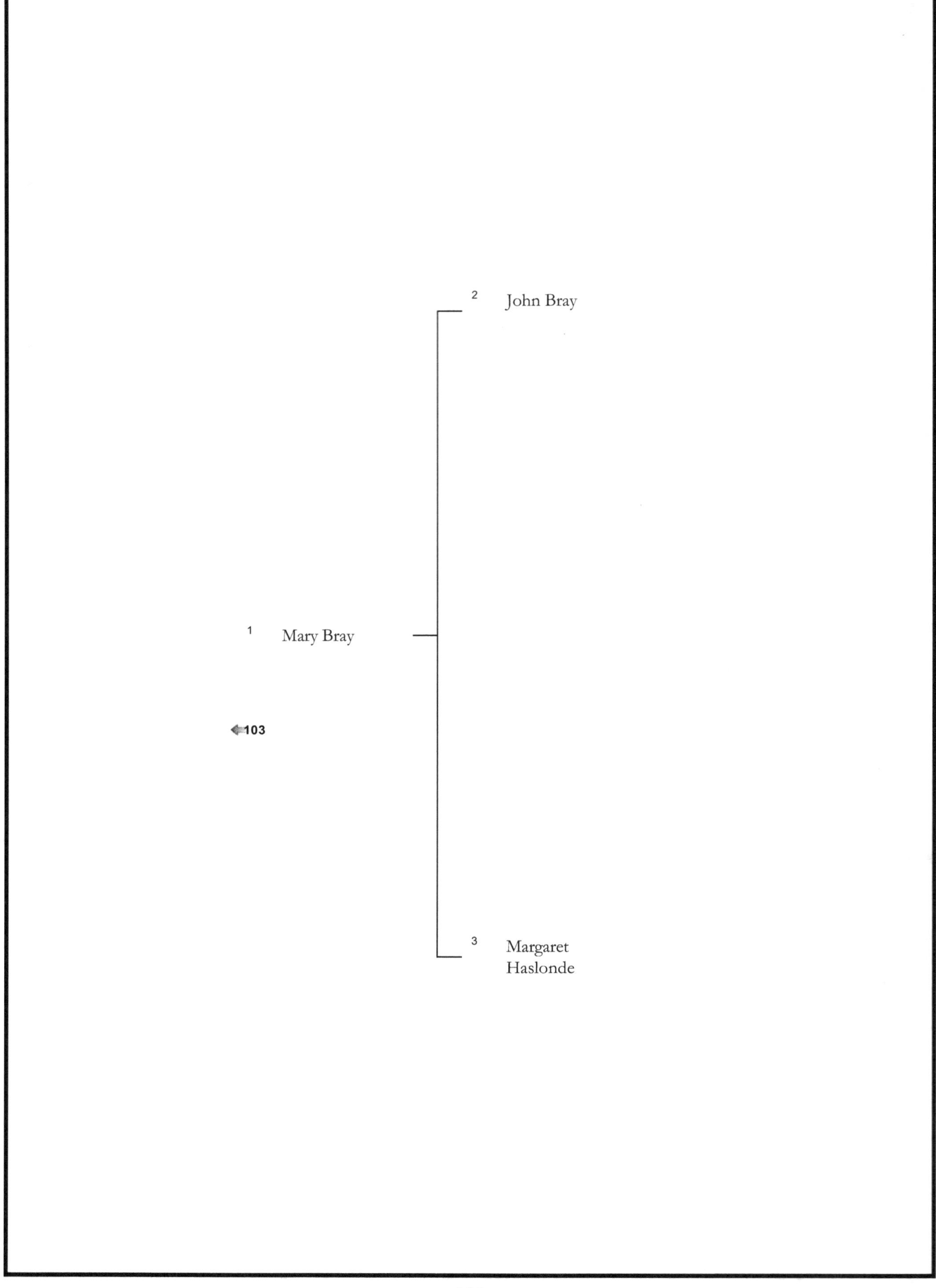

1 Mary Bray
2 John Bray
3 Margaret Haslonde
103

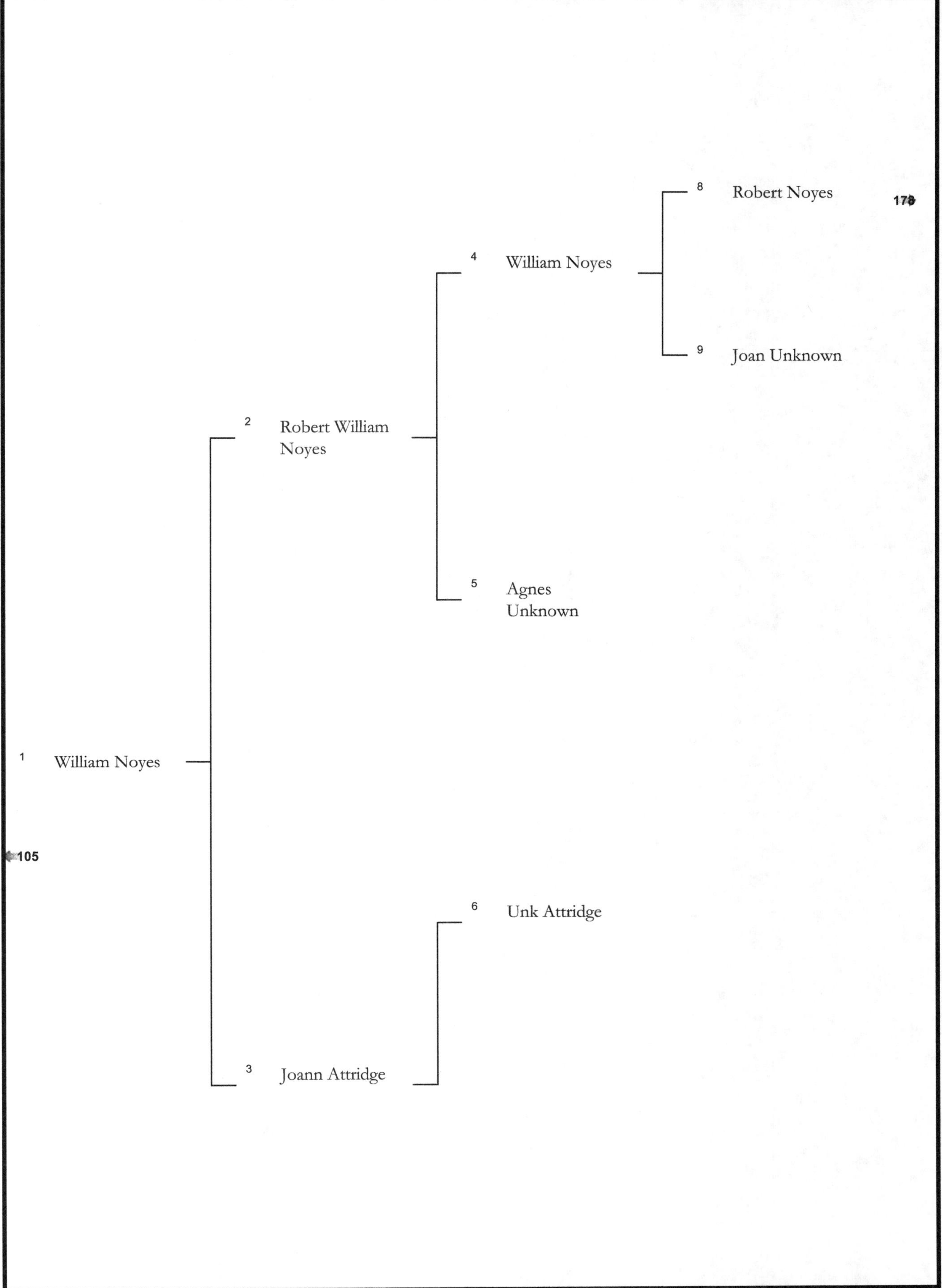

8 Robert Noyes
173
4 William Noyes
9 Joan Unknown
2 Robert William Noyes
5 Agnes Unknown
1 William Noyes
105
6 Unk Attridge
3 Joann Attridge

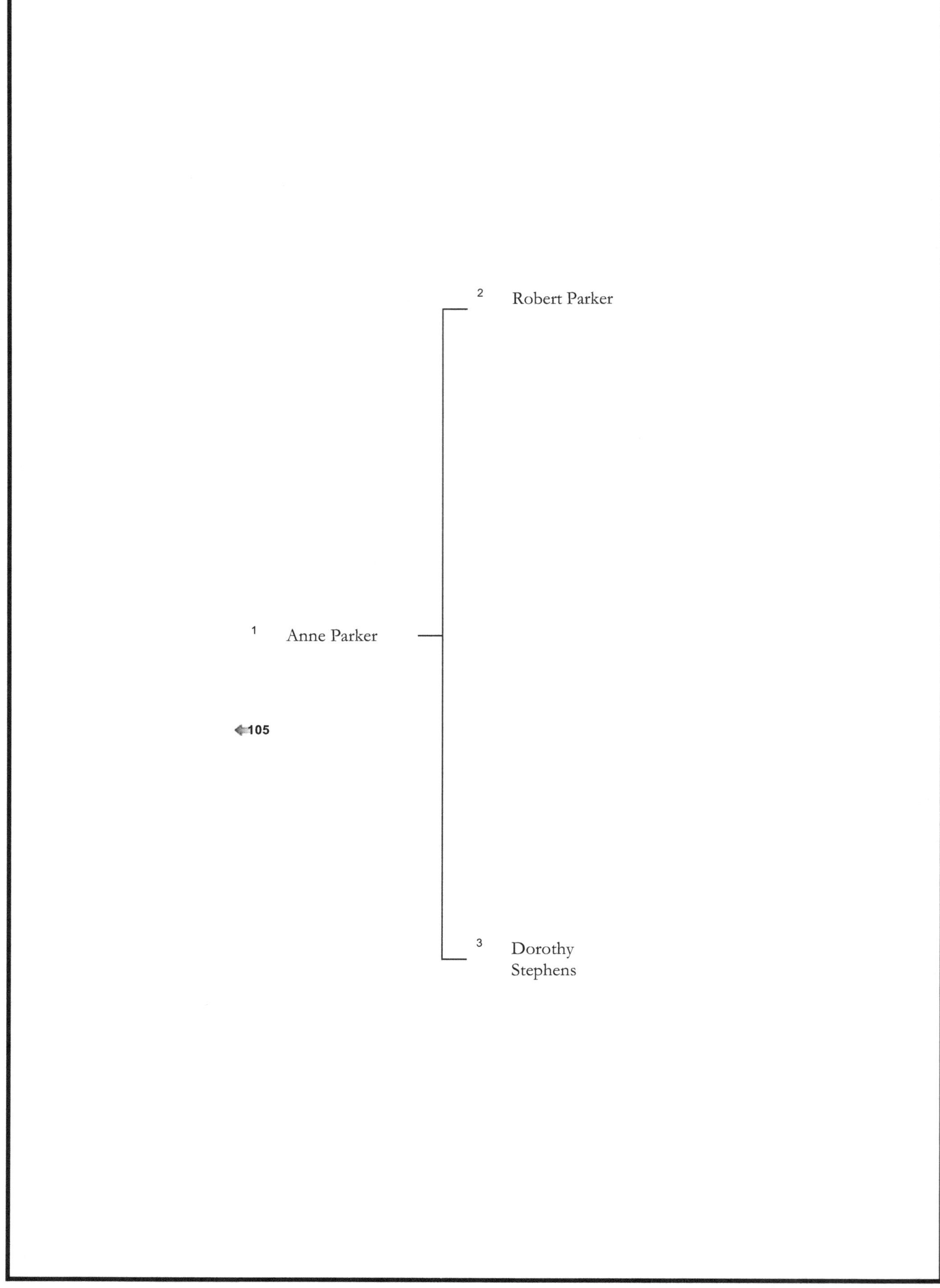

2 Robert Parker
1 Anne Parker
105
3 Dorothy Stephens

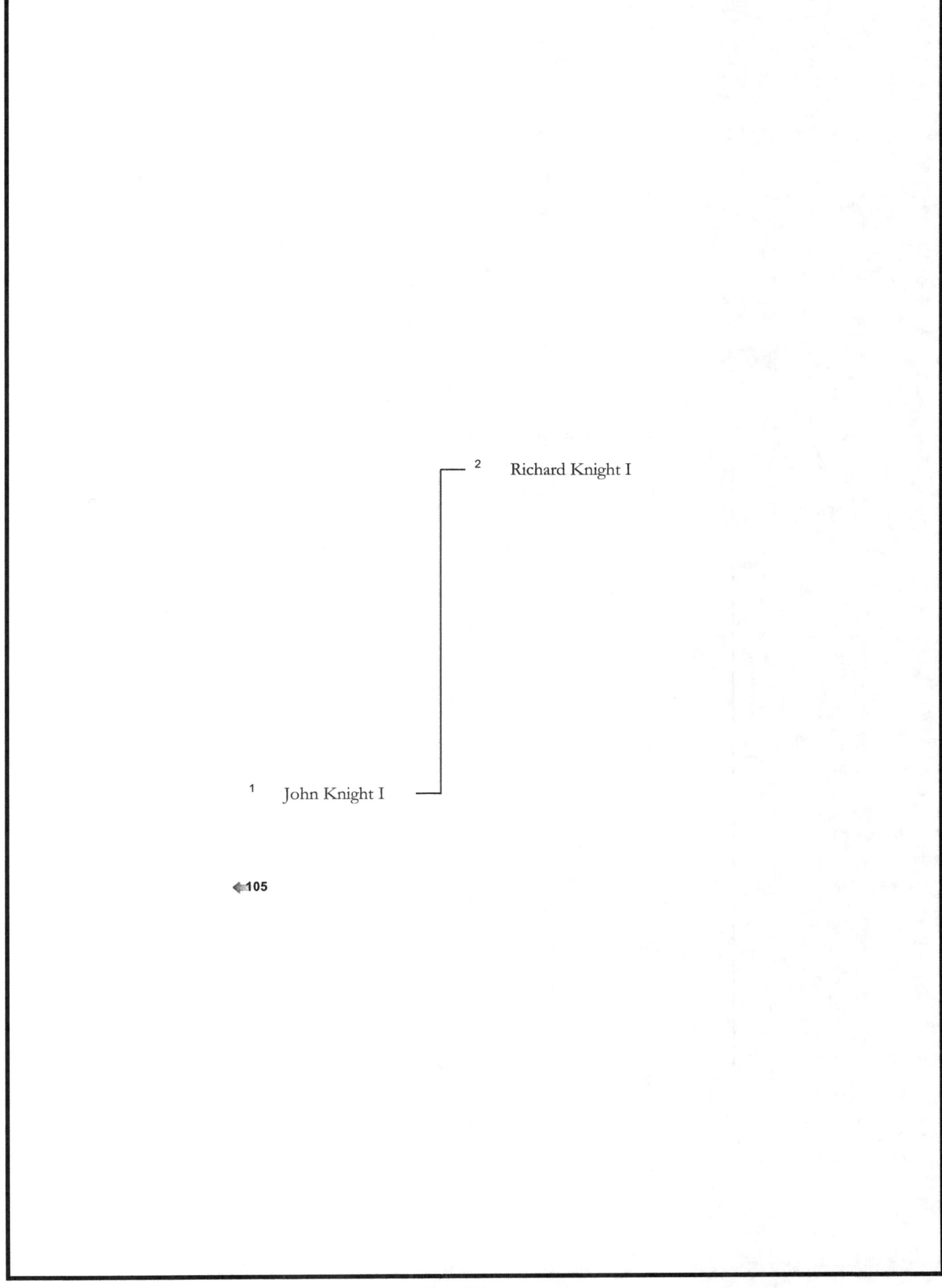

2 Richard Knight I
1 John Knight I
105

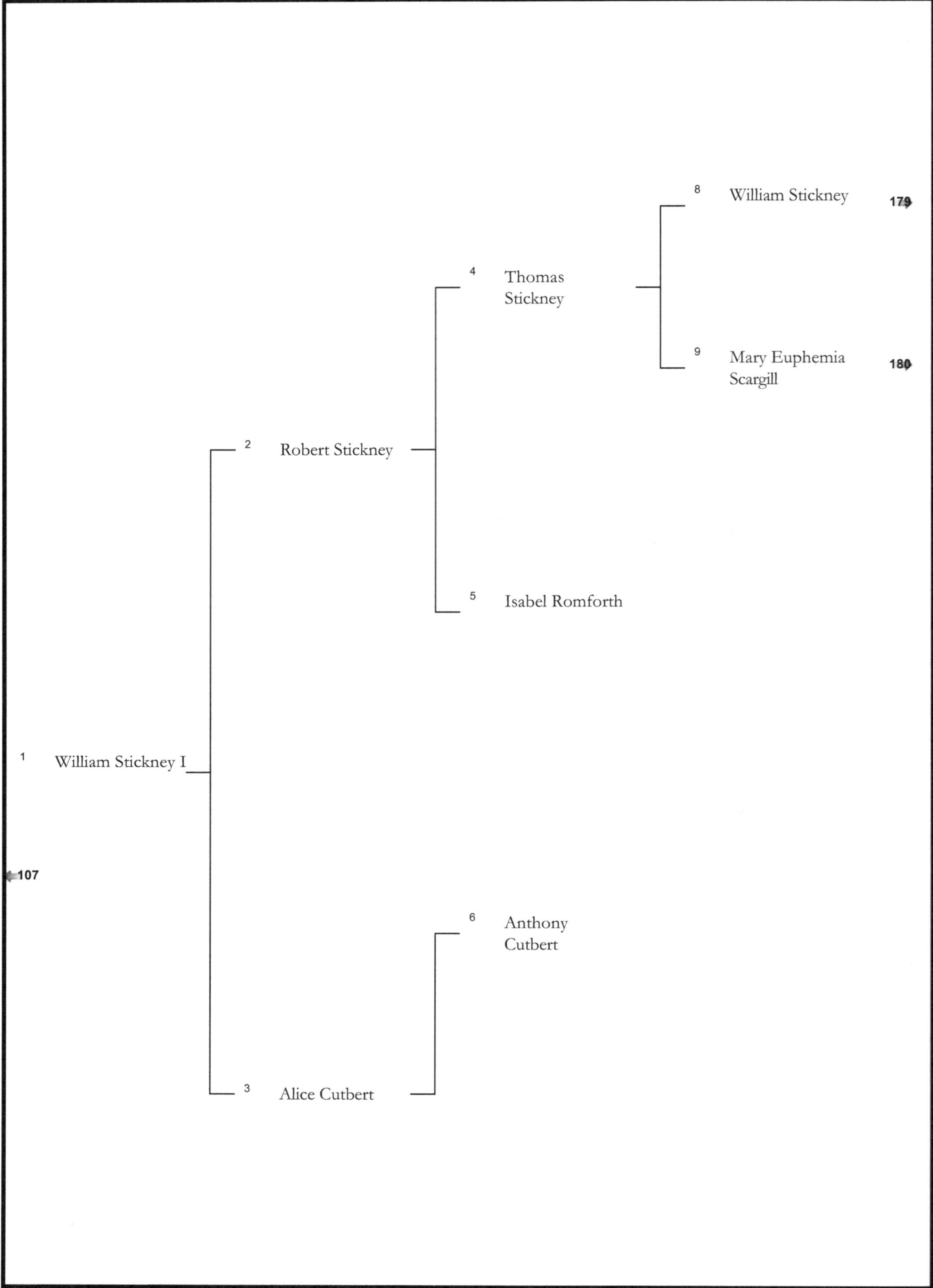

1 William Stickney I
107
2 Robert Stickney
4 Thomas Stickney
8 William Stickney 179
9 Mary Euphemia Scargill 180
5 Isabel Romforth
3 Alice Cutbert
6 Anthony Cutbert

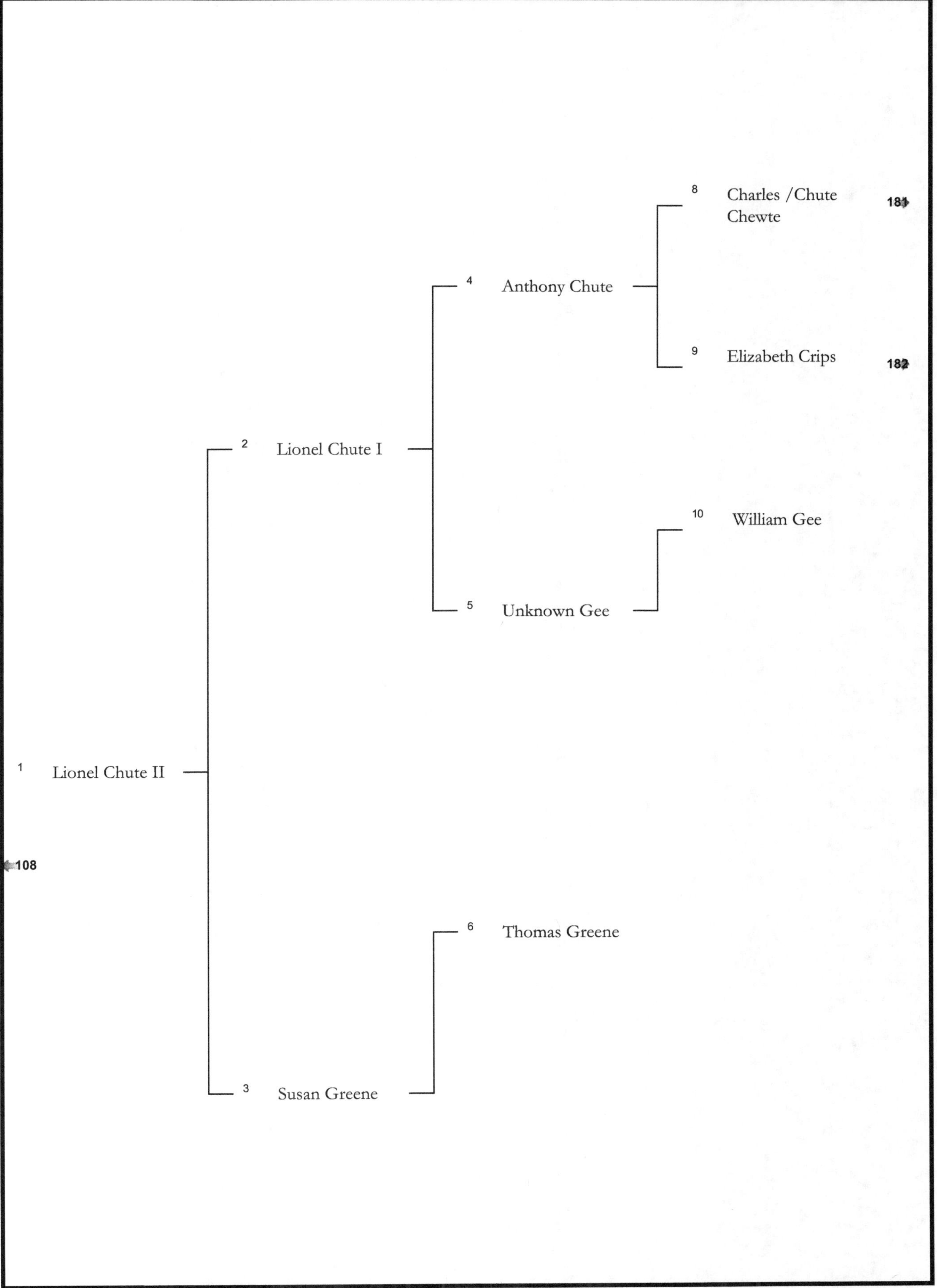

1 Lionel Chute II
2 Lionel Chute I
3 Susan Greene
4 Anthony Chute
5 Unknown Gee
6 Thomas Greene
8 Charles /Chute Chewte
181
9 Elizabeth Crips
182
10 William Gee
108

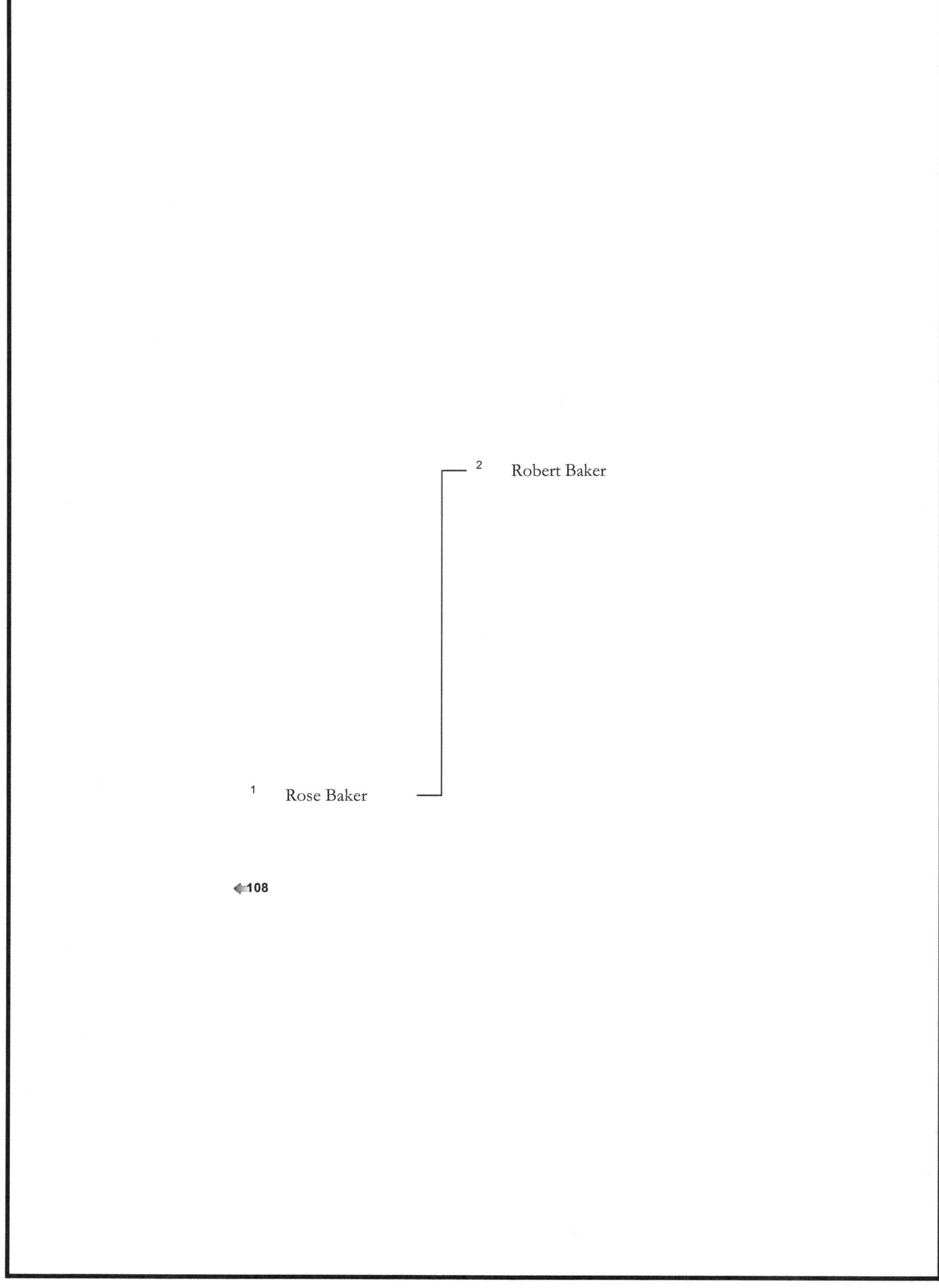

2 Robert Baker
1 Rose Baker
108

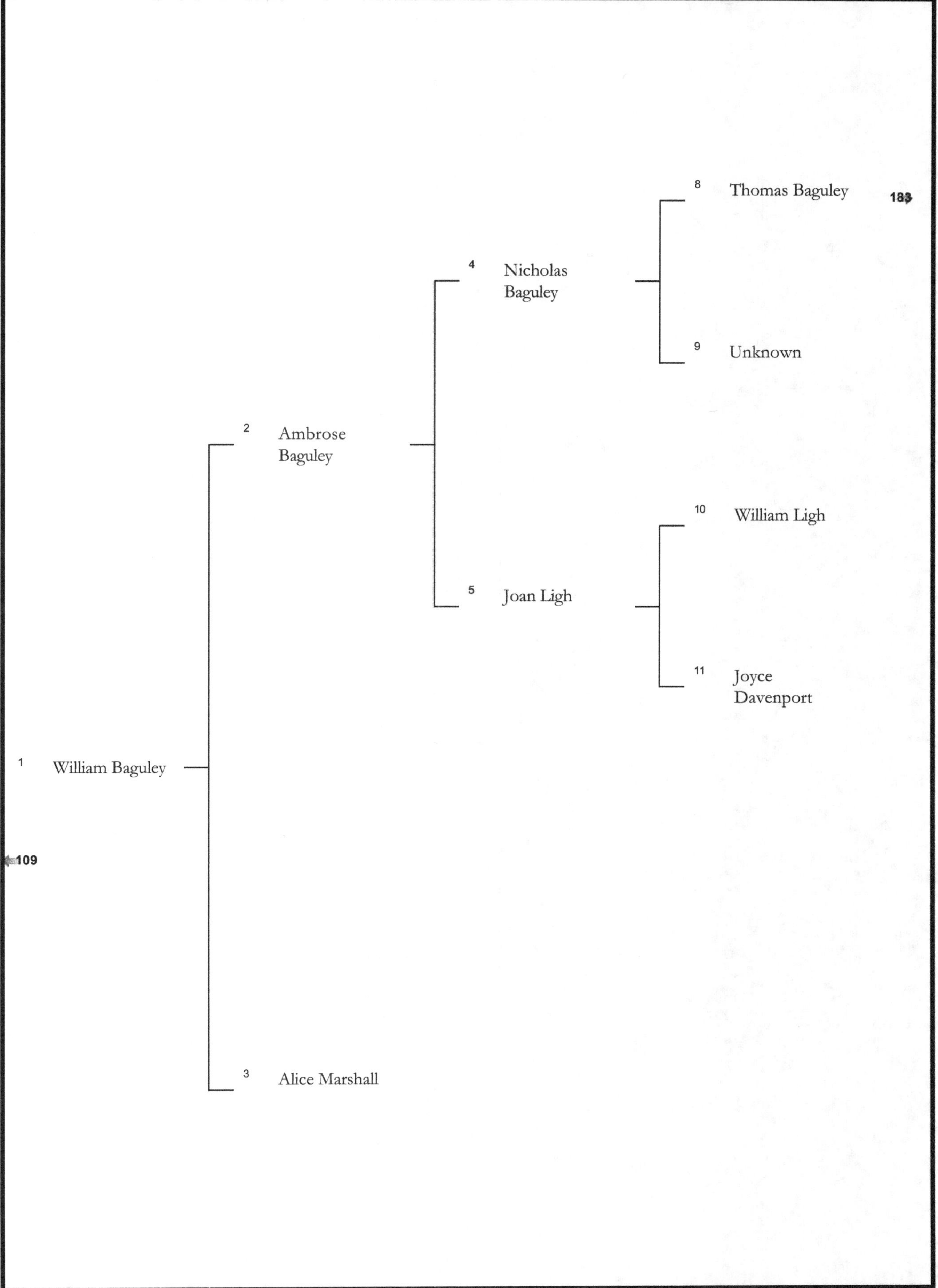

8 Thomas Baguley
183
4 Nicholas Baguley
9 Unknown
2 Ambrose Baguley
10 William Ligh
5 Joan Ligh
11 Joyce Davenport
1 William Baguley
109
3 Alice Marshall

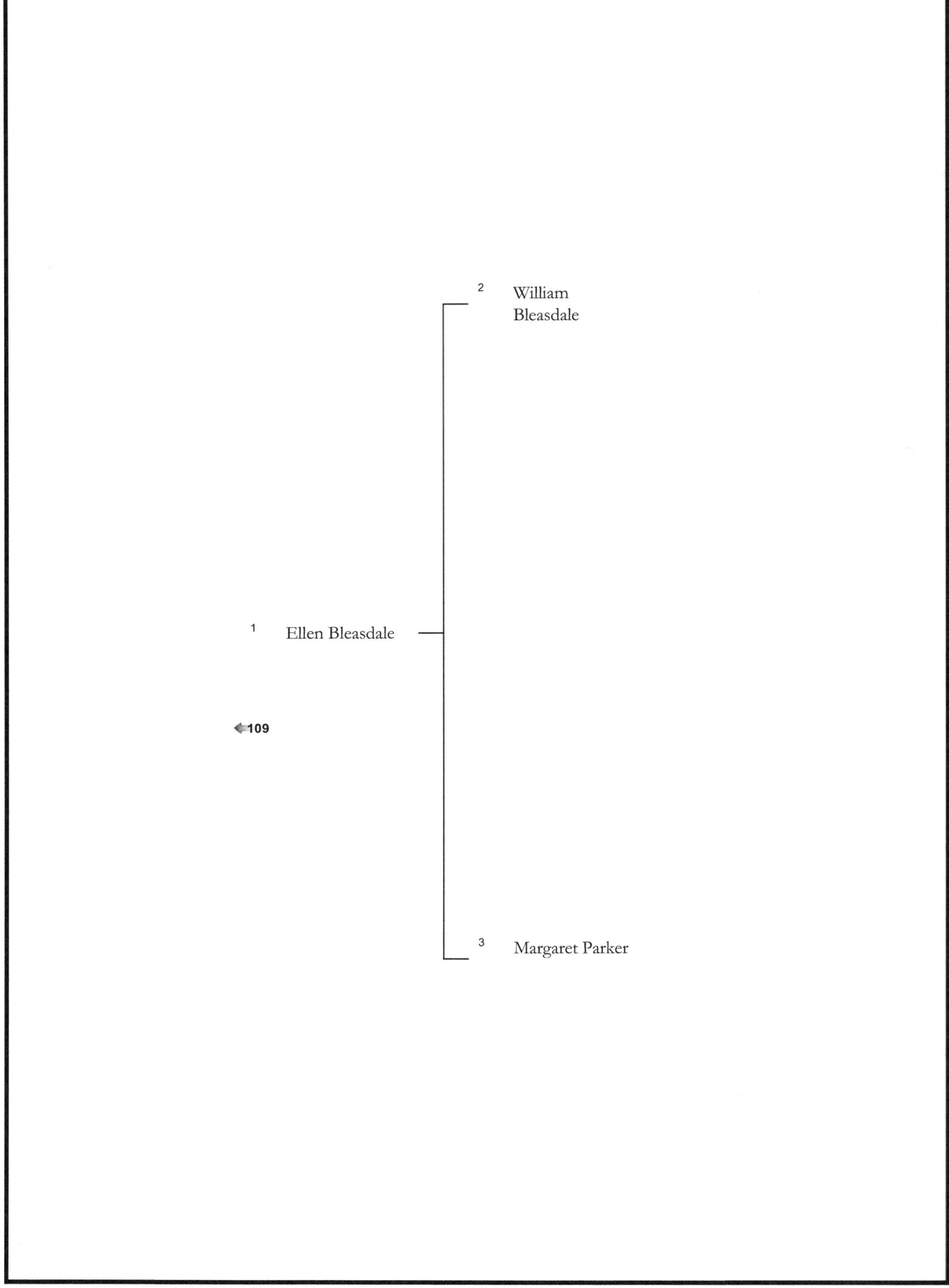
2 William
Bleasdale

1 Ellen Bleasdale

109

3 Margaret Parker

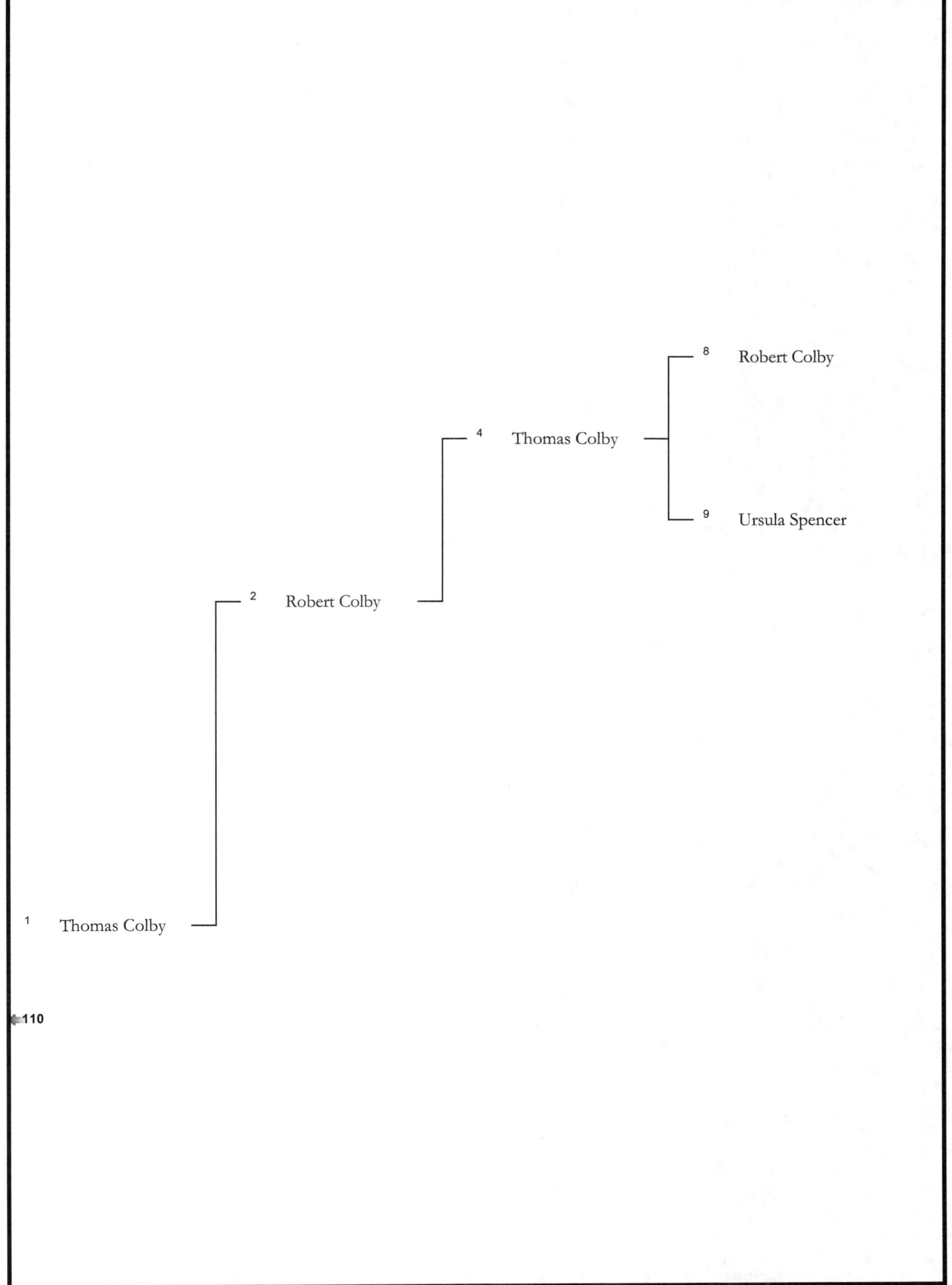

8 Robert Colby
4 Thomas Colby
9 Ursula Spencer
2 Robert Colby
1 Thomas Colby
110

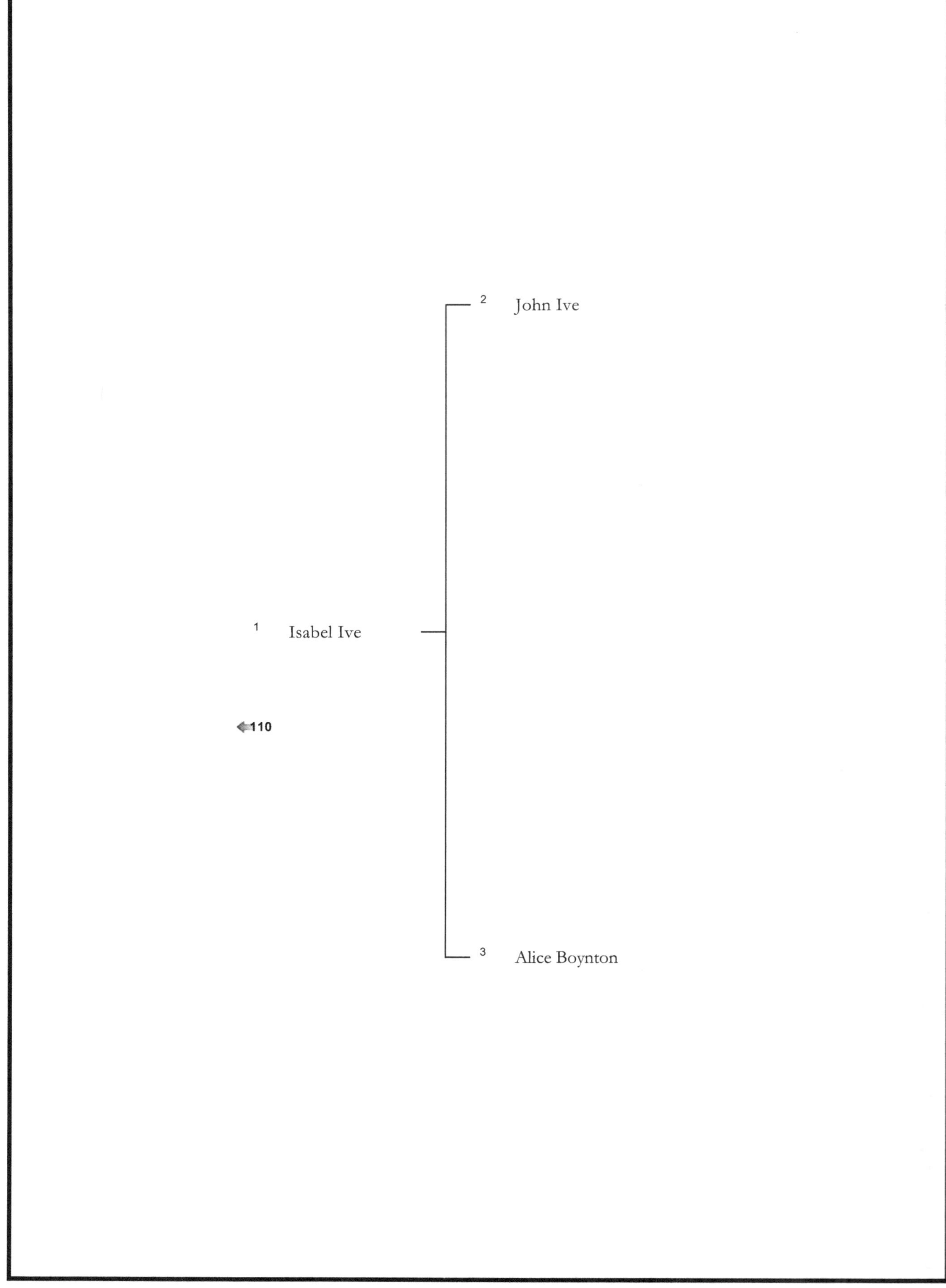

2 John Ive
1 Isabel Ive
110
3 Alice Boynton

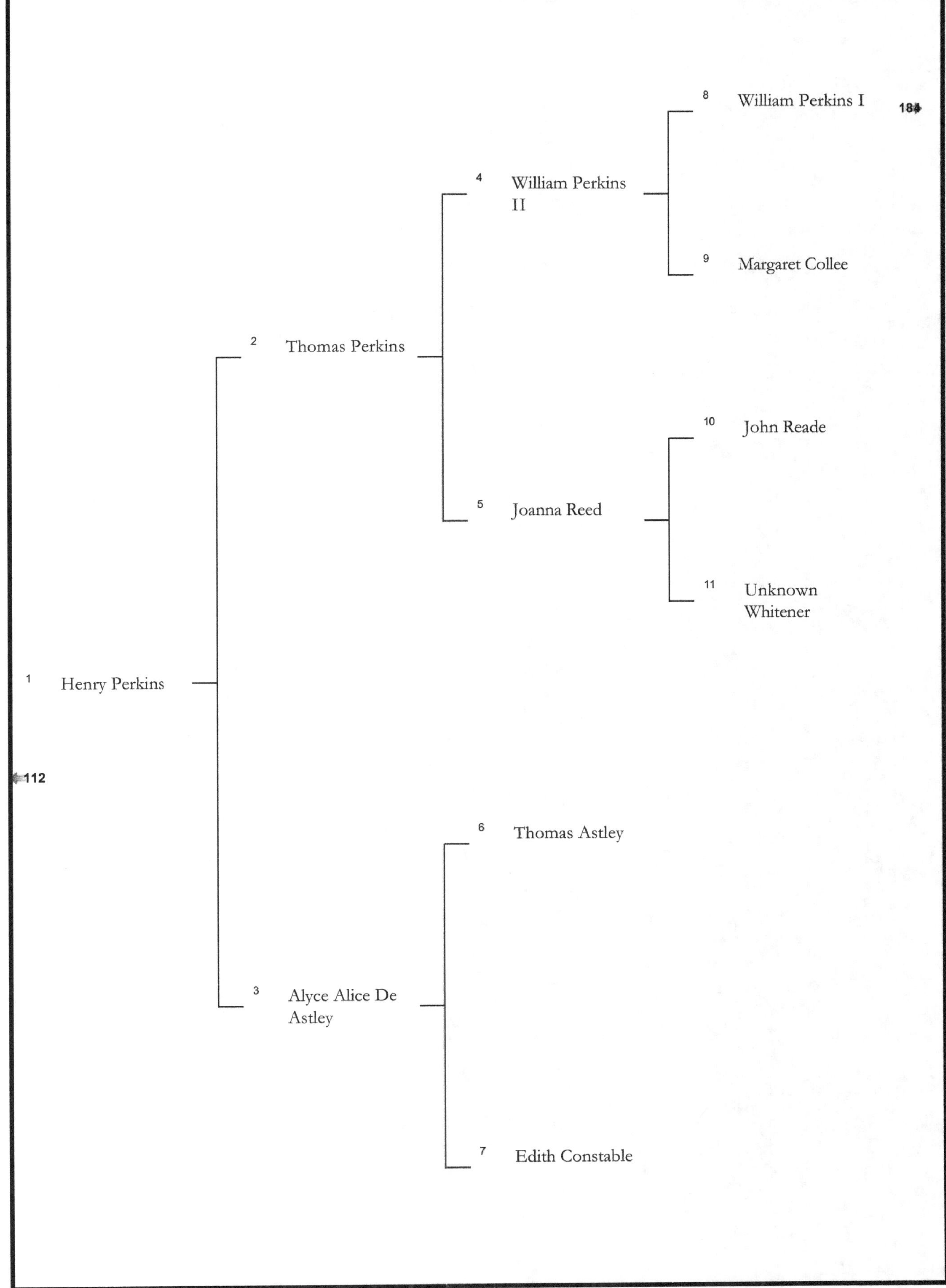

8 William Perkins I
18#
4 William Perkins II
9 Margaret Collee
2 Thomas Perkins
10 John Reade
5 Joanna Reed
11 Unknown Whitener
1 Henry Perkins
112
6 Thomas Astley
3 Alyce Alice De Astley
7 Edith Constable

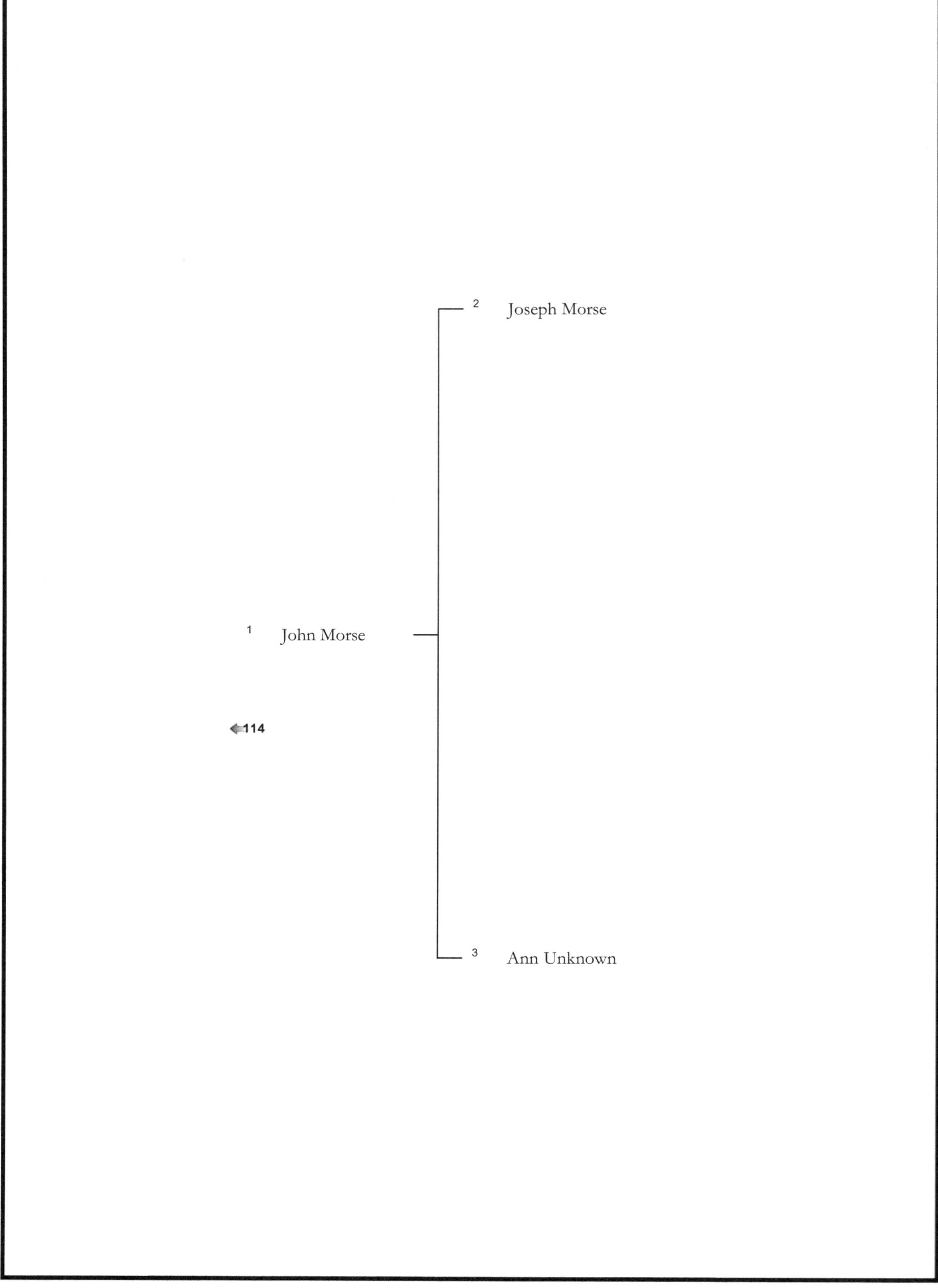

1 John Morse
2 Joseph Morse
3 Ann Unknown
114

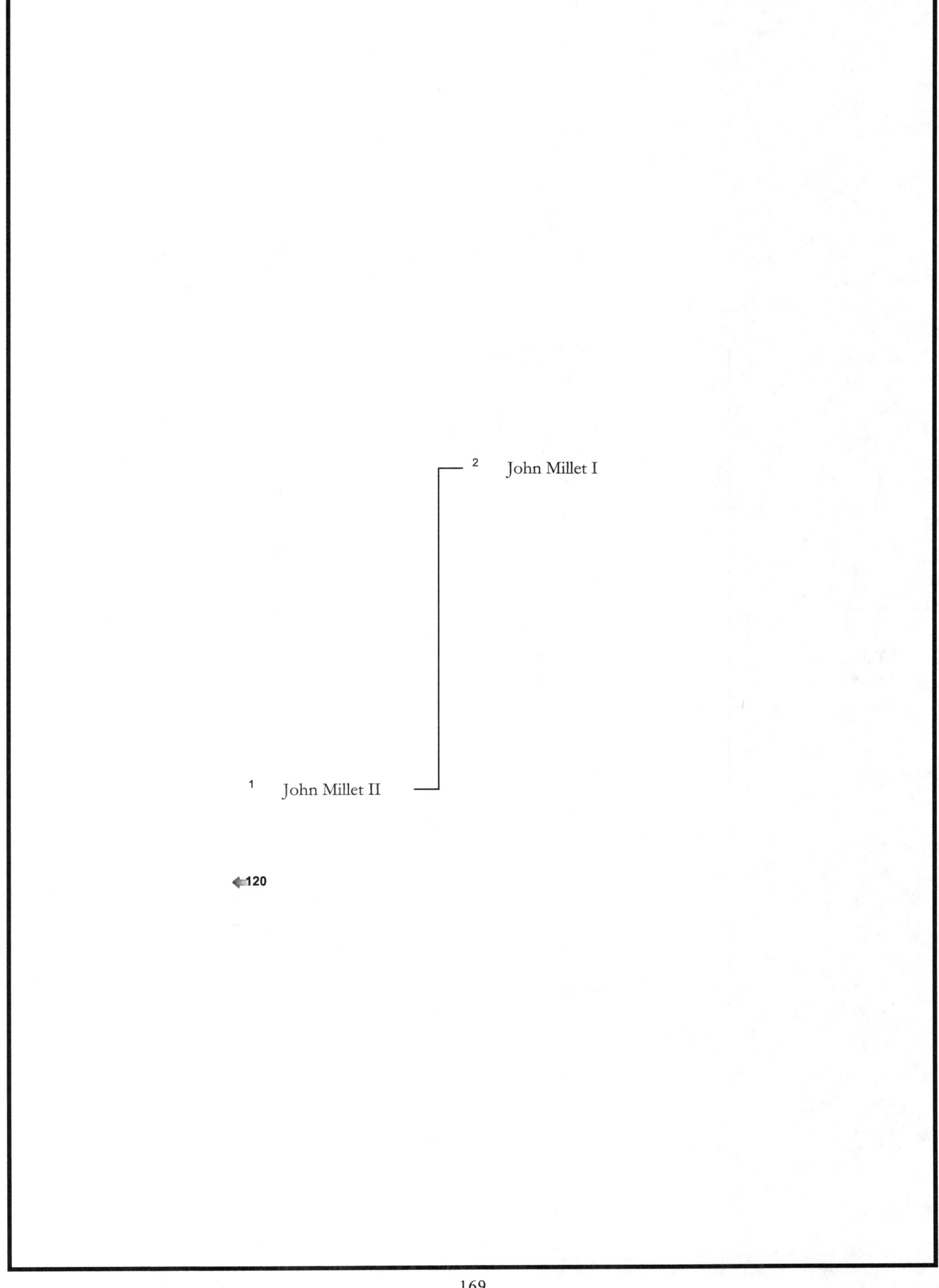

2 John Millet I
1 John Millet II
120

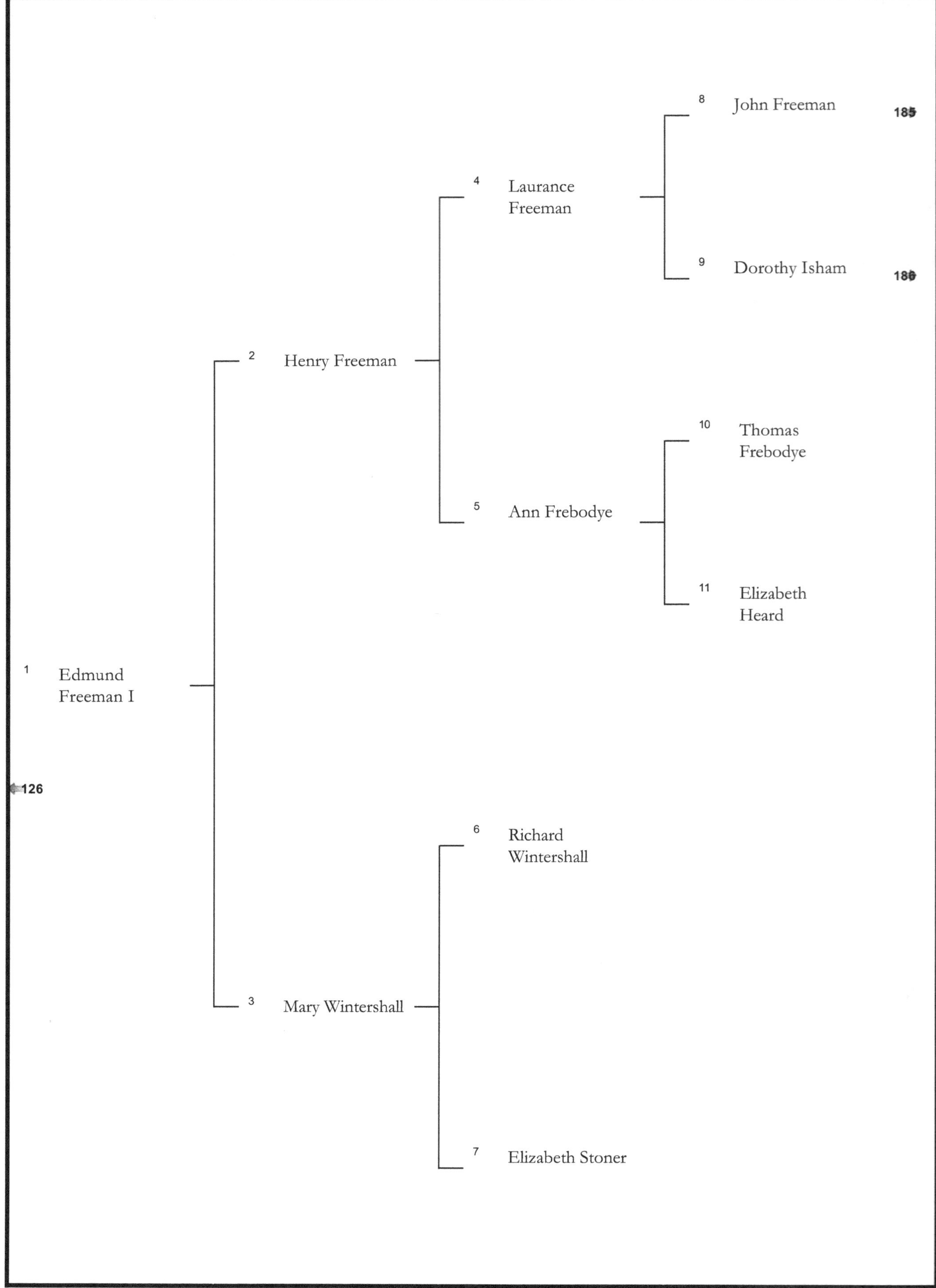

1 Edmund Freeman I
126
2 Henry Freeman
3 Mary Wintershall
4 Laurance Freeman
5 Ann Frebodye
6 Richard Wintershall
7 Elizabeth Stoner
8 John Freeman 185
9 Dorothy Isham 186
10 Thomas Frebodye
11 Elizabeth Heard

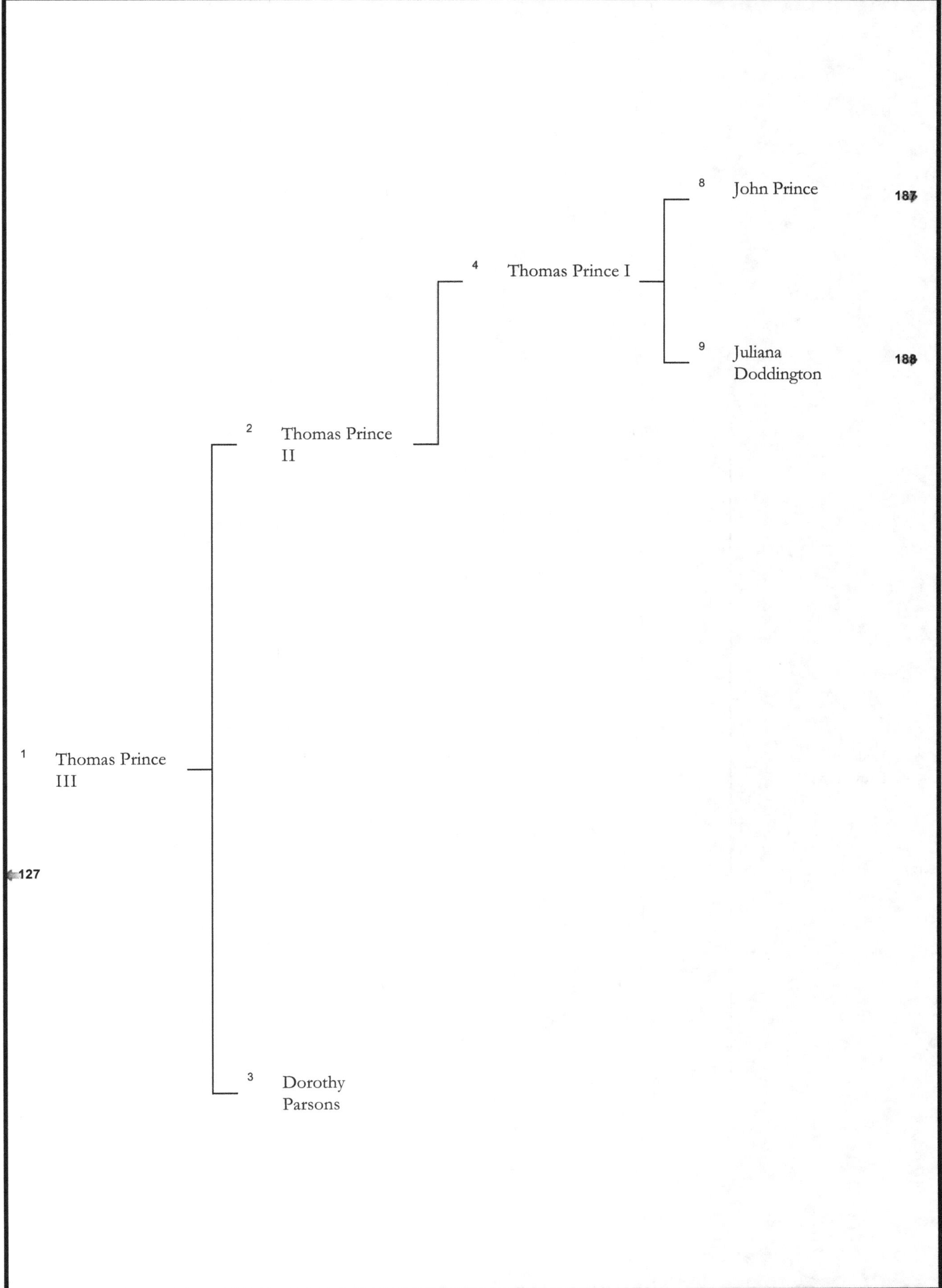

1 Thomas Prince III
127
2 Thomas Prince II
3 Dorothy Parsons
4 Thomas Prince I
8 John Prince
187
9 Juliana Doddington
188

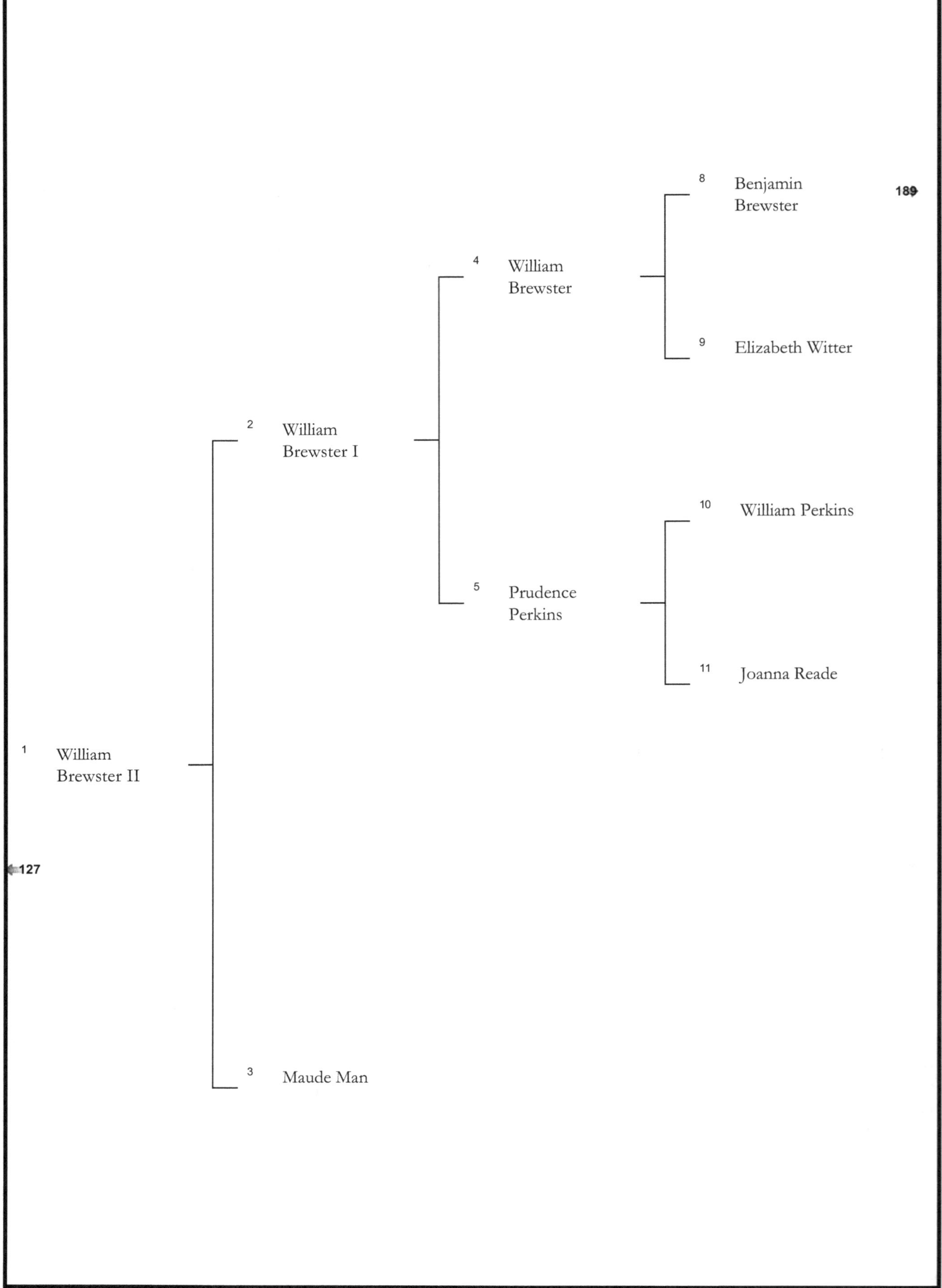
8 Benjamin Brewster
189
4 William Brewster
9 Elizabeth Witter
2 William Brewster I
10 William Perkins
5 Prudence Perkins
11 Joanna Reade
1 William Brewster II
127
3 Maude Man

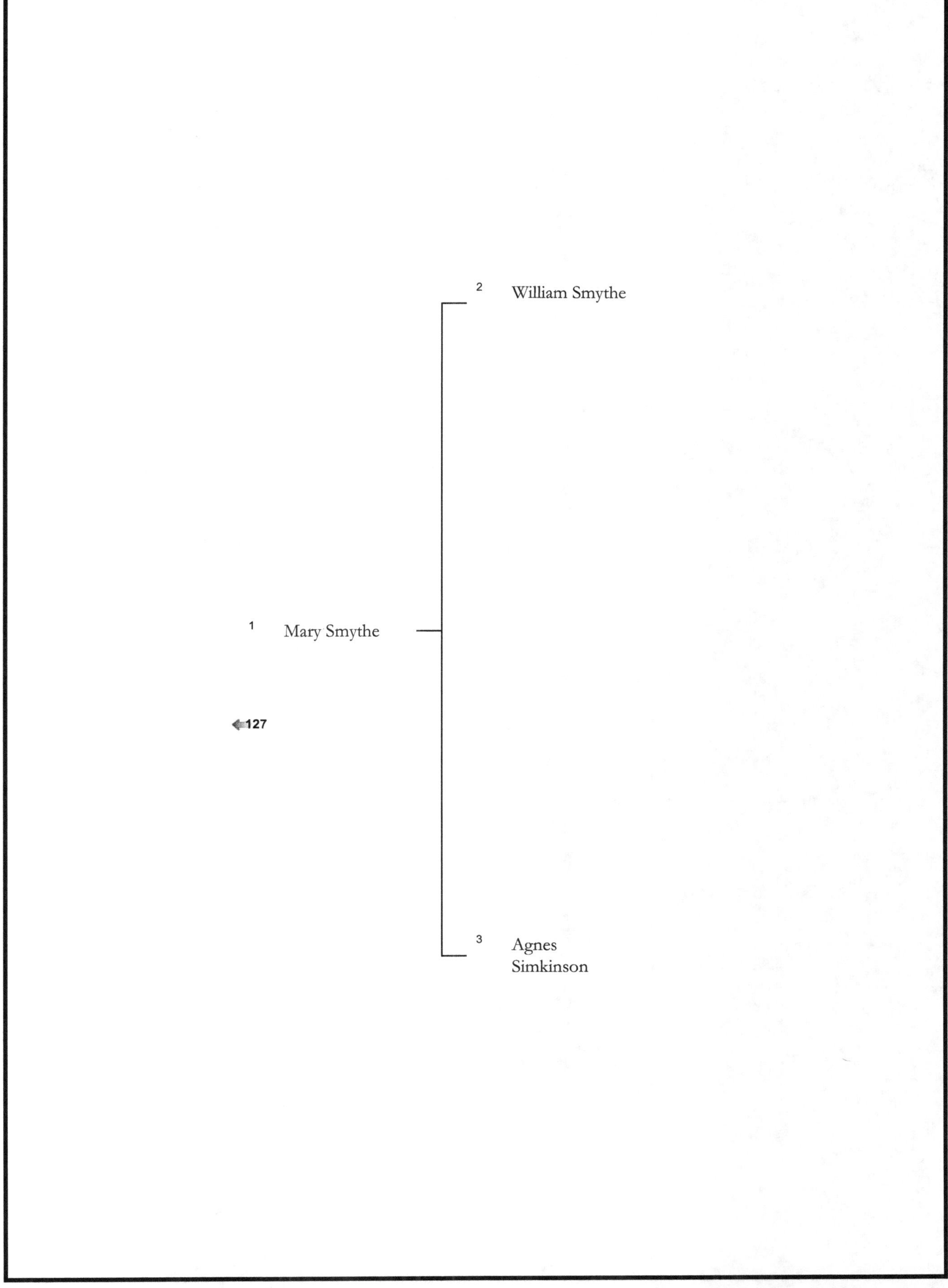

2 William Smythe
1 Mary Smythe
127
3 Agnes
Simkinson

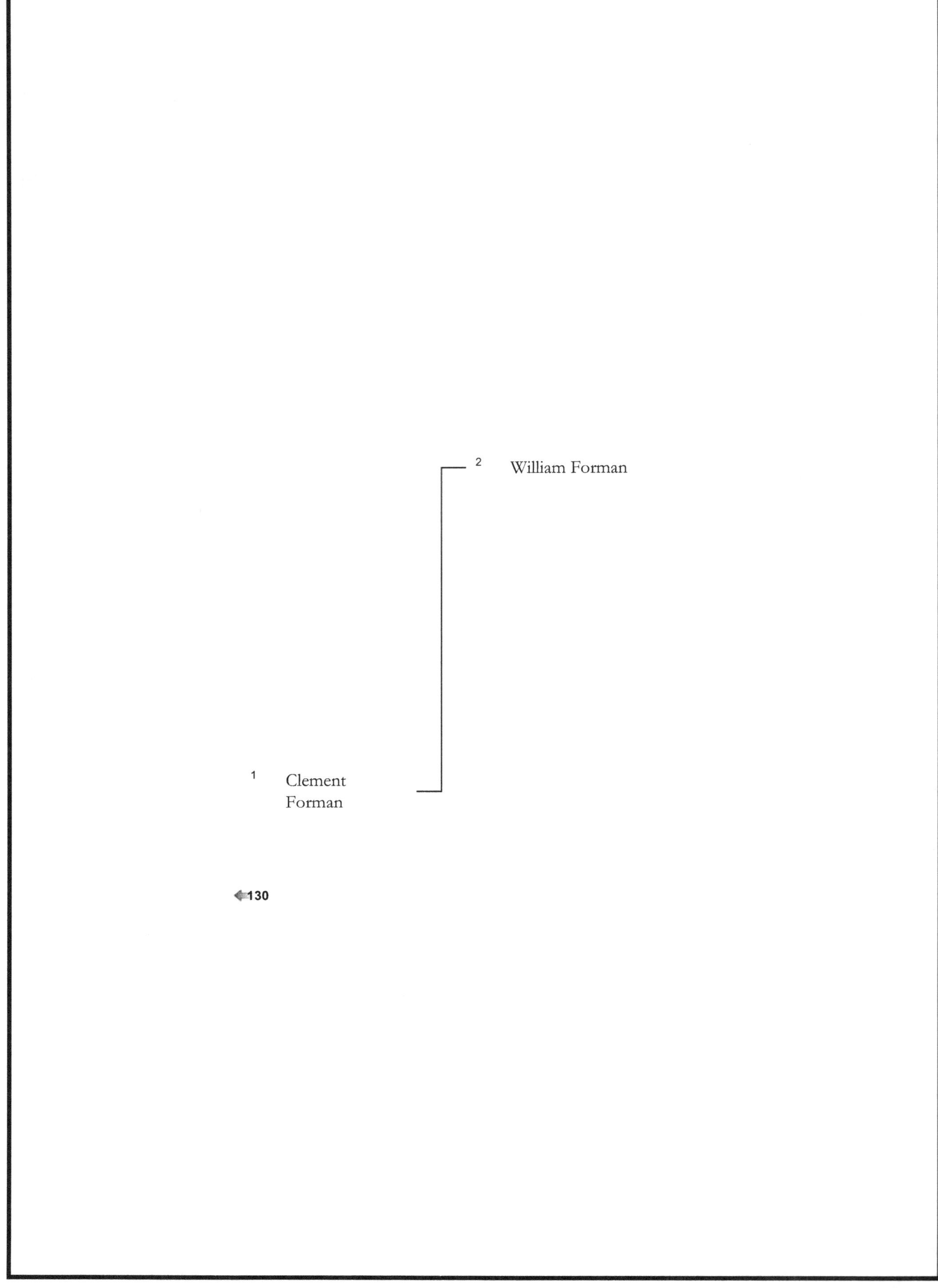

2 William Forman
1 Clement
Forman
130

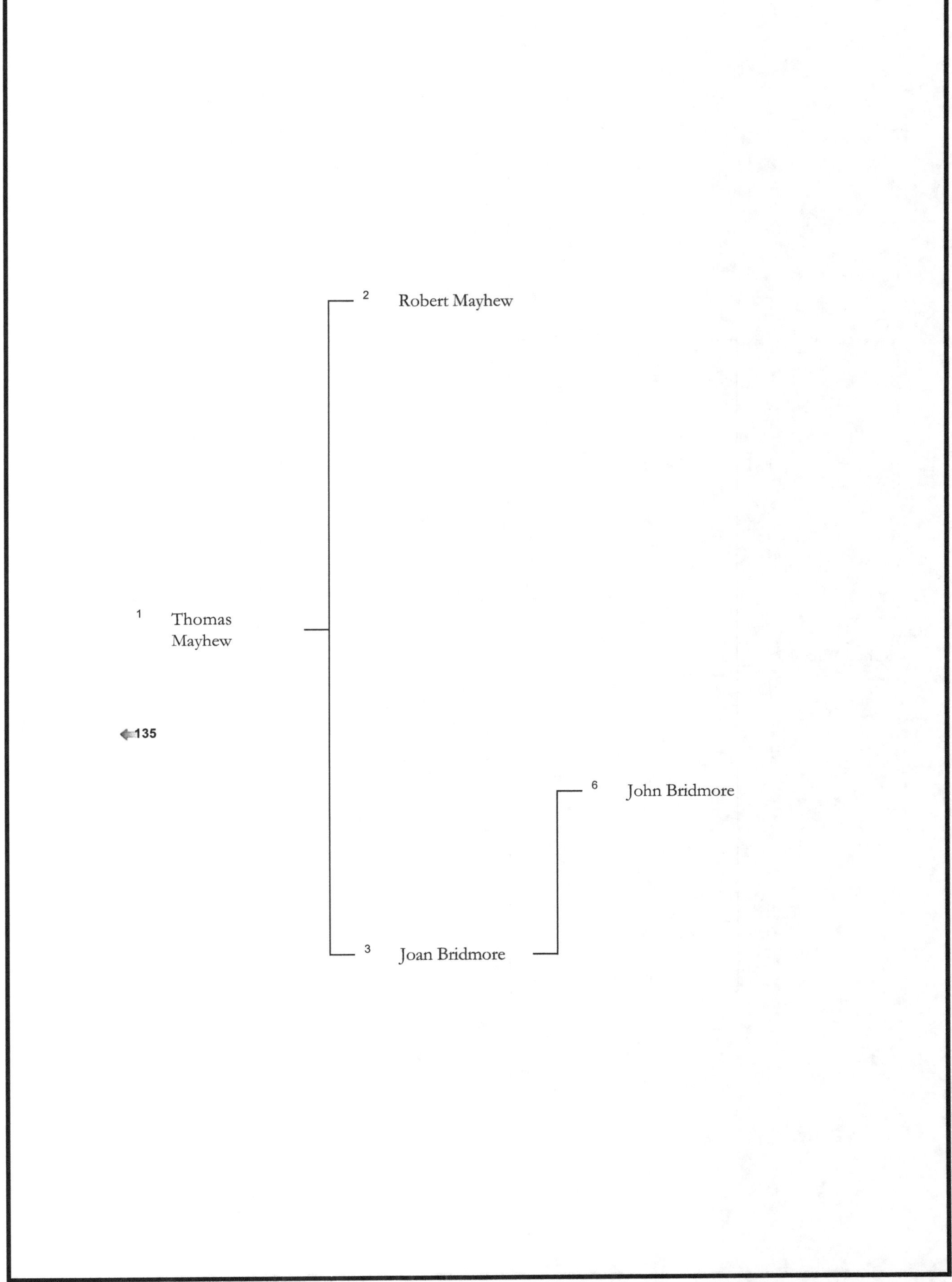

1 Thomas Mayhew
2 Robert Mayhew
3 Joan Bridmore
6 John Bridmore
135

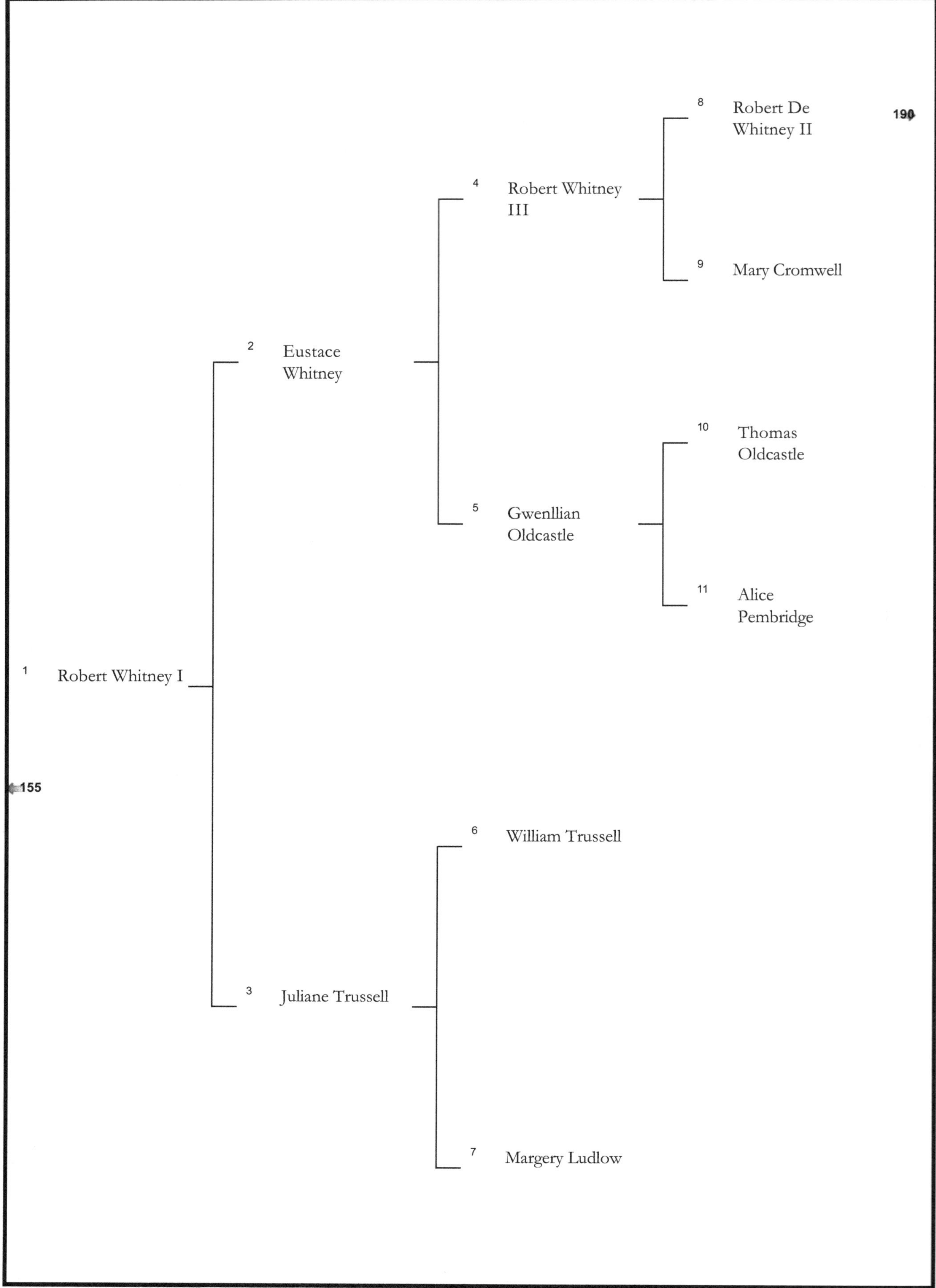

1 Robert Whitney I
2 Eustace Whitney
3 Juliane Trussell
4 Robert Whitney III
5 Gwenllian Oldcastle
6 William Trussell
7 Margery Ludlow
8 Robert De Whitney II
9 Mary Cromwell
10 Thomas Oldcastle
11 Alice Pembridge
155

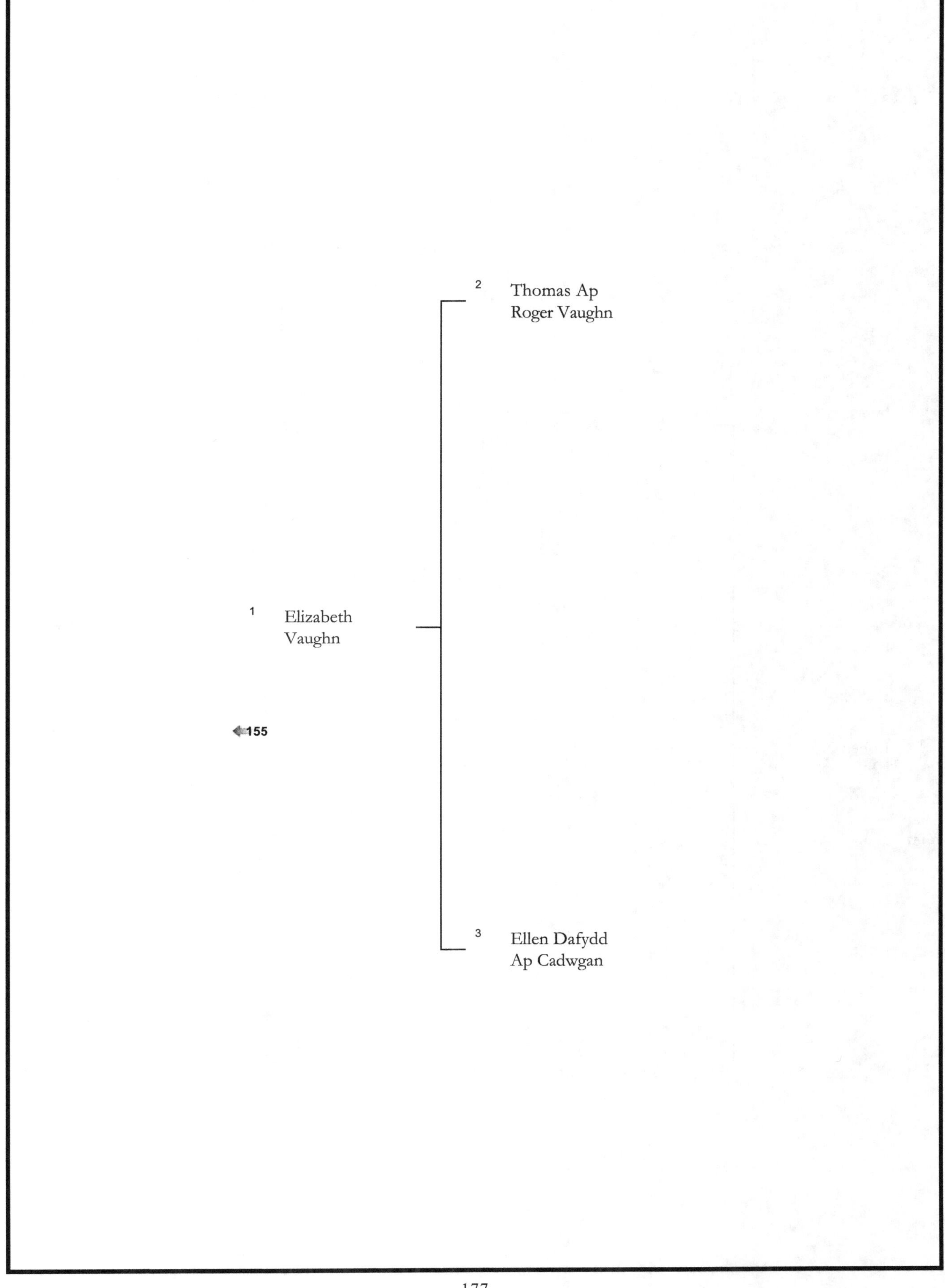

1 Elizabeth Vaughn
2 Thomas Ap Roger Vaughn
3 Ellen Dafydd Ap Cadwgan
155

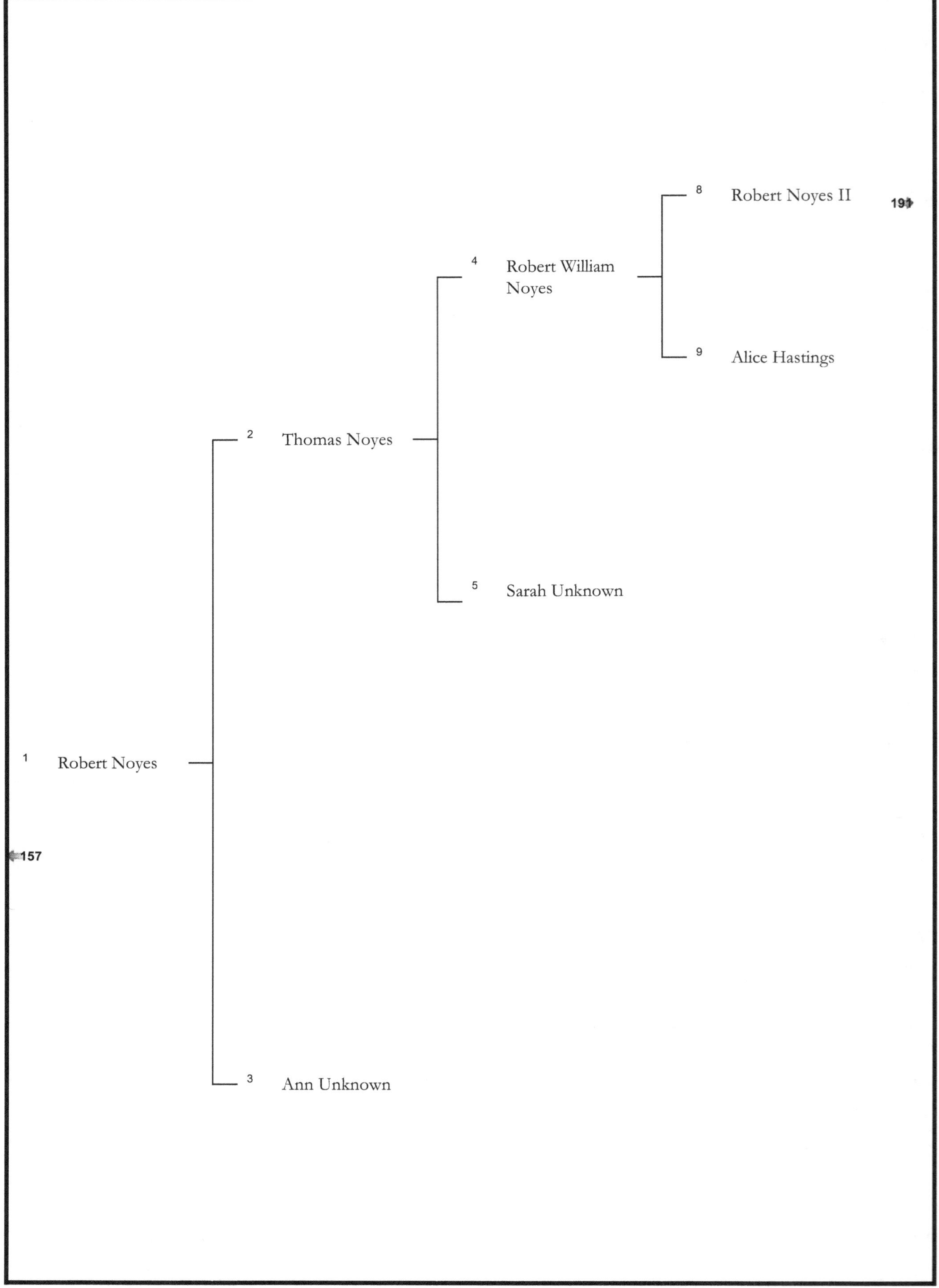

8 Robert Noyes II
19?
4 Robert William Noyes
9 Alice Hastings
2 Thomas Noyes
5 Sarah Unknown
1 Robert Noyes
157
3 Ann Unknown

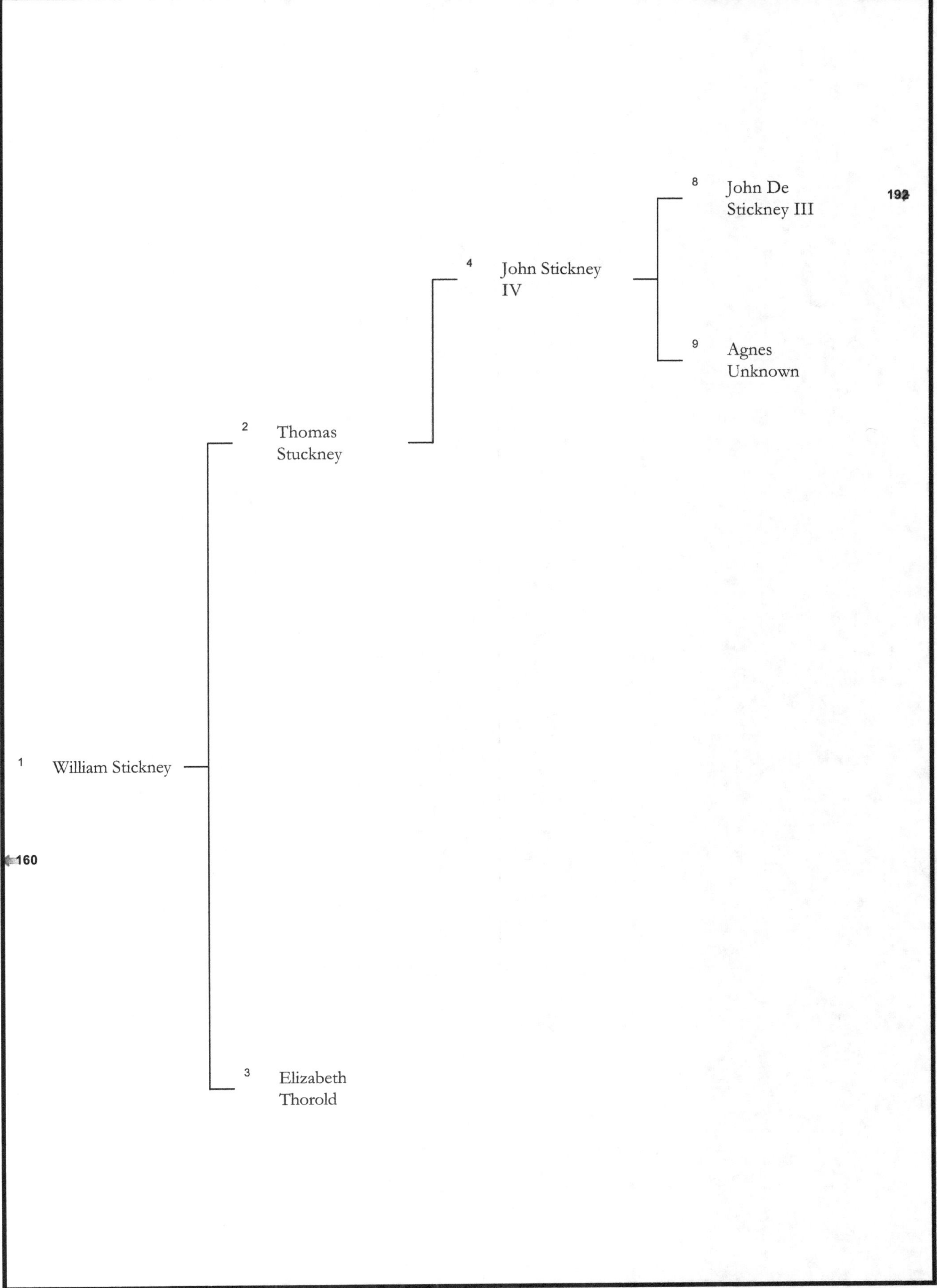

192
1 William Stickney
2 Thomas Stuckney
3 Elizabeth Thorold
4 John Stickney IV
8 John De Stickney III
9 Agnes Unknown
160

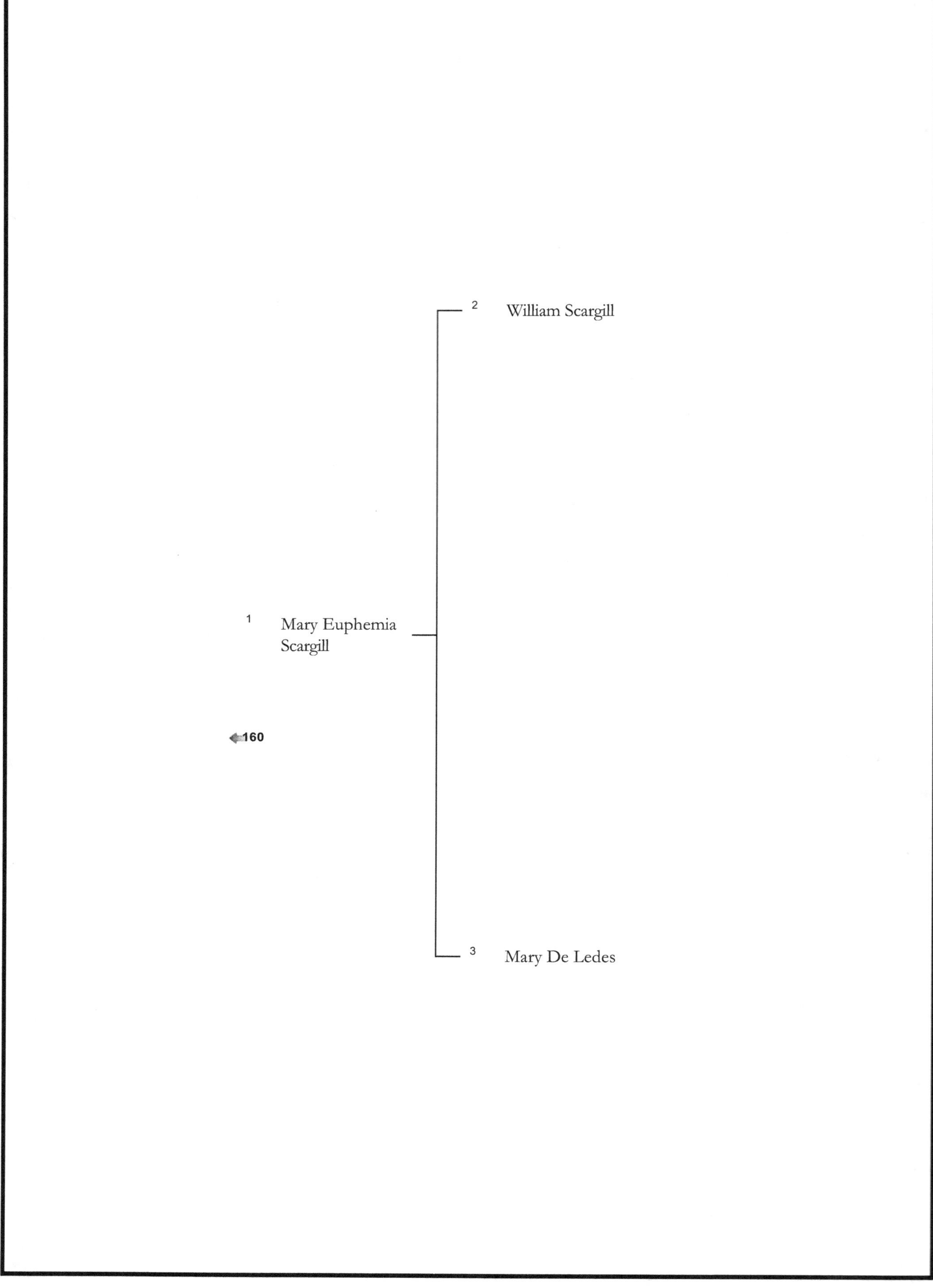

2 William Scargill
1 Mary Euphemia Scargill
160
3 Mary De Ledes

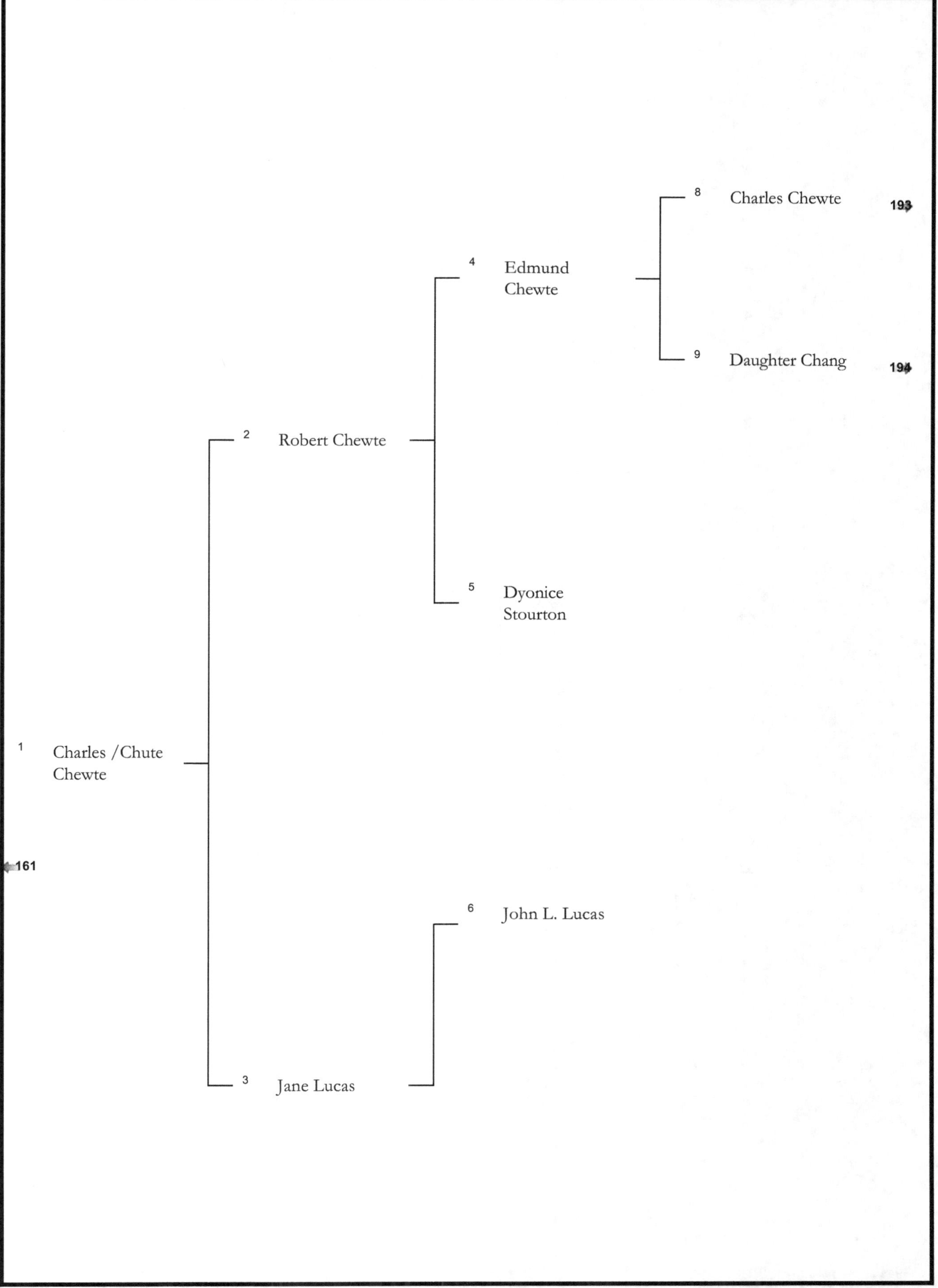

1
Charles /Chute Chewte
161
2
Robert Chewte
3
Jane Lucas
4
Edmund Chewte
5
Dyonice Stourton
6
John L. Lucas
8
Charles Chewte
193
9
Daughter Chang
194

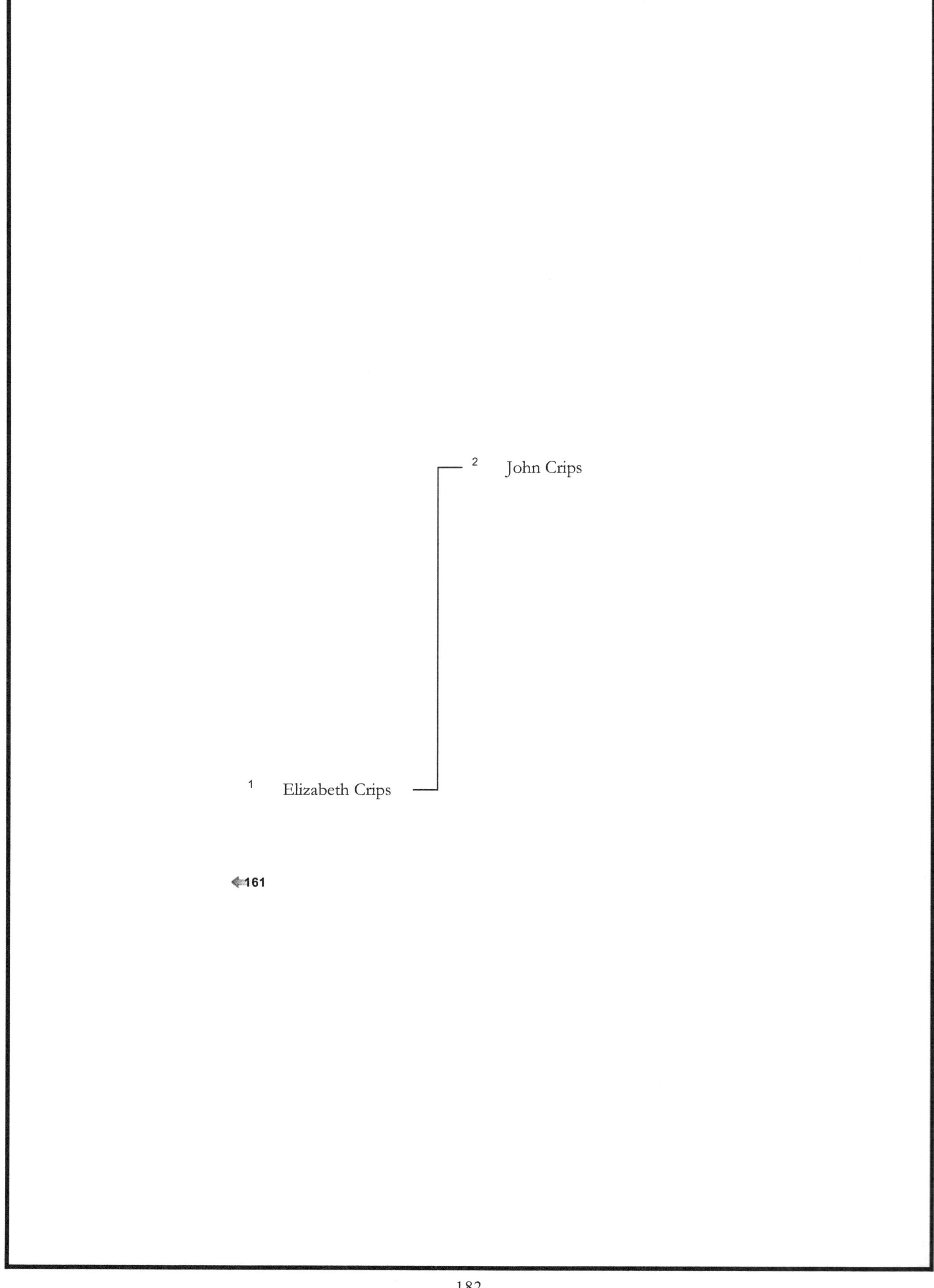

2 John Crips
1 Elizabeth Crips
161

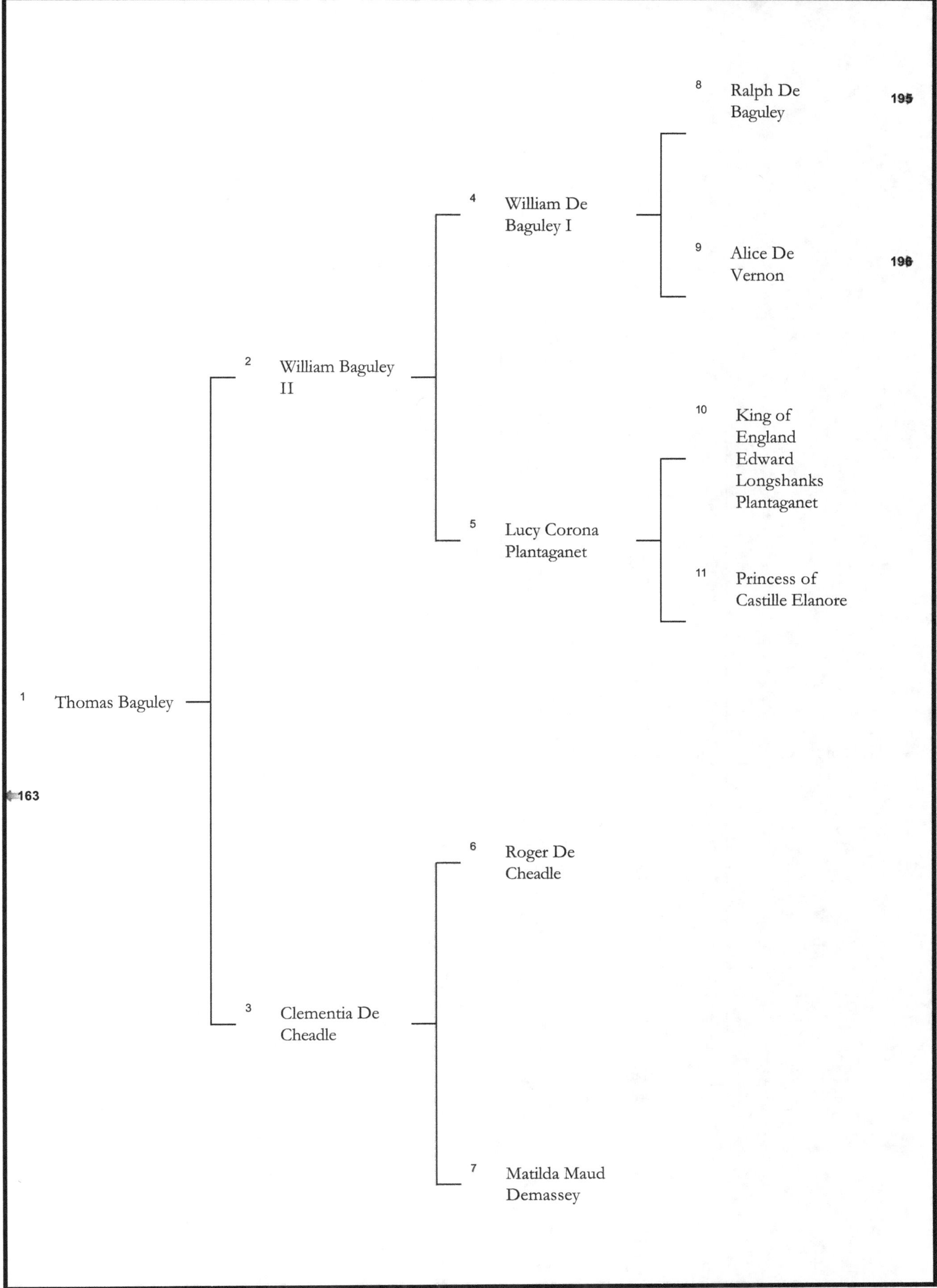

1 Thomas Baguley

2 William Baguley II

3 Clementia De Cheadle

4 William De Baguley I

5 Lucy Corona Plantaganet

6 Roger De Cheadle

7 Matilda Maud Demassey

8 Ralph De Baguley
195

9 Alice De Vernon
196

10 King of England Edward Longshanks Plantaganet

11 Princess of Castille Elanore

163

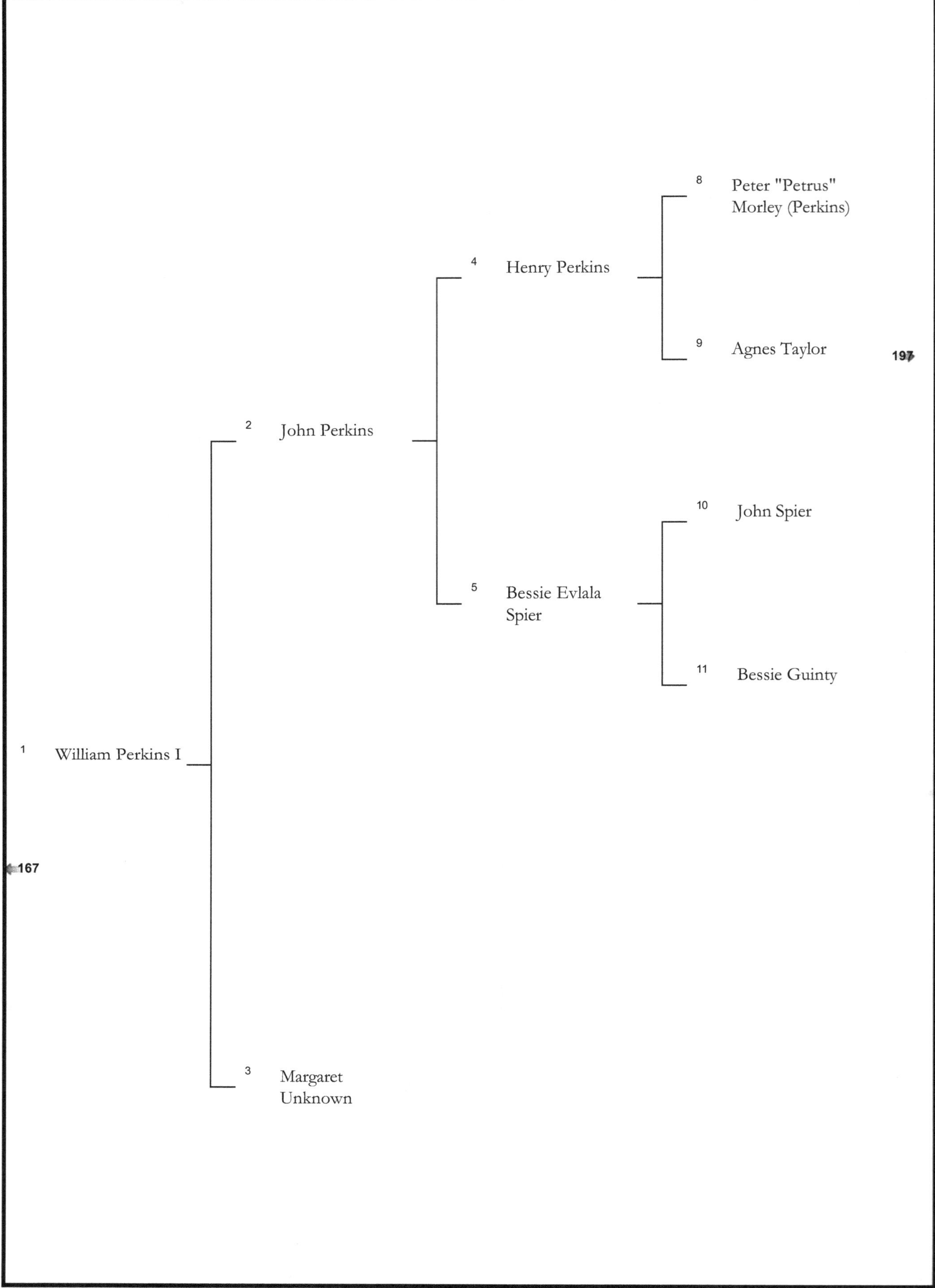

8 Peter "Petrus" Morley (Perkins)
4 Henry Perkins
9 Agnes Taylor
197
2 John Perkins
10 John Spier
5 Bessie Evlala Spier
11 Bessie Guinty
1 William Perkins I
167
3 Margaret Unknown

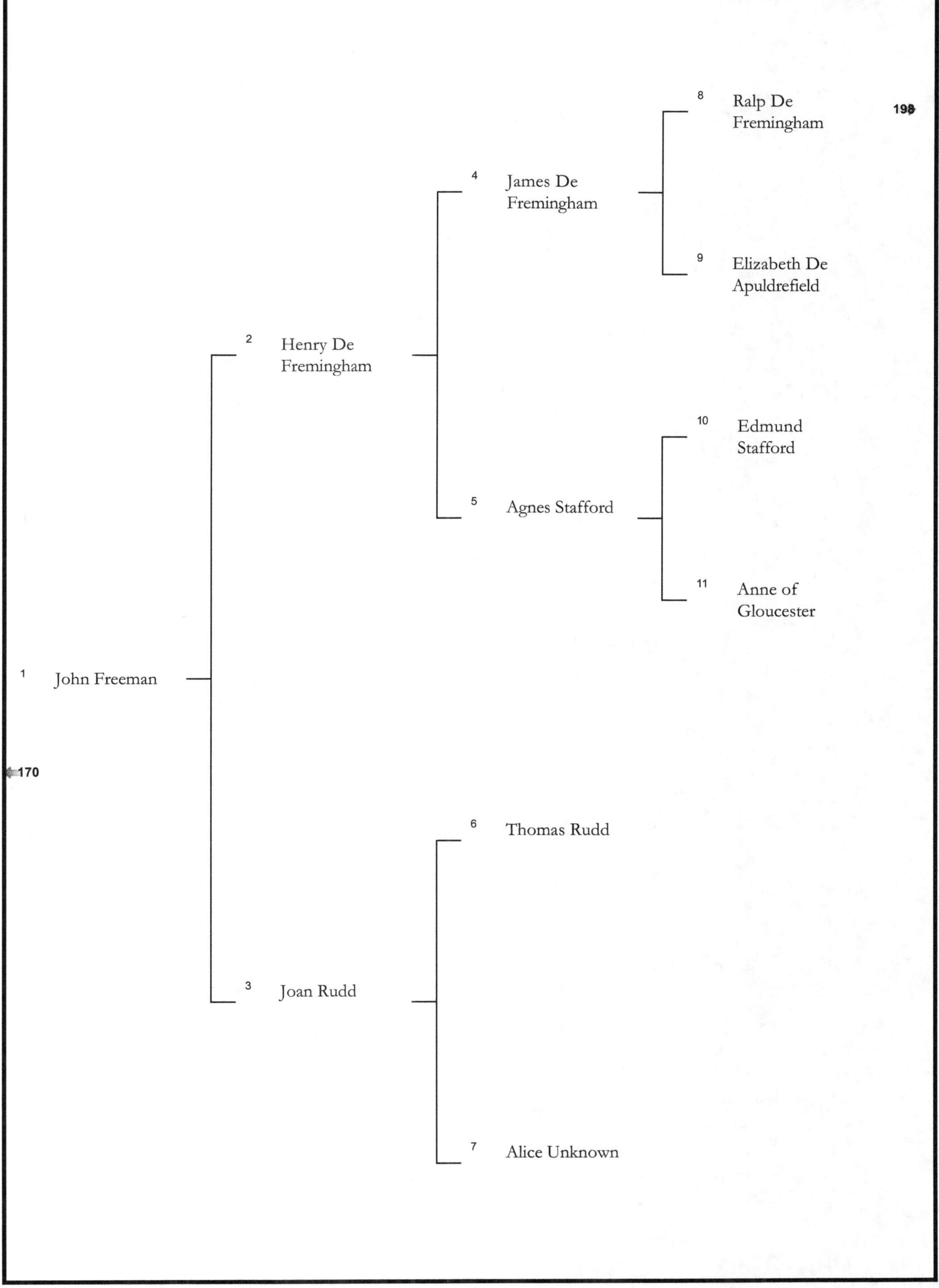

1 John Freeman
2 Henry De Fremingham
3 Joan Rudd
4 James De Fremingham
5 Agnes Stafford
6 Thomas Rudd
7 Alice Unknown
8 Ralp De Fremingham
9 Elizabeth De Apuldrefield
10 Edmund Stafford
11 Anne of Gloucester
195
170

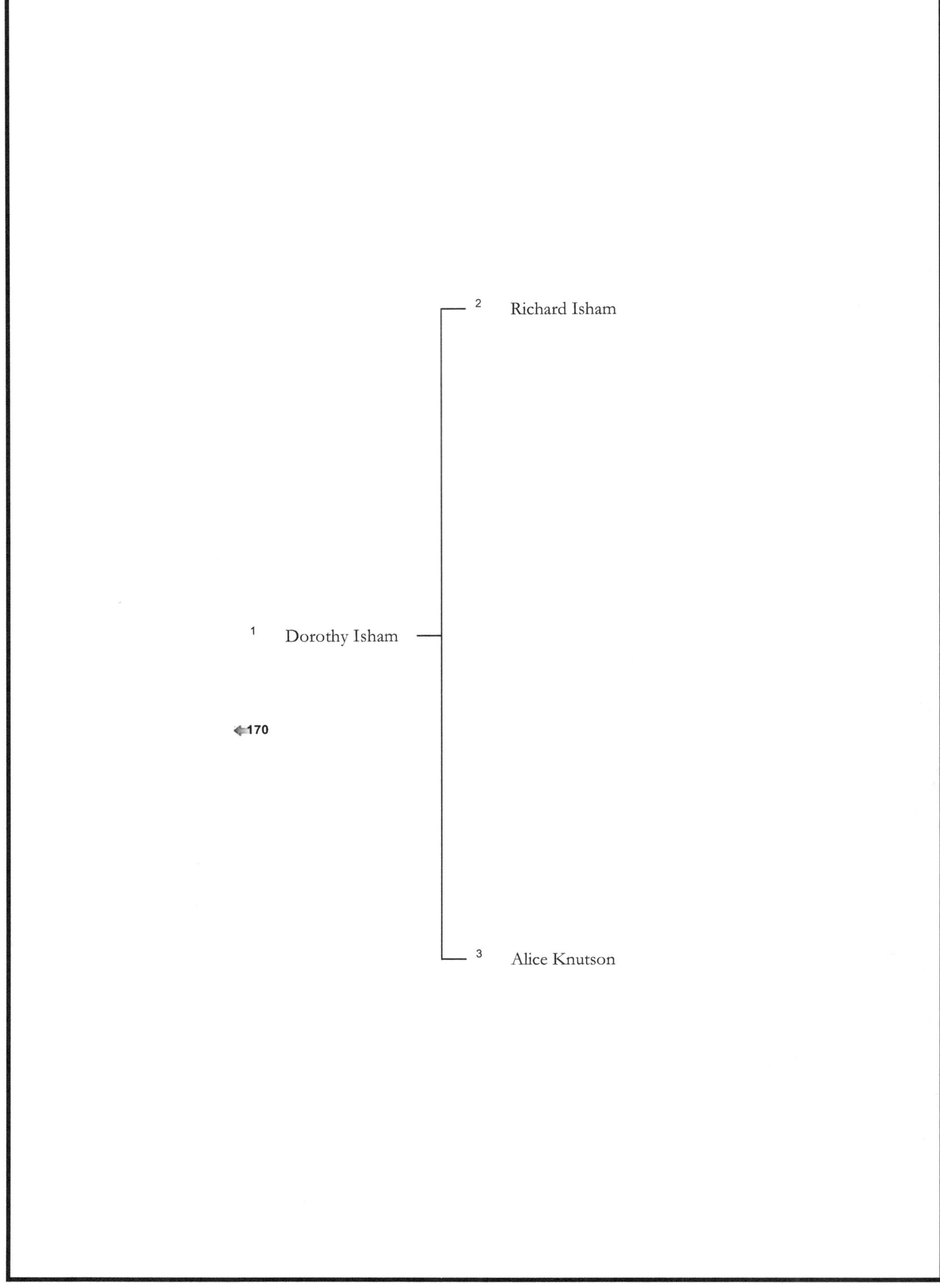

2 Richard Isham
1 Dorothy Isham
170
3 Alice Knutson

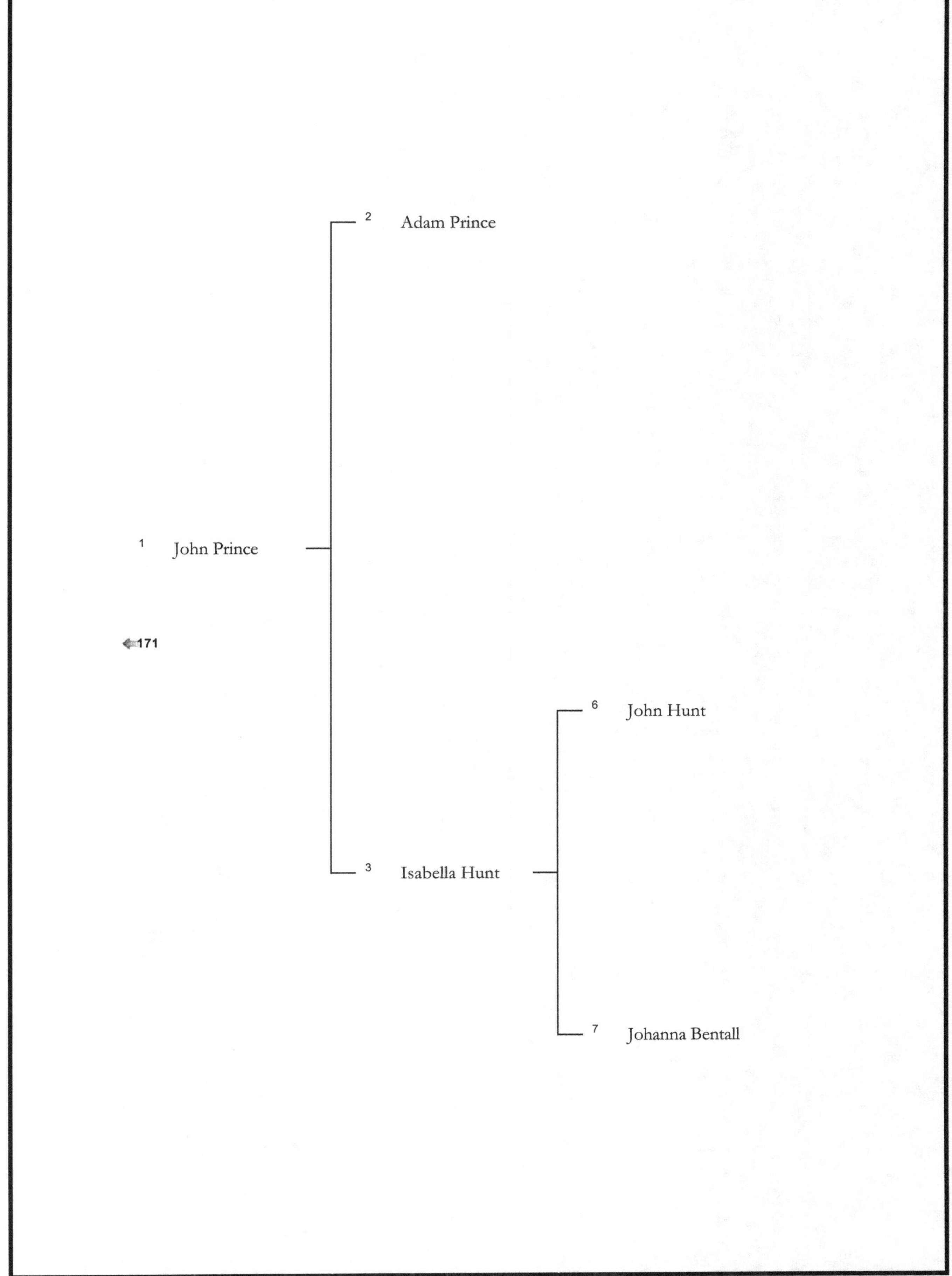

1 John Prince
2 Adam Prince
3 Isabella Hunt
6 John Hunt
7 Johanna Bentall
171

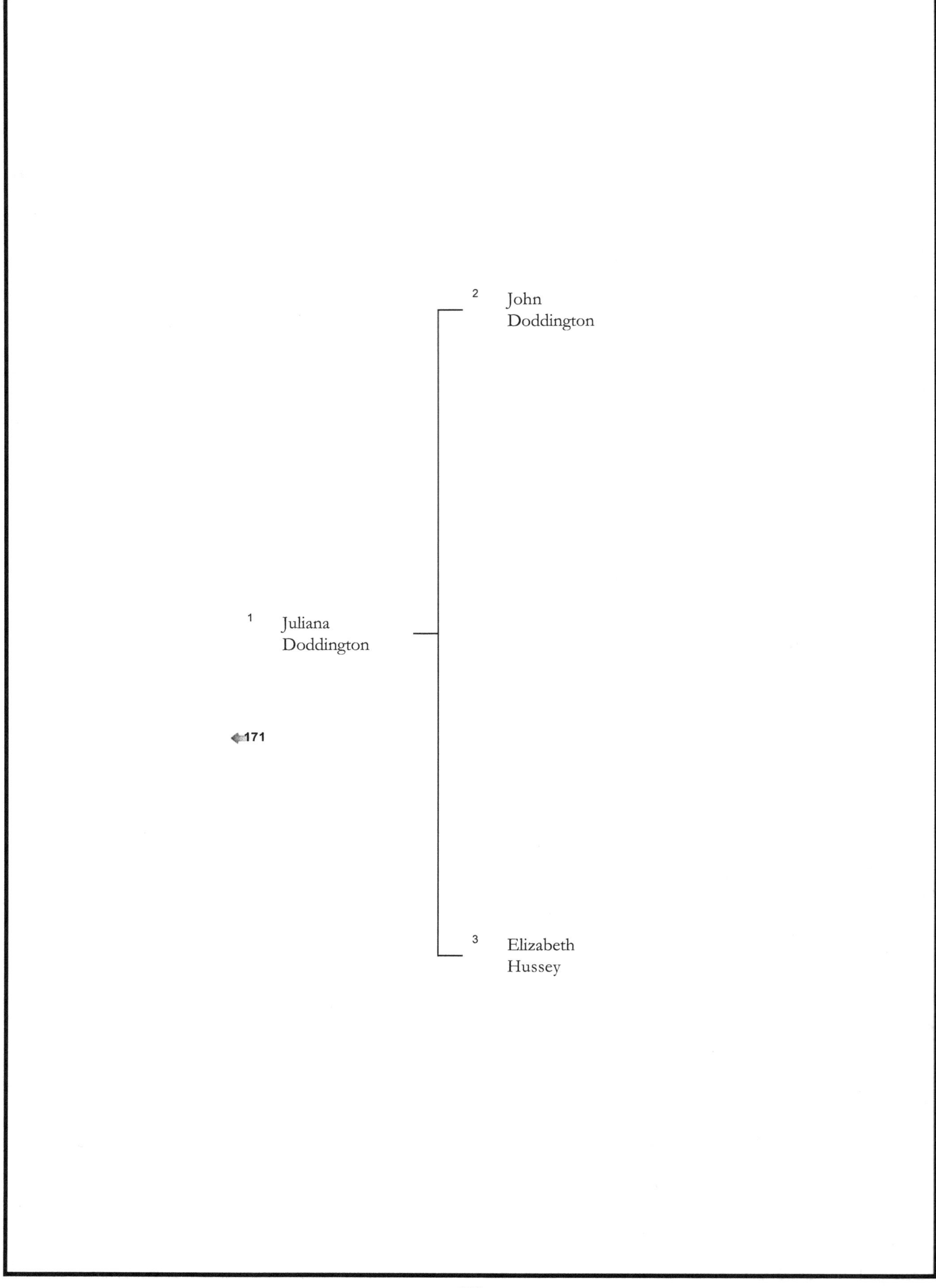

1 Juliana Doddington
2 John Doddington
3 Elizabeth Hussey
171

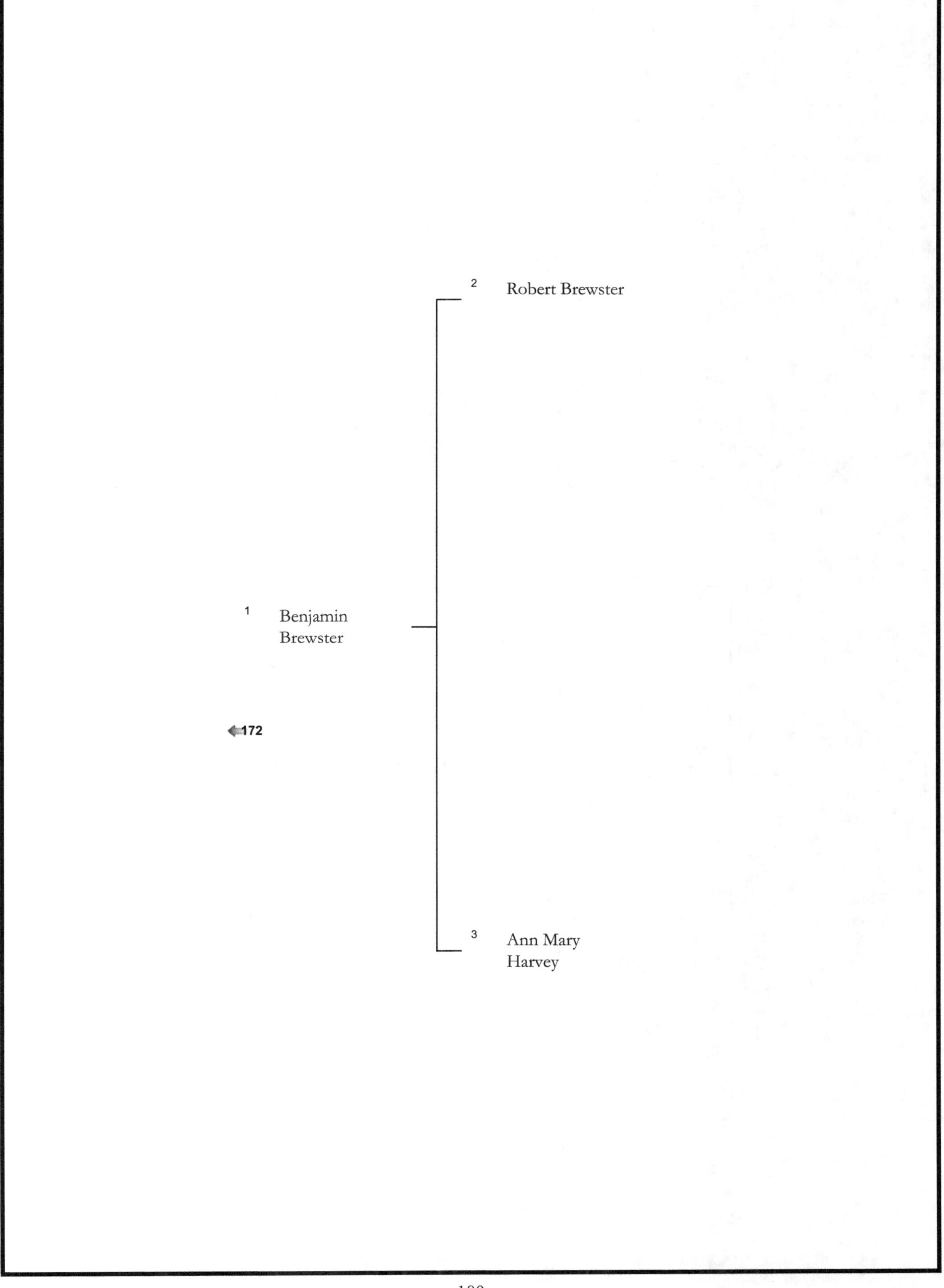

2 Robert Brewster
1 Benjamin Brewster
172
3 Ann Mary Harvey

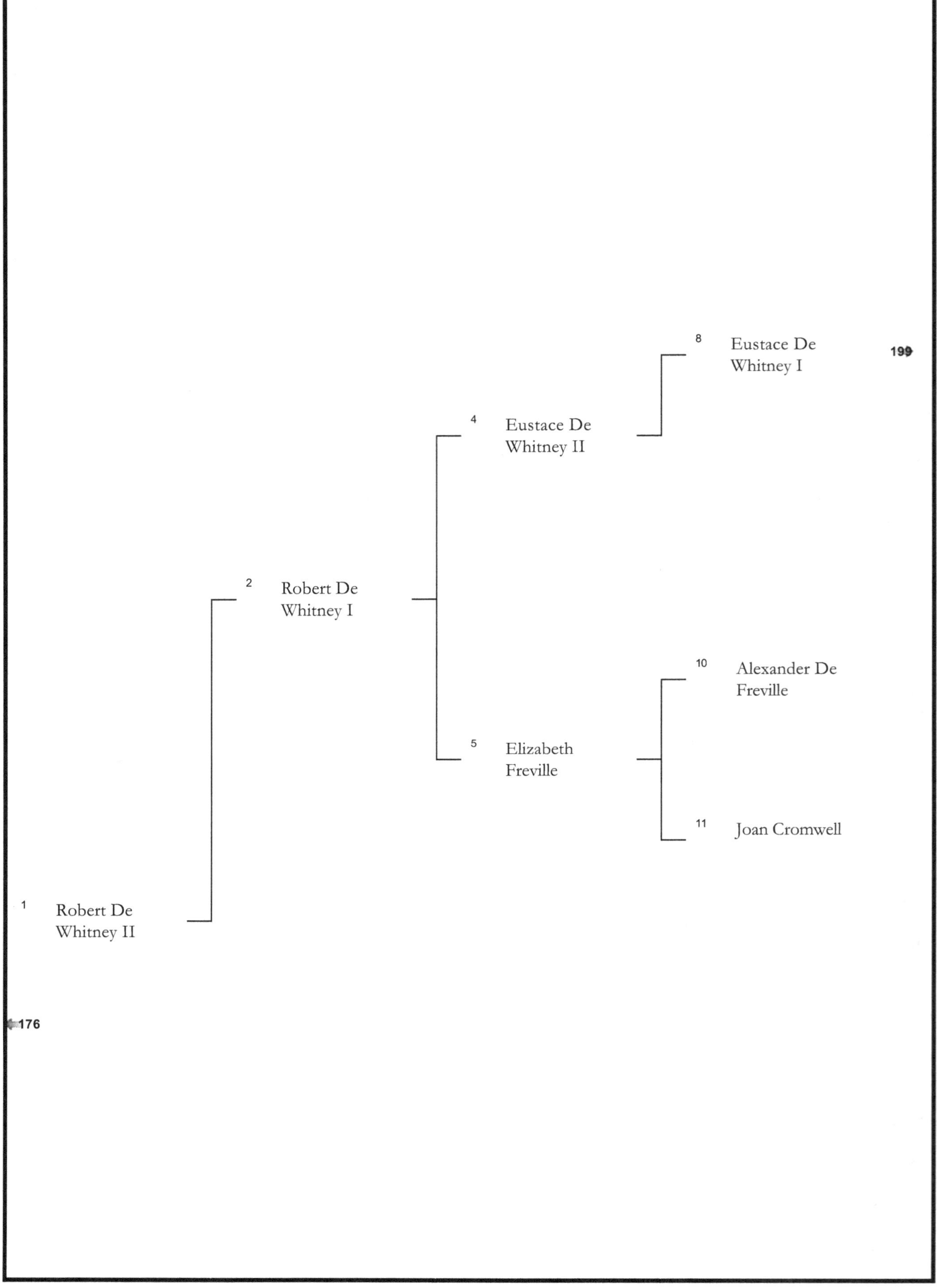

8 Eustace De Whitney I
199
4 Eustace De Whitney II
2 Robert De Whitney I
10 Alexander De Freville
5 Elizabeth Freville
11 Joan Cromwell
1 Robert De Whitney II
176

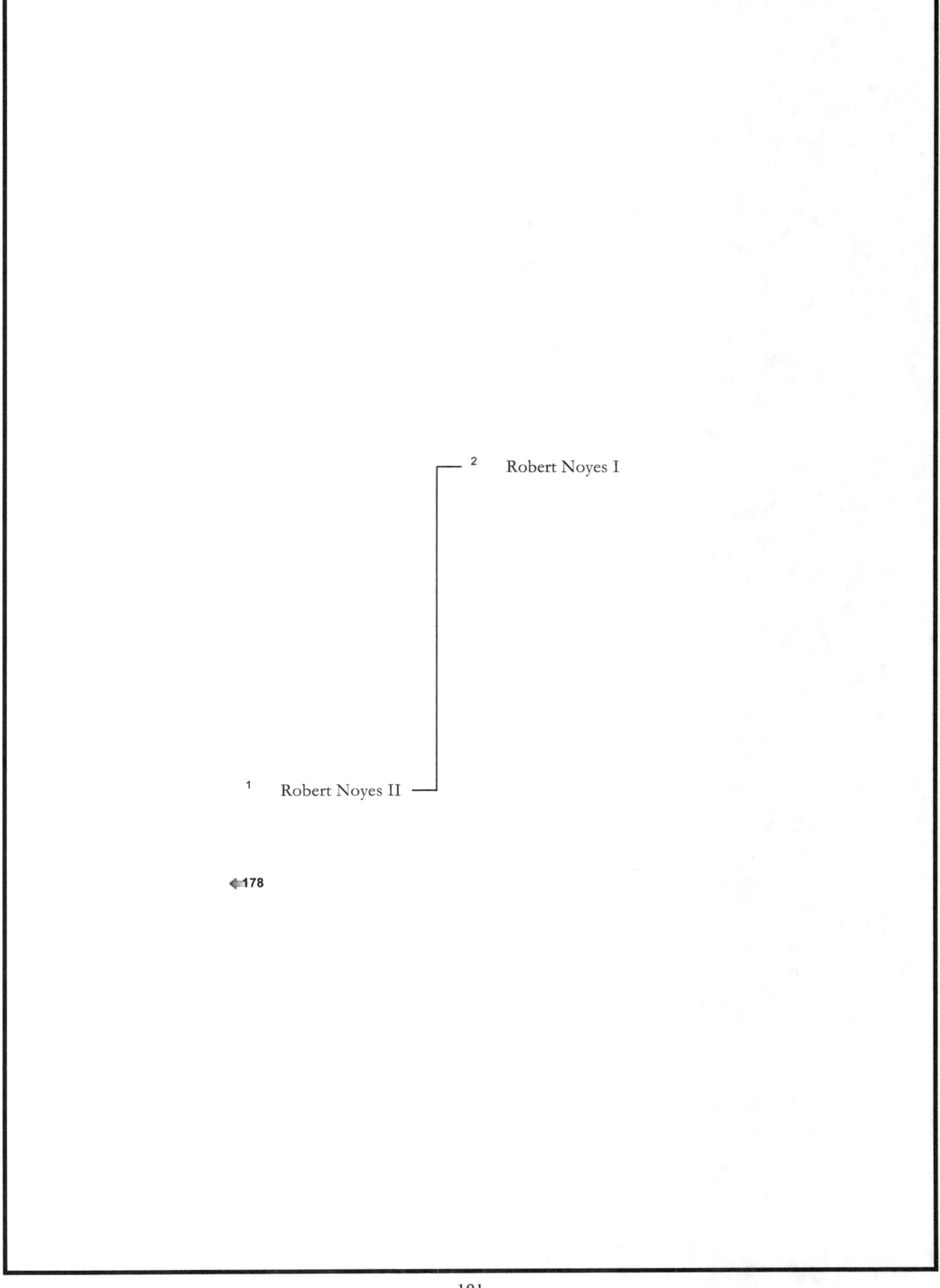

2   Robert Noyes I
1   Robert Noyes II
178

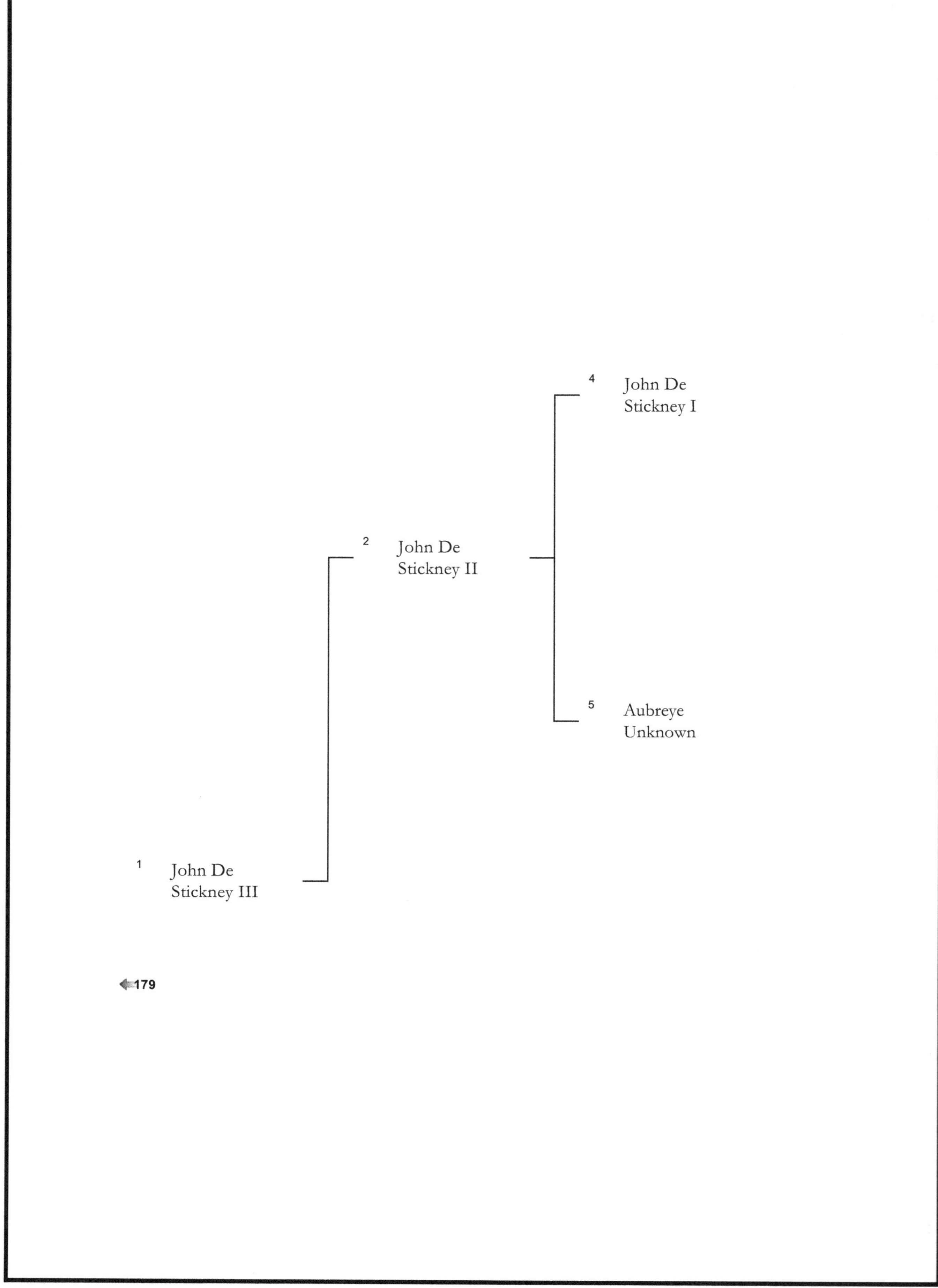

4
John De
Stickney I

2
John De
Stickney II

5
Aubreye
Unknown

1
John De
Stickney III

179

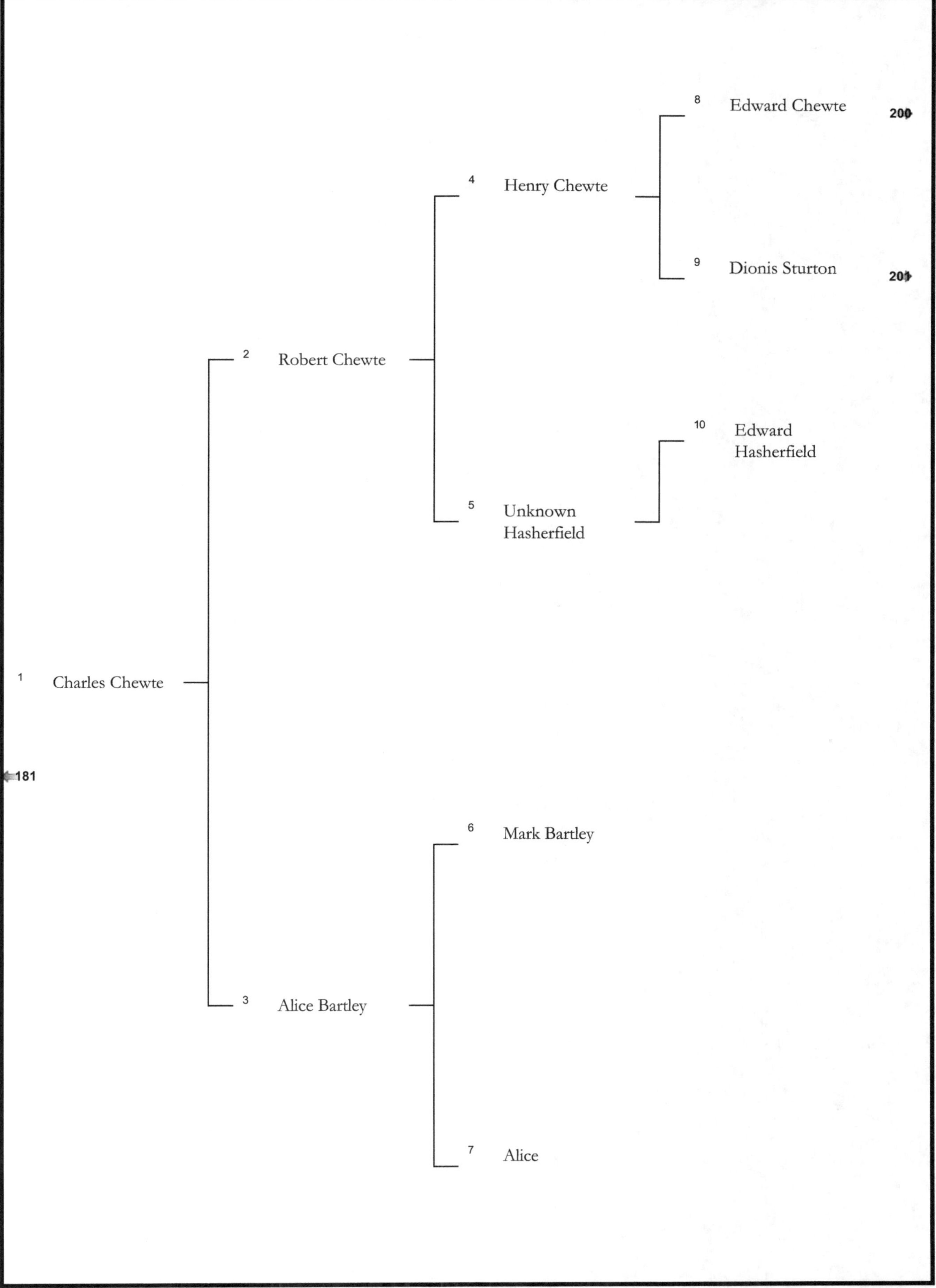

1 Charles Chewte
181
2 Robert Chewte
3 Alice Bartley
4 Henry Chewte
5 Unknown Hasherfield
6 Mark Bartley
7 Alice
8 Edward Chewte
200
9 Dionis Sturton
201
10 Edward Hasherfield

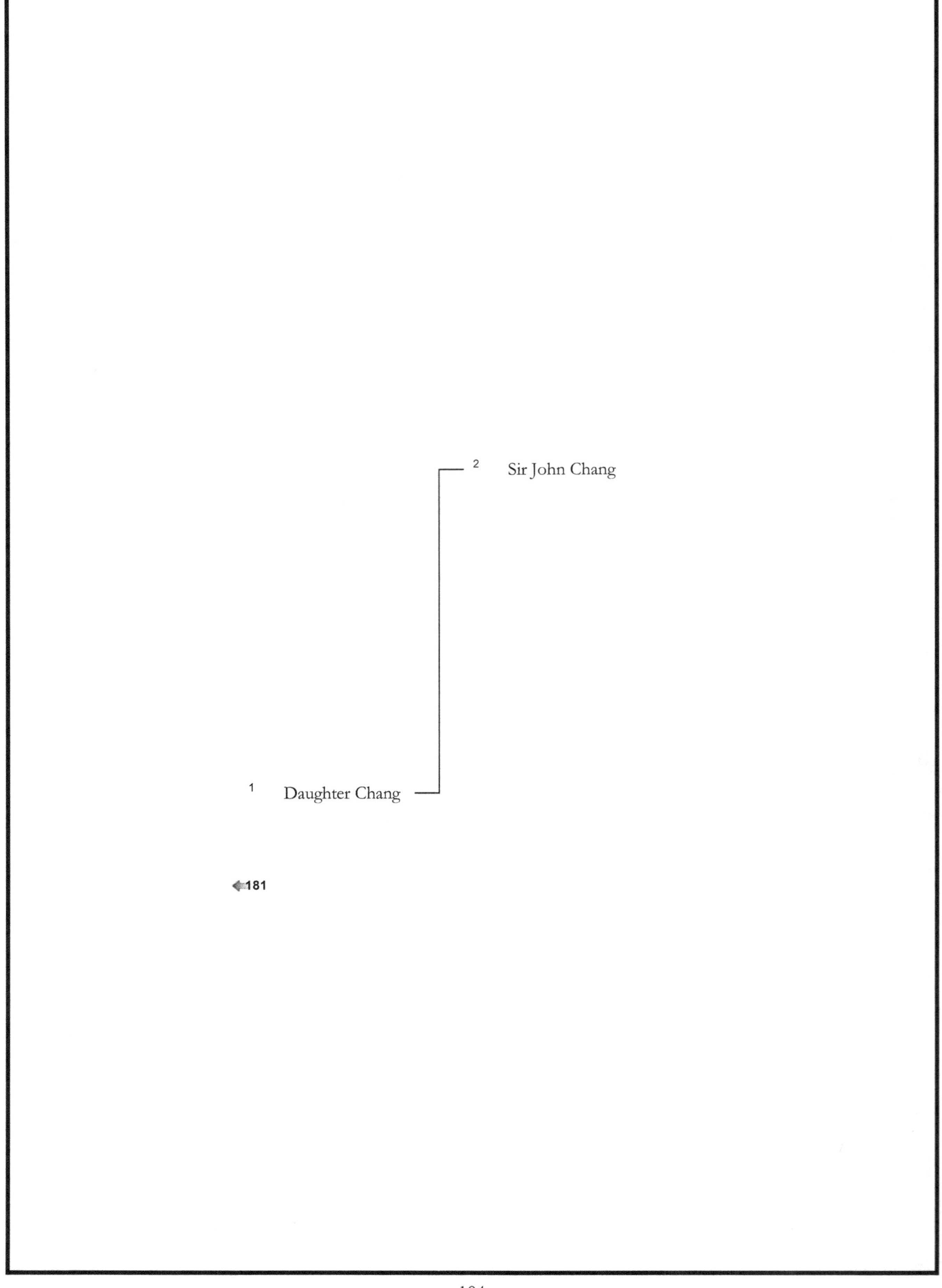

181

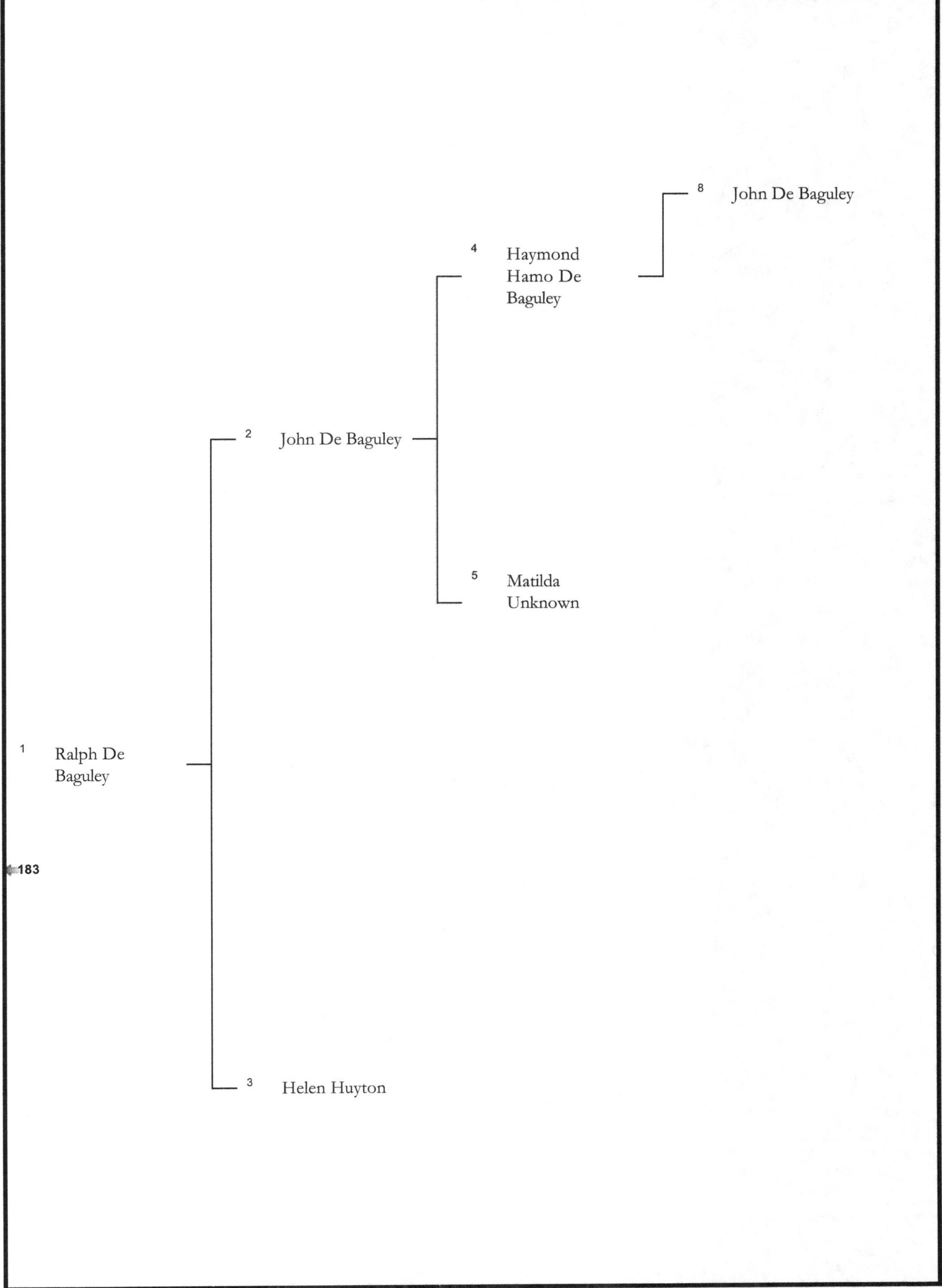

8   John De Baguley

4   Haymond Hamo De Baguley

2   John De Baguley

5   Matilda Unknown

1   Ralph De Baguley

183

3   Helen Huyton

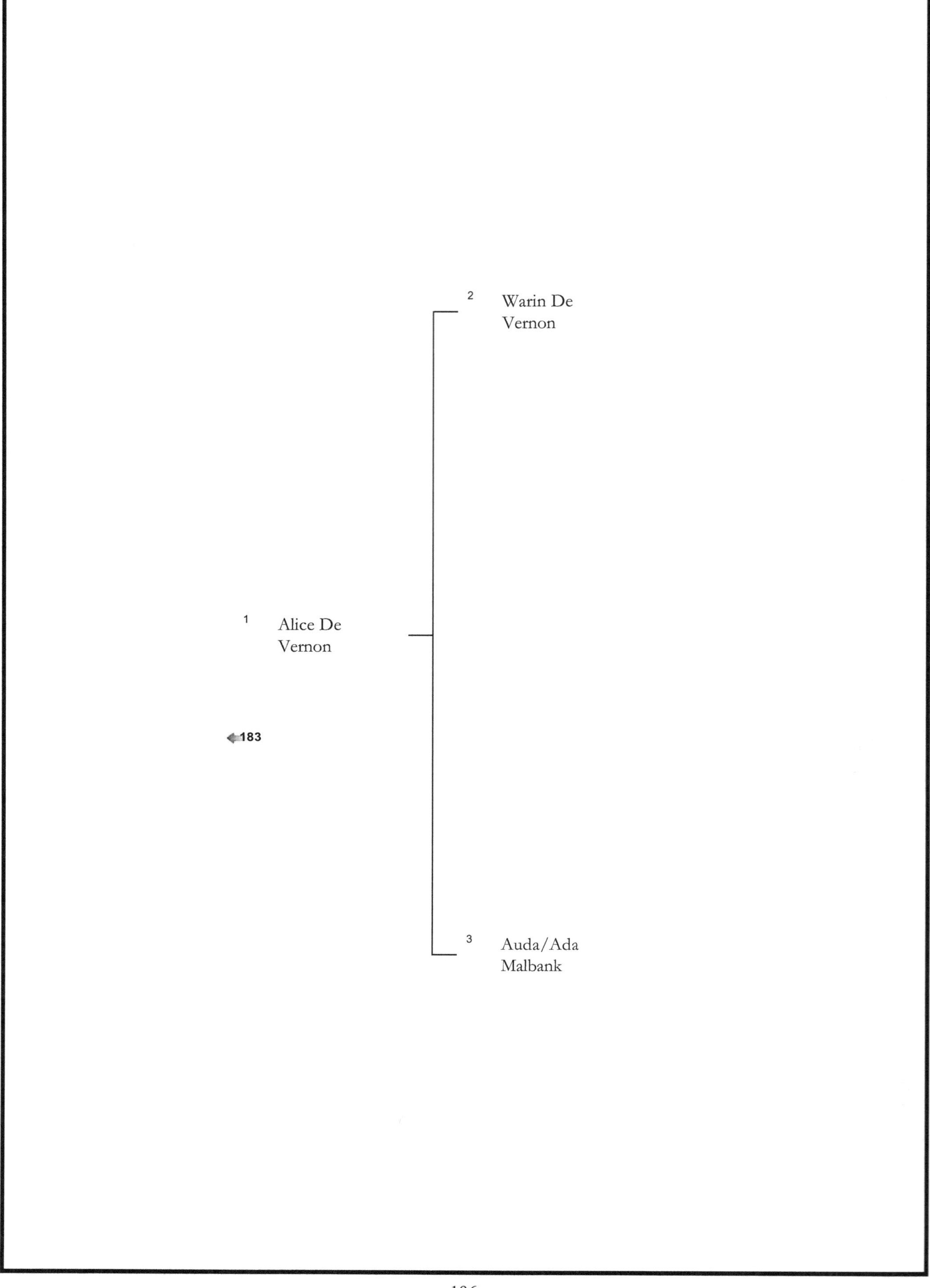

1 Alice De Vernon
2 Warin De Vernon
3 Auda/Ada Malbank
183

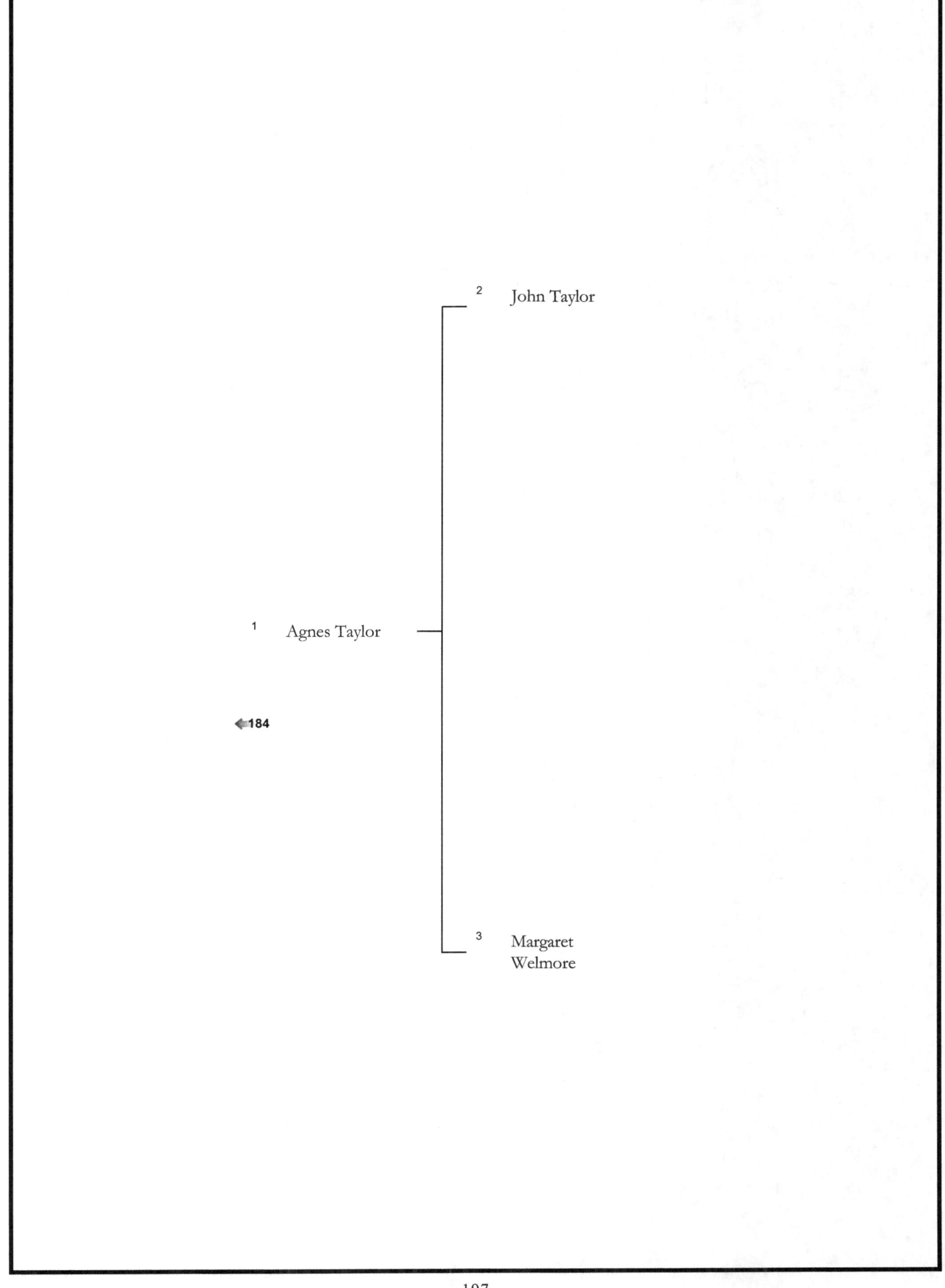

1 Agnes Taylor
2 John Taylor
3 Margaret Welmore
184

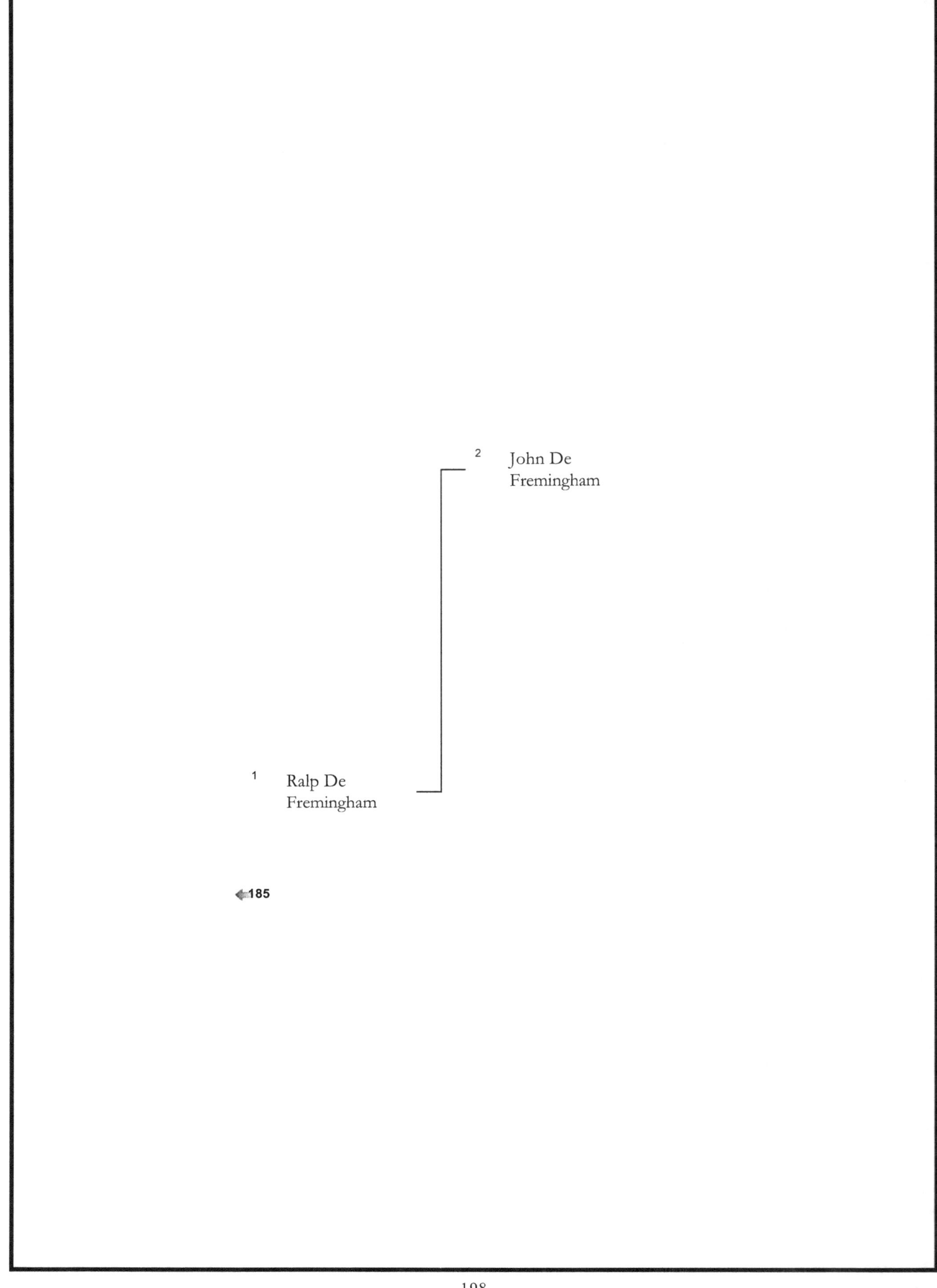

185

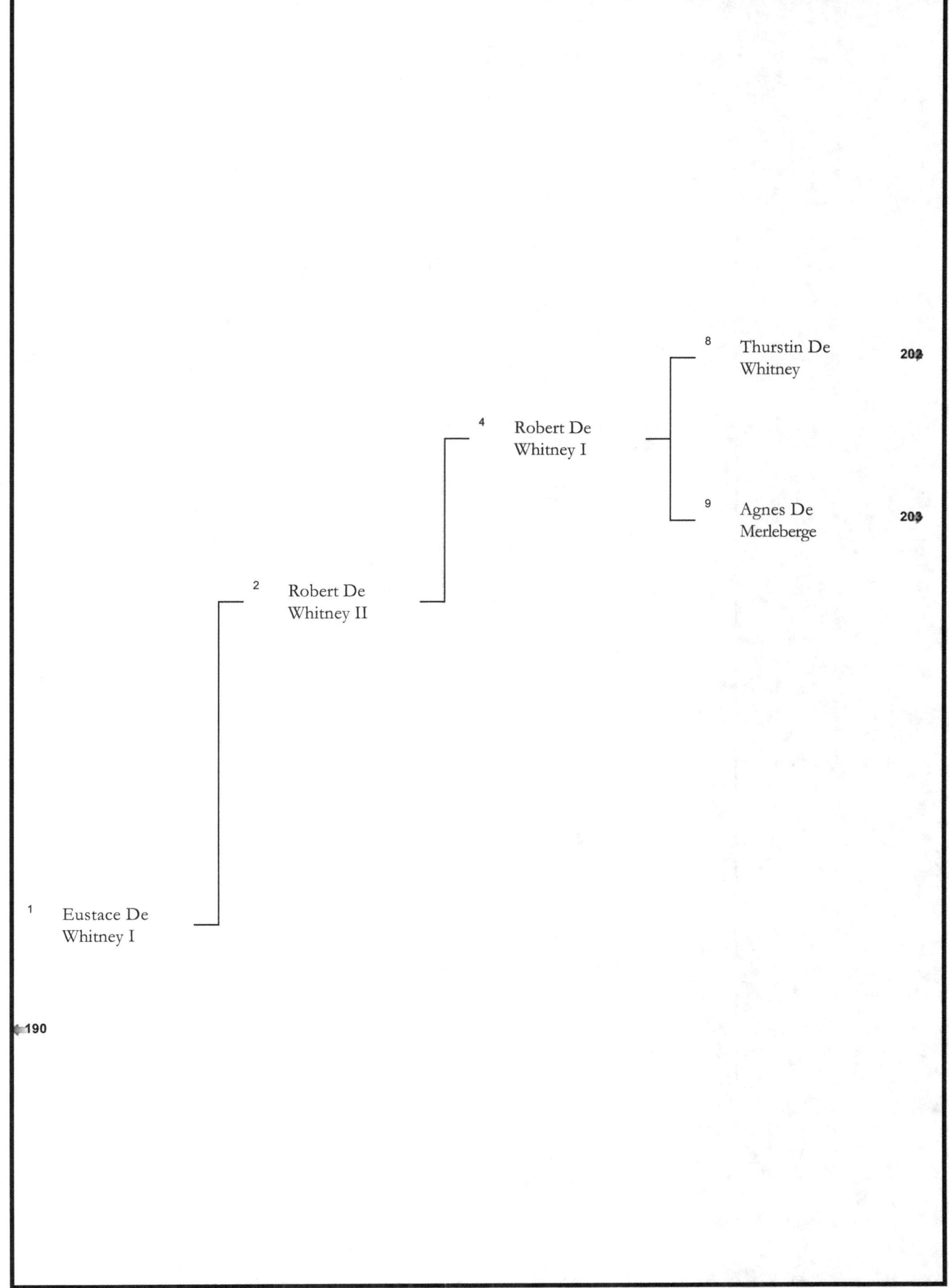

1 Eustace De Whitney I
2 Robert De Whitney II
4 Robert De Whitney I
8 Thurstin De Whitney
9 Agnes De Merleberge
202
203
190

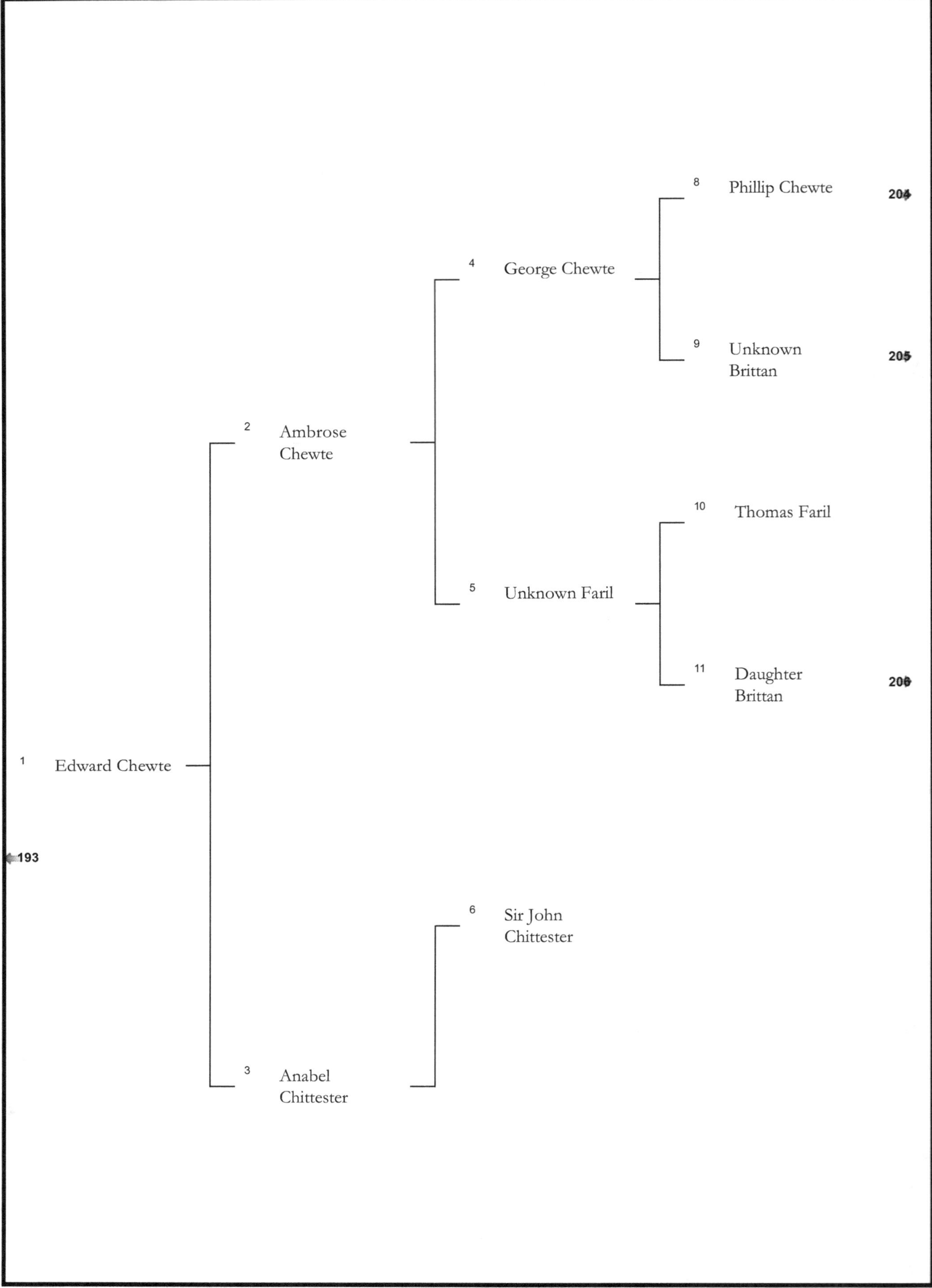

1 Edward Chewte
193
2 Ambrose Chewte
3 Anabel Chittester
4 George Chewte
5 Unknown Faril
6 Sir John Chittester
8 Phillip Chewte 204
9 Unknown Brittan 205
10 Thomas Faril
11 Daughter Brittan 206

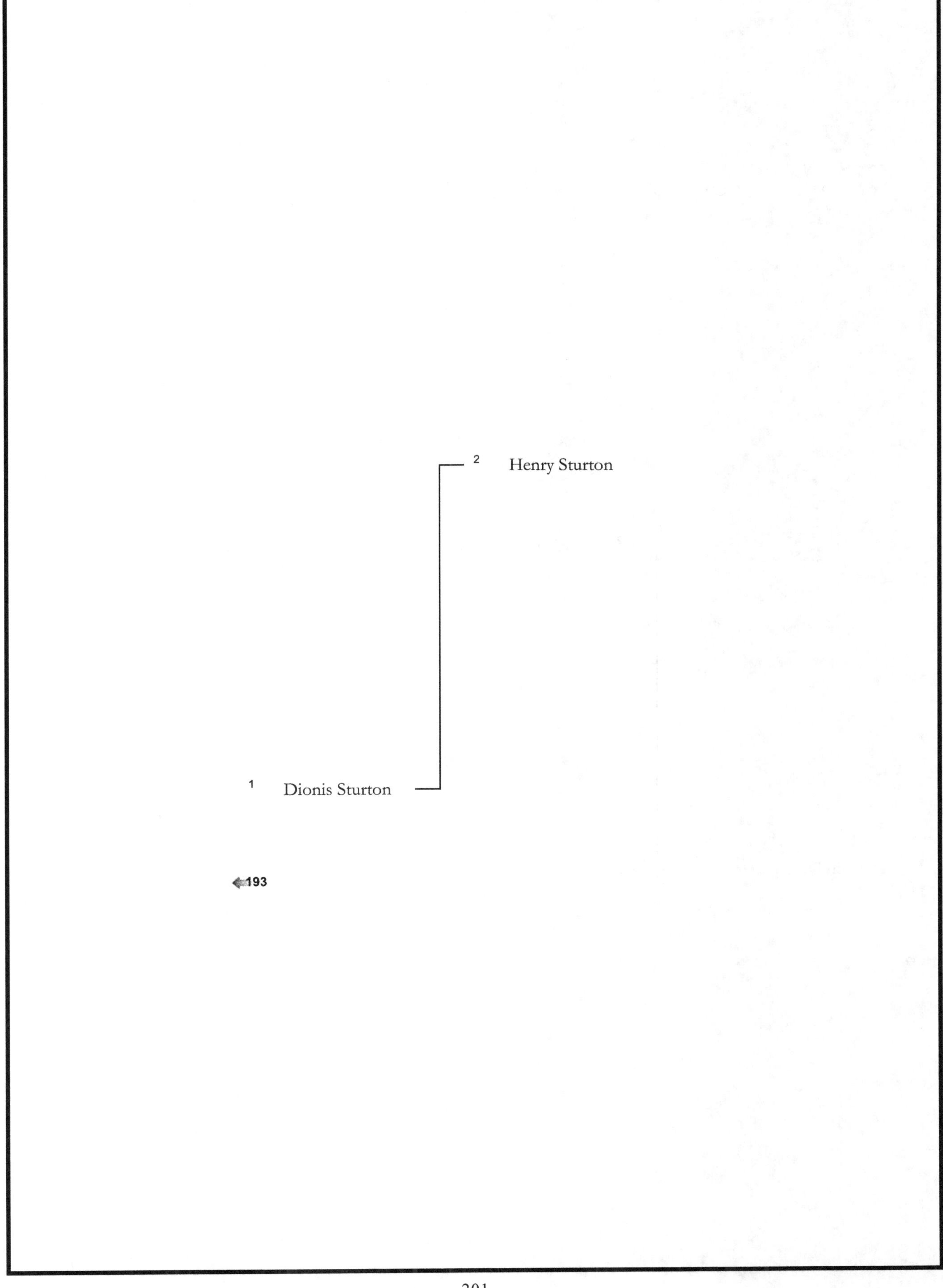

193

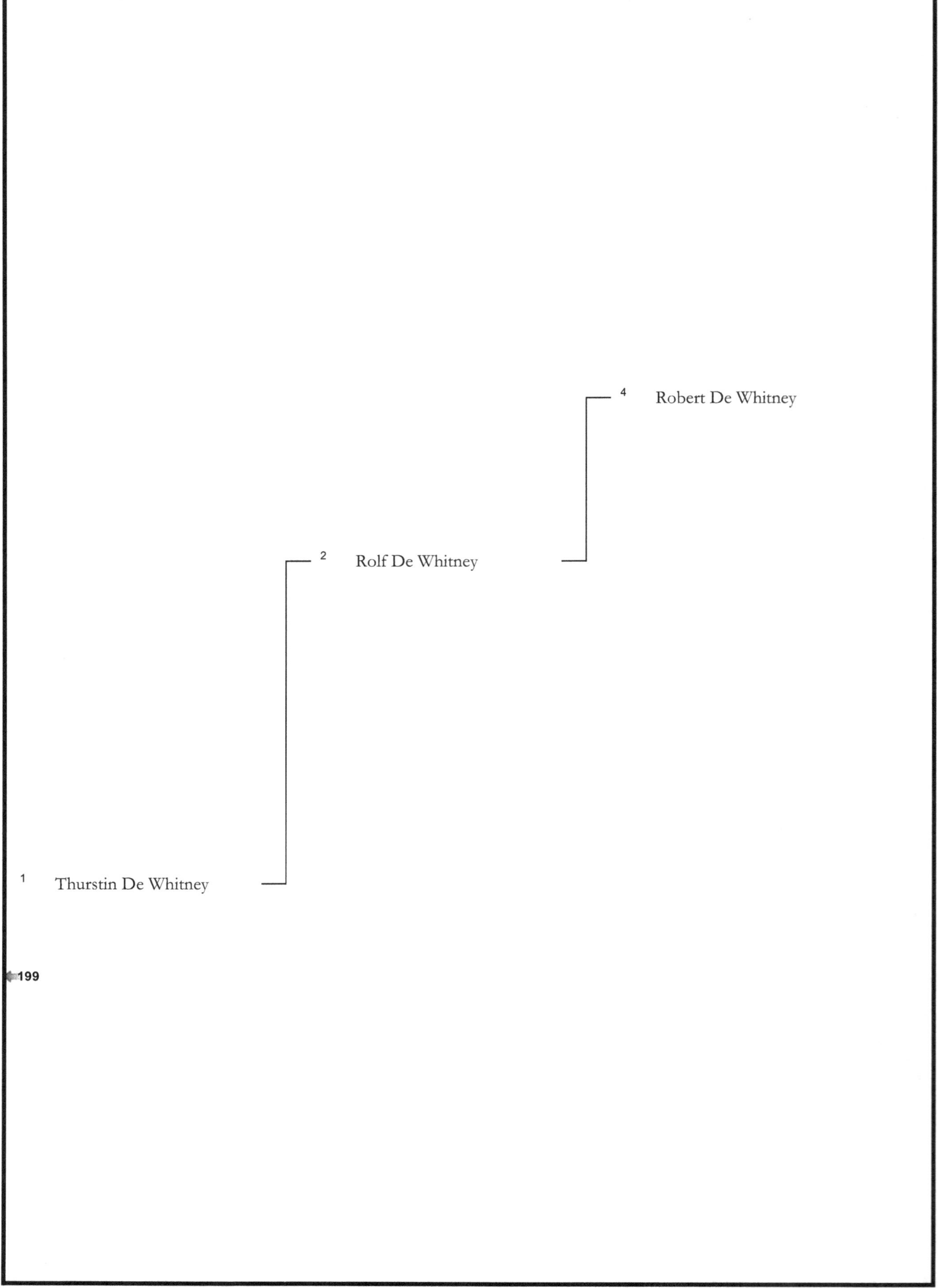

4 Robert De Whitney
2 Rolf De Whitney
1 Thurstin De Whitney

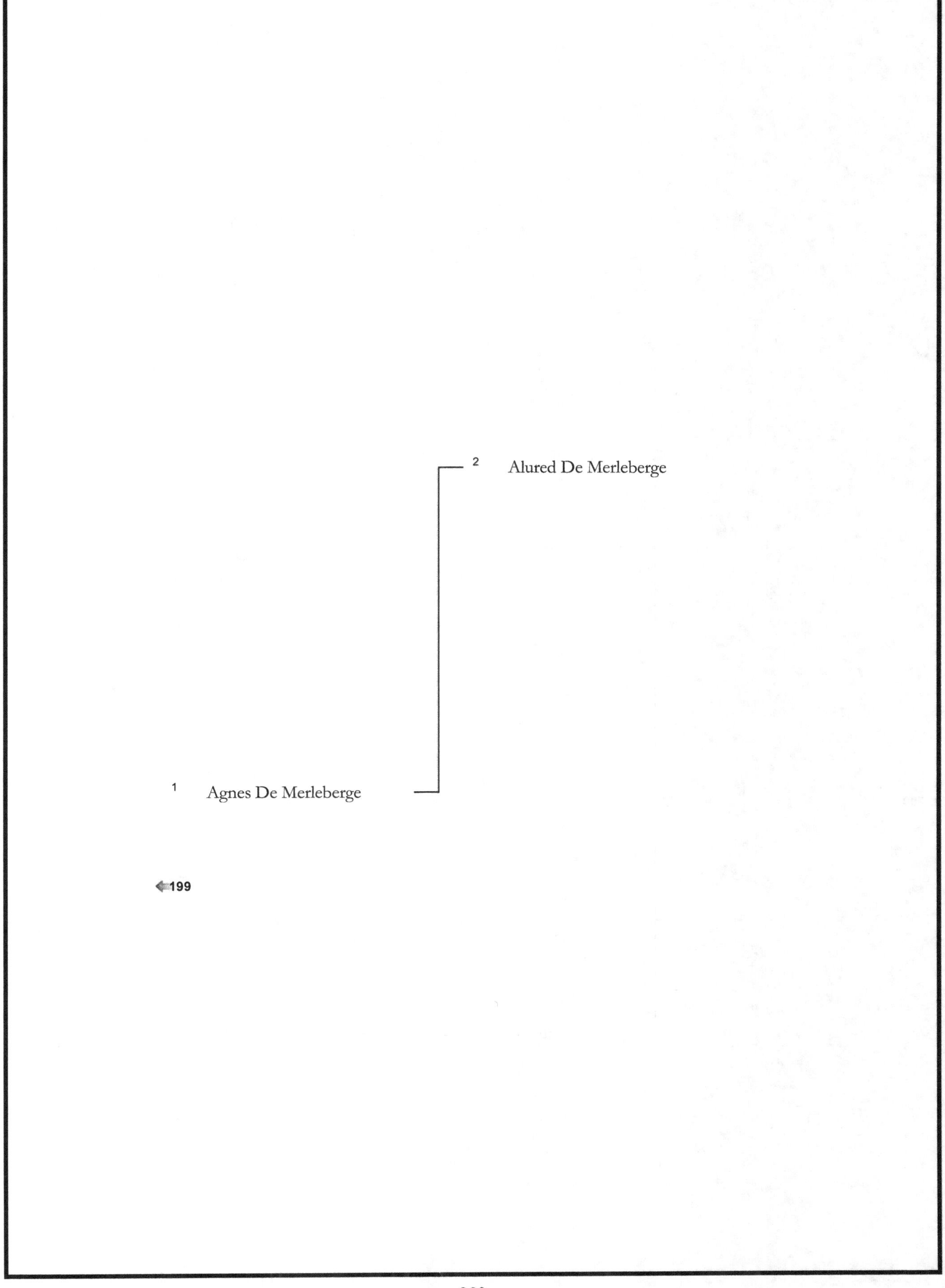

2   Alured De Merleberge
1   Agnes De Merleberge
199

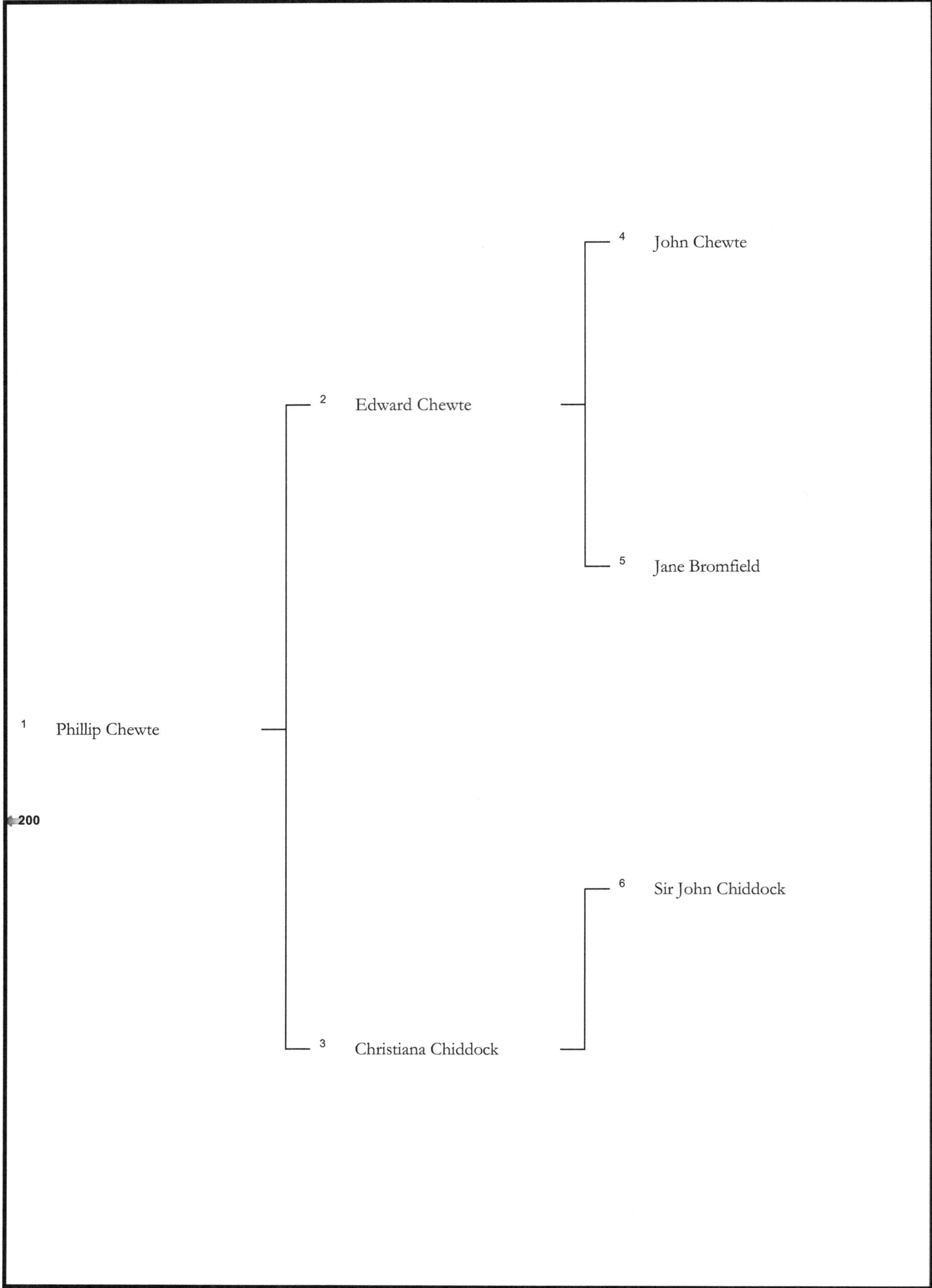

1 Phillip Chewte
2 Edward Chewte
3 Christiana Chiddock
4 John Chewte
5 Jane Bromfield
6 Sir John Chiddock
200

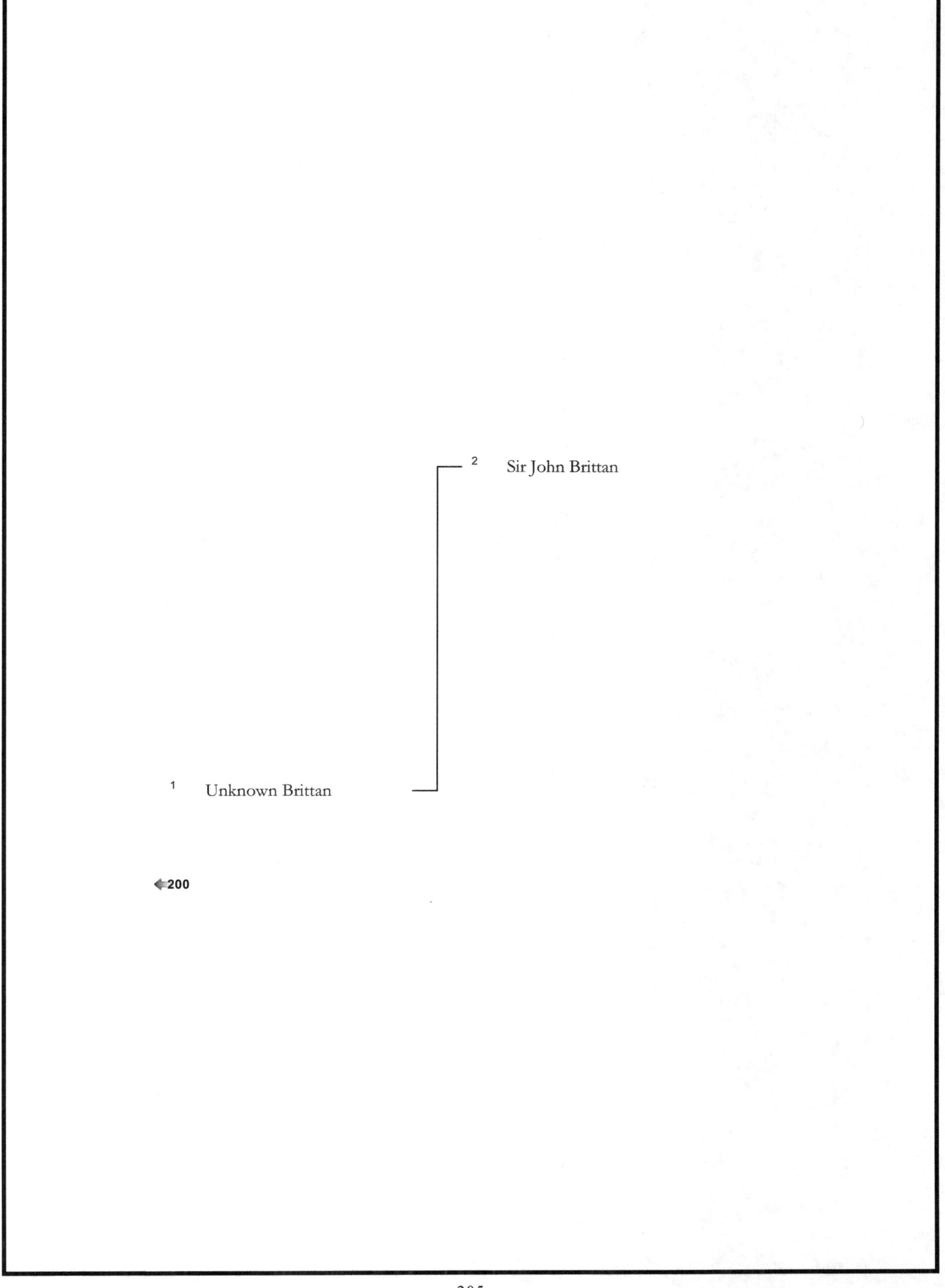

2   Sir John Brittan
1   Unknown Brittan
200

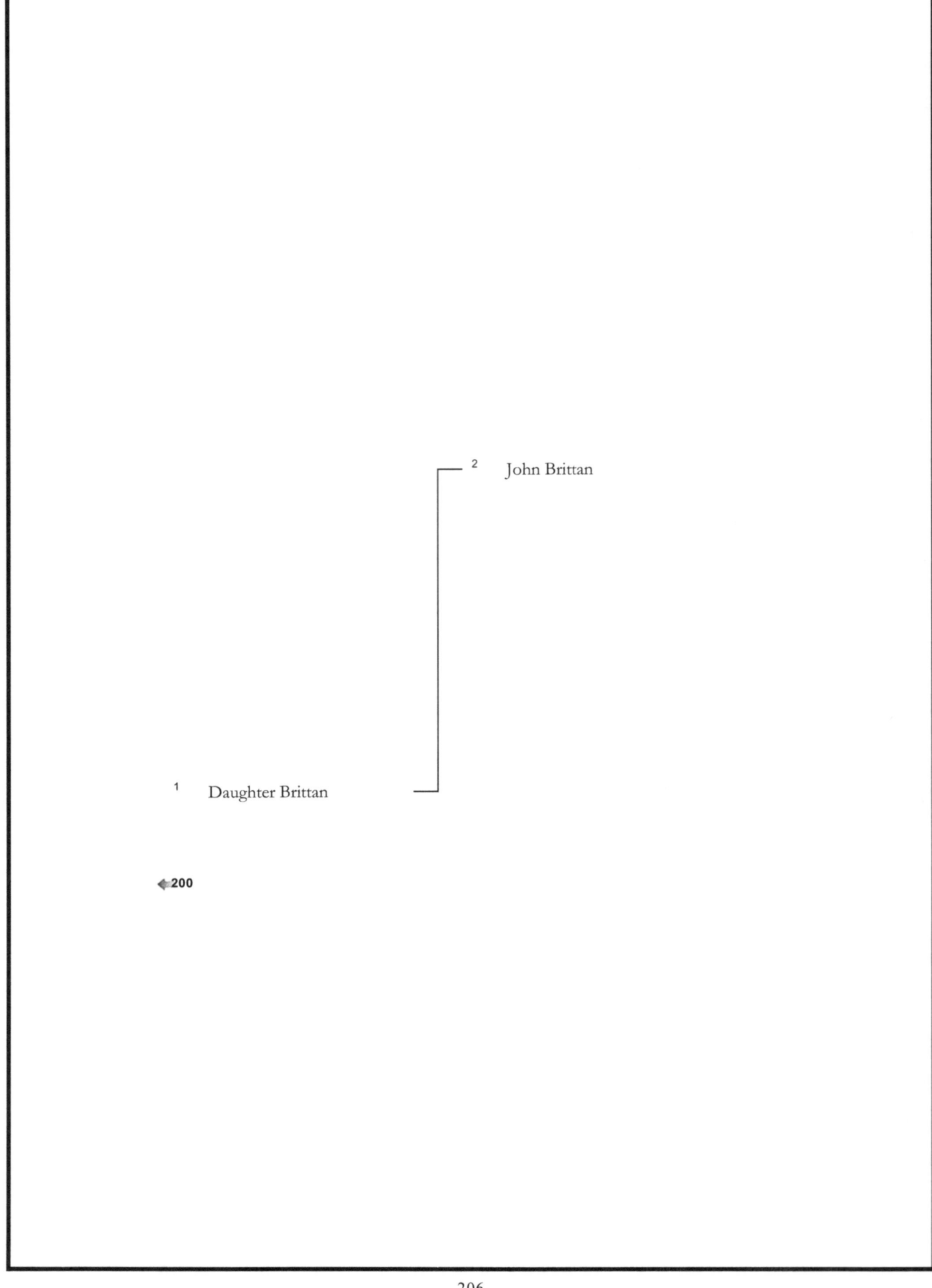

2 John Brittan
1 Daughter Brittan
200

FAMILY TREE/PEDIGREE CHART INDEX OF DIRECT ANCESTORS

The following is an Index of all direct ancestors (alphabetical by their complete last and first names) found in the family tree/pedigree charts. Additional variants, usages, and references of the ancestors' first, middle, and last names may be viewed within the indexed narratives for their respective parental and **GENERATION** entries in *Volumes 1* and *2.*

W

ANNEXES

The following annexes contain additional historical notes, summary lists, and reference items that may be helpful or of interest.

GENEALOGICALLY RELATED GEOGRAPHICAL DATA FOR WASHINGTON, COUNTY MAINE

Many towns and areas within the colonies have changed names over the years, and in some cases the states and counties to which they belong. For instance, Maine was part of the state of Massachusetts until 1820. As Washington County, Maine, was being settled, the areas that would later become towns were named as Plantations followed by a number. The following list notes the original Plantation name and the current name of the towns. Even within this list, some towns broke off from other towns over the years, which creates some variances and challenges in some genealogical records and histories. For example, Jonesport incorporated on February 3, 1832, from a portion of Jonesborough (Jonesboro). On April 7, 1925, Jonesport then set off land to form the town of Beals. Other towns like Centerville, which incorporated in 1842, became an unorganized township in 2004.

PLANTATIONS EAST OF MACHIAS

Plantation Number	Current Town Name
1	Perry
2	Dennysville, Pembroke
4	Robbinson
5	Calais
8	Eastport, Lubec
9	Trescott
10	Edmunds
11	Cutler
12	Whitney
13	Marion

PLANTATIONS WEST OF MACHIAS

Plantation Number	Current Town Name
4	Steuben
5	Harrington, Milbridge
6	Addison
11	Cherryfield
12	Columbia
13	Columbia Falls
22	Jonesboro, Jonesport, Beals, Roques Bluff

IMMIGRANT ANCESTOR ARRIVALS, SHIP NAMES, AND DATES

Our immigrant ancestors faced long and treacherous journeys by ship to come to the American colonies and between 1620 and 1640 there were supposedly over 300 ships that came to New England. Based on historical records and references, the following is a summary (listed alphabetically by last name) of the immigrant ancestor, the name of the ship they arrived on, and the year. For many of the male ancestors, their wives and children often accompanied them and that is noted in the narrative for each family if known. If they came on different vessels, that is noted below.

- WILLIAM BARNES- *Globe* 1635
- JOHN BENSON - *Confidence* 1638
- MARY BREWSTER - *Anne* 1623
- WILLIAM BREWSTER III - *Mayflower* 1620
- WILLIAM CHADBOURNE I - *Pied Cow* 1634
- WILLIAM COPP - *Blessing* 1635
- ANTHONY EAMES - *Recovery* 1653
- RALPH FARNUM - *James* 1635
- EDMUND FREEMAN III - *Abigail* 1635
- THOMAS GARDNER I - *Elizabeth* 1635
- JOHN GODDARD - *Pied Cow* 1634
- EDMUND GOODENOW- *Confidence* 1638
- JOHN GREENAWAY - *The Mary and The John* 1630
- THOMAS HATCH - *Hercules* 1634
- RICHARD INGERSOLL - *Mayflower* 1629
- EDWARD IRESON - *Abigail* 1635
- JOHN KELLEY I - *Hector* 1635
- RICHARD KNIGHT II - *James* 1635
- JOHN KNIGHT I - *James* 1635
- JOHN LEAVITT - *Diligent* 1630
- JOHN LIBBY - *Hercules* 1635
- AGNES LITTLEFIELD - *Bevis* 1638
- THOMAS LOMBARD - *The Mary And The John* 1630
- ROBERT LONG - *Defence* 1635
- MARY LYNDE - *Abigail* 1635
- HUGH MASON - *Frances* 1634
- THOMAS MILLET - *Elizabeth* 1635
- ANTHONY MORSE II - *James* 1635
- NICHOLAS NOYES - *The Mary and The John* 1633

- THOMAS PAGE - *Increase* 1635
- WILLIAM PALMER I - *Fortune* 1621
- FRANCES PALMER - *Anne* 1623
- JOHN PERKINS - *Lyon* 1631
- THOMAS PHILBROOK I - *Arabella* 1630
- DANIEL POORE - *Bevis* 1638
- QUINTON PRAY - *Ann Cleve* 1643
- THOMAS PRENCE V - *Fortune* 1621
- WILLIAM REED - *Assurance of Zion* 1637
- ABRAHAM RIDEOUT - *Chandler* by 1716
- HENRY ROWLEY - *Charles* 1632
- JOHN S. SAWYER - 'A ship commanded by Captain Parker' 1636
- JOHN WHITE - *Lyon* 1632
- JOHN WHITNEY - *Elizabeth and Anne* 1635

MILITARY RECORDS

For genealogical purposes, the ancestors who served in the military – and service was often expected and mandatory – left vital information and details about their lives and their families in their military and war records. The summary below (listed alphabetically by last name) notes some of the ancestors, their rank, and military campaign service and more details may often be found in the family narratives.

- ORLANDO BAGLEY II, Ensign, Colonial Armed Forces
- JACOB BAGLEY, Revolutionary War and Continental Service against Canada
- JOHN BAGLEY I, Private, War of 1812
- CHRISTOPHER HENRY BENNER, Revolutionary War
- JOSEPH BENSON, Narragansett Indian Fight
- DAVID BUTLER, Captain, French and Indian War
- SAMUEL COLSON II, Revolutionary War
- NATHANIEL COX, Revolutionary War
- TRISTRAM DODGE I, Sergeant, Colonial Armed Forces 1676
- JOHN FREEMAN, Indian Wars
- DOMINICUS JORDAN, Indian Wars
- EBENEZER JORDAN, Revolutionary War
- THOMAS KELLEY, Revolutionary War
- SAMUEL KNOWLES, Against Canada 1759
- JOSEPH LIBBY, Revolutionary War
- DANIEL LOOK, Revolutionary War
- HUGH MASON, Indian Wars

- JOSIAH NOYES, French and Indian Wars
- JOHN OAKS, Revolutionary War and War of 1812
- JONATHON OAKS, Battle of Quebec
- JAMES PENDLETON, Captain, King Phillip's War
- JAMES PHILBROOK, Revolutionary War
- JOHN SAWYER, Revolutionary War
- BENJAMIN SHAW II, Revolutionary War
- EDMUND STEVENS, Revolutionary War
- GEORGE TENNEY, Revolutionary War
- JOHN WHITE, Captain, Revolutionary War
- TILLY WHITE, Private, Revolutionary War

BIBLIOGRAPHY

The following is a sampling of the hundreds of books, official government documents, church and civil society records, categories of records, and other references used to document the information provided and trace the Bagleys and related families in *Volumes 1-3*.

BOOKS, GOVERNMENT RECORDS, CHURCH AND CIVIL SOCIETY RECORDS, AND OTHER RESOURCES

17th Century Colonial Ancestors (1983)

A Dictionary of English and Welsh Surnames (1910)

A Genealogical and Heraldic Dictionary of the Landed Gentry of Great Britain (1840)

A Genealogy of the Philbrick and Philbrook Families: Descended from the Emigrant, Thomas Philbrick, 1583-1667

A Notebook on the Descendants of Elder William Brewster of Plymouth Colony (1985)

Abington Town and Vital Records

Abstracts of Death Notices and Miscellaneous News Articles (1833-1852 and 1833)

Albermarle County, North Carolina Records

Aldrich Genealogy (1971)

American Ancestry, Vol 1,2,3,4,17 (1882-1897)

American Antiquarian Society

American Colonists in English Records (1961)

American Marriages Before 1699 (1979)

Ancestors and Descendants of Thomas Millet (1959)

Ancestral Lines of 54 Families (1935)

Ancestral Lines Revised (1981)

Ancestral Roots of 60 Colonists (2006)

Ancestry.com - https://www.ancestry.com/

Anglo-Saxon Bishops, Kings and Nobles (1899)

Anglo–Saxon Chronicle, Years 853–901

Annals of The Caledonians, Picts and Scots of Strathclyde, Cumberland (1828)

Bagley Cemetery Records

Barnstable Town Records

Beverly Vital Records

Birth records

Book of The Radclyffes

Boston Vital Records

Bounty Land Records #7742-160-50

Braintree Vital Records

Brian Pendleton and His Descendants (1911)

Burke's Guide to The Royal Family (1973)

Canadian Census 1851-1881

Cemetery records

Cemetery Records from Parsonsfield, Maine
Centerville Town Records
Church records
Clayton Library Center for Genealogical Research, Houston, Texas
Columbia/Columbia Falls Town Records
Colonial censuses
Colonial Families (1928)
Colonial Families of America, Vol. 15 (1935)
Colonial Families of The U.S., Vol. 1- 3 (1902)
Common pleas court records
Continental Army records
Continental censuses
County censuses
County Genealogies: Pedigrees of Hertfordshire Families (1844)
Cox Families of Holderness (1939)
Cross Index of Ancestral Roots of 60 U.S. Colonists (1964)
Curwens of Workington Hall (1880)
Daniel Goodwin of Ancient Kittery, Maine and His Descendants (1985)
Daughters of the American Revolution Genealogical Research System
Daughters of the American Revolution Library
Death records
Dennysville Town Records
Descendants of Captain Hugh Mason (1937)
Descendants of Isaac Cummings (1930)
Descendants of John White of Wenham and Lancaster (1900)
Descendants of John Whitmarsh (1916)
Descendants of Matthew Coe (1894)
Descendants of Richard Austin of Charlestown, Massachusetts 1638 (1951)
Descendants of Richard Knowles (1974)
Descendants of Thomas Tenney (1904)
Descendants of William Sawyer (1889)
Dictionary of National Biography (1885)
Directory of Ancestral Heads of New England Families 1620-1700 (1964)
Dodge Genealogy (1904)
Dorchester Vital Records
Dover Branch of Leighton Family (1944)
Dover Vital Records
Eames - Ames Early Genealogy (1931)
Early Families of Limington, Maine (1984)
Early Families of Weymouth (1984)
Early Jonesborough Families of Washington County, Maine (2004)
Early Pioneers of Massachusetts (1900)

Early Records of Lancaster, Massachusetts 1643-1725 (1884)

Early Sargents of New England (1922)

Edmonds Town Records

English Ancestors of Epes Sargent (1928)

Essex Antiquarian (1897-1910)

Essex County Historical Collections, Vol. 2 and 4

European Ancestry of The Prescott Family in America (1977)

Families Related to the Bagley and Floyd Families (1990)

Family of Hugh Mason (1930)

Family Records

Federal census records

Fidelity oaths

Findagrave.com - https://www.findagrave.com/

Fine assessments

Forbes and Furbish Genealogy (1892)

Founders and Patriots: Checklist of The Founding Ancestors (1983)

Founders of Early American Families (1926)

Founders of Early American Families: Emigrants from Europe 1607-1657 (1975)

Freeman Genealogy (1875)

Freeman lists

Genealogical Account of The Descendants of John Kelly (1886)

Genealogical and Family History of New Hampshire (1908)

Genealogical and Personal Memoirs of Early Families of Massachusetts (1910)

Genealogical and Personal Memoirs Relating to The Families of Boston (1907)

Genealogical Dictionary of Maine and New Hampshire (1976)

Genealogical Dictionary of New England (1860)

Genealogical Dictionary of Rhode Island (1969)

Genealogical Gleanings in England, Vol. II (1901)

Genealogical History of The Hatch Family (1925)

Genealogical Register of Plymouth Families (1985)

Genealogical Register of The First Settlers of New Hampshire (1983)

Genealogies of the Early Families of Weymouth (1984)

Genealogies of The Families And Descendants of The Early Settlers of Watertown, Massachusetts, Including Waltham And Weston : To Which is Appended The Early History of The Town (1860)

Genealogy and Estates of Charlestown (1879)

Genealogy and Family History of New Hampshire (1908)

Genealogy and History of Watertown, Vol. 1 (1855)

Genealogy and Memoirs of Families of Massachusetts (1910)

Genealogy of Maine (1905)

Genealogy of Massachusetts (1910)

Genealogy of Rhode Island Families (1985)

Genealogy.com - https://www.genealogy.com/

Geneanet.org - https://en.geneanet.org/

Geni.com - https://www.geni.com/

George Aldrich Genealogy (1972)

Gloucester Vital Records

Hayward-Howard and Littlefield (1970)

Historical Memoranda of Ancient Dover New Hampshire (1900)

History of Boothbay (1984)

History of England Before the Norman Conquest (1895)

History of Martha's Vineyard (1966)

History of Parsonsfield, Maine 1771–1888 (1981)

History of the Town of Hingham (1893)

History of Watertown (1855)

History of Wells and Kennebunk (1875)

History of York, Maine (1931)

Hull Vital Records

Images of America: Jonesport and Beals (1999)

Immigrant Ancestors: A List of 2,500 Immigrants to America Before 1750

Immigration records

Indentured servant lists

Ingersoll Genealogy (1926)

International Genealogical Index (IGI)

Inventories and wills from probate records

Isaac Cummings, of Topsfield, Mass., and Some of His Descendants (1899)

James Family Association

Job Judkins of Boston (1962)

Job Judkins of Boston and His Descendants (1962)

John Bagley, War of 1812, Pension Index #SO(19542), #S(12620)

John Perkins of Ipswich (1889)

JohnCardinal.com - http://johncardinal.com/

Jonesboro Town Records

Jonesport Town Records

Jury lists

Kittery Tax List, 1760

Knowles: The Descendants of Richard Knowles (1974)

Lancaster Town Records

Lancaster Vital Records

Land patents

Land records

Land warrants

Leavitts of America (1924)

London, England Visitations and Vital Records

Loyalist lists

Lynn Vital Records
Maine Families In 1790 (1989)
Maine Farmer: Marriage Notices from the Maine Farmer 1833-1852 (1996)
Maine Genealogical Recorder, Vol. 8-9 (1895)
Maine Genealogical Society
Maine Genealogy (1907)
Maine in the War
Maine Probate Abstracts (1991)
Maine State Archives
Maine Wills 1640-1760 (1887)
Maine Wills and Abstracts
Maine, A History, Vol. 5 (1931)
Marriage records
Massachusetts Colonial Names
Massachusetts Genealogy (1910)
Massachusetts Magazine, Vol. 1, No 7
Massachusetts Soldiers and Sailors of The Revolutionary War, Vol. 17 (1908)
Massachusetts State Archives
Matthew Pratt and Descendants (1889)
Mayflower Descendants and Their Marriages (1985)
Mayhew Family Tree (1855)
Memorial of the 100th Anniversary of the Settlement of Dennysville, Maine (1886)
Mendo Vital Records
Merchant lists
Military records
Minuteman lists
Morse Genealogy (1903)
Mortality schedules
Muster rolls
My Tribe, O'Flaherty, Francis Jr., Cited on The O'Flaherty Genealogical Project
Nantucket Vital Records
National Genealogical Society
National Mormon Family History Center, Salt Lake City, Utah
National Order Founders and Patriots Register
National Society of The Daughters of Colonial Wars
New England Family and Genealogical Memorial (1915)
New England Genealogical Dictionary
New England Genealogical Recorder
New England Historical and Genealogical Register, Vol. 6, 32, 38, 46, 53, 67, 70, 78, 79, 93, 106, 113
New England Library of Genealogical and Personal History (1902)
New England Marriages Prior To 1700 (1985)
Newbury Vital Records

Newspapers

North Yarmouth Vital Records

Noyes Genealogy (1904)

Oaths of allegiance

Of Mary Brewster (1984)

Old Eliot (Book One 1897-1899), (Book Two 1900-1905), (Book Three 1906-)

Old Families of Amesbury and Salisbury (1897)

Old Kittery and Her Families (1903)

Parkers in America

PBS: Colonial House 2003-2004, Historical Background and Ancestry -
https://www.thirteen.org/wnet/colonialhouse/history/1628.html

Pedigree Register, Vol. 3 (1913)

Pedigrees From Plea Rolls (1905)

Pedigrees of The County Families of Yorkshire (1874)

Pension rolls

Petition lists

Pioneers of Maine and New Hampshire (1965)

Pioneers on Maine Rivers (1973)

Pipe Rolls of Lancashire

Planters of The Commonwealth (1930)

Plymouth Colony Vital Records

Plymouth Vital Records

Portland in the Past With Historical Notes of Old Falmouth (1886)

Pre-U.S. jurisdiction records

Prescott Memorial (1870)

Province & Court Records of Maine, Vol. I 1636-1668 and Vol. VI, 1718/19-1727 (1929)

Quit rents

Rebel lists

Records of The First and Second Churches of Berwick, Maine

Reed Genealogy, Descendants of William Reed (Reade) (1955)

Regimental rolls and accounts

Register of St Bees

Registers of Enlistments Roll #1

Rent rolls

Residence lists

Revolutionary War Records

Richard Austin of Charlestown (1968)

Robert Randall and Descendants (1909)

Roots of The Past in Washington County

Rowley Vital Records

Roxbury Vital Records

Salem Town Records

Salisbury and Amesbury, Descendants of John Kelly of Newbury (1886)

Scottish Kings: A Revised Chronology of Scottish History, 1005-1625, with Notices of the Principal Events, Tables of Regnal Years, Pedigrees, Tables, Calendars, Etc (1906)

Servant schedules

Soldiers, Sailors and Patriots of The Revolutionary War - Maine (1983)

Some Descendants of John Benson (1920)

Some Descendants of Orlando Bagley of Amesbury, Massachusetts (1973)

Some Pedigrees from the Visitation of Kent, 1663-68 (1887)

Somerset, England, Parish Records

Southeastern Massachusetts Old Families, Vol. 1-3 (1912)

State censuses

State papers

Surrey, England, Visitations

Tax lists

Territorial censuses

The Ancestry and Posterity of Joseph Smith and Emma Hale Smith (1929)

The Bagley Family Martin Allardyoe (1916)

The Chadbourne Family Association

The Colby Family in Early America (1970)

The Complete Peerage of England, Scotland, Ireland, Great Britain and the United Kingdom (1910)

The Descent of John Prescott from Alfred The Great (1948)

The Dodge Family Association

The English Ancestry and Homes of the Pilgrim Fathers: who came to Plymouth on the "Mayflower" in 1620, the "Fortune" in 1621 and the "Anne" and "The Little James" in 1623 (1965)

The families of Laura Bagley Donovan Guptill of Addison, Maine (1982)

The Families of Standish and Prescott of Standish Parish (1948)

The Genealogy and Estates of Charlestown (1879)

The Goodwins of Kittery, York Co., Maine (1898)

The Historical Antiquities of Hertfordshire (1700)

The History of Wells and Kennebunk (1797)

The Libby Family in America (1882)

The Lineage and Ancestry of HRH Prince Charles, Prince of Wales (1977)

The Mary and The John (1971)

The Mason Family (1972)

The Mayflower Society

The Pioneers of Massachusetts: A Descriptive List, Drawn from Records of the Colonies, Towns, and Churches, and Other Contemporaneous Documents (1900)

The Royal Daughters of England (1910)

The Royal House of Stuart (1969)

The Scots Peerage: The Complete Peerage; Burke's Guide (1904)

The Tenney Family (1904)

The Wilder Connection (1992)

These Names of Ours (1938)

Thomas Philbrook and Family (1884)

Topographical Dictionary of 2,885 English Emigrants (1963)

Town records

Tristram Dodge and Descendants (1886)

U.S. Army Records 1798-1914

U.S. Census 1790-1940

U.S. Immigration and Naturalization Records

United States Library of Congress, Washington, DC

United States National Archives, Washington, DC

Veteran schedules

Visitation of Lancashire 1533

Visitations of Yorkshire 1584, 1612

Vital Records of Berwick, South Berwick, and North Berwick, Maine

Vital Records of Kittery, Maine

Voter lists

War of 1812 Records

Wells, The Frontier Town of Maine, Vol. 1 & 2 (1970)

Westmoreland Pipe Rolls

White Family Quarterly, Descendants of John of Wenham and Lancaster (1903)

Whiting Town Records

WikiTree.com - https://www.wikitree.com/

Wilder Family History (1878)

William Lewis of Stoke-By-Nayland (1932)

William Sargent and Descendants (1899)

William Sawyer (1898)

Wiltshire Visitations 1565, 1623

Worcester County Massachusetts, Vol. 1 (1907)

Yarmouth Town Records